Lecture Notes in Computer Science 15753

Founding Editors

Gerhard Goos
Juris Hartmanis

Editorial Board Members

Elisa Bertino, *Purdue University, West Lafayette, IN, USA*
Wen Gao, *Peking University, Beijing, China*
Bernhard Steffen, *TU Dortmund University, Dortmund, Germany*
Moti Yung, *Columbia University, New York, NY, USA*

The series Lecture Notes in Computer Science (LNCS), including its subseries Lecture Notes in Artificial Intelligence (LNAI) and Lecture Notes in Bioinformatics (LNBI), has established itself as a medium for the publication of new developments in computer science and information technology research, teaching, and education.

LNCS enjoys close cooperation with the computer science R & D community, the series counts many renowned academics among its volume editors and paper authors, and collaborates with prestigious societies. Its mission is to serve this international community by providing an invaluable service, mainly focused on the publication of conference and workshop proceedings and postproceedings. LNCS commenced publication in 1973.

Bernhard Haslhofer · Java Xu · Friedhelm Victor ·
Massimo Bartoletti · Andrea Bracciali ·
Kanta Matsuura · Jarek Nabrzyski ·
Vero Estrada-Galiñanes · Claudio Tessone ·
Jurlind Budurushi · Karola Marky
Editors

Financial Cryptography and Data Security

FC 2025 International Workshops

CAAW 2025 and WTSC 2025
Miyakojima, Japan, April 18, 2025
Revised Selected Papers, Part I

Editors
Bernhard Haslhofer
Complexity Science Hub
Vienna, Austria

Friedhelm Victor
TRM Labs
San Francisco, CA, USA

Andrea Bracciali
Università di Torino
Turin, Italy

Jarek Nabrzyski
University of Notre Dame
Notre Dame, IN, USA

Claudio Tessone
University of Zurich
Zurich, Switzerland

Karola Marky
Ruhr-Universität Bochum
Bochum, Germany

Java Xu
University College London
London, UK

Massimo Bartoletti
Università degli Studi di Cagliari
Cagliari, Italy

Kanta Matsuura
The University of Tokyo
Tokyo, Japan

Vero Estrada-Galiñanes
Neuchâtel, Switzerland

Jurlind Budurushi
University of Karlsruhe
Karlsruhe, Germany

ISSN 0302-9743　　　　　　　ISSN 1611-3349　(electronic)
Lecture Notes in Computer Science
ISBN 978-3-032-00491-8　　　ISBN 978-3-032-00492-5　(eBook)
https://doi.org/10.1007/978-3-032-00492-5

© International Financial Cryptography Association 2026
Chapter "SoK: Modelling Data Storage and Availability" is licensed under the terms of the Creative Commons Attribution 4.0 International License (http://creativecommons.org/licenses/by/4.0/). For further details see license information in the chapter.

This work is subject to copyright. All rights are solely and exclusively licensed by the Publisher, whether the whole or part of the material is concerned, specifically the rights of translation, reprinting, reuse of illustrations, recitation, broadcasting, reproduction on microfilms or in any other physical way, and transmission or information storage and retrieval, electronic adaptation, computer software, or by similar or dissimilar methodology now known or hereafter developed.
The use of general descriptive names, registered names, trademarks, service marks, etc. in this publication does not imply, even in the absence of a specific statement, that such names are exempt from the relevant protective laws and regulations and therefore free for general use.
The publisher, the authors and the editors are safe to assume that the advice and information in this book are believed to be true and accurate at the date of publication. Neither the publisher nor the authors or the editors give a warranty, expressed or implied, with respect to the material contained herein or for any errors or omissions that may have been made. The publisher remains neutral with regard to jurisdictional claims in published maps and institutional affiliations.

This Springer imprint is published by the registered company Springer Nature Switzerland AG
The registered company address is: Gewerbestrasse 11, 6330 Cham, Switzerland

If disposing of this product, please recycle the paper.

CAAW 2025 Preface

These proceedings collect the papers accepted at the Fourth International Cryptoasset Analytics Workshop (CAAW 2025), held in conjunction with the Financial Cryptography and Data Security 2025 conference (FC 2025) in Miyakojima, Japan, in April 2025. CAAW provided an interdisciplinary forum for researchers to present their newest findings on cryptoassets and their ecosystems, to learn about novel analytics methods spanning peer-to-peer networks, consensus, on-chain, and off-chain layers, and to discuss open challenges and future directions. In recognition of the breadth of the field, CAAW 2025 also addressed cross-cutting issues in law, ethics, privacy, and security.

This year, CAAW received 23 submissions. After a rigorous double-blind peer review, with an average of four reviews per paper, followed by discussion, nine full papers were finally accepted for presentation and inclusion in these proceedings. We are grateful to the multidisciplinary Programme Committee for their generous effort and to all authors for preparing high-quality submissions. Revised versions of the accepted papers, following workshop discussions, are collected in the present volume.

Accepted papers analyzed a broad spectrum of phenomena in the cryptoasset ecosystem, ranging from payment-channel dynamics and inscription "booms" to price-oracle accuracy and zero-knowledge rollup benchmarks. Key recent developments addressed by papers and discussed at the workshop included Layer-2 protocols, support for zero-knowledge technology, models of smart-contract computation, and off-chain performance measurements. By weaving together these technical, empirical, and societal threads, the workshop provided a holistic view of cryptoasset analytics – one that not only advanced measurement and methodology but also informed the broader conversation around governance, ethics, and the future of decentralized systems.

The technical program was rounded out by two invited keynote talks. Brad Bachu (Uniswap Labs) spoke on "Empirical Research in Crypto: Challenges and Opportunities," reflecting on methodological rigor and data-driven insight in DeFi research. Owen Vaughan (independent blockchain researcher) presented "Bringing DeFi to Bitcoin," showcasing advances in zero-knowledge proofs and verifiable computation to extend Bitcoin's capabilities. Their perspectives framed many of the themes addressed in the peer-reviewed contributions.

We are grateful to the Financial Cryptography 2025 organizers for hosting CAAW, and to our sponsors for their generous support. Our heartfelt thanks go to all authors for submitting high-quality work, to the Programme Committee for their careful and constructive reviews, and to all workshop participants for lively discussions and feedback.

CAAW 2025 was supported by

April 2025

Bernhard Haslhofer
Friedhelm Victor
Java Xu

CAAW 2025 Organization

Organizing Committee

Bernhard Haslhofer	Complexity Science Hub, Austria
Friedhelm Victor	TRM Labs, USA
Jiahua Xu	Exponential Science, and University College London, UK

Program Committee

Svetlana Abramova	Complexity Science Hub, Austria
Rachit Agarwal	IIT Kanpur, India
Lukas Aumayr	TU Wien, Austria
Stefano Balietti	University of Mannheim, Germany
Massimo Bartoletti	University of Cagliari, Italy
Andrea Bracciali	University of Turin, Italy
Carlo Campajola	University College London, UK
Andrea Canidio	CoW DAO, Portugal
Diego Castejon	IMDEA Software Institute, Spain
Yebo Feng	Nanyang Technological University, Singapore
Robin Fritsch	ETH Zurich, Switzerland
Martin Harrigan	South East Technological University, Ireland
Lioba Heimbach	ETH Zürich, Switzerland
Walter Hernandez	DLT Science Foundation and UCL, UK
Juraj Hledik	European Commission, Italy
Aljosha Judmayer	SBA Research, Austria
Kwok Yan Lam	Nanyang Technological University, Singapore
Sheng-Nan Li	University of Zürich, Switzerland
Christos Makridis	Stanford University, USA
Riccardo Marchesin	University of Trento, Italy
Johnnatan Messias	MPI-SWS, Germany
Malte Möser	Chainalysis, USA
Vabuk Pahari	MPI-SWS, Germany
Masarah Paquet-Clouston	Université de Montréal, Canada
Arash Pourdamghani	TU Berlin, Germany
Julien Prat	CREST, École Polytechnique, France
Pietro Saggese	IMT School for Advanced Studies Lucca, Italy

István András Seres	Eötvös Loránd University, Hungary
Sandeep Shukla	IIT Kanpur, India
Natkamon Tovanich	CREST, École Polytechnique, France
Kentaroh Toyoda	IHPC, A*STAR SIMTech, Singapore
Nicolò Vallarano	Universität Zürich, Switzerland
Dimitrios Vasilopoulos	IMDEA Software Institute, Spain
Saravanan Vijayakumaran	IIT Bombay, India
Stefan Voigt	København Universitet, Denmark
Viet Anh Vu	University of Cambridge, UK
Christoph Wegener	Leuphana University, Germany
Cong Wu	University of Hong Kong, China
Marcus Wunsch	Zurich University of Applied Sciences, Switzerland
Aviv Yaish	Yale University, USA
Michelle Yeo	National University of Singapore, Singapore
Francesco Zola	Vicomtech, Spain

WTSC 2025

9th International Workshop on Trusted Smart Contracts

Preface

These proceedings collect the papers accepted at the Ninth Workshop on Trusted Smart Contracts (WTSC25 - http://fc25.ifca.ai/wtsc/), associated to the Financial Cryptography and Data Security 2025 international conference. WTSC25 was hosted this year on the beautiful island of Miyakojima, Japan.

The WTSC series' main focus is on *smart contracts*, i.e. self-enforcing agreements in the form of executable programs, and, more generally, on *decentralised applications* that interoperate with (possibly specialised) blockchain systems. The WTSC series aims to address the *scientific foundations* of Trusted Smart Contract engineering and their applications, i.e., the development of contracts and applications that enjoy some verifiable "correctness" properties. Correctness, safety, privacy, authentication, efficiency, sustainability, resilience and trust in smart contracts and decentralised applications are all topics of interest. We discuss open problems, proposed solutions, new and decentralised business models and use cases, as well as visions of future developments, amongst a research community that is growing around these themes. WTSC is supported by a multi-disciplinary and diverse Program Committee that comprises members from universities, companies and research institutions from several countries worldwide. The association to FC25 provided, once again, an ideal context for running our workshop.

This year WTSC received twelve submissions by about twenty authors. Given the high quality of submission, eight papers were finally accepted after double-blind peer review, with an average of four reviews per paper, some followed by discussion, providing constructive feedback to the authors of all submitted papers. We want to commend the generous effort by the PC. Revised papers after the discussion at the workshop are collected in the present volume. Accepted papers analysed attacks on main chains, formalisation and exploitation of incentives and cryptoeconomics, a formalisation of proof-of-space, privacy over decentralised finance, tokenisation security, fee mechanisms and a SoK on data management. The long-term, fruitful collaboration with the Workshop on Coordination of Decentralized Finance (CoDecFin) series provided this year a joint invited talk - *Can smart contracts make real-world assets more valuable?* by Jason Teutsch, Truebit, and a panel - *Crypto-Agility and PQC migration for Blockchain*, chaired by Shin'ichiro Matsuo on the migration to quantum-resistant blockchains.

Once again, WTSC 2025's chairs would like to thank everyone for their effort and valuable contributions: authors, program committee members, reviewers and participants, as well as the support by IFCA, the FC25 chairs and committee, and Ray Hirschfeld for the usual exceptional organisation and coordination of the whole FC event and series.

May 2025

Massimo Bartoletti
Andrea Bracciali

WTSC 2025 Organization

Program Committee

Monika di Angelo	Vienna University of Technology, Austria
Igor Artamonov	Emerald, USA
Fadi Barbara	University of Turin, Italy
Marco Benedetti	Banca d'Italia, Italy
Massimo Bartoletti	University of Cagliari, Italy
Stefano Bistarelli	University of Perugia, Italy
Andrea Bracciali	University of Turin, Italy
Daniel Broby	Asian Institute of Management, Philippines
Martin Chapman	King's College London, UK
James Chapman	IOG, UK
Nicola Dimitri	University of Siena, Italy
Nadia Fabrizio	University of Bergamo, Italy
Josselin Feist	Trail of Bits, USA
Oliver Giudice	Banca d'Italia, Italy
Geoffrey Goodell	University College London, UK
Davide Grossi	University of Groningen, The Netherlands
Bernhard Haslhofer	Complexity Science Hub, Austria
Yoichi Hirai	BedRock Systems GmbH, Germany
Michela Iezzi	Banca d'Italia, Italy
Enrique Larraia	Heliax, Spain
Andrew Lewis-Pye	London School of Economics, UK
Akaki Mamageishvili	Offchain Labs, Switzerland
Carla Mascia	Datacrypto, USA
Patrick McCorry	Arbitrum, UK
Sihem Mesnager	University of Paris VIII, France
Bud Mishra	New York University, USA
Alex Norta	Tallinn University of Technology, Estonia
Akira Otsuka	Institute of Information Security, Japan
Massimiliano Sala	University of Trento, Italy
Jason Teutsch	Truebit, USA
Sara Tucci Piergiovanni	Paris-Saclay University, France
Polina Vinogradova	IOG, Canada
Philip Wadler	University of Edinburgh, UK
Yilei Wang	Qufu University, China
Tim Weingärtner	Lucerne University, Switzerland

Santiago Zanella-Béguelin Microsoft, UK
Dionysis Zindros Stanford University, USA

WTSC25 was partially supported by
EUPEX - European Project for Exascale (https://eupex.eu/)
SERICS - Security and Rights in the Cyberspace (https://serics.eu/)

Contents – Part I

On the Lifecycle of a Lightning Network Payment Channel 1
   *Florian Grötschla, Lioba Heimbach, Severin Richner,
and Roger Wattenhofer*

The Writing Is on the Wall: Analyzing the Boom of Inscriptions and Its
Impact on EVM-Compatible Blockchains 17
   *Johnnatan Messias, Krzysztof Gogol, Maria Inés Silva,
and Benjamin Livshits*

Price Oracle Accuracy Across Blockchains: A Measurement and Analysis 32
   Robin Gansäuer, Hichem Ben Aoun, Jan Droll, and Hannes Hartenstein

A Public Dataset For the ZKsync Rollup 47
   Maria Inês Silva, Johnnatan Messias, and Benjamin Livshits

Early Observations of Based Rollups: A Case Study of Taiko 63
   Jan Gorzny, Phillip Kemper, and Martin Derka

What Drives Liquidity on Decentralized Exchanges? Evidence
from the Uniswap Protocol 78
   *Brian Zhu, Dingyue Liu, Xin Wan, Gordon Liao, Ciamac Moallemi,
and Brad Bachu*

Liquidity Fragmentation or Optimization? Analyzing Automated Market
Makers Across Ethereum and Rollups 94
   *Krzysztof M. Gogol, Manvir Schneider, Claudio J. Tessone,
and Benjamin Livshits*

Quantifying Price Improvement in Order Flow Auctions 111
   Brad Bachu, Xin Wan, and Ciamac C. Moallemi

Short Paper: Atomic Execution is Not Enough for Arbitrage Profit
Extraction in Shared Sequencers 127
   Maria Inês Silva and Benjamin Livshits

Revisiting Bitcoin's Merkle Tree Security: Practical Implications
and an Attack on Core Chain 137
   Yogev Bar-On

A Quantitative Notion of Economic Security for Smart Contract
Compositions 147
    Emily Priyadarshini and Massimo Bartoletti

Hollow Victory: How Malicious Proposers Exploit Validator Incentives
in Optimistic Rollup Dispute Games 164
    Suhyeon Lee

A Formalization of Signum's Consensus 180
    Fausto Spoto

Monero's Decentralized P2P Exchanges: Functionality, Adoption,
and Privacy Risks 200
    Yannik Kopyciok, Friedhelm Victor, and Stefan Schmid

Toward a Secure Tokenized Green Credit Management System: Case
Study of WREGIS 216
    Mahmudun Nabi and Reihaneh Safavi-Naini

Parallel Execution Fee Mechanisms 245
    Abdoulaye Ndiaye

SoK: Modelling Data Storage and Availability 263
    Carlo Brunetta and Massimiliano Sala

Author Index 281

Contents – Part II

Optimizing Liveness for Blockchain-Based Sealed-Bid Auctions in Rational Settings 1
    Maozhou Huang, Xiangyu Su, Mario Larangeira, and Keisuke Tanaka

Blockchain-Based Carbon Footprint Management 29
    Umut Pekel and Oğuz Yayla

An Analysis of Financial Stability Risk Propagation Through Leveraged Staking Activities 50
    Takaya Sugino, Benjamin Kraner, James Angel, Shin'ichiro Matsuo, and Rohil Paruchuri

SCOOP: CoSt-effective COngestiOn Attacks in Payment Channel Networks 69
    Mohammed Ababneh, Kartick Kolachala, and Roopa Vishwanathan

Universal Blockchain Assets 84
    Owen Vaughan

Private Electronic Payments with Self-custody and Zero-Knowledge Verified Reissuance 100
    Daniele Friolo, Geoffrey Goodell, D. R. Toliver, and Hazem Danny Nakib

Rayls: A Novel Design for CBDCs 122
    Mario Yaksetig and Jiayu Xu

Hybrid Stabilization Protocol for Cross-Chain Digital Assets Using Adaptor Signatures and AI-Driven Arbitrage 138
    Shengwei You, Andrey Kuehlkamp, and Jarek Nabrzyski

Intmax2: A ZK-Rollup with Minimal Onchain Data and Computation Costs Featuring Decentralized Aggregators 162
    Erik Rybakken, Leona Hioki, Mario Yaksetig, Denisa Diaconescu, František Silváši, and Julian Sutherland

Quest Love: A First Look at Blockchain Loyalty Programs 196
    Joseph Al-Chami and Jeremy Clark

SoK: Designing a Curriculum for Open Finance 212
    Daniel Broby and Eduardo T. Valencia Jr.

3+ Seat Risk-Limiting Audits for Single Transferable Vote Elections 226
   Michelle Blom, Alexander Ek, Peter J. Stuckey, Vanessa Teague, and Damjan Vukcevic

Doing More with Less: Mismatch-Based Risk-Limiting Audits 241
   Alexander Ek, Michelle Blom, Philip B. Stark, Peter J. Stuckey, Vanessa J. Teague, and Damjan Vukcevic

Voting Without Self-voting 256
   Peter B. Rønne

Anamorphic Voting: Ballot Freedom Against Dishonest Authorities 266
   Rosario Giustolisi, Mohammadamin Rakeei, and Gabriele Lenzini

E2Easy: a Simple Lattice-Based in-Person End-to-End Voting Scheme 281
   Eduardo L. Cominetti, Marcos A. Simplicio, Diego F. Aranha, Paulo Matias, and Roberto Araújo

Security Analysis of the Australian Capital Territory's eVACS 2020/2024 Paperless Direct Recording Electronic Voting System 297
   Chris Culnane, Andrew Conway, Vanessa Teague, and Ty Wilson-Brown

opn.vote: A Publicly Verifiable Blockchain-Based eVoting System 306
   Felix Maduakor, Thi Van Thao Doan, and Joerg Mitzlaff

Enhancing Helios for Elections at Qatar University 309
   Jurlind Budurushi, Khalid Abdallah, Farhan Al Sadi, Hosam Zarouk, Abdelwahab Almasri, and Armstrong Nhlabatsi

Author Index 313

On the Lifecycle of a Lightning Network Payment Channel

Florian Grötschla[✉], Lioba Heimbach, Severin Richner, and Roger Wattenhofer

ETH Zurich, Zürich, Switzerland
{fgroetschla,hlioba,richners,wattenhofer}@ethz.ch

Abstract. The *Bitcoin Lightning Network*, launched in 2018, serves as a *layer 2* scaling solution for Bitcoin. The Lightning Network allows users to establish channels between each other and subsequently exchange off-chain payments. Together, these channels form a network that facilitates payments between parties even if they do not have a channel in common. The Lightning Network has gained popularity over the past five years as it offers an attractive alternative to on-chain transactions by substantially reducing transaction costs and processing times. Nevertheless, due to the privacy-centric design of the Lightning Network, little is understood about its inner workings. In this work, we conduct a measurement study of the Lightning Network to shed light on the lifecycle of channels. By combining Lightning gossip messages with on-chain Bitcoin data, we investigate the lifecycle of a channel from its opening through its lifetime to its closing. In particular, our analysis offers unique insights into the utilization patterns of the Lightning Network. Even more so, through decoding the channel closing transactions, we obtain the first dataset of Lightning Network payments, observe the imbalance of channels during the closing, and investigate whether both parties are involved in the closing, or one closes the channel unilaterally. For instance, we find nearly 60% of cooperatively closed channels are resurrected, i.e., their outputs were used to fund another channel.

Keywords: Bitcoin · layer 2 · Lightning Network

1 Introduction

The inception of Bitcoin in 2008 marked the creation of the first decentralized cryptocurrency. While the introduction of Bitcoin permanently impacted the way society regards money and finance, cryptocurrencies such as Bitcoin are also known for their extremely small throughput. To tackle this issue, *payment channels* were introduced [10, 12, 18, 19, 23, 27]. The idea is that instead of settling every transaction on the Bitcoin blockchain directly, Alice and Bob create a payment channel between each other on the blockchain and lock an amount of

---

F. Grötschla—The authors of this work are listed alphabetically.

BTC in the channel, namely, the *channel capacity*. With the payment channel, Alice and Bob can exchange payments directly. Even more, multiple payment channels together form a *payment channel network* that allows users to route their payments across various channels. Thus, users are not required to set up a channel with every individual they wish to exchange payments with but can take advantage of the existing network of channels. To compensate the owners of channels involved in facilitating a transaction, transactions pay a small fee. The *Lightning Network* is a payment network implementation on top of Bitcoin. Nodes in the Lightning Network *gossip* with each other to exchange information about the nodes and channels in the network. For example, when Alice and Bob create a payment channel between themselves, they might choose to announce the channel in the network such that other nodes in the network know about this channel and can potentially use it to route their transaction. Thanks to these messages, the size and structure of the *public* network, that is, nodes and channels that announce themselves, is generally well understood. There are currently more than 13,000 nodes with 50,000 payment channels that hold over 70M USD [3].

Privacy for payments is a key component of the Lightning Network. When Alice sends a payment to Charlie, the Lightning Network is designed so that no other node should be able to know the source and the target of the payment, even if they were involved in routing the transaction. Thus, little is understood of the network's activity and usage as most transactions are not broadcast on the Bitcoin blockchain but rather kept between the two endpoints of a channel [13, 15, 28]. We show that despite these mechanisms, we can extract information on the usage of Lightning channels by analyzing the traces left in gossip messages from the Lightning network and Bitcoin transactions that manage these channels on the blockchain. We do so by matching transaction outputs with the possible transaction blueprints provided by Lightning and identifying the code paths used to claim funds from these outputs. This can tell us, among other things, whether a channel was closed cooperatively, if one party tried to steal funds by broadcasting an old state to the blockchain, or if the output of a closed channel was used to open a new one.

Contribution. We present an empirical study of the lifecycle and usage of Lightning Network payment channels. Through an analysis of off-chain Lightning gossip messages and on-chain Bitcoin data, we provide the following insights:

- Our longitudinal study of *channel openings* over time quantifies the number of channels opened, the size of channels, and the proportion of publicly announced channels.
- Through an analysis of gossip messages, we reason about the *usage of channels during their lifetime* and find indicators to predict the direction of the net flow of routed payments in a channel.
- The traces of a channel's closing transaction further allow us to quantify the sizes of any unsettled Lightning Network payments at the time of the closing. We obtained, to the best of our knowledge, the *first dataset of Lightning payment sizes* comprising 21,168 payments.

– Our in-depth study of *channel closings* reveals the channel imbalances at the closing time and the closing type, e.g., whether the channel was closed unilaterally or cooperatively.

2 Lightning Network

The Lightning Network is a layer 2 protocol designed to scale Bitcoin: a network of bidirectional payment channels enables off-chain transfer of Bitcoin. Each payment channel established by two nodes in the network represents an edge in the network and allows them to exchange payments by agreeing on updated channel states. In practical terms, each channel has a fixed amount of Bitcoin known as its capacity, which remains constant throughout its operation. However, the ownership distribution of Bitcoin within the channel can change with each transaction. For example, if node A sends node B an amount x of Bitcoin, the balance on A's side of the channel decreases by x, while the balance on B's side increases by the same amount.

The underlying mechanism that enables this balance updating process without requiring on-chain transactions is the creation of off-chain commitments. These commitments are essentially signed transactions that reflect the updated balances of the channel but are not broadcast to the Bitcoin blockchain unless the channel is closed. This off-chain nature significantly reduces the load on the Bitcoin blockchain, enabling faster and cheaper transactions. When a payment is made over the Lightning Network, it can be routed through multiple channels to reach its final destination. This is possible due to the interconnected nature of the network, where multiple channels between various nodes form a complex web. Payments can thus be routed across the network, from the sender to the receiver, through intermediary nodes that facilitate the transaction. Each intermediary node deducts a small fee for forwarding the payment, providing an economic incentive to participate in the network.

Importantly, the Lightning Network enables instant and low-cost transactions. The network is further designed to protect the privacy of transactions. Since transactions occur off-chain, they are not recorded on the Bitcoin blockchain, enhancing user privacy. In addition, the origin and destination of transactions routed through the network are difficult to trace for an observer, adding an extra layer of privacy.

2.1 Channel Lifecycle

A payment channel in the Lightning Network is created through a *funding transaction*, maintained/updated by *commitment transactions*, and closed by a *closing transaction*. Generally, only the funding and closing transactions are validated on-chain. Commitment transactions, on the other hand, are held by the nodes involved in the channel and only posted on-chain when a channel is unilaterally closed by one party. The unilateral closing of a channel leads to a timelocked output for that party's funds.

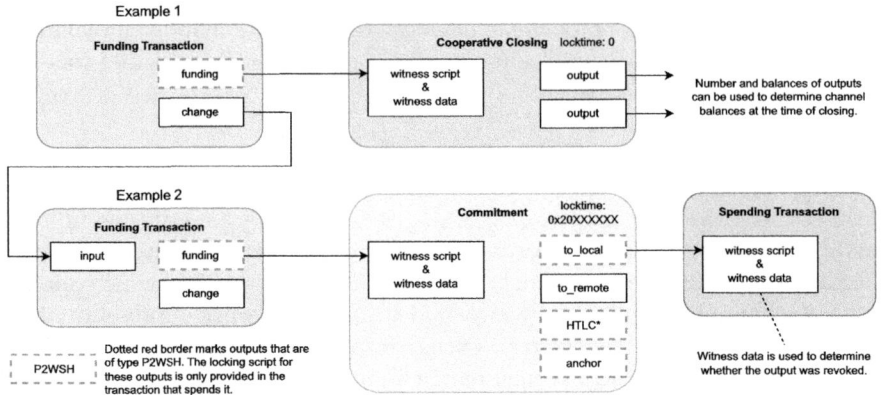

Fig. 1. Two exemplary funding transactions. Cooperative closings spend the 2-of-2-multisig output from the funding transaction and do not have a locktime, while commitments use the locktime field to encode the commitment number. By analyzing the outputs from the commitment, we can classify them into multiple types; some of them are used to send funds to the owner of the commitment (after some timeout), while others represent HTLCs or enable fee bumping. Following the local output for the commitment owner to the spending transaction lets us identify whether the commitment has been revoked. We further analyze whether outputs were used to directly fund other channels. Here, the funding transaction in Example 1 has a change output that funds another channel (i.e., Example 2).

Funding Transaction. A funding transaction is a Pay-to-Witness-Script-Hash (P2WSH) transaction using a specified script for the output, which represents the channel [23]. Thus, on the Bitcoin blockchain, a Lightning Network channel is represented by a single P2WSH output containing the hash of a 2-of-2 multi-signature scheme as the locking script. We also refer to this as the multisig or channel address. The transaction can generally have multiple outputs, with some of them taking the role of "change". The script for the funding transaction is defined as follows:

Script Funding

```
1: 2 <pubkey1> <pubkey2> 2 OP_CHECKMULTISIG
```

The two public keys correspond to the private keys held by the two channel endpoints, and the output can only be spent when both agree. Importantly, transactions of this kind are not unique to Lightning channel openings [15] but heuristics to identify private channels have been developed (cf. Section 3) (Fig. 1).

Closing Transaction. A channel is can either be closed *cooperatively* or *non-cooperatively*. If the channel is closed cooperatively, both parties agree on channel balances and jointly decide to close the channel. Both nodes sign a closing transaction that spends the channel funds to their respective wallets. As soon as the transaction is confirmed on the blockchain parties can spend their funds. Otherwise, if the channel is closed non-cooperatively, the party wishing to close the channel submits a commitment transaction to the blockchain. The other node is then given a time window to revoke that transaction (in case an old commitment transaction was submitted that does not reflect the latest status of the channel balances, referred to as *prior state cheating*). If the commitment transaction becomes revoked, all channel funds are awarded to the revoking node as a punishment for not following the protocol. If, however, the time window expires without a revocation, the node can spend the channel funds according to the balances from the submitted commitment transaction.

Commitment Transaction. Commitment transactions update the channel balances, and the most recent commitment transaction always represents the current balances between the channel's nodes. These commitment transactions are usually not published on-chain and, thus, allow for fast and inexpensive Bitcoin transfers inside the channel without needing to pay fees on the Bitcoin blockchain. Further, the channel participants sign each commitment transaction. Thereby, invalidating the previous commitment transaction which is essential as it allows for any old commitment transaction to be revoked. A commitment might be broadcast for various reasons. For example, when one channel party is unresponsive and the other wants to recover its funds. In this case, the broadcaster has to wait for a timeout to pass before they can access their funds, giving the other party time to invalidate an outdated and replaced commitment. This is referred to as *prior state cheating* and results in all funds being given to the party that invalidated the outdated commitment. If no such invalidation takes place, the funds can be accessed by the broadcaster after the timeout.

3 Data Collection and Classification

We collect data from the Lightning Network gossip data as well as the Bitcoin blockchain data. Our data ranges from 1 January 2019 to 23 September 2023, but utilize shortened data ranges for parts of the analysis.

Bitcoin Blockchain Transactions. To gather Bitcoin transactions related to channel openings and closings, we utilize the Blockstream Esplora API [2]. In particular, we start with public channels that are announced through gossip messages and retrieve their funding transactions. These are used as a starting point for the private channel discovery and to scan their transaction outputs for usage in later transactions. As most outputs are of type P2WSH as specified in the protocol, the locking scripts are concealed until their usage as a transaction input. Therefore, starting from the funding transactions, we scan all outputs and their usages to detect the closing and spending transactions to infer the type of the transaction output and store further details such as the block height and time the following transaction took place.

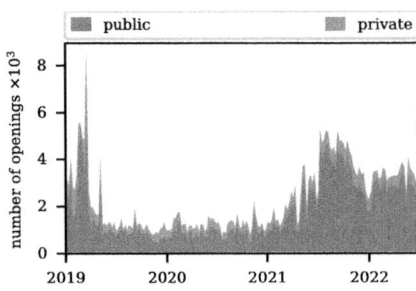 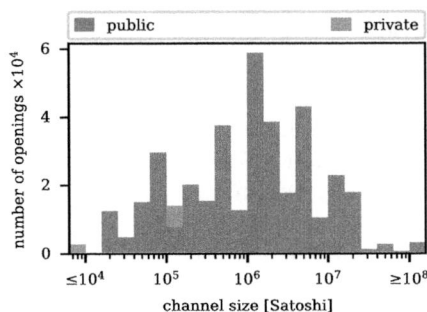

Fig. 2. Weekly number of public and private channel openings.

Fig. 3. Private and public channel opening sizes.

Private Channel Detection. While *public* channels announce themselves through gossip messages, *private* channels are never gossiped about publicly. Various heuristics for private Lightning channel detection exist [14,20,26]. These are primarily focused on identifying potential funding transactions. We use the following heuristic proposed by Kappos et al. [15] to identify these channels and calculate associated statistics:

1. We apply the "Property Heuristic" to identify Bitcoin transactions that are likely used as Lightning funding transactions. The heuristic includes checking the number, size, and kind of transaction outputs, as well as their compliance with the Lightning specification.
2. To identify private channels, we employ the "Tracing Heuristic" that detects "peeling chains" – sequences of channel opening and closing transactions that are linked within the Bitcoin transaction graph. This heuristic tracks the flow of funds by following the closing and change outputs of channel funding transactions to determine if they are reused in subsequent channel funding transactions. Such reuse suggests that a single entity is involved in both channels. The heuristic can also be applied in reverse to trace the origins of the funding inputs. Channels identified through this method that do not appear in the Lightning Network's gossip protocol data are classified as private, as they are not publicly announced.

Given that we lack information about whether these channels map to any nodes in the publicly accessible network, we limit ourselves to deriving statistics based solely on on-chain data.

Transaction Output Classification. To deduce the output type, we evaluate the locking script and cross-reference it with known output types within the Lightning specification [1]. These types encompass *local* outputs, which represent funds time-locked for the commitment owner, *remote* outputs, allocated to the other channel party for direct spending, HTLCs designed for non-confirmed transactions, and anchors enabling fee bumping. In the case of local outputs, we further investigate the path employed for script unlocking, enabling the assessment of potential revocations in instances of prior state cheating. Outputs that remain unspent are categorized as *unspent*, as their output type cannot be inferred without a spending transaction that provides the witness data.

4 Channel Lifecycle

4.1 Channel Opening

The life of a channel begins when its funding transaction is created. In Fig. 2, we show the weekly number of public and private channel openings. In 2020, there were consistently around 5,000 channel openings per month. There is a notable increase in 2021, reaching 15,000 monthly openings, ahead of a slight decline. The increase and subsequent decline in nodes could be related to the adoption of Bitcoin as a legal tender in El Salvador on 5 June 2021 [4]. Other reasons could also factor in, for example low transaction fees could incentivize the opening of new channels. However, especially the uptick of new channels in the beginning of 2021 coincides with rising transaction fees, which counters this argument. Beyond this timeframe, we could also not find a significant correlation. Throughout the period we investigate, private channels constituted approximately 22% of all channel openings. Figure 3 further visualizes the channel sizes for private and public channels. We consider the amount of Satoshis (1 Satoshi = 10^{-8} Bitcoin) locked in these public and private channels over the entire timeframe. These channels vary widely in size, ranging from four to eight digits of Satoshis, which, as of May 2024, one Satoshi is less than a thousandth USD. Interestingly, private channels tend to have lower average volumes. The reasons for this could be attributed to factors such as specific use cases, privacy considerations within the network, or user preferences when engaging in private channel transactions.

4.2 Channel Lifetime

In the following, we focus on the lifetime of the channels. We start by investigating the size of the Lightning Network in terms of the number of active nodes (cf. Figure 4a) and the number of active channels (cf. Figure 4b). We consider a node to be active if it is involved in at least one open public payment channel. Importantly, for nodes, we only identify public nodes as private nodes are not active in the gossip network. From the start of 2019 until the end of our data period, i.e., 1 July 2022, we observe that the number of active nodes is generally increasing. Notably, there is a significant increase in mid-2021 and a significant drop in the number of nodes in early 2022. Again, we speculate that this could be due to the usage of the Lightning Network in El Salvador. Further, the drop in the number of active nodes in 2022 coincides with an unusually high number of channels closing during that time period (cf. Section 4.3). We note that the number of active nodes peaked at around 12,500 at the beginning of 2022 and dropped to just over 7,500 by mid-2022. Similarly, the number of active channels, namely, the number of open channels, is increasing during our data period. However, less so than the number of nodes—indicating that the average node

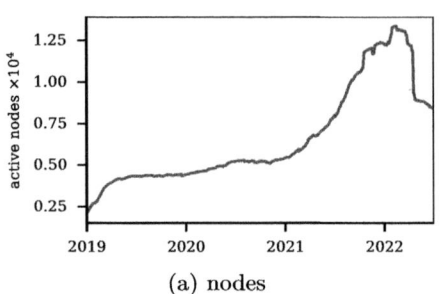 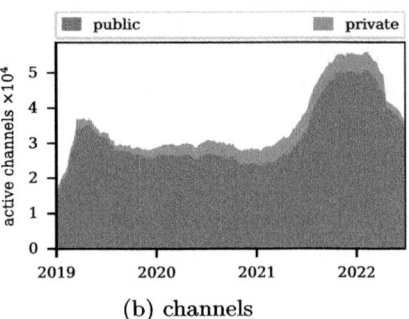

Fig. 4. Number of public nodes (cf. Figure 4a), as well as public and private channels (cf. Figure 4b) over time.

is involved in fewer public channels in mid-2022 (with four) than at the beginning of 2019 (with six). The number of public channels peaked at over 45,000 in early 2022. For the channels, we also include the number of private channels and observe that the number of private channels is always less than 20% of the number of public channels. Further, the proportion of private channels peaked in early 2021 and has decreased since then. We further notice a small discrepancy between the proportion of private channel openings (cf. Figure 2) and their proportion of the network. This discrepancy is a result of the short channel lifetime of private channels as we will see in Sect. 4.3.

Gossip Message Analysis. We continue by investigating the gossip messages broadcast on the network. Due to gaps in the lngossip [9] dataset, we restrict the following analysis, which depends on these network messages, to a period without gaps, i.e., 1 January 2020 to 1 July 2021. Recall that there are several types of gossip messages, we focus on `channel_update` messages here. In more detail, we study the channel updates and analyze whether they give us any insights into traffic patterns in the network. We start with the frequency of channel updates. Every time either channel side adjusts the fees and parameters used for routing, they will broadcast a `channel_update` message in the network. Our analysis considers such a message to be an update if the parameters are not identical to the previous message. Figure 5 plots a histogram of the mean daily number of channel updates during their lifetime. On average, the channels have 0.69 daily updates, while the median is only 0.05. This discrepancy by a factor of ten between the mean and the median indicates an extremely skewed dataset. That is, there are few channels with many updates and many channels with little to no updates. However, updating channel parameters can be essential to optimize participation in routing. For one, the channel parameters need to be competitive to attract traffic, but just as importantly, the channel parameters are used to avoid the channel becoming depleted by guiding payment flow in the right direction. Note that once a channel active in routing becomes depleted, it is generally closed and reopened, which is costly. Thus, frequent channel updates can indicate that the channel is being actively used in routing transactions through

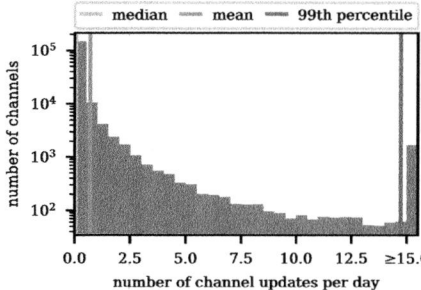 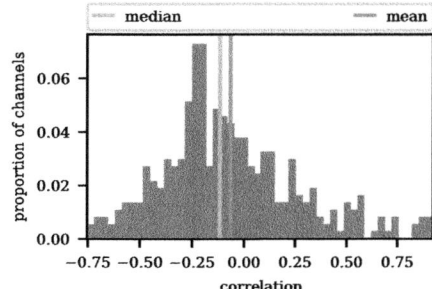

Fig. 5. Daily number of channel updates. The median, mean, and 99th percentile are indicated by vertical lines.

Fig. 6. Correlation between proportional fee set by the two channel sides for channels with ≥100 updates by each side.

the Lightning Network. We, however, find that only 8.9% of the public channels update their parameters at least once per day on average and would expect at least one update per day for channels that forward a couple of transactions per day on average. The 99th percentile of channels update their parameters at least 14.7 times a day. We thus believe that these channels actively participate in forwarding transactions through the network.

Channel Fees. When updating the fees for routing, nodes specify a *base* (i.e., a flat rate charged per transaction) and a *proportional* (i.e., a rate charged proportional to the transaction size) fee. We will now focus on the proportional fee, as one method of rebalancing a depleted channel is fee management. If one's outbound liquidity is getting low, a strategy is to increase the fees to disincentive nodes from using your outbound liquidity. The opposite could be done at the other channel end. Thus, the proportional fee moving in opposite directions could hint at the net direction of transactions sent through the channel as well as the liquidity imbalance of the channel. To test this hypothesis, we consider all channels with at least 100 updates from either side and plot the correlation between the proportional fee time series from both sides in Fig. 6. We find that both the mean and median of the proportional fee correlation across the analyzed channels are negative—in line with our hypothesis. However, there are also channels with a strong correlation between the proportional fees from either side over time. This could be a sign that both channel sides want traffic regardless of the direction and rely on other rebalancing strategies.

HTLC Analysis. Our preceding analysis provides insight into which channels might be involved in routing and the possible direction of flows in channels that we learn by analyzing the gossip messages. However, while the gossip messages allow us to reason about the traffic in the network, they do not offer precise information about the transactions routed through the network. The design of the Lightning Network aims to prevent this information from ever being revealed, but there is an exception during the channel closing. *Hashed timelock contracts (HTLCs)* are the centerpiece of every Lightning Network payment, as they allow

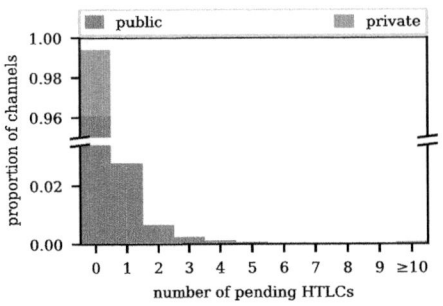 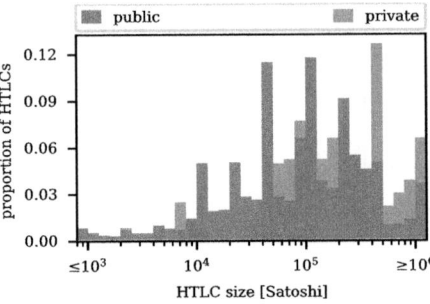

(a) Number of unsettled HTLCs for public and private channels during the closing.

(b) Size of unsettled HTLCs for public and private channels.

Fig. 7. Number of unsettled HTLCs (cf. Figure 7a) and Fig. 7b.

for secure and atomic, that is, the entire transaction succeeds or fails, routing through the network. We note that HTLCs are used for both single-hop and multi-hop payments. Importantly, an HTLC represents an unconfirmed transaction, and its size thus corresponds to that of said transaction. In rare cases, these HTLCs are settled on-chain, where the HTLC is not consolidated before the channel is closed. Thus, in these cases, we can observe the size and number of transactions in the channel. In Fig. 7, we present an analysis of exactly these HTLCs. In total, we observe 20,804 unconfirmed HTLCs in public channel closings and 364 in private channel closings. Figure 7a visualizes the number of unconfirmed HTLCs per channel during the closing. For the vast majority of channels, 96% of public and 99% of private channels, there are no unconfirmed HTLCs when the channel is closed. For private channels, all remaining channels have precisely one open HTLC. While it is not immediately clear that these are all single-hop payments, it is highly likely to be the case given that none of the 364 private channels with unsettled HTLCs have more than one unsettled HTLC, which is more likely to happen when the channel is involved in routing transactions. Finally, these unsettled HTLCs offer a unique insight into the size of Lightning transactions. Figure 7b plots the size of these HTLCs for public and private channels. We start by noting that the HTLCs greatly vary in size and that those unsettled HTLCs we observe for private channels are larger than those in public ones on average. The average HTLC size in private channels is 360,000 Satoshis, whereas it is 230,000 Satoshis in public channels. This could be related to the fact that a larger proportion of unsettled HTLCs in private channels represent single-hop payments. That is, the parties went through the effort of setting up a channel as they were expecting to exchange funds, as opposed to multi-hop payments, where the parties use the existing network to exchange funds. We further notice that there are peaks for the transaction sizes. Many HTLCs are close to round numbers such as 1,000, 2,000, 3,000, or 10,000, indicating that individuals are generally more likely to send payments with these "round" sizes through the network. The amounts are usually a few Satoshis larger than these multiples, which could be due to fees added on top.

4.3 Channel Closing

We proceed with an analysis of the end of the channel lifetime: its closing. Figure 8 provides an overview of channel lifetime for public and private instances. Generally, their distribution follows a similar trend. However, extremely short-lived channels make up a more significant proportion of private channels, whereas long-lived channels account for a bigger proportion of public channels. Thus, the average lifetime of public channels is 143 days, which exceeds the average lifetime of private channels at only 125 days. Potentially, some private might have been opened for testing or rebalancing purposes and were thus not announced publicly.

Closing Frequency. In Fig. 9, we plot the weekly number of channel closings for public and private channels over time. While initially, private channels take up a larger proportion of channel closings, the number and distribution of channel closings is relatively stable until mid-2021 with approximately 1,000 channel closings per week. From then on the number of channel closings starts to increase and stabilizes at more than 2,000 weekly channel closings. With one week in mid-2022 exhibiting an abnormally high number of (private) channel closings at more than 6,000. We previously noticed this spike in channel closings due to a drop in the number of nodes and channels in the network at this time (cf. Figure 4).

Closing Types. In the following, we investigate the closing type of channels. Recall that we distinguish between two different types: *cooperative* and *unilateral* (through a commitment transaction). Cooperative closings are bilaterally agreed upon by both channel endpoints through an on-chain transaction. In this case, all funds locked in the channel are directly accessible to both parties. In this case, the number of channel outputs is either one, i.e., all channel funds are with one party, or two otherwise. We will identify the first case as `coopx1` and the second case as `coopx2` throughout. For unilateral channel closings, one party publishes a commitment on the blockchain. The party then has to wait for the passing of a timelock before the funds can be accessed. The timeout allows the other party to publish a revocation if an outdated commitment was published. For closings that were not revoked, we differentiate between three cases by the number of types of outputs: `local`, `local + remote`, and `remote` (cf. Section 2.1). With `local`, we identify all unilateral closings, where all funds are with the party that submitted the commitment, and the output has a timelock. With `remote`, we denote channels that only have one remote output, which does not have a timelock and can be spent immediately by the party that did not submit a commitment. In the case of `local + remote`, both outputs exist. Finally, we group all revoked unilateral closings as `revoked` regardless of the number and type of outputs given their sparse occurrence. Figure 10 visualizes the share of these aforementioned channel closing types for public and private channels, respectively. For public channels (cf. Figure 10a), cooperative closings make up the biggest proportion. Together, they account for more than 50% of all closings,

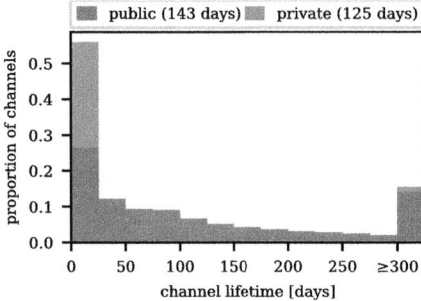 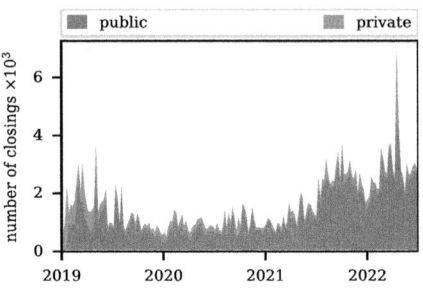

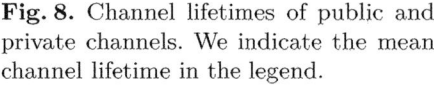

Fig. 8. Channel lifetimes of public and private channels. We indicate the mean channel lifetime in the legend.

Fig. 9. Weekly public and private channel closings over time. Notice the spike in closings in mid-2022.

of which cooperative closings with two outputs, denoted as coopx2, are 60% and those with one output, coopx1, are 40%. Interestingly, a more significant proportion of channels is closed cooperatively with two outputs than with one at the end of our collection window as opposed to the beginning. Thus, by mid-2022, channels are closed before either side is entirely depleted. Unilateral closings make up slightly less than half of all closings for public channels. For these, the proportion of closing with a single timelocked output, i.e., local, is initially significant and declines over time, whereas those unilateral closings with two outputs, i.e., local + remote, increase over time. With slightly less than 10% of all closings, unilateral remote closings make up a surprisingly large proportion given that the channel party that will not receive any funds goes through the effort of unilaterally closing the channel. Overall, we notice that by the end of our data analysis period, more public channels are closed before they become entirely unbalanced than in early 2019. Finally, we note that revocations are extremely rare, with a mere 103 observed during our data collection window and thus not visible in Fig. 10a.

Private Channel Closings. For private channels (cf. Figure 10b), we observe a different pattern. Cooperative closings also make up around 50% of closings, but the relative increase in those with two outputs cannot be observed. Unilateral closings also account for around 50% of closings over time. Here, unilateral closings are almost equally split between those with a single remote output and those with a single local output. Furthermore, the variations in the relative proportions of channel closings are minimal, especially in comparison to the public channels. Finally, as with public channels, revocations are extremely rare, with 78 occurrences during our time window. A further question is whether the channels are reopened, i.e., whether the channel closing is a means to rebalance the channel on-chain. We find that for 35% of the closed public channels, at least one of its outputs was used to fund another public channel. In contrast, only 14% of closed private channels fund another private channel. The reopenings are even

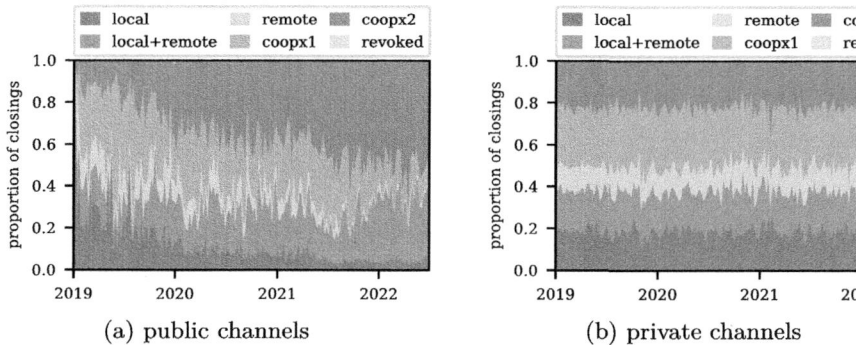

Fig. 10. Closing outputs for public and private channels. `local`, `local + remote`, `remote`, and `revoked` are types of unilateral channel closings, `coopx1`, and `coopx2` cooperative channel closings. `revoked` closings are extremely rare.

more pronounced when only considering cooperatively closed channels. 56% of closed public channel outputs refund a channel and 33% for private channels.

5 Related Work

Lightning Network Topology. A line of research studies the topology of the Lightning Network. From a theoretical point of view, multiple works study the strategic placement of nodes to route transactions and maximize fee collection efficiently [5,8,11]. Avarikioti et al. [6] further game-theoretically study the Nash equilibrium topology of the Lightning Network. From an empirical point of view, Seres et al. [25] and Lin et al. [17] present early measurement studies of the Lightning Network topology using Lightning Network gossip messages and comment on high centralization in the network. Subsequent work by Zabka et al. [29] takes an in-depth look at the network's centrality to find that the Lightning Network's centrality is increasing. As opposed to investigating the Lightning Network topology, we focus on investigating the lifecycle and usage of the Lightning Network payment channels. Zabka et al. [30] analyze Lightning Network gossip messages to analyze the Lightning Network in further detail. Their work reveals the client implementations used by nodes in the network, as well as their geographical location. Our work combines these gossip messages with on-chain data to investigate the various stages of a channel's lifetime.

Lightning Network De-anonymization. Multiple works have investigated to what extent Lightning Network de-anonymization is possible. Herrera et al. [14] employ probing transactions to unveil channel balances, while Tikhomirov et al. [26] de-anonymize network participants. Romiti et al. [24] conduct a cross-layer analysis, combining off- and on-chain data, to de-anonymize participants in Lightning channels. In a similar fashion, Kappos et al. [15] and Nowostawski et al. [20] leverage the on-chain data not only to de-anonymize participants but also to identify private channels. We leverage these heuristics to identify private channels and analyze the lifecycles of both public and private channels. Our analysis reveals channel usage patterns, which were previously unexplored.

Rebalancing. Imbalanced channels are a challenge in the Lightning Network, as they only allow payments to flow in one direction. While the most simple but costly solution to rebalancing a channel is to close and reopen the channel, other (off-chain) rebalancing solutions have been studied and proposed [7,16,21,22].

6 Conclusion

Previous Lightning Network measurement studies mainly focused on the network topology and network overview statistics, given the privacy protection for transfers in the network. We leverage data leaked through fee updates and on-chain channel closings to extend the understanding of the usage of the Lightning Network by providing further insights into the lifecycle of channels. Our analysis is the first to reveal insights into the usage of private and public payment channels (e.g., routing, rebalancing, etc.) in combination with an analysis on whether channels are closed cooperatively or unilaterally and possibly reopened. Even more so, we present the first dataset of payments routed through the network and offer novel insights into the routing activity in the network.

References

1. Bolt #3: Bitcoin transaction and script formats. https://github.com/lightning/bolts/blob/master/03-transactions.md, Accessed 22 May 2024
2. Esplora http api. https://github.com/Blockstream/esplora/blob/master/API.md Accessed 20 Mar 2024
3. Lightning networ search and analysis engine. https://1ml.com/ Accessed 22 May 2024
4. Alvarez, F.E., Argente, D., Van Patten, D.: Are cryptocurrencies currencies? bitcoin as legal tender in el salvador. Technical Report, National Bureau of Economic Research (2022)
5. Avarikioti, G., Wang, Y., Wattenhofer, R.: Algorithmic channel design. In: 29th International Symposium on Algorithms and Computation (ISAAC 2018), vol. 123, pp. 16–1. Schloss Dagstuhl-Leibniz-Zentrum für Informatik (2018)
6. Avarikioti, Z., Heimbach, L., Wang, Y., Wattenhofer, R.: Ride the lightning: the game theory of payment channels. In: Financial Cryptography and Data Security, pp. 264–283. Springer (2020)
7. Conoscenti, M., Vetro, A., De Martin, J.C.: Hubs, rebalancing and service providers in the lightning network. IEEE Access **7**, 132828–132840 (2019)
8. Davis, V., Harrison, B.: Learning a scalable algorithm for improving betweenness in the lightning network. In: 2022 Fourth International Conference on Blockchain Computing and Applications (BCCA), pp. 119–126. IEEE (2022)
9. Decker, C.: Lightning network research: topology datasets. https://doi.org/10.5281/zenodo.4088530, https://github.com/lnresearch/topology, Accessed 20 May 2024

10. Decker, C., Wattenhofer, R.: A fast and scalable payment network with bitcoin duplex micropayment channels. In: Pelc, A., Schwarzmann, A.A. (eds.) Stabilization, Safety, and Security of Distributed Systems, pp. 3–18. Springer International Publishing, Cham (2015)
11. Ersoy, O., Roos, S., Erkin, Z.: How to profit from payments channels. In: International Conference on Financial Cryptography and Data Security, pp. 284–303. Springer (2020)
12. Green, M., Miers, I.: Bolt: Anonymous payment channels for decentralized currencies. In: Proceedings of the 2017 ACM SIGSAC Conference on Computer and Communications Security, pp. 473–489. ACM (2017)
13. Guo, Y., Tong, J., Feng, C.: A measurement study of bitcoin lightning network. In: 2019 IEEE International Conference on Blockchain (Blockchain), pp. 202–211. IEEE (2019)
14. Herrera-Joancomartí, J., Navarro-Arribas, G., Ranchal-Pedrosa, A., Pérez-Solà, C., Garcia-Alfaro, J.: On the difficulty of hiding the balance of lightning network channels. In: Proceedings of the 2019 ACM Asia Conference on Computer and Communications Security, pp. 602–612 (2019)
15. Kappos, G., et al.: An empirical analysis of privacy in the lightning network. In: Financial Cryptography and Data Security, pp. 167–186. Springer (2021)
16. Khalil, R., Gervais, A.: Revive: rebalancing off-blockchain payment networks. In: Proceedings of the 2017 ACM SIGSAC Conference on Computer and Communications Security, pp. 439–453 (2017)
17. Lin, J.H., Primicerio, K., Squartini, T., Decker, C., Tessone, C.J.: Lightning network: a second path towards centralisation of the bitcoin economy. New J. Phys. **22**, 83022 (2020)
18. Miller, A., Bentov, I., Bakshi, S., Kumaresan, R., McCorry, P.: Sprites and state channels: payment networks that go faster than lightning. In: Financial Cryptography and Data Security - 23rd International Conference, FC, pp. 508–526 (2019)
19. Nadarajah, S., Chu, J.: On the inefficiency of bitcoin. Econ. Lett. **150**, 6–9 (2017)
20. Nowostawski, M., Tøn, J.: Evaluating methods for the identification of off-chain transactions in the lightning network. Appl. Sci. **9** (2019)
21. Papadis, N., Tassiulas, L.: Blockchain-based payment channel networks: challenges and recent advances. IEEE Access **8**, 227596–227609 (2020)
22. Pickhardt, R., Nowostawski, M.: Imbalance measure and proactive channel rebalancing algorithm for the lightning network. In: 2020 IEEE International Conference on Blockchain and Cryptocurrency (ICBC), pp. 1–5. IEEE (2020)
23. Poon, J., Dryja, T.: The bitcoin lightning network: scalable off-chain instant payments (2015)
24. Romiti, M., Victor, F., Moreno-Sanchez, P., Nordholt, P.S., Haslhofer, B., Maffei, M.: Cross-layer deanonymization methods in the lightning protocol. In: Financial Cryptography and Data Security, pp. 187–204. Springer (2021)
25. Seres, I.A., Gulyás, L., Nagy, D.A., Burcsi, P.: Topological analysis of bitcoin's lightning network. In: Mathematical Research for Blockchain Economy, pp. 1–12. Springer (2020)
26. Tikhomirov, S., Moreno-Sanchez, P., Maffei, M.: A quantitative analysis of security, anonymity and scalability for the lightning network. In: 2020 IEEE European Symposium on Security and Privacy Workshops (EuroS&PW), pp. 387–396. IEEE (2020)
27. Vranken, H.: Sustainability of bitcoin and blockchains. Curr. Opin. Environ. Sustain. **28**, 1–9 (2017)

28. Zabka, P., Foerster, K.T., Schmid, S., Decker, C.: Empirical evaluation of nodes and channels of the lightning network. Pervasive Mob. Comput. **83**, 101584 (2022)
29. Zabka, P., Förster, K.T., Decker, C., Schmid, S.: Short paper: a centrality analysis of the lightning network. In: Financial Cryptography and Data Security, pp. 374–385. Springer (2022)
30. Zabka, P., Förster, K.T., Schmid, S., Decker, C.: Node classification and geographical analysis of the lightning cryptocurrency network. In: International Conference on Distributed Computing and Networking, pp. 126–135. ACM (2021)

The Writing Is on the Wall: Analyzing the Boom of Inscriptions and Its Impact on EVM-Compatible Blockchains

Johnnatan Messias[1](✉)[iD], Krzysztof Gogol[2][iD], Maria Inés Silva[3,5][iD], and Benjamin Livshits[4][iD]

[1] MPI-SWS, Saarbrücken, Germany
johnme@mpi-sws.org
[2] University of Zurich, Zürich, Switzerland
[3] NOVA Information Management School, Lisbon, Portugal
[4] Imperial College London, London, UK
[5] Matter Labs, Berlin, Germany

Abstract. This paper examines inscription-related transactions on Ethereum and major EVM-compatible rollups, assessing their impact on scalability during transaction surges. Our results show that, on certain days, inscriptions accounted for nearly 90% of transactions on Arbitrum and ZKsync Era, while 53% on Ethereum, with 99% of these inscriptions involving meme coin minting. Furthermore, we show that ZKsync and Arbitrum saw lower median gas fees during these surges. ZKsync Era, a ZK-rollup, showed a greater fee reduction than the optimistic rollups studied—Arbitrum, Base, and Optimism.

1 Introduction

Layer-2 (L2) scaling solutions have emerged as a response to the scalability challenges of Layer-1 (L1) blockchains such as Bitcoin and Ethereum. These solutions aim to enhance transaction throughput and cost efficiency while inheriting the security guarantees of their underlying L1 blockchain. L2s execute transactions off-chain and subsequently settling state transitions on an L1 blockchain.

Despite their increasing adoption, most L2 solutions had not undergone significant stress testing until late 2023, when an unprecedented spike in transaction volume occurred. This surge was largely driven by the emergence of *inscriptions*, a phenomenon inspired by Bitcoin ordinals [27]. Ordinals, introduced in March 2023 [5], enable the assignment of unique identifiers to individual satoshis, effectively transforming them into Non-Fungible Tokens (NFTs). This concept extended beyond Bitcoin, reaching Ethereum and its major L2 rollups, where inscriptions allowed users to embed arbitrary data, such as text, images, or code, directly onto the blockchain. By late 2023, inscription transactions accounted for over 80% of all transactions on some Ethereum Virtual Machine (EVM) chains [1], significantly influencing network performance, transaction costs, and user behavior.

Most of this work was performed while the authors were at Matter Labs.

This rapid increase in transaction volume led to temporary service disruptions, with certain rollups experiencing downtime of approximately 78 min [12, 23]. However, during this surge, Zero Knowledge (ZK) rollups—one type of L2 blockchain—offered notably lower gas costs compared to Ethereum, making them an attractive alternative for inscription trading. Furthermore, Ethereum's Dencun upgrade in March 2024 introduced *blobs* as temporary data storage, reducing gas fees for rollups but raising concerns about the long-term availability of inscription-related data [20]. Since blobs are designed for ephemeral state verification, inscription-related data may not persist on-chain, relying instead on off-chain indexers managed by platform creators.

In this paper, we investigate the performance and user behavior of EVM-compatible chains during the inscription boom. Our study focuses on Ethereum and its four major rollups—Arbitrum, Base, Optimism, and ZKsync Era. We address the following research questions:

What Caused the Transaction Surge on EVM Chains at the End of 2023? We analyze transaction data of Ethereum and its four major rollups. We identified that these transactions were due to inscription-based meme coins and were minted and traded at significantly lower costs compared to Bitcoin ordinals or Ethereum inscriptions. Our findings indicate that these inscriptions adopted modified versions of the BRC-20 standard [22,27,30], facilitating their integration into NFT marketplaces [7,13,32]. Specifically, on December 17, 2023, over 88% of all transactions on ZKsync Era were due to inscriptions. Other blockchains also exhibited a high percentage of inscription-related transactions. Arbitrum recorded the highest percentage, with over 89%, followed by Ethereum at over 53%, Base at over 37%, and Optimism, with over 35% of the total inscription transactions.

What Impact did Inscription Transactions have on the Cost and Performance of EVM Blockchains? We evaluate how inscription-driven transaction spikes affected network stability, gas fees, and transaction throughput. Our analysis shows that, unlike Ethereum, where transaction surges led to increased gas fees, some rollups experienced reduced median transaction costs. We also compare the cost efficiency of ZK rollups versus optimistic rollups.

Why did Users Choose Inscription-Based Meme Coins Over ERC-20 Tokens? We examine the user interaction with inscriptions, finding that inscription transactions predominantly involved minting rather than trading. Across all analyzed chains, over 99% of inscription-related transactions were for minting activities, with some tokens, such as *zrc-20 sync*, sustaining trading activity beyond the initial boom. For example, in comparison to the overall number of inscription transactions, the percentage of inscription minting or claiming activities was as follows: Arbitrum at 99.82%, Base at 99.99%, Ethereum at 99.92%, Optimism at 99.98%, and ZKsync Era at 99.91%.

To promote scientific reproducibility, we make our datasets and analysis scripts publicly available [17]. By providing insights into the inscription-driven stress test of EVM chains, our study contributes to the broader understanding of

Table 1. Example of inscriptions data recorded on-chain: *protocol name, operation, token name (Tick), total supply,* and *maximum amount of tokens minted each round (Limit)*.

Protocol	Tick	Operation	Total Supply	Limit	JSON data
zrc-20	sync	deploy	21×10^6	4	{"p":"zrc-20","op":"deploy","tick":"sync","amt":"21000000","limit":"4"}
zrc-20	sync	transfer	—	4	{"p": "zrc-20", "op": "transfer", "tick": "sync", "amt": "4"}
zrc-20	sync	mint	—	4	{"p":"zrc-20","op":"mint","tick":"sync","amt":"4"}
zrc-20	zksi	deploy	21×10^8	1×10^4	{"p":"zrc-20","op":"deploy","tick":"zksi","max":"2100000000","limt":"10000"}
zrc-20	zkss	deploy	21×10^6	1×10^3	{"p":"zrc-20","op":"deploy","tick":"zkss","max":"21000000","lim":"1000"}
zrc-20	zkss	sell	—	1000	{"p":"zrc-20","op":"sell","orderMessage":[{"amt":10000,"nonce":"62..."},
zrc-20	zkzk	deploy	21×10^6	21×10^6	{"p":"zks-20","op":"deploy","tick":"zkzk","max":"21000000","lim":"21000000"}
era-20	bgnt	deploy	21×10^6	5	{"p":"era-20","op":"deploy","tick":"bgnt","max":"21000000","lim": "5"}
era-20	bgnt	deploy	21×10^6	5	{"p":"era-20","op":"deploy","tick":"bgnt","max":"21000000","lim": "5"}
era-20	bgnt	list	—	5	{"p":"era-20","op":"list","tick":"bgnt","amt":"250","price":"1500000000000000"}
era-20	bgnt	buy	—	—	{"p":"era-20","op":"buy","tx":"0xda..."}
layer-2	$L2	claim	—	1000	{"p":"layer2-20","op":"claim","tick":"$L2","amt":"1000"}

blockchain scalability, economic incentives, and data availability in the evolving blockchain ecosystem.

2 Background on Inscriptions

Inscriptions involve the recording of arbitrary data on the blockchain. On EVM-compatible chains, users encode *HEX* data into the transaction input *call data* (refer to column *JSON* in Table 1), usually also setting the transaction's *from* and *to* attributes with the same user addresses. This structure constitutes a self-transfer made from a user to their own address.

2.1 Operation Types

There are various protocol standards that define the structure of inscriptions. *BRC-20* was the first standard proposed for Bitcoin, and includes three main types of operations: *deploy, mint,* and *transfer,* each encoded in a single transaction [26]. The protocol standards on EVM-compatible chains extend this set of operations by adding, for example, *claim, list, buy, sell,* among others.

Deploy. The *deploy* action specifies the protocol name, token tick, total supply, and the maximum amount of tokens a user can mint (or claim) per transaction. Table 1 shows examples of inscriptions' data recorded on-chain. For example, to deploy an inscription, a transaction containing a *deploy* action should be recorded on-chain, marking the initiation of an inscription event. In the case of a *zrc-20 sync* inscription (see first row in Table 1), the protocol specifies a total supply of 21 million inscriptions and a limit of 4 tokens minted per transaction.

Mint. After the transaction that deploys the inscription persists in the chain, users can issue a *mint* action to actually mint (or in this case claim ownership) of the tokens. To initiate this, users need to issue a transaction with an input call data encoded to *HEX code,* specifying the protocol and tick that jointly identify the inscription-based token. In the same transaction, users provide the number of tokens they want to claim (refer to column *Limit* in Table 1) that must not exceed the maximum limit specified in *deploy* operation for the given protocol-tick pair. The off-chain *indexer* is responsible for ensuring the integrity and user balances of inscription-based tokens.

Claim. Similarly to *mint*, it allows users to mint and claim ownership of a new inscription token. This operation is used, for example, within the *layer2-20* standard to mint a new inscription token, *$L2*. The $L2 token is a multi-L2 inscription token that its inscription creator allows to be minted on multiple blockchains. However, there is just one *deploy* operation that defines the token's maximum supply. The *off-chain indexer* maintained by the creator is responsible for ensuring the integrity of data in these circumstances.

Transfer. Once users successfully mint the inscriptions, they can transfer ownership of their inscription tokens to another address. To do so, they typically issue a transaction to another address and add the data formatting standard of a *transfer* to the input call data. The receiving address will then possess ownership of these inscriptions. The inscription token is also identified by a protocol standard and a token name (*tick*). Tokens with the same names (ticks) can be deployed multiple times using various protocol standards.

List. It enables users to list their inscriptions on marketplaces [7,8,13,32]. Users specify the quantity of tokens and their price (in Ether) that they are willing to receive in exchange for their inscriptions from interested buyers.

Buy. This operation is used to purchase inscription tokens from marketplaces. It references the transaction that listed the inscription on the marketplace. The *buy* operation specifies only protocol standards, as the token name (*tick*), amount, and price are declared in the *list* operation.

Sell. It is used for selling inscriptions, this operation specifies the protocols and the order message containing seller and signer details, as well as the amount of tokens being sold and their prices.

2.2 Comparison with NFTs and ERC-20 s

In this section, we discuss the distinctions between inscriptions and established *Ethereum Request for Comments (ERC)* standards such as ERC-20 [10] and ERC-721 [11] concerning tokens and Non-Fungible Token (NFT), respectively.

Comparison with NFTs. In the Ethereum blockchain, NFTs [21,25] are created through smart contracts. Each user receives a unique *token ID*, affirming their ownership of a specific asset. These assets, which can be JPEG files or CryptoPunk images [21], are stored off-chain on a server or on the InterPlanetar File System (IPFS) [14].

In contrast to NFTs, inscription-based tokens do not rely on any smart contract and, thus, do not allow upgrades. The link to the asset file is inscribed into the transaction data. In a blockchain with a maximal native token supply, such as Bitcoin, the amount of inscription is bound by the blockchain network limits. In contrast, NFTs based on smart contracts are free from such limitations, theoretically allowing for unlimited minting. Also, each inscription is allocated a position in the blockchain, which creates the opportunity to derive the additional value of the inscription from the location within the block.

Table 2. Data set used to analyze inscription events on five blockchains.

Chain	Start date	End date	# of Issuers	# of Blocks	# of Inscriptions
Arbitrum	June 17th, 2023	April 30th, 2024	118,544	3,575,299	16,309,035
Base	July 28th, 2023	April 30th, 2024	79,573	780,770	2,020,661
Ethereum	June 14th, 2023	April 30th, 2024	245,008	930,824	6,493,580
Optimism	June 18th, 2023	April 30th, 2024	49,112	588,053	1,475,663
ZKsync Era	June 18th, 2023	April 30th, 2024	481,687	2,809,054	17,161,306

Comparison with ERC-20. The other application of inscriptions is to create ERC-20-style tokens. As inscription-based tokens are not reliant on smart contracts, they are not susceptible to the risk of smart contract upgrades, and their maximal circulating supply is declared once in the *deploy* operation. The minting and transfer of each new inscription-based token can be tracked directly on the blockchain and cannot be altered.

However, due to their lack of smart contract support, inscription-based tokens offer limited functionality. They are primarily utilized for speculative purposes and fall into the category of meme-coins [26]. Based on the inscriptions technology, it is possible to mint a single NFT-style token or a group of tokens with a predefined token supply in circulation. Nevertheless, it is the off-chain indexer, managed by the token's creator, responsible for ensuring the data integrity of minted tokens. Trading of inscription-based tokens predominantly occurs within inscriptions marketplaces since they are not compatible with the ERC-20 standard required by Decentralized Exchanges (DEXs) [29].

3 Data Collection

We analyze the inscriptions data recorded on Ethereum and its major EVM-compatible rollups: ZKsync Era, Arbitrum, Optimism, and Base. From these L2s, ZKsync Era is a ZK rollup, whereas other chains are optimistic rollups.

We then collected blockchain data from various sources and made them and our scripts available in a public repository [17]. For ZKsync, we use data obtained from their official archive node and a Web3-compatible API for ZKsync Era [9]. For Arbitrum, Base, Ethereum, and Optimism, we use data sources from Nansen BigQuery [19]. These data sources enable us to collect comprehensive data containing all information recorded on the evaluated chains. This includes data about blocks, transactions, and events (or logs triggered during the execution of smart contracts) specifically related to inscriptions. Table 2 provides an overview of the specifics of our dataset.

Our focus is on blockchain data associated with inscriptions. While a significant portion of inscriptions involves the issuance of self-transfer transactions (i.e., where issuers initiate a transfer to their own address), we adopt a broader perspective. This involves considering instances where inscriptions are added to the chain, irrespective of whether through a self-transfer or not. This is important to capture the total fees users spent on inscriptions.

To identify these inscriptions, we specifically search for transactions with input call data starting with "`0x646174613a`", representing "`data:`" in ASCII.

Table 3. Inscription transactions per issuers.

Protocol	# of Issuers	Mean	Std.	Median	Min	Max
Arbitrum	118,544	137.57	676.76	6	1	38,050
Base	79,573	25.39	154.91	3	1	19,674
Ethereum	245,008	26.50	245.60	3	1	67,713
Optimism	49,112	30.04	168.05	3	1	19,612
ZKsync Era	481,687	35.62	245.35	3	1	40,770

This criterion allows us to recognize inscriptions within the blockchain. The blockchains with the most number of transaction inscriptions in our dataset were ZKsync Era and Arbitrum. In total, we found 17,054,466 transactions containing inscriptions in our ZKsync Era data set issued by 481,687 addresses and added to 2,809,054 blocks. Similarly, we identified 16,309,035 transactions containing inscriptions in Arbitrum, issued by 118,544 addresses and added to 3,575,299 blocks. The average number of inscriptions per block are 6.07 and 4.56 for ZKsync Era and Arbitrum, respectively. We provide similar statistics for Base, Ethereum, and Optimism chains in Table 2. This dataset forms the basis for our empirical analysis of inscriptions.

The distribution of inscription transactions per address is highly skewed towards a few participants, as shown in Table 3. Most inscription issuers initiated at least three transactions related to inscriptions. Arbitrum exhibited the highest median, with at least six transactions per issuer. Table 3 also highlights that a small number of issuers were responsible for a significant fraction of the total inscriptions. For instance, a single issuer accounted for 67,713 transactions to claim their inscriptions, followed by ZKsync Era with 40,770 transactions. These are likely bots accounts.

4 Empirical Analysis

In this section, we present our empirical analysis of the inscriptions recorded on Ethereum and its major EVM-compatible rollups: Arbitrum, Base, Optimism, and ZKsync Era. We characterize the inscription protocols, operations, tokens, and their trading dynamics. Then, we investigate the impact of sudden surges in inscription transactions on the blockchains' performance.

4.1 Overall Transactions

Our analysis shows multiple spikes in inscription transaction counts occurred on Arbitrum (November 25th, December 15th, 16th, and 18th) and ZKsync Era (November 17th, 16th, 17th, and December 21st) as shown in Fig. 1a. During peak periods, inscriptions dominated daily transactions, comprising nearly 90% on ZKsync Era and Arbitrum (December 16th, 2023), over 53% on Ethereum (January 14th, 2023), and almost 35% on Optimism and Base (January 24th, 2024). Figure 1billustrates those peaks. Due to this high activity of inscriptions on-chain, some rollups were not prepared to handle the surge in transactions, leading to downtimes and delays in the processing of transactions [12,23]. Next, we investigate the protocols and operations that contribute to these observed spikes.

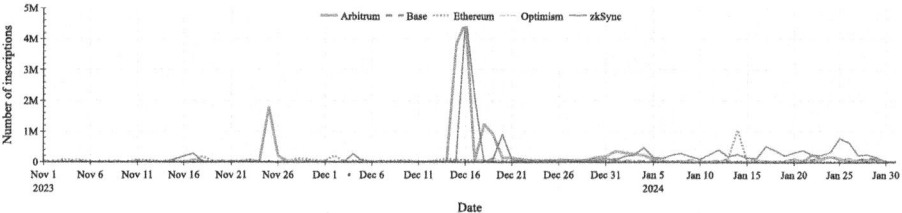

(a) Absolute number of inscriptions.

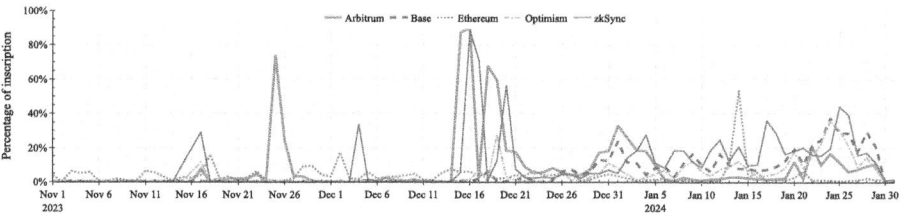

(b) Percentage of inscriptions in comparison to the overall number of transactions.

Fig. 1. Daily distribution of inscription transactions in our data set: (a) absolute number of inscription transactions; and (b) percentage of inscription transactions compared to the total number of transactions.

4.2 Inscriptions Characterization

Our analysis indicates that inscription tokens are uniquely unified by a protocol-tick pair. Therefore, we aggregated data using this pair to identify the top inscriptions tokens. Figure 2 illustrates the breakdown of inscription transactions based on protocol, operation, and the leading token. In the following, we provide our observations for each of these categories.

Protocols. Our initial observation reveals, in (Fig. 2 row *Top Protocols*), that each blockchain contains a particular leading inscription protocol, similar to *BRC-20* on Bitcoin [27,30], constituting between 54% and 93% of transactions. In addition, blockchain-specific standards such as *FAIR-20* for Arbitrum, *ERC-20* for Ethereum, and *ZRC-20* for ZKsync Era appear the most. The *LAYER2-20* protocol is present across all studied L2s, being the dominant inscription protocol on Base and Optimism, and the second largest on ZKsync Era.

Operations. Recall from §2 that both *claim* and *mint* operation types work similarly. Thus, if evaluated together they account for approximately 99% of all inscription transactions in all chains we studied. From Fig. 2 row *Top Operations*, a small number of transactions are attributed to the *list* operation, used for listing inscriptions for sale in an inscription marketplace, and the *deploy* operation, which declares the token on the chain along with its token supply. The low percentage of *transfer*, *sell*, and *buy* transactions suggests that inscription tokens are not yet actively traded on EVM chains.

Tokens. From our analysis (Fig. 2, row *Top Tokens*), we observe that various protocols deploy and mint tokens with the same tick symbols. To account for this, we identify each token using a protocol-tick pair. Our findings indicate

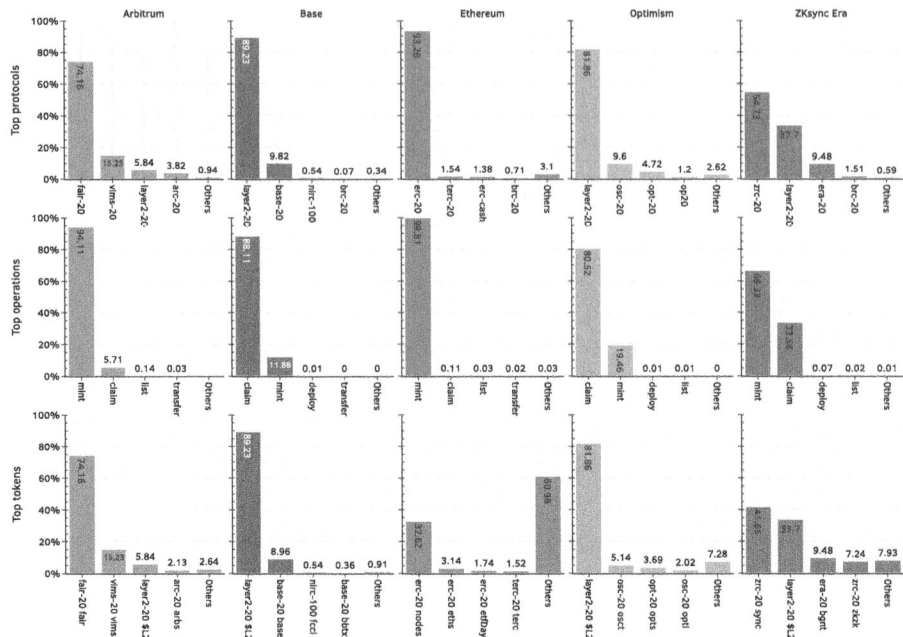

Fig. 2. Percentage breakdown of the top 3 inscriptions attributes — protocol, operations, and tokens — for the chains analyzed in our study: Arbitrum, Base, Ethereum, Optimism and ZKsync Era.

that Arbitrum, Base, and Optimism each have a dominant token, comprising between 74% and 89% of inscription transactions on their respective platforms. In contrast, the token distribution on Ethereum is more diverse, with the *ERC-20 NODES* token contributing approximately 32% of the transactions, while all other tokens individually represent less than 3.14%. On ZKsync Era, the top four tokens account for over 92% of inscription transactions, also indicating token distribution concentration when compared to other chains. Notably, the token *LAYER2-20 $L2* is present across all rollups and is also the dominant token on both Base and Optimism.

4.3 Inscription Trading

We analyze the trading behavior of two inscription tokens within the ZKsync Era: *zrc-20 sync* (the predominant token) and *era-20 bgnt* (a smaller but noteworthy token due to its completed minting process). Our analysis, presented in Fig. 3, shows their respective trading activities. Notably, *era-20 bgnt* has a higher level of trading activity compared to *zrc-20 sync*. Specifically, we observed 477 transfer transactions for *zrc-20 sync*, along with the corresponding token median prices as shown in Fig. 3a, and 1148 buy transactions for *era-20 bgnt*, with corresponding median prices depicted in Fig. 3b

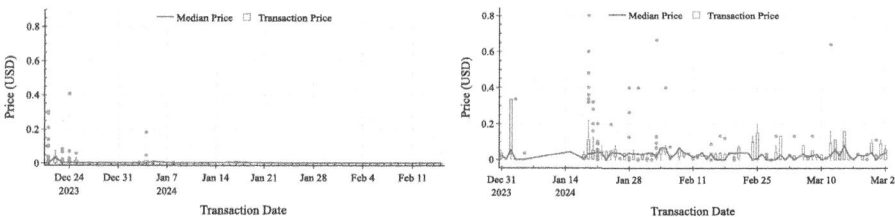

(a) *Transfer transactions of zrc-20 sync.* (b) Buy transactions of *era-20 bgnt.*

Fig. 3. Price per token at every transaction on ZKsync Era considering *zrc-20 sync* and *era-20 bgnt* tokens.

Table 4. Inscription operations cost in GWei for major tokens.

Chain	Token	Operation	Total (in ETH)	Mean	Std.	Median	Min	Max
Arbitrum	fair-20 fair	mint	0.77	74.10	305.72	60.87	0	488,849.89
Arbitrum	layer2-20 $L2	claim	0.03	40.12	18.83	34.77	0.57	500.85
Base	layer2-20 $L2	claim	0.0016	1.03	8.27	0.02	0	2199.20
Ethereum	erc-20 nodes	mint	0.19	176.70	7015.97	99.32	0.01	1,351,757.78
Optimism	layer2-20 $L2	claim	0.0009	0.78	3.04	0.11	0	1617.84
ZKsync Era	zrc-20 sync	mint	88.86	12,684.59	3795.42	12,748.95	0	1,097,718.16
ZKsync Era	era-20 bgnt	mint	11.31	7114.49	2525.91	6292.83	0.32	244,836.15
ZKsync Era	era-20 bgnt	list	0.015	4839.49	9528.53	272.57	0	60,807.7
ZKsync Era	layer2-20 $L2	claim	0.017	29.63	6.90	28.38	0.42	2001.14

Our analysis shows that the price of *zrc-20 sync* oscillated between $0.10 and $0.4, while *era-20 bgnt* ranged from $0.10 to $0.8. The trading of the *era-20 bgnt* token continued from its minting throughout the entire studied period. As the trades occur in batches of 4 or 5 tokens, they provide minimal compensation to the seller to cover the gas fees necessary to mint and list the inscriptions. However, trading inscriptions at such low prices is feasible due to the low gas fees on rollups, which ranged at ZKsync Era from $0.05 to $0.25 (see Fig. 4).

Next, we analyze how spikes in inscription transactions influence gas fees across the network. Table 4 presents a breakdown of fees incurred during inscription operations. Recall that, in the first transaction, *deploy*, the maximum number of tokens that can be minted or claimed in a single transaction is specified. Then, we calculate the average fee per single token for each operation. We found that the mint operation is more efficient than *claim*, although both have a similar functionality. The interesting comparison provides *claim* operation for *layer2-20 $L2* token, as it is operating across all rollups. Its mining (claiming) operation had a lower median fee on Optimism and Base, followed by ZKsync Era and Arbitrum.

4.4 Impact on Gas Fees

This section analyzes the impact of daily transaction volumes on the median gas fee per transaction. Unlike L1 blockchains, rollups are expected to offer lower gas fees with increasing transaction counts due to their scaling mechanism. As more L2 transactions can be compressed into a single batch stored in the L1 network,

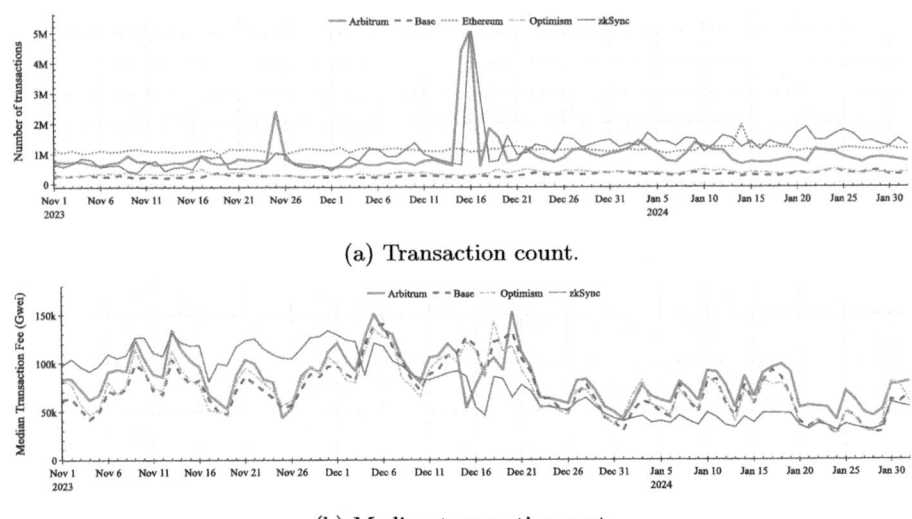

Fig. 4. Daily transaction count and median transaction cost in USD paid by the user: (a) transactions count; and (b) median transaction cost.

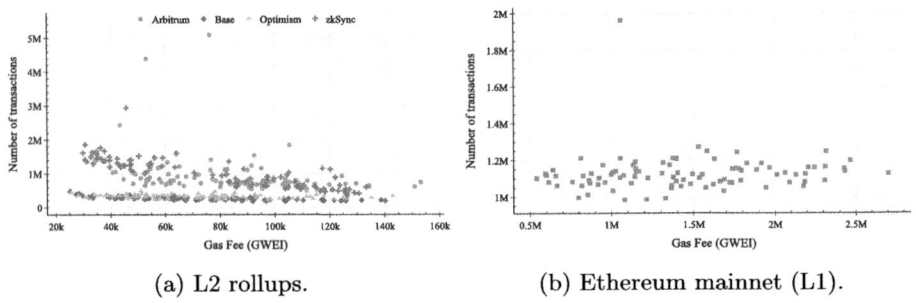

Fig. 5. Distribution of gas fees in GWei relative to transaction count: (a) L2 rollups; and (b) Ethereum mainnet.

gas fees tend to decrease. In particular, spikes in daily transaction counts on specific days resulted in a decrease in median gas fees per transaction for other users, as shown in Fig. 4. Fees on L2 rollups are linked to compression and are also affected by the fees of L1 Ethereum.

Further analysis of the relationship between transaction count and median gas fee is presented in Fig. 5. Generally, gas fees with more transactions on rollups either remain unchanged (Base, Optimism) or decrease (Arbitrum, ZKsync). Conversely, on Ethereum, gas fees tend to increase with higher transaction counts. Additionally, ZKsync demonstrates higher efficiency in reducing gas fees compared to Arbitrum, attributable to its ZK rollup design, while Arbitrum, like Base and Optimism, is an optimistic rollup. Thus, unlike L1 blockchains, gas costs on ZK rollups decrease with a larger transaction volume, as observed on November 17, December 5, December 17, and December 20 on ZKsync Era.

5 Discussion

In this section, we discuss various aspects of inscriptions, starting with the impact of blobs on inscription ownership. We then explore whether inscriptions are beneficial or detrimental to the blockchain ecosystem. Finally, we address the potential for *pump-and-dump* schemes [16,28] associated with inscriptions.

Impact of Blobs on Inscription Ownership. As inscriptions are appended to transactions as arbitrary data within the input call data, there is no assurance of perpetual availability of this data in the future. Blobs, initially designed to increase the efficiency of Ethereum rollups [2], were used to issue new inscription directly in Ethereum blockchains, called *BlobScriptions* [1]. Yet, blob data is intended to be stored by Ethereum nodes for 18 days, during which rollup operators or other parties verify their transactions. After this period, BlobScriptions disappear from the Ethereum blockchain and are only stored (and available) in the indexer of the creator protocol, outside the blockchain. Similarly, rollups are not required to store (outside of blobs) the transaction input data used by rollup-based inscriptions, raising questions about the ownership of inscriptions.

Inscriptions: Good or Bad? A report by Binance on BRC-20 highlights that the unexpected surge in transactions resulted in an increase in transaction fees for many blockchains [22]. The report suggests that such an increase in fees can be seen as a natural progression in blockchain adoption. Therefore, attribution of this spike solely to BRC-20s is considered irrelevant. More concerning, however, is that other protocols, such as Arbitrum, experienced downtime of approximately 78 min [23], while ZKsync Era saw an increase in Transaction-per-Second (TPS), with nearly 96% of all transactions being related to inscriptions over the course of several hours. Thus, causing users to worry about delayed transaction inclusion. This sparked a broader debate within the blockchain community about whether ordinals and inscriptions truly benefit users.

Challenges and Opportunities for Trading Inscription. Inscriptions are not compatible with ERC-20 tokens. Therefore cannot be traded on traditional decentralized exchanges based on Automated Market Makers (AMMs) such as Uniswap [3], which is the base for trading tokens with low market capitalization. Today, inscriptions are listed at NFT-marketplaces in a limited-order book type, reducing their liquidity [7,13,32]. Also, for many inscription-based meme-coins, their minting process may still be ongoing, and new tokens could continue to be minted until the token limit specified in the *deploy* operation is reached. Furthermore, wrapping inscription-based meme coins into ERC-20 tokens could allow these inscriptions to be listed on DEXs, attracting meme-coin traders who are not familiar with NFT marketplaces. We see this as the next evolution of inscriptions if they are intended to stay.

Hope or Hype? During minting periods, platforms utilized various channels to engage users, including communities, influencers, and specific chains that amplified them. Consequently, numerous users issued inscriptions across different platforms [7,13,32]. Understanding user expectations, often influenced by Fear-Of-Missing-Out (FOMO), regarding inscriptions is crucial. For instance, *are inscrip-*

tions more about hope or hype? This question relates to whether inscriptions are a novel concept or just a passing trend. In the case of Bitcoin, there was a significant surge in interest and user participation during the BRC-20 movement, followed by a subsequent decline in enthusiasm over the following months [26,27]. Our work shows similar results for EVM-compatible chains: *inscriptions peak initially but witness a decline in user interest over time*, as shown in Sect. 4.1. The evolution of inscriptions fuels discussions on innovative features and integration with tokens and NFTs. Despite potential profitability, marketplace platforms encounter challenges in translating inscriptions into substantial profits for users, particularly across different chains. Due to the nature of inscriptions, which rely on off-chain applications, there is currently no mechanism to prevent users from purchasing previously sold inscriptions. Additionally, users can utilize software programs to automatically claim the majority of inscriptions during the minting or claiming period. Hence, *should inscriptions be distributed directly to wallets, similar to traditional airdrop methods* [18]*?*

Addressing these questions could potentially improve inscriptions, transforming them into a promising addition to the blockchain ecosystem.

6 Related Work

In this section, we review the existing literature and related works pertinent to our study on inscriptions within EVM-compatible chains.

Social Phenomena on Financial Markets. The impact of social phenomena on financial markets has received some research attention recently. In traditional finance, the GameStop short-squeeze event from 2021 highlighted how online social movements can lead to significant shifts in trading behavior and even impact established financial institutions [31]. Later, various authors analyzed this unprecedented event in more detail. Vasileiou et al. [24] found a causal link between the stock performance in early 2021 and the Google Trend Index for the stock, thus showing the impact of online interest in the stock in its price performance. Following this, Anand and Pathak [4] and Zheng et al. [31] focussed their analysis on the activity of the subreddit *r/wallstreetbets* (where the majority of the social activity related to GameStop was occurring during that time). Their findings further corroborate the link between stock performance and the subreddit's social media activity and sentiment.

Social Phenomena on Decentralized Finance. Even though the introduction of ordinals and inscriptions is fairly recent, there has been some work towards understanding these phenomena. Wang et al. [26,27] conducted a comprehensive analysis of BRC-20 tokens within the Bitcoin network. Their investigation revealed a notable surge in interest and user participation during the BRC-20 movement. The study involved a comparison between these BRCs and the widely-used Ethereum ERC-20 tokens, employing metrics such as average price return, volatility, and other relevant factors. The study highlighted a significant influx of users into the BRC market within a month, coupled with a subsequent decline in enthusiasm over the following months. In essence, users displayed a tendency to lose interest after the initial surge. In the broader context, the research emphasized that, despite the hype, BRC-based tokens constituted only a modest fraction of the overall market size when juxtaposed with ERC-like tokens on the Ethereum platform. Our paper also analyses the broader market dynamics of inscriptions during their boom, however, we expand the study to the top EVM chains instead of focussing on Bitcoin ordinals.

Li et al. [15] also looked at BRC-20 tokens within the Bitcoin network. However, they perform a comparative analysis between Bitcoin inscriptions and NFTs focussed on technical implementation details, function, and use cases. They additionally provide an in-depth historical overview of Bitcoin-related NFTs. While our paper also involves a characterization of inscriptions and their functions, our focus remains on EVM Layer 2 s rather than Bitcoin.

Finally, Bertucci [6] analyzed the impact of ordinals on transaction fees in Bitcoin. They found that ordinal inscriptions typically have lower fee rates than regular transactions, which indicates careful fee-setting by ordinal users. They also concluded that the rise of ordinal transactions has increased non-inscription transaction fee rates and total block fees, thus increasing miners' revenue. We do a similar fee investigation in our paper. Yet, we look at inscriptions in EVM chains instead of Bitcoin.

Novelty of our Approach. To the best of our knowledge, this is the first work to conduct an in-depth analysis of inscriptions in multi EVM-compatible chains and the user dynamics that arose from the inscription boom observed in the end of 2023 and early 2024. While Bitcoin originally set the stage for this user trend [26,27], EVM chains have witnessed substantial adoption as well. The absence of analysis in this domain introduces a notable gap in the existing research landscape, which we address in this paper.

7 Conclusion

The inscriptions boom between December 2023 and January 2024 was the first real-life stress test for various EVM-compatible blockchains. Our study of Ethereum, Arbitrum, Base, Optimism, and ZKsync Era during this period revealed stark differences between L1, L2 blockchains, and among rollups.

First, we observed that, on specific peak days, transactions related to inscriptions accounted for nearly 90% on Arbitrum and ZKsync Era, and over 53% on Ethereum, and almost 35% on Optimism and Base. The surge in on-chain inscriptions overwhelmed some rollups, causing their instability due to the increased transaction volume. This resulted in downtimes and delays in transaction processing.

We further found that 99% of these inscription transactions across all examined blockchains were driven by the claim or minting of inscription-based memecoins, followed by a modest amount of trading activity, mostly associated with listing operations on marketplaces. All chains show a dominant token that represents more than 74% of all inscription transactions.

Looking at the impact of inscriptions on gas fees, we concluded that gas fees on rollups either remained stable or decreased during the transaction volume peak. Particularly, the median transaction fee remained the same on Base and Optimism, and decreased on Arbitrum and ZKsync Era. On the other hand, Ethereum experienced a rise in fees, which is not surprising. Unlike L1 blockchains, rollups are designed to offer lower gas fees as transaction counts increase, due to their ability to compress multiple L2 transactions into a single batch on the L1 network.

Moreover, the future of inscriptions as a stable market for token trading in EVM-chains is still not cemented. For instance, Data Availability (DA) and User Interface (UI) issues can complicate interactions with inscriptions, highlighting how nascent the market still is. It is nevertheless an interesting trend and a lot of innovation can still occur to turn the space into a more mature one.

Finally, to promote scientific reproducibility and facilitate further research, we made our data set and scripts publicly available [17].

References

1. Dune dashboard - EVM inscriptions (2024), https://dune.com/hildobby/inscriptions
2. Ethereum roadmap (2024), https://ethereum.org/en/roadmap/
3. Adams, H., Zinsmeister, N., Salem, M., Keefer, R., Robinson, D.: Uniswap v3 core (2021)
4. Anand, A., Pathak, J.: The role of reddit in the gamestop short squeeze. Econ. Lett. **211**, 110249 (2022)
5. Anonymous: Brc-20 experiment (2023), https://domo-2.gitbook.io/brc-20-experiment/
6. Bertucci, L.: Bitcoin ordinals: determinants and impact on total transaction fees. Available at SSRN 4486127 (2023)
7. BigInt: BigInt. https://bigint.co/inscriptions (2024), Accessed 22 May 2024
8. Binance: Binance NFT marketplace to support bitcoin NFTs. https://www.binance.com/en/blog/nft/binance-nft-marketplace-to-support-bitcoin-nfts-4250480174684233711 (2024), Accessed 22 May 2024
9. Community, Z.: ZKsync Public RPCs. https://docs.zksync.io/zksync-era/ecosystem/node-providers#public-rpcs (2025), Accessed 28 Feb 2025
10. Corwin Smith: ERC-20 token standard. https://ethereum.org/en/developers/docs/standards/tokens/erc-20 (2024), Accessed 22 May 2024
11. Corwin Smith: ERC-721 non-fungible token standard. https://ethereum.org/en/developers/docs/standards/tokens/erc-721 (2024), Accessed 22 May 2024
12. Haig, S.: Mantle's throughput peaks at 200 TPS as inscriptions expand across layer 2s. https://thedefiant.io/news/defi/mantle-s-throughput-peaks-at-200-tps-as-inscriptions-expand-across-layer-2s (2024), Accessed 23 May 2024
13. Insacribe: Incentivized mainnet. https://inscribe.app/app (2024), Accessed 22 May 2024
14. Labs, P.: Ipfs powers the distributed web. https://ipfs.tech (2024), Accessed 22 May 2024
15. Li, N., Qi, M., Wang, Q., Chen, S.: Bitcoin inscriptions: foundations and beyond, January 2024. https://doi.org/10.48550/arXiv.2401.17581, http://arxiv.org/abs/2401.17581, arXiv:2401.17581 [cs]

16. Li, T., Shin, D., Wang, B.: Cryptocurrency pump-and-dump schemes. Available at SSRN 3267041 (2021)
17. Messias, J., Gogol, K., Silva, M.I., Livshits, B.: Data set and scripts used for analyzing "inscriptions" on EVM-based chains. https://github.com/johnnatan-messias/research-inscriptions-boom (2025)
18. Messias, J., Yaish, A., Livshits, B.: Airdrops: giving money away is harder than it seems. arXiv preprint arXiv:2312.02752 (2023)
19. Nansen: nansen query: empowering crypto teams with in-depth blockchain data. https://www.nansen.ai/query (2024), Accessed 22 May 2024
20. Park, S., et al.: Impact of EIP-4844 on Ethereum: consensus security, Ethereum Usage, Rollup transaction dynamics, and blob gas fee markets, May 2024. https://doi.org/10.48550/arXiv.2405.03183, http://arxiv.org/abs/2405.03183, arXiv:2405.03183 [cs, math]
21. Schaar, L., Kampakis, S.: Non-fungible tokens as an alternative investment: evidence from cryptopunks. J. Br. Blockchain Assoc. (2022)
22. Shivam sharm: BRC-20 tokens: a primer. https://www.binance.com/en/research/analysis/brc-20-tokens-a-primer (2023), Accessed 15 Jan 2023
23. Tom blackstone: arbitrum network went offline for 78 minutes because of inscriptions. https://cointelegraph.com/news/arbitrum-network-goes-offline-december-15 (2023), Accessed 15 Jan 2023
24. Vasileiou, E., Bartzou, E., Tzanakis, P.: Explaining gamestop short squeeze using intraday data and google searches. Forthcoming J. Prediction Mark. (2021)
25. Wang, Q., Li, R., Wang, Q., Chen, S.: Non-fungible token (NFT): overview, evaluation, opportunities and challenges. arXiv preprint arXiv:2105.07447 (2021)
26. Wang, Q., Yu, G.: Brc-20: hope or hype. arXiv preprint arXiv:2310.10652 (2023)
27. Wang, Q., Yu, G.: Understanding brc-20: Hope or hype. Available at SSRN 4590451 (2023)
28. Xu, J., Livshits, B.: The anatomy of a cryptocurrency {Pump-and-Dump} scheme. In: 28th USENIX Security Symposium (USENIX Security 19), pp. 1609–1625 (2019)
29. Xu, J., Paruch, K., Cousaert, S., Feng, Y.: Sok: decentralized exchanges (dex) with automated market maker (amm) protocols. ACM Comput. Surv. **55**(11), 1–50 (2023)
30. Yu, G., Wang, Q.: Bridging brc-20 to ethereum. arXiv preprint arXiv:2310.10065 (2023)
31. Zheng, X., Tian, H., Wan, Z., Wang, X., Zeng, D.D., Wang, F.Y.: Game starts at gamestop: characterizing the collective behaviors and social dynamics in the short squeeze episode. IEEE Trans. Comput. Soc. Syst. **9**(1), 45–58 (2021)
32. ZKS market: a tool to inscribe zrc-20. https://zksmarket.ink (2024), Accessed 22 May 2024

Price Oracle Accuracy Across Blockchains: A Measurement and Analysis

Robin Gansäuer[✉][iD], Hichem Ben Aoun[iD], Jan Droll[iD], and Hannes Hartenstein[iD]

KASTEL Security Research Labs, Karlsruhe Institute of Technology, Karlsruhe, Germany
{robin.gansaeuer,hichem.aoun}@student.kit.edu,
{jan.droll,hannes.hartenstein}@kit.edu

Abstract. Decentralized finance depends on accurate price oracles to ensure reliable smart contract operations. Chainlink, a leading decentralized oracle network, bridges blockchains with off-chain data via price feeds. This study quantifies Chainlink's accuracy by comparing its price feeds across eight networks to centralized exchanges for two trading pairs, using mean absolute percentage error analysis and descriptive statistics. The results reveal performance variability. For instance, Polygon achieves high accuracy, while Ethereum and ZKsync exhibit greater deviations under market volatility. The study discusses trade-offs between threshold and heartbeat configurations, emphasizing their complementary roles in balancing accuracy and efficiency. In addition, arbitrage implications and inefficiencies are identified.

Keywords: Price Oracle · Accuracy · Blockchain · DeFi · Chainlink

1 Introduction

The rapid evolution of decentralized finance (DeFi) underscores the pivotal role of accurate off-chain data in enabling reliable smart contract operations. Price oracles, which bridge on-chain systems and external data sources, facilitate autonomous smart contract execution without dependence on centralized authorities. Such decentralized systems enhance the security and transparency underpinning DeFi platforms. However, inaccuracies in price data pose significant risks, including arbitrage opportunities, market manipulation, and the malfunctioning of automated financial services.

Despite their foundational importance, price oracles remain understudied in a comprehensive, cross-platform context. Prior research has largely been confined to isolated blockchain environments or specific exchanges, leaving gaps in understanding their performance across diverse ecosystems. Centralized exchanges (CEXs), known for their high liquidity and consistent pricing, are

---

R. Gansäuer and H. Ben Aoun contributed equally to this work.

widely regarded as reliable benchmarks for financial data. By contrast, decentralized oracle networks (DONs), such as Chainlink, aggregate off-chain data from multiple sources and deliver it on-chain via mechanisms like data feeds. Nevertheless, their capacity to ensure precise and consistent price information across heterogeneous blockchains remains insufficiently explored.

To bridge these gaps, this study systematically examines the accuracy of Chainlink's price feeds by comparing them against CEX benchmarks and evaluating the impact of parameters such as blockchain selection, deviation thresholds, and heartbeat intervals. The investigation is guided by two key research questions:

- RQ1: *How do blockchain selection, deviation thresholds, and heartbeat intervals affect price updates of Chainlink Price Feeds?*
- RQ2: *How accurately do Chainlink Price Feeds reflect off-chain price data, based on benchmarks from selected CEXs across blockchains?*

Addressing these questions, the study compares Chainlink's price feeds with data from two CEXs, evaluating their precision and consistency across a variety of blockchain networks using data from the full month of December 2024. While Chainlink serves as the focal point, the findings contribute to a broader understanding of price oracle functionality and accuracy within the DeFi ecosystem. By addressing both the diversity of platforms and the operational mechanisms of oracles, this research provides insight into the critical role of decentralized oracles in ensuring the stability and security of DeFi platforms.

The structure of this paper is as follows: Sect. 2 provides basic information on price oracles and decentralized oracle networks at the example of Chainlink. Section 3 reviews related work and identifies key research gaps. Section 4 outlines the methodological framework designed to address the research questions. Section 5 presents the empirical findings, while Sect. 6 discusses their broader implications, study limitations, and directions for future work.

2 Background on Price Oracles: Chainlink

Chainlink offers a notable approach to overcome the *oracle problem* [3], a fundamental challenge in blockchain technology where smart contracts are unable to interact directly with off-chain data in a trustworthy fashion. These contracts, which enforce agreements based on predefined conditions, operate within a blockchain's environment. However, blockchains are intentionally isolated from external data to preserve their security and decentralization [5]. This isolation creates a challenge for smart contracts that require real-world information, such as financial market prices, weather data, or supply chain information, to function correctly.

To address this issue, Chainlink proposes a *decentralized oracle network* that connects blockchains to external data sources. By establishing this connection, smart contracts are empowered to execute transactions incorporating real-world data, while striving to maintain the intended decentralization of blockchain systems. The core of Chainlink's system relies on *data feeds*, which aggregate and deliver data from multiple independent oracles, intending to ensure data integrity and availability. These features are particularly crucial for DeFi applications, such as lending platforms, synthetic asset protocols and decentralized exchanges [5].

Architecture. Chainlink operates through a dual-layer architecture comprising *off-chain* and *on-chain* components that work in close tandem to enable the transmission of external data to smart contracts. This layered approach is designed to reduce the risks of erroneous or malicious data interference [3,5].

The off-chain component is driven by a decentralized network of *Chainlink nodes*, which fetch data from external sources, perform computations and transmit the results to the blockchain. This decentralized structure seeks to reduce reliance on single points of failure and to enhance resilience against potential adversarial actions. Once processed, the aggregated data is relayed via *on-chain aggregator contracts* for smart contract execution [5].

The on-chain component enhances data reliability by evaluating oracle performance, matching smart contract data requests with suitable nodes, and consolidating inputs from multiple oracles into a single output [5].

Data Feeds, Thresholds, Heartbeats, and Rounds. A key service of Chainlink is its *data feeds*, which aggregate and provide real-world price data for various assets. These feeds are relevant for DeFi applications that rely on real-world pricing information to execute smart contracts. They operate on a *push-based design*, where updates are pushed to the blockchain based on specific conditions. Updates are triggered by the following conditions:[1]

- Deviation thresholds, in short thresholds: Update triggered by specified price change compared to the price currently reported on-chain. These thresholds are intended to ensure prompt reflection of market movements, enabling smart contracts to respond.
- Heartbeats: Periodic updates ensure data reliability during low market volatility, preventing outdated pricing from impacting smart contracts.

When a threshold is reached and a corresponding Chainlink node detects it, a new round is initiated to aggregate oracle data of the Chainlink nodes. Rounds are numbered, and therefore, one can associate reported prices to rounds. Values for thresholds and heartbeats need to be configured to provide timely and relevant data while optimizing network load and transaction costs. In Subsect. 5.1, we analyze deviation thresholds and heartbeat intervals for various blockchains, while in Subsect. 5.2, we analyze price accuracy, and in Subsect. 5.3, we relate threshold and heartbeat configuration to price accuracy [2].

---

[1] See https://docs.chain.link/architecture-overview/architecture-decentralized-model.

3 Related Work

3.1 State of the Art

Research on Chainlink Price Feeds is limited but critical due to their foundational role in DeFi. Key studies by Nadler et al. [11], Vakhmyanin and Volkovich [12], and Gogol et al. [7] provide valuable insights.

Nadler et al. [11] conducted an extensive study of Chainlink oracles on Ethereum, analyzing over 150 million data points from 40 price feeds. Their investigation highlighted how heartbeat intervals and deviation thresholds impact oracle price accuracy. While effective in stable conditions, these mechanisms caused significant delays during periods of market volatility, exposing smart contracts to stale and unreliable data. Their update types and rounds structure analysis is foundational but focuses solely on the Ethereum blockchain [11].

Vakhmyanin and Volkovich [12] explored Layer-2 ecosystems, focusing on the Mycelium platform on Arbitrum. They found that Chainlink's 2.5% deviation threshold delayed updates during volatile conditions, creating arbitrage opportunities for high-frequency traders. The study emphasized the difficulty of maintaining oracle accuracy in fast-changing environments [12].

Gogol et al. [7] analyzed arbitrage opportunities across Layer-2 networks, including Arbitrum, Optimism, Base, and ZKsync. They identified over 500,000 unexploited arbitrage events and revealed how gas fees and block production times shape price discrepancies. However, their work does not address Chainlink's specific configurations or its potential role in reducing inefficiencies [7].

3.2 Research Gaps

While significant progress has been made in understanding Chainlink oracles in DeFi, key gaps remain.

First, Nadler et al. [11] focus on Ethereum-based oracles, leaving the performance of Chainlink Price Feeds on other ecosystems, such as Layer-1 blockchains like Avalanche and Layer-2 solutions like Arbitrum, largely unexplored. These ecosystems introduce varying conditions, such as differing block times and transaction costs, that could significantly impact oracle behavior and require a broader cross-blockchain evaluation [11].

Second, while studies have examined mechanisms like heartbeat intervals and deviation thresholds, their effectiveness across different blockchain environments and under varying market conditions remains insufficiently explored. Gogol et al. [7] address arbitrage dynamics, highlighting the influence of cross-rollup conditions and market variability, but do not analyze how these mechanisms directly affect Chainlink's accuracy or reliability in practice [7].

Third, no rigorous comparison has been made between Chainlink and CEXs such as Coinbase and Kraken across multiple blockchains. While prior research notes deviations during market volatility, the extent of Chainlink's accuracy and latency compared to CEXs remains unquantified, particularly under diverse and challenging conditions. Such comparisons are crucial for a thorough assessment of Chainlink's reliability and performance as a decentralized data provider.

4 Methods

This study adopts an adapted version of the *Knowledge Discovery in Databases (KDD)* process [6] to evaluate the accuracy of Chainlink Price Feeds compared to CEXs. Data was continuously collected for the entire month of December 2024 using a custom-built agent, capturing real-time price movements. This period was chosen due to practical constraints. The KDD framework comprises six stages: *Data Sourcing, Selection, Preprocessing, Transformation, Data Mining,* and *Interpretation and Evaluation*. To support this, the *Medallion Architecture* [4] organizes data into three layers: *bronze* (raw data), *silver* (cleaned data), and *gold* (refined dataset).

4.1 Data Sourcing and Selection

BTC/USD and ETH/USD trading pairs were chosen for their high liquidity, relevance in cryptocurrency markets, and availability across Chainlink and CEXs. Chainlink price data was accessed via public *Remote Procedure Call (RPC)* endpoints, capturing updates every second to ensure high-frequency data collection. For CEXs, websocket connections facilitated continuous, low-latency price streams. All data points were timestamped upon retrieval from the RPC, forming the *bronze layer*.

Coinbase and Kraken were selected for their high market share and provision of free websocket access to USD-based trading pairs. We did not choose Binance because it does not offer trading pairs that include fiat currency, specifically USD. For Chainlink, price feeds spanned Layer 1 blockchains such as Ethereum, Avalanche, Binance Smart Chain (BSC), and Celo, alongside Layer 2 solutions including Arbitrum, Polygon, ZKsync, and Linea. These networks were chosen for their accessibility via public RPC endpoints, ensuring consistent and reliable data retrieval. To enhance reliability, we used a list of at least five RPCs as fallback options, with Llama RPC as the primary for consistency and Infura RPC as the final fallback.

4.2 Preprocessing and Transformation

The preprocessing phase ensured that raw data was systematically prepared for analysis. Missing values, occurring due to occasional delays in data updates, were handled conservatively to maintain data integrity. Temporal alignment across data sources was achieved by synchronizing timestamps to a unified one-second precision. These steps were executed using *Databricks* with *Apache Spark* on *Azure*, enabling large-scale data processing.

In the transformation phase, semi-structured data from the *bronze layer* was cleaned and converted into structured formats in the *silver layer* and further refined into an analysis-ready dataset in the *gold layer*. Data from Chainlink feeds and CEXs was aggregated to one-second intervals to enable consistent comparisons, ensuring alignment of update frequencies.

4.3 Data Mining

In the data mining phase, statistical methods were applied to assess the accuracy of Chainlink Price Feeds compared to CEX prices. Price accuracy was evaluated using the *Mean Absolute Percentage Error (MAPE)*, which quantified percentage-based deviations between Chainlink's price feeds and CEX prices from Coinbase, Kraken, and their weighted average. In addition, Pearson correlation coefficients are computed to quantify the impact of threshold and heartbeat parameters on price deviations.

4.4 Interpretation and Evaluation

The comparison framework, illustrated in Fig. 1, is organized into two primary components: the *Analysis Component* and the *Comparison Component*.

The *Analysis Component* focuses on update types and round analysis, categorizing Chainlink price updates into mechanisms such as *threshold, heartbeat*, and *unknown*. This structured approach ensures a detailed and comprehensive understanding of the mechanisms driving Chainlink's price feeds.

The *Comparison Component* evaluates the accuracy of Chainlink Price Feeds for BTC/USD and ETH/USD against benchmark data from Coinbase and Kraken. Using *MAPE* and Pearson correlation, this component assesses deviations and examines how well Chainlink updates align with reference data under varying network configurations.

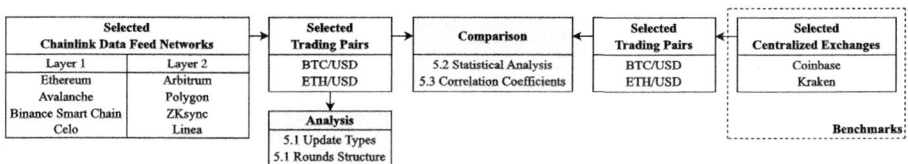

Fig. 1. Comparison Framework: Analyzing Chainlink Feeds Against CEX Benchmarks.

Table 1. Chainlink Data Feed Networks and Trading Pair Configurations.

	Layer 1 Networks				Layer 2 Networks		
Network	Trading Pair	Threshold (%)	Heartbeat (s)	Network	Trading Pair	Threshold (%)	Heartbeat (s)
Ethereum	BTC/USD	±0.5	3,600	Arbitrum	BTC/USD	±0.05	86,400
	ETH/USD	±0.5	3,600		ETH/USD	±0.05	86,400
Avalanche	BTC/USD	±0.1	86,400	Polygon	BTC/USD	±0.0	60
	ETH/USD	±0.1	86,400		ETH/USD	±0.0	60
BSC	BTC/USD	±0.1	60	ZKsync	BTC/USD	±0.5	86,400
	ETH/USD	±0.1	60		ETH/USD	±0.5	86,400
Celo	BTC/USD	±0.1	86,400	Linea	BTC/USD	±0.5	86,400
	ETH/USD	±0.1	86,400		ETH/USD	±0.5	86,400

5 Results

5.1 Analysis of Update Types and Rounds Structure

In this subsection, we examine how threshold and heartbeat configurations affect the temporal distribution of price updates across different data feed networks. Figure 1 shows the different data feed networks we focus on, while Table 1 details their respective configurations. All networks specify both threshold- and heartbeat update mechanisms, though the specific parameter values differ. Most networks use threshold values above 0% and 60-second heartbeat intervals. Polygon stands out as the only network configured with a 0% threshold, leading to updates at the smallest price movements. Based on heartbeat and threshold configurations, we group the networks into four categories: long heartbeat with large threshold, moderate heartbeat with large threshold, and short heartbeat with small threshold. Polygon, due to its unique threshold configuration, forms a distinct fourth group.

For visual analysis, we utilize scatter plots as in [11]: The plots show the price difference (deviation) of the update relative to the current round price on the vertical axis and the time since the last update normalized by the heartbeat interval on the horizontal axis. Indicated are the types of update: threshold, heartbeat, or unknown (for the case of an update that we cannot relate to threshold or heartbeat).

The first group consists of Arbitrum, ZKsync, Linea, Avalanche, and Celo. These networks make use of a long heartbeat interval of 86,400 s (24 h). The deviation thresholds are set to $\pm 0.05\%$, $\pm 0.1\%$ or $\pm 0.5\%$. As shown in Fig. 2 for the BTC/USD trading pair on ZKsync, updates occur predominantly close to the beginning of the heartbeat interval, triggered by significant market movements that exceed the threshold. Thus, a "long heartbeat interval" actually indicates reliance primarily on deviation threshold-driven updates.

The second group consists solely of Ethereum that adopts a hybrid mechanism with a moderate heartbeat interval of 3,600 s (one hour). In Ethereum, a larger deviation threshold of $\pm 0.5\%$ is used. The on-chain price data feed shows a more dispersed update pattern, as seen in Fig. 3 for the BTC/USD trading pair. Updates occur inside and outside the threshold corridor, primarily influenced by threshold-driven updates. The temporal distribution of updates is wider and shows a more balanced distribution across the heartbeat interval. This balance reflects an approach of optimizing for a consistent update frequency while accommodating significant price movements to ensure robust performance in its decentralized price feed system.

The third group consists of BSC that incorporates short heartbeat intervals of 60 s and a price threshold of $\pm 0.1\%$. Figure 4 illustrates the hybrid update mechanism, where most updates are time-driven. This approach ensures frequent updates while responding to market fluctuations, providing adaptability to both stable and volatile conditions. The update distribution for BSC shows periodic peaks that do not correspond to its heartbeat interval, suggesting a periodicity within the heartbeat interval. This hybrid approach makes BSC particularly flexible in accommodating a range of market dynamics.

The fourth group is represented by Polygon, where the deviation threshold is set to 0%, meaning updates could potentially occur at every new block whenever the off-chain price changes. However, as shown in Fig. 5 for the BTC/USD trading pair, this expected behavior is not fully reflected in the observed update distribution. Instead, we find a periodicity similar to group three. Only a few updates appear to coincide with the heartbeat interval during price stability, while threshold-triggered updates dominate during periods of market activity, ensuring both data accuracy and consistency of on-chain information.

The diversity in update distributions across networks demonstrates the adaptability of Chainlink's system, balancing market responsiveness with consistent data availability. This flexibility allows the architecture to adapt to varying network requirements and market conditions. However, given the different update strategies, one is wondering whether all of these strategies lead to accurate price information. We address this aspect in the next subsections.

5.2 Statistical Analysis of Price Accuracy

The statistical analysis in this section focuses on the accuracy of Chainlink's price feeds in replicating CEX price movements. Price movements should gener-

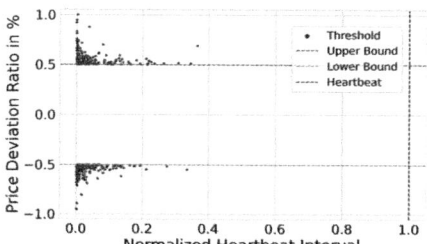

Fig. 2. Long heartbeat interval: updates of BTC/USD on ZKsync (threshold: ±0.5%, heartbeat: 86,400 s) for December 2024.

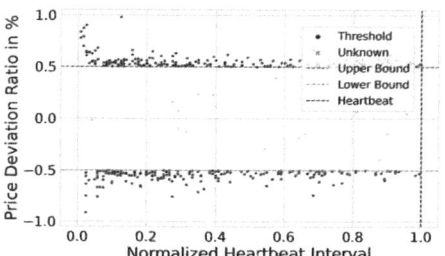

Fig. 3. Moderate heartbeat interval: updates of BTC/USD on Ethereum (threshold: ±0.5%, heartbeat: 3,600 s) for December 2024.

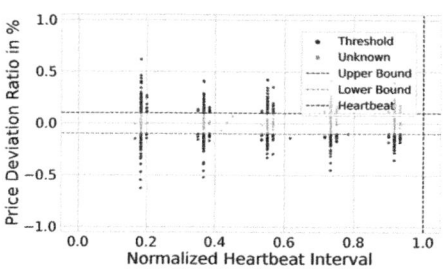

Fig. 4. Short heartbeat interval: updates of BTC/USD on BSC (threshold: ±0.1%, heartbeat: 60 s) December 2024.

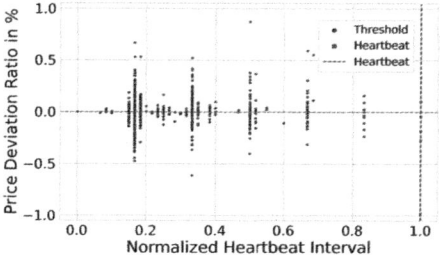

Fig. 5. Short heartbeat interval: updates of BTC/USD on Polygon (threshold: ±0.0%, heartbeat: 60 s) December 2024.

ally remain within the predefined upper and lower bounds that result from the configuration of the deviation threshold and the heartbeat interval. The reported price on Chainlink, the upper and lower bounds of the respective configuration, and the prices reported by Kraken and Coinbase are depicted in Figs. 6, 7, 8 and 9 for ZKsync, Ethereum, BSC, and Polygon, respectively. The figures show data from a randomly chosen 12-hour window from 00:00 UTC until 12:00 UTC on 2024-12-03, as shorter intervals lack sufficient rounds and larger timeframes reduce the visibility of price deviations. The results illustrate varying levels of fidelity across networks, with notable discrepancies and fluctuations in some cases, while others demonstrate high accuracy and stability.

Figure 6 reveals considerable price fluctuations on the ZKsync network. Centralized exchange prices frequently diverge between the upper and lower bounds, indicating significant volatility. While Chainlink's price feed effectively remains within the defined threshold, the wide range between the bounds illustrates the challenge of capturing precise market movements during volatile conditions. This observation is critical, as it highlights the limitations of relying solely on predefined bounds in such scenarios, where centralized exchanges exhibit inconsistent price behavior. The results suggest that while ZKsync's configuration ensures

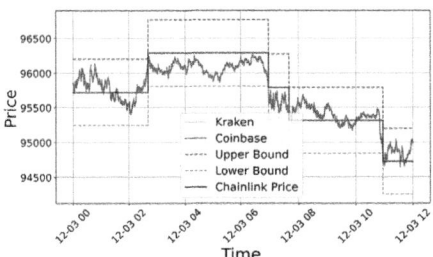

Fig. 6. Price and thresholds of BTC/USD on ZKsync (threshold: ±0.5%, heartbeat: 86,400 s) over time (12h).

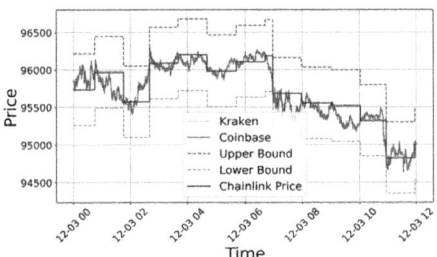

Fig. 7. Price and thresholds of BTC/USD on Ethereum (threshold: ±0.5%, heartbeat: 3,600 s) over time (12h).

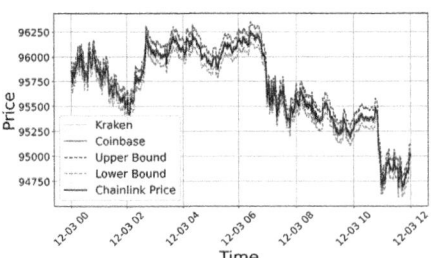

Fig. 8. Price and thresholds of BTC/USD on BSC (threshold: ±0.1%, heartbeat: 60 s) over time (12h).

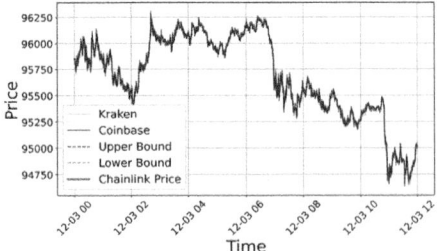

Fig. 9. Price and thresholds of BTC/USD on Polygon (threshold: ±0.0%, heartbeat: 60 s) over time (12h).

adherence to the threshold, it may struggle to accurately replicate real-time market prices during rapid fluctuations.

Similarly, Fig. 7 depicts the behavior of Chainlink's price feeds on the Ethereum network. Configured with a wider threshold of ±0.5%, the upper and lower bounds show substantial variability compared to the actual prices on Coinbase and Kraken. This variability, combined with frequent deviations between the bounds, suggests that the Ethereum configuration prioritizes update efficiency over strict adherence to real-time CEX prices. The Chainlink feed, while staying within the thresholds, captures a generalized trend rather than replicating precise market fluctuations. This trade-off between accuracy and stability is particularly evident in scenarios of increased market activity, where CEX prices reflect frequent and sharp changes.

In contrast, Fig. 8 provides an intermediate perspective, showing Chainlink's performance on the BSC network. Although the price feed adheres to the threshold bounds, the deviation between the upper and lower bounds remains narrower than the deviation observed on ZKsync and Ethereum. This suggests a more balanced approach, where the Chainlink feed effectively captures real-time market trends while maintaining a reasonable level of stability. The results indicate that BSC's configuration balances accuracy and resilience.

Lastly, Fig. 9 highlights the exceptional performance regarding accuracy of Chainlink's price feeds on the Polygon network. Due to the defined price threshold of 0% (i.e., each deviation triggers an update), the Chainlink prices align almost perfectly with those of Coinbase and Kraken, with minimal deviation due to block time restrictions. The graph demonstrates a seamless replication of the centralized exchange prices, suggesting that Chainlink effectively captures real-time market movements without significant lag or error. This precise alignment underscores the robustness of the Chainlink mechanism on Polygon, particularly in maintaining data accuracy even during periods of high market activity.

The histogram in Fig. 10 presents a comparative analysis, using MAPE, based on the data of the full month of December, across multiple networks for three categories: Weighted CEXs (by transaction volume), Coinbase, and Kraken. The price deviation ratio was calculated by taking the absolute difference between the Chainlink price and the CEX price, divided by the Chainlink price. This resulted in a deviation value for each recorded data point. These values were subsequently averaged, grouped by network and trading pair to receive the MAPE. It reveals significant disparities in the accuracy of Chainlink's price feeds, with ZKsync exhibiting the highest MAPE across all categories, indicating substantial deviations from CEX prices. In contrast, BSC and Polygon consistently achieve the lowest MAPE values, demonstrating superior accuracy and alignment with market prices. Networks like Avalanche and Linea fall into a middle ground, showing moderate deviations. This analysis highlights the impact of network-specific configurations on price feed fidelity, emphasizing the need for tailored adjustments.

Overall, the analysis reveals significant differences in the accuracy of Chainlink's price feeds across networks. Polygon demonstrates exceptional alignment

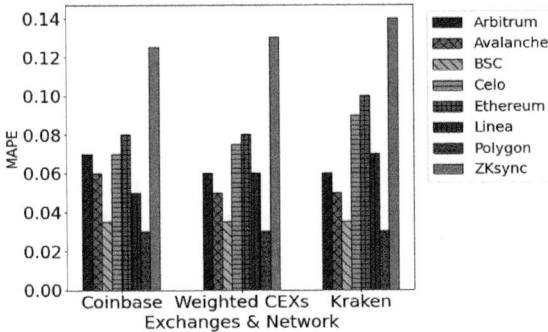

Fig. 10. MAPE for Accuracy Comparison by Exchange and Network.

with CEX prices, while Avalanche strikes a balance between stability and accuracy. In contrast, Ethereum and ZKsync exhibit larger deviations, particularly during volatile conditions, reflecting the trade-offs of their configurations. The comparative MAPE analysis further underscores these disparities, highlighting Polygon and Arbitrum as the most accurate networks and ZKsync as the least.

5.3 Correlation of Update Parameters and Price Accuracy

To understand the influence of the configuration of the deviation threshold and the heartbeat interval on the price deviation ratio, we computed the corresponding Pearson correlation coefficients as descriptive statistics. The Pearson correlation coefficient was used to assess how changes in the deviation threshold and heartbeat interval influence the price deviation ratio, quantifying the strength and direction of the relationship between these parameters. The Pearson correlation coefficient for the threshold metric evaluates to 0.66 and indicates a strong positive relationship between the deviation threshold configuration and the discrepancy between the weighted price of the CEXs (weighted by transaction volume) and Chainlink's price feeds. This value suggests that as the threshold increases, the magnitude of price discrepancies also increases proportionally. For the heartbeat metric, the Pearson correlation coefficient is 0.27, which means a somewhat weak positive relationship with the weighted CEX price discrepancy. Please note again that we use the correlation coefficient as a descriptive statistic and refrain from inference.

6 Discussion

In December 2024, the observed mean absolute percentage error for the eight analyzed Chainlink data feed networks is smaller than 0.14 for all networks, and smaller than 0.1 for all observed networks but ZKsync. Thus, generally speaking, the average tracking error appears to be reasonably small. However, the update mechanism should react quickly on the one hand and should not induce unnecessary transactions on the other hand. In the following subsections, we discuss this trade-off, further implications, limitations, and future work.

Tradeoffs. The analysis of MAPE values provides some context on the accuracy of Chainlink Price Feeds across blockchains. Polygon stands out as the most accurate, achieving consistently low MAPE values. Notably, it operates with an average block time of just 2.1 s, significantly shorter than most other networks. This rapid block time facilitates frequent updates, enhancing alignment with off-chain prices. Such exceptional performance underscores the effectiveness of frequent updates, raising the question of whether higher thresholds remain justified. The answer depends on network-specific factors, such as block time and transaction costs. For Polygon, the threshold of 0%[2] eliminates deviation, but this approach may not be feasible on networks with higher costs or slower block times.

In contrast, ZKsync exhibits the highest MAPE values, reflecting significant deviations from off-chain prices. This is due to its higher threshold and longer heartbeat intervals. Avalanche and Linea occupy a middle ground, with moderate MAPE values indicating a balance between accuracy and efficiency. Arbitrum also demonstrates high accuracy, performing comparably with Polygon, particularly in aligning with CEX prices.

The interplay between the threshold and heartbeat parameters highlights their distinct yet complementary roles, borrowing concepts of safety and liveness from the field of distributed computing. While the threshold acts as a safety condition, ensuring that updates are triggered only when deviations exceed a predefined limit ("nothing bad has happened") [8], the heartbeat serves as a liveness condition, guaranteeing that updates eventually occur to restore alignment ("eventually something good will happen") [1]. Removing the heartbeat would be problematic, as it ensures eventual recovery from discrepancies, even in low-volatility markets. Without it, price updates could stall for extended periods, causing outdated on-chain prices that increase the risk of incorrect liquidations and arbitrage exploits, without ever being corrected. Conversely, a poorly calibrated threshold can lead to larger inaccuracies, especially during high-volatility conditions. These principles are supported by the update patterns observed across networks. All networks showed few updates triggered by the heartbeat, reinforcing its role as a safety net rather than a primary driver of updates. Without the heartbeat, there is no assurance that discrepancies will be corrected in a timely manner, highlighting its indispensability in maintaining data accuracy.

The tradeoff between oracle accuracy and operator costs is critical. Higher accuracy demands frequent updates, lower deviation thresholds, and shorter heartbeat intervals, increasing on-chain fees and computational expenses. Conversely, raising thresholds or extending heartbeats reduces costs but risks delayed updates and larger discrepancies between on-chain and off-chain values. While minimizing the threshold can significantly cut costs, eliminating it entirely would trigger updates for every minor price change, making operations economically

---

[2] At the time of publication, the threshold on Polygon has been increased to 0.1% for BTC/USD and ETH/USD.

unfeasible, especially for high transaction cost blockchains. These costs would ultimately shift to users.

To balance accuracy and cost, a dynamic threshold adjustment could provide a more effective solution. By adapting the threshold based on factors such as the rate of price change at the update trigger, market volatility, network congestion, and trading volume, oracles could optimize updates to reflect meaningful price shifts while avoiding unnecessary transactions.

Implications for Practice and Research. From a practice perspective, the findings highlight a potential vulnerability in DeFi systems, where price deviations, even as low as an average of 0.15%, can lead to substantial arbitrage profits in scenarios involving high trading volumes. For instance, if Chainlink's BTC/USD price feed deviates on average by 0.15% compared to CEX prices, an arbitrageur could exploit this by purchasing BTC on a DeFi platform at the lower oracle price and immediately selling it at the higher market price after an update. With significant trading volumes (e.g., $10 million), a deviation of 0.15% translates into a profit of $15,000 per arbitrage cycle, compounded across multiple transactions. Empirical evidence confirms that such inefficiencies are actively exploited in practice. Recent research indicates that about 52% of Ethereum blocks contain at least one flashbots transaction, with 98.68% of liquidations on AAVE and Compound explicitly depending on Chainlink oracle updates occurring within the same block [9]. In addition, approximately 85% of these bundles consist precisely of one oracle update immediately followed by a liquidation, illustrating traders' already existing strategic exploitation of oracle update timing to maximize profitability [9]. Such practices potentially result in liquidity providers incurring losses as their provided liquidity is depleted to fund trades executed at suboptimal prices. This systematic exploitation underscores the necessity for refining oracle mechanisms, such as optimizing deviation thresholds and heartbeat intervals. Yet, even when such inefficiencies are detected, their exploitability can be limited by transaction costs, slippage, and protocol configurations like liquidation penalties, highlighting the need to assess the practical feasibility of these solutions at the ecosystem level [10].

From a research perspective, these findings underscore the need to examine how oracle discrepancies impact the broader DeFi ecosystem, particularly in terms of financial burden distribution between stakeholders such as liquidity providers, governance participants and end-users. Quantifying these losses under varying conditions provides critical information on the stability of the protocol. Adaptive oracle mechanisms, capable of dynamically adjusting thresholds and update intervals based on metrics like market volatility and trading volume, also warrant evaluation for their role in mitigating price deviations effectively.

Furthermore, the systemic implications of oracle discrepancies, including their effects on liquidity pools, derivatives pricing, and AMM strategies, highlight potential vulnerabilities that propagate losses across interconnected protocols. The economic and ethical dimensions of arbitrage require scrutiny, focusing on whether arbitrage profits enhance capital efficiency or destabilize protocols. The potential shift from push-based data feeds to pull-based data streams also raises questions about trade-offs in latency, coordination, and computational costs, offering a critical perspective on optimizing decentralized price feed systems. However, the ecosystem cannot rely solely on pull-based oracles for data that is needed by many users simultaneously. In such cases, each user would redundantly request the same datapoint, introducing inefficiencies and imposing constraints on the underlying infrastructure. When the data flow follows a one-to-many connection, with a single datapoint serving multiple users, a push-based model remains the more scalable and efficient solution.

Limitations and Future Work. Our research presents several limitations and opportunities for future work. The data collection for one month, conducted during the moderately volatile period of December 2024, provides valuable information but may not fully capture the impacts of extreme market conditions, such as high volatility spikes, severe congestion, or periods of low activity. Extending the study over varying market cycles would provide a more holistic understanding of oracle performance and resilience. The analysis was limited to two trading pairs, both involving a fiat currency (BTC/USD and ETH/USD), which, while significant, may not reflect the unique dynamics of crypto-to-crypto trading pairs. Including a broader set of trading pairs, such as ETH/BTC or stablecoin-to-crypto pairs, could reveal additional complexities and patterns in price feed behavior. Reliance on CEXs for price comparisons does not fully account for deviations from DEX prices, which may result from differing liquidity, slippage, or arbitrage. Moreover, while indexed data effectively highlights overall network trends, it may obscure network-specific behaviors, such as block time variability affecting price update latency and accuracy. Closer analysis of these discrepancies could enhance our understanding of how market structures and network mechanics influence oracle reliability.

7 Conclusion

This study provides an evaluation of the accuracy of Chainlink's price oracles across diverse blockchain networks. By comparing price feeds with data from centralized exchanges, the findings reveal how threshold and heartbeat parameters interact to balance price accuracy with update frequency.

The analysis examines different approaches of oracle configurations. For instance, Polygon's 0% threshold-driven updates achieve high accuracy with minimal deviations, while larger threshold values on ZKsync and Ethereum present challenges under volatility. Avalanche exemplifies a balanced approach, maintaining stability while reflecting real-time market trends. These findings underscore Chainlink's architectural adaptability across diverse market and network conditions.

Our findings identify potential vulnerabilities in DeFi systems that rely on push-based data feeds. Even small deviations in oracle accuracy might lead to arbitrage opportunities and systemic inefficiencies. Whether these vulnerabilities are actually exploitable is subject to further research. However, adaptive oracle mechanisms capable of dynamically tuning parameters to match market volatility and the adoption of pull-based data streams could significantly improve resilience.

References

1. Alpern, B., Schneider, F.B.: Recognizing safety and liveness. Distrib. Comput. **2**(3), 117–126 (1987). https://doi.org/10.1007/BF01782772
2. Breidenbach, L., et al.: Chainlink 2.0: next steps in the evolution of decentralized oracle networks. Chainlink Labs **1**, 1–136 (2021). https://research.chain.link/whitepaper-v2.pdf
3. Caldarelli, G.: Understanding the blockchain oracle problem: a call for action. Information **11**(11), 509 (2020). https://doi.org/10.3390/info11110509
4. Databricks: What is the Medallion Lakehouse Architecture? (2020). https://docs.databricks.com/en/lakehouse/medallion.html. Accessed 17 Jan 2025
5. Ellis, S., Juels, A., Nazarov, S.: Chainlink: a decentralized oracle network. Whitepaper (2017). https://research.chain.link/whitepaper-v1.pdf
6. Fayyad, U., Piatetsky-Shapiro, G., Smyth, P.: From data mining to knowledge discovery in databases. AI Mag. **17**(3), 37–54 (1996). https://doi.org/10.1609/aimag.v17i3.1230
7. Gogol, K., Messias, J., Miori, D., Tessone, C., Livshits, B.: Cross-rollup MEV: non-atomic arbitrage across L2 blockchains. arXiv preprint arXiv:2406.02172 (2024). https://doi.org/10.48550/arXiv.2406.02172
8. Lamport, L.: Proving the correctness of multiprocess programs. IEEE Trans. Softw. Eng. **SE-3**(2), 125–143 (1977). https://doi.org/10.1109/TSE.1977.229904
9. Messias, J., Pahari, V., Chandrasekaran, B., Gummadi, K.P., Loiseau, P.: Dissecting Bitcoin and Ethereum transactions: On the lack of transaction contention and prioritization transparency in blockchains. In: Financial Cryptography and Data Security, pp. 221–240 (2024). https://doi.org/10.1007/978-3-031-47751-5_13
10. Muck, M., Schmidl, T., Wolf, J.: Wish or reality? On the exploitability of triangular arbitrage in cryptocurrency markets. Financ. Res. Lett. **73**, 106508 (2025). https://doi.org/10.1016/j.frl.2024.106508
11. Nadler, M., Schuler, K., Schär, F.: Blockchain price oracles: Accuracy and violation recovery. Available at SSRN (2023). https://doi.org/10.2139/ssrn.4700164
12. Vakhmyanin, I., Volkovich, Y.: Price arbitrage for DeFi derivatives. In: Proceedings of the IEEE International Conference on Blockchain and Cryptocurrency (ICBC), pp. 1–4 (2023). https://doi.org/10.1109/ICBC56567.2023.10174884

A Public Dataset For the ZKsync Rollup

Maria Inês Silva[1,4], Johnnatan Messias[2(✉)], and Benjamin Livshits[3]

[1] NOVA Information Management School, Lisbon, Portugal
[2] MPI-SWS, Saarbrücken, Germany
[3] Imperial College London, London, UK
[4] Matter Labs, Berlin, Germany

Abstract. Despite blockchain data being publicly available, practical challenges and high costs often hinder its effective use by researchers, thus limiting data-driven research and exploration in the blockchain space. This is especially true when it comes to Layer-2 (L2) ecosystems, and ZKsync, in particular. To address these issues, we have curated a dataset from 1 year of activity extracted from a ZKsync Era archive node and made it freely available to external parties. We provide details on this dataset and how it was created, showcase a few example analyses that can be performed with it, and discuss some future research directions.

1 Introduction

The blockchain ecosystem is built on the principles of decentralization and transparency. However, a significant challenge remains for end users and non-technical researchers: *blockchain data is not easily accessible*. This challenge hinders the widespread adoption of blockchain technology, which should be more easily accessible.

Currently, blockchain data can be obtained by deploying an archive node in the case of chains based on Ethereum Virtual Machine (EVM) [5,9,27,30], or a full node for Bitcoin [8]. However, this requires high bandwidth and a high-speed storage machine to keep the blockchain fully synced. In other words, individual deployment of archive nodes is not a practical solution. Additionally, users can gather the data through Remote Procedure Calls (RPCs) providers. However, collecting data this way can be challenging for some non-technical users and researchers and is usually costly. Alternatively, users can depend on external data sources such as Etherscan, Arbiscan, Dune, ZettaBlock, Nansen, and similar platforms. Although they may provide an interesting solution, they may prove costly in the long run and do not meet the requirements of specific end-users, particularly those engaged in research that relies on quickly and cheaply accessible data.

MI. Silva and J. Messias contributed equally to this work. Most of this work was performed while the authors were at Matter Labs. The authors also acknowledge the help of Igor Borodin from Matter Labs and his assistance in hosting the dataset.

© International Financial Cryptography Association 2026
B. Haslhofer et al. (Eds.): FC 2025 Workshops, LNCS 15753, pp. 47–62, 2026.
https://doi.org/10.1007/978-3-032-00492-5_4

We believe that anyone requiring blockchain data should have a straightforward and hassle-free way to access it without worrying about infrastructure or hardware. This data has significant value for research purposes, such as alerting and measurement analysis [17,22], Airdrop designs and analyzes [12,26], analyzing Maximal-Extractable Value (MEV) [15,16,24,36,39,42], Automated Market Maker (AMM) [13,37], and potentially improving the adoption of particular chains such as ZKsync and other Layer-2 blockchains (L2s) rollups within the research scope [23]. In addition, it can contribute to the growth of these ecosystems as more researchers become involved in the field.

In a recent talk, a company named Paradigm emphasized that to empower the blockchain community with the necessary data analysis capabilities, we must make blockchain data more accessible [3]. By ensuring that these data are available affordably, quickly, and with minimal effort, we can effectively address the challenge of data unavailability in our ecosystem. They introduced a novel EVM blockchain node developed in Rust, known as *Reth*, that can be applied to EVM-compatible blockchains. Paradigm provided an endpoint to their archive node, allowing anyone to make requests to their node. Similar initiatives have been provided by Matter Labs and other companies interested in making blockchain data more accessible [5,27,30]. Nevertheless, users would need to build high-efficiency code to gather all the necessary data, which could invalidate this process for some users due to network delays or lack of coding skills.

More recently, Paradigm [32,33], BigQuery [11] and other research groups [22, 24] have made blockchain data accessible and available by providing them in an easy-to-download and-load schema. In that sense, we followed through and decided to make a ZKsync dataset fully available and accessible to any user or researcher. Therefore, we provide 1 year of ZKsync data covering the period of February 14th, 2023, (block 1) and March 24th, 2024, (block 29,710,983). More details of the dataset are available in Sect. 2.

1.1 Why ZKsync Era Data?

Launched in March 2023, ZKsync Era is a L2 scaling solution for the Ethereum blockchain that utilizes Zero-Knowledge Proof (ZKP) for efficient transaction processing. ZKsync Era is also an EVM-based rollup, ensuring compatibility with existing Ethereum smart contracts. In July 2024, ZKsync Era ranked among the top five ZKP chains with a Total Value Locked (TVL) estimated at 1.23 billion USD [20]. This scaling solution improves Ethereum by processing transactions in batches using ZKP, which helps maintain low transaction fees and encourages user participation.

In this sense, rollups are a key strategy to scale the Ethereum ecosystem [10]. In fact, these L2 chains have become an important part of the ecosystem in the last few years by pushing new innovations and absorbing a significant portion of user activity. At the same time, there are still many unexplored questions when it comes to these L2 blockchains, and existing research on them is fairly limited.

Given the growing role of L2 chains in the Ethereum ecosystem, we believe there is an opportunity for researchers to conduct research and expand our understanding of these L2 blockchains, such as ZKsync. By making a 1-year ZKsync Era data easily available to external groups, we hope to advance ZKsync-related research and knowledge about L2 chains, more generally.

1.2 Contributions

▶ *Public Availability of ZKsync Data.* To facilitate scientific use of our collected ZKsync Era dataset, we have made it available in a public GitHub repository [1]. This consists of a one-year dataset containing information regarding blocks, transactions, receipts, and logs. Dataset details are presented in Sect. 2.

▶ *Facilitating Research and Analysis.* We demonstrated potential applications of this dataset in research and advocating for the adoption of specific blockchain technologies like ZKsync and L2 rollups in general in Sect. 3.

▶ *Practical Implications for Users and Researchers.* We address challenges associated with data gathering via RPCs and external platforms like Etherscan, Arbiscan, and others, which may be slow and costly. We also provide an easy-to-download and easy-to-load dataset of ZKsync Era, along with Jupyter notebooks to facilitate this onboarding process [1]. Table 1 describes the code utilized to load and process our dataset. All the analyses conducted in this paper can be easily reproduced using our code, which will be available in a GitHub repository. See Sects. 2 and 3 for details.

1.3 Paper Organization

This paper is organized as follows. Section 2 details our dataset and its data schema, together with the necessary background to understand the context of blockchain data in general. Section 3 provides examples of analyses that can be achieved using this dataset, such as regarding transaction fees and gas usage, events derived from transaction logs, token swaps, and more. Furthermore, Sect. 4 discusses open problems and future directions for which this dataset could be useful. Finally, we present the conclusion of our work in Sect. 5.

2 Data Schema and Processing

In this section, we present our ZKsync dataset in detail. The dataset covers the period of February 14th, 2023, (block number 1) and March 24th, 2024, (block number 29,710,983) corresponding to 1 year of data. It contains 327,174,035 transactions and 1,631,772 contracts deployed during this time period which triggered 2,044,221,151 events on-chain. Transactions were issued by 7,322,502 unique users. This dataset enables researchers or blockchain enthusiasts to explore all the activities that occurred in the ZKsync Era since its deployment.

We gathered our dataset from a ZKsync Era archive node as raw data. This data consists of all the information regarding blocks, transactions, receipts, and logs. Then, we conducted a pre-processing step to allow anyone to use the

Table 1. Description of the code used for analysis in this paper. These notebook files are available in our GitHub repository [1] in the directory ./zksync-data-dump/notebooks/ and show how to interact and process our ZKsync dataset.

Notebook file	Description
01-zksync-data.ipynb	It computes the basic statistics of the dataset and provides analyses used in Sect. 2. We use four main sources of data: *blocks*, *transactions*, *transaction receipts*, and *logs*.
02-data-exploration-fees.ipynb	It analyses gas usage and transaction fees for ZKsync used in Sect. 3.1. We use two main sources of data: *blocks* and *transaction receipts*.
03-data-exploration-contracts.ipynb	It analyzes the contract deployment and events triggered on ZKsync described in Sect. 3.2. We use one main source of data: *transaction logs* but also load *blocks* data to extract timestamps information.
04-data-exploration-swaps.ipynb	It analyzes the swap events on ZKsync described in Sect. 3.3. We use one main source of data: *transaction logs* but also load *blocks* data to extract timestamps.

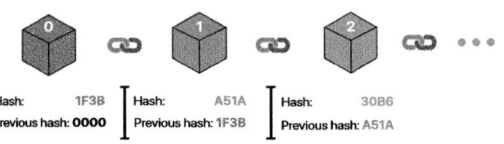

Fig. 1. Illustration of blocks connected to each other forming the blockchain.

dataset. This step consists of formatting the data in a parquet format that can be easily accessible through well-known libraries available in Python, for example, Pandas [31] and Polars [35]. Due to the high volume of data (i.e., around 200 GB), we focus on using Polars for better processing, memory management, and *Lazy evaluation* [19,34], allowing straightforward data processing on a local laptop. Next, we discuss each of the different data types separately.

2.1 Blocks

Blocks are sequential units of data within a blockchain, each identified by a unique hash. They contain a list of transactions, metadata such as timestamps, and the hash of the previous block (*parentHash*), which links them in a chain back to the genesis block (block number 0) as shown in Fig. 1. This chain of blocks forms the blockchain. Blocks ensure transaction security, network consensus, and efficient data storage and processing within blockchain networks. In our dataset, blocks should be sorted according to the attribute *block number* to maintain the correct order of the blocks on the blockchain.

2.2 Transactions

Transactions are digital interactions that involve the transfer of assets, the recording of data, or the execution of smart contracts between parties on blockchains like those based on EVM. Each transaction is initiated by a user, authenticated through cryptographic signatures, and sent to a decentralized network of nodes for validation. Once verified, transactions are grouped into blocks and added to the blockchain via a consensus mechanism, ensuring that they are secure, immutable, transparent, and free of intermediaries, forming the core of the blockchain system.

In rollups, such as ZKsync, transactions are aggregated and processed off the underlying blockchain (e.g., Ethereum, a Layer-1 blockchain (L1)) to enhance scalability and reduce costs. Rollups bundle multiple transactions into a single batch, which is then submitted to the underlying blockchain as one transaction. This method reduces the load on the underlying chain while ensuring transaction security and finality through cryptographic proofs, such as ZKP used by ZKsync or validity checks. By processing transactions off-chain and periodically committing the results to the underlying chain, rollups improve throughput and efficiency without compromising the security and decentralization of the blockchain.

Transactions are identified by a unique transaction hash. When issuing a transaction, the user needs to specify parameters such as the recipient address (which can also be a smart contract and the functions the user wants to call), the number of tokens to transfer, the gas price, and the gas limit. The gas price represents the fee the user is willing to pay per unit of gas, while the gas limit is the maximum amount of gas the user is willing to consume for the transaction, a mechanism introduced to prevent infinite loops or excessive resource consumption.

In our dataset, transactions should be sorted by the *blockNumber* and *transactionIndex* attributes to maintain the correct order of the transactions on the blockchain.

2.3 Transactions Receipts

Besides the transaction data, our dataset also contains a table of transaction receipts. These transaction receipts provide a comprehensive summary of the outcome and effects of a transaction once it is processed and included in a block. They include the transaction hash, block number, and block hash to identify and verify the transaction, along with the sender (*from*) and recipient (*to*) addresses. The receipts also detail the cumulative gas used by the transaction and all preceding transactions in the block, the actual gas used by the specific transaction, and the final gas price paid by the user. By multiplying the actual gas used by the gas price, we have the actual transaction fee the user paid.

Additional information includes *logs* for event logging (discussed next), the transaction status (success or failure), and the effective gas price paid. These receipts are crucial for users and developers to understand, audit, and interact with transactions and smart contracts on the blockchain. For example, they provide essential elements for analyzing, monitoring, and verifying transaction fees spent by users.

Similarly to transactions, in our dataset, transaction receipt data should be sorted by attributes *blockNumber* and *transactionIndex* to maintain the correct order of the transactions on the blockchain.

2.4 Transactions Logs

In this section, we discuss the attributes of the transaction logs data in the ZKsync dataset in detail. Transaction logs are systematic records of events generated during the execution of transactions, particularly in interactions involving smart contracts. Each log entry contains *log index*, *data*, and *topics*, crucial to identifying and categorizing specific events such as token transfers, approvals, swaps, minting, and voting.

These logs are emitted using the *emit* keyword within the smart contract code and play a pivotal role in monitoring activities, triggering actions within decentralized applications, and enabling event-driven programming. For instance, Decentralized Exchanges (DEXs) emit events upon trade executions, enabling user interfaces to update displays with current trade information. These logs are stored in transaction receipts, offering a gas-efficient method to capture transient event data without permanently altering the blockchain's state. Among the vast array of data accessible on EVM-based blockchains, transaction logs stand out as crucial sources of information for researchers, developers, and users. They facilitate analyses of various token transfer patterns and support blockchain analysis research, which is the focus of our contributions.

In our dataset, transaction logs should be sorted by the *blockNumber*, *transactionIndex*, and *logIndex* attributes to maintain the correct order in which they are stored on the blockchain. This is particularly important when analyzing the different states of a blockchain before and after the execution of a transaction that triggers a smart contract function.

Topics Attributes. The interpretation of the *topics* attributes ($topics_0$, $topics_1$, $topics_2$, and $topics_3$) depends on the implementation details of the invoked function within a smart contract. Typically, $topics_0$ represents the event name, while subsequent topics represent indexed parameters of the event. The "data" attribute contains non-indexed event parameters. For example, in the context of a token transfer event, $topics_0$ might indicate the event name *Transfer*, $topics_1$ and $topics_2$ could respectively denote sender and receiver addresses, and *data* would typically represent the number of tokens transferred.

Hashing and Signatures. $topics_0$ corresponds to the hashed function signature using *keccak256* [7]. This signature consists of the function name followed by its parameter types. For example, the signature of a typical *Transfer* event is *Transfer(address,address,uint256)*. After hashing it with keccak256, the result becomes *0xddf2 ··· b3ef*,[1] which is the $topics_0$. Below is a Python code snippet demonstrating how to verify if a given signature matches $topics_0$:

```
import web3
def check_sig(sig, topics_0):
    return web3.Web3.keccak(text=sig).hex() == topics_0
```

---

[1] We shortened $topics_0$ to *0xddf252ad ··· f523b3ef* for better visualization in the paper.

Event Mapping. We provide a mapping of the top 90 most frequently invoked events within the ZKsync dataset in our GitHub repository under `./src/utils.py#events_dict`. This mapping facilitates the parsing of the majority of events in our dataset. The mapping is structured as a dictionary where the $topics_0$ hex value serves as the key, and the corresponding value is a dictionary containing the parsed event name and its function signature. For instance, the Transfer event is represented as follows within the map:

```
events_dict ["0
    xddf252ad1be2c89b69c2b068fc378daa952ba7f163c4a11628f55a4df523b3ef"]
    = {
    "name": "Transfer",
    "signature": "Transfer(address,address,uint256)"}
```

2.5 L2 to L1 Logs

L2 to L1 logs are messages emitted by the ZKsync L2 network and transmitted to the Ethereum L1 network. They are essential for maintaining communication between the two layers, ensuring the security and integrity of transactions and data transfers. In ZKsync, the L1 smart contract verifies these communications by checking the messages alongside the ZKP. The only *provable* part of the communication from L2 to L1 is the native L2 to L1 logs emitted by the Virtual Machine (VM). These logs can be generated using the *to_l1 opcode* [4]. We refer the reader to the ZKsync documentation for more details [2].

3 Example Analyses

This section demonstrates some analyses that can be performed using our ZKsync dataset. Each subsection concentrates on a specific topic and utilizes their respective data (e.g., blocks, transactions, receipts, and logs). In this paper, we consider all activity that starts with block 561,367, the first block on April 1st, until block 29,710,983, the last block in the ZKsync dataset.

This section should serve as a starting point for other researchers wishing to use this dataset for their research. The code for generating this analysis is discussed in Table 1 and will be available in a GitHub repository.

3.1 Gas Usage and Transaction Fees

To start, we look into transactions, gas usage, and fees. All results are generated from two main sources of data, namely blocks and transaction receipts. Note that we are using the transaction receipts instead of the transaction data because the receipts are the source of the actual units of gas used and the final transaction fee paid by users.

Figure 2 shows the daily transactions executed in ZKsync Era over the period analyzed. The network processed an average of 905,194 transactions daily, with a significant spike in December 2023 that accounts for 5,362,921 transactions in a single day. This spike was due to a boom in inscriptions, which became very popular for memecoin traders around this time. Messias *et al.* [23] did a comprehensive review of this phenomenon across various rollups. Since the spike stabilized, we have seen a slight increase in daily transactions, which are now hovering around 1.2 million transactions per day.

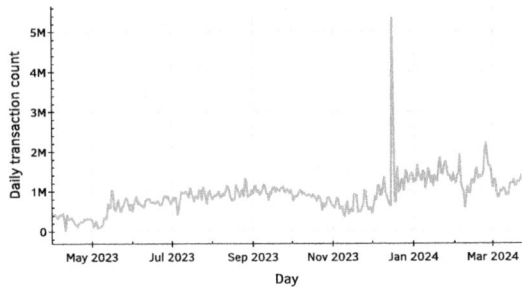

Fig. 2. Total transactions executed per day.

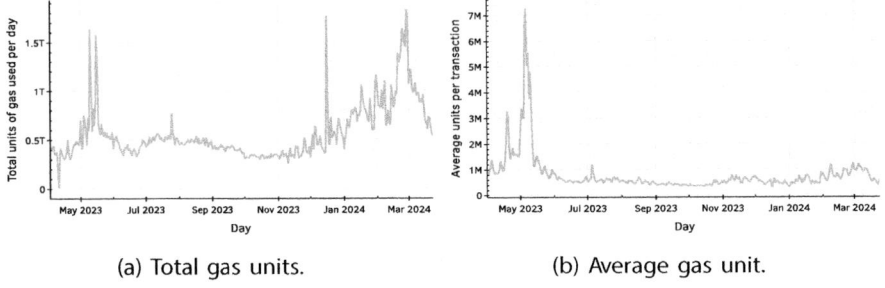

(a) Total gas units.

(b) Average gas unit.

Fig. 3. Comparison of gas unit usage over time: (a) Total gas units used per day; and (b) Average gas units used per transaction.

Considering gas usage, Fig. 3a illustrates the total number of gas units used each day in the ZKsync Era. On average, the network has processed 567,111,979,658 gas units per day in the last year. However, gas usage has been relatively volatile. Particularly, it has experienced three significant spikes of more than 1.5 trillion gas units per day, which we detail next.

May 2023. 30% of all gas used during the month of May 2023 can be attributed to the *zkApes airdrop*. The address receiving the most gas units was the *SyncSwap router* contract, which is used to execute swaps in the largest DEX in ZKsync Era. During this time, we see more than 10%

December 2023. This was caused by the inscriptions boom we discussed before [23].

March 2024. The gas utilization during this spike is much more distributed among transaction receivers, with the top receivers being DEX routers, such as the *SyncSwap V2 router* and the *Mute.io router* (which recently re-branded to Koi), and token contracts, such as *USDC.e* and *SOUL*. This dispersed distribution of gas usage coupled with the observed steady growth in both gas usage and transaction count up to the spike suggests that it is due to the increased trading activity on ZKsync Era.

We can further contextualize gas utilization by looking at Fig. 3b, which shows the average number of gas units used per transaction. We see that in May 2023, transactions were using on average a significantly higher number of gas units (reaching 7,265,323 units per transaction) compared to the average over the 1-year period (784,149 units).

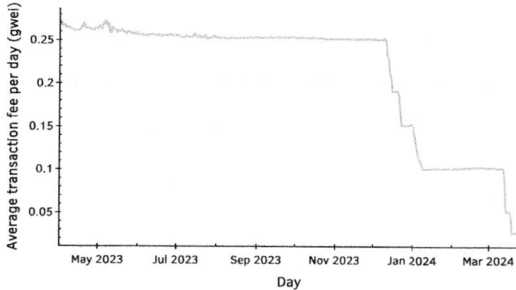

Fig. 4. Average transaction fee in gwei per unit of gas by day.

Finally, we can look at the transaction fees. Figure 4 shows the average transaction fees over time. In other words, this is the cost that users have paid, on average, to submit one unit of gas to ZKsync Era. Transaction fees were fairly stable during 2023, with an average of 0.25 gwei per gas unit.

However, in late 2023, a key upgrade led to a significant decrease in ZKsync transaction fees. Concretely, the implementation of the new prover, Boojum [21], marked a significantly reduced hardware requirement to run a Zero-Knowledge (ZK) prover and thus allowed a reduction of transaction fees to 0.1 gwei per unit of gas.

Then, in March 2024, the Dencun upgrade was implemented and deployed on the Ethereum mainnet. This upgrade, brought in EIP-4844, introduced a new type of transaction that can store "blobs" of data in the beacon node for 14 days [41]. Blobs have their independent fee model and submitting data as blobs is much cheaper than the previously used call-data [29]. ZKsync Era was one of the first rollups using blobs to publish the data related to its state changes, thus further reducing transaction fees to 0.025 gwei per unit of gas.

3.2 Events and Contract Deployments

Events are an important source of additional data about activity on EVM chains. They correspond to data emitted by smart contracts and stored on-chain. Next, we analyze this data and report on some specific events. Recall that events can be obtained from the logs data in the ZKsync dataset as discussed in Sect. 2.

Figure 5 shows the top 15 event types with the most emitted events during the period under analysis. Different contracts may emit the same event type, so what distinguishes them is the event's function signature and, thus, its respective hash.

There is a significant overrepresentation of the top 4 event types, with *Transfer* events being by far the most significant type (70.9% of all events are Transfer events). This is not unexpected as this event is emitted every time an ERC-20 token is transferred between two addresses in ZKsync Era. This occurs in simple token transfers and other standard contract operations such as swaps in DEXs.

Before looking at *Transfer* events in more detail, we should highlight a particularity in how ZKsync Era implements transaction fee collection. In this chain, every transaction generates two additional ETH transfers—one for the initial payment of the transaction fees from the transaction submitter and another with a transaction fee refund (after all L1 and proving costs are accounted for). These transaction fee

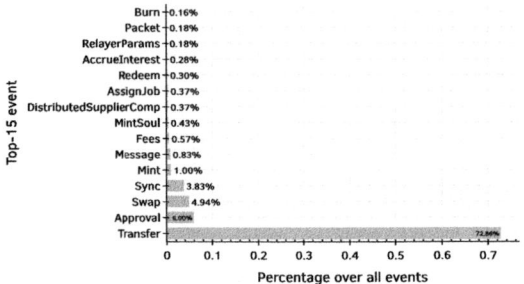

Fig. 5. Top 15 event types with the highest number of events emitted between April 1st, 2023 and March 24th, 2024, and their percentage over all events emitted. Percentages *include* ETH transfers generated from transaction fee payments.

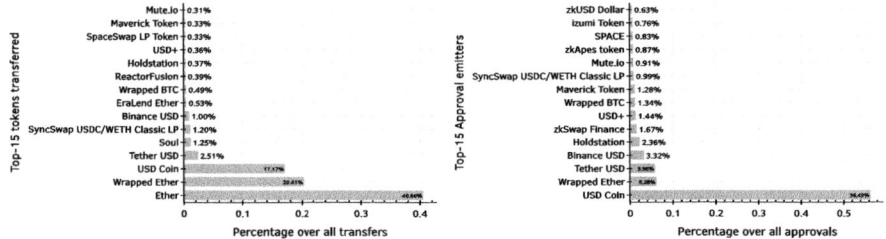

(a) Top 15 ERC-20 tokens with the highest number of Transfer events emitted.

(b) Top 15 contracts with the highest number of Approval events emitted.

Fig. 6. Percentage of the top 15 contracts with the highest Transfer and Approval events emitted between April 1st, 2023 and March 24th, 2024: (a) Transfer events, where percentages *exclude* ETH transfers generated from transaction fee payments; and (b) Approval events.

transfers always appear as ETH transfers from or to the address $0x8001$[2] and thus generate *Transfer* events. These specific events account for 38.2% of all events emitted, and if we exclude them entirely from the event dataset, Transfer events only account for 56.1% of these filtered events.

After filtering the Transfer events generated by fee management ETH transfers, we can explore the top tokens transferred by examining the contract address that emitted the event. Figure 6a displays the 15 tokens most frequently transferred during the period. Native ETH, Wrapped ETH, and Bridged USDC (USDC.e) are the most transfers, accounting collectively for 78.4%. We can also see some other stablecoins, such as Tether USD or Binance USD, and Liquidity Provider (LP) tokens associated with DEXs on ZKsync Era, such as SyncSwap and SpaceSwap.

Approvals are the second-largest event type, with 6% of events emitted. Similarly to the Transfer events, we can see which contracts emit these events. Figure 6b shows these top 15 emitters.

---

[2] We shortened this address for better visualization in the paper.

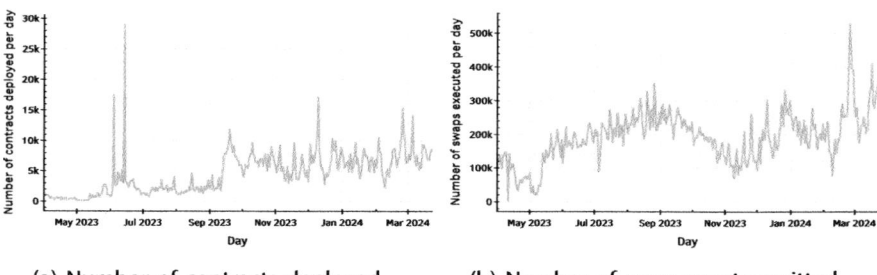

(a) Number of contracts deployed.   (b) Number of swap events emitted.

Fig. 7. Daily total number of contracts deployed (in a) and daily number of swap events emitted (in b) on ZKsync Era.

The top emitters are also ERC-20 token contracts, and these events represent an owner "approving" a spender to transfer a predefined amount of tokens they hold. This is common in bridged assets, for example, as is the case of Bridged USDC (USDC.e) and Wrapped ETH, the top 2 emitters.

Swaps and *Syncs* are the third and fourth most frequently emitted event types, accounting for 4.9% and 3.8% of all events emitted, respectively. These events are a key source of data for analyzing DEXs. However, we will explore these more in-depth in the next subsection.

Finally, we examine contract deployments. Every time a contract is deployed, a specific event type is emitted, which allows us to easily track this metric. Although this event type is not among the 15 most emitted event types, it is still an important metric for network activity. In ZKsync, the contract deployment event is named *ContractDeployed*.

Figure 7a shows the number of contracts deployed on ZKsync each day. Before September 2023, developers averaged 2510 contract deployments per day. However, there were two major spikes during this time, the first reaching 29,114 and the second reaching 17,602 contract deployments in a single day. Then, after September 2023, contract deployments increased to a daily average of 6672.

3.3 Swaps

After a high-level look at these events, we now focus on a specific event relevant to understanding activity on DEXs—the *Swap* event. Recall that swap events account for 4.9% of all events emitted on ZKsync.

Swap events are emitted every time a successful swap is performed in a DEX. These events contain information about the contract that emits the event, the amounts of each token being traded, and the wallets involved in the trade.

Figure 7b shows the number of swap events emitted each day during the analyzed period, which is equivalent to the number of swaps performed each day on ZKsync DEXs. We have a long-term trend of increasing the number of daily swaps, with a peak around March 2024 (which reached 531,819 swaps in a single day). During this year, users performed an average of 192,009 swaps per day.

We also see which LP contract was involved in the swap by looking at the contract address that emitted the event. Depending on the DEXs protocol, this may be the

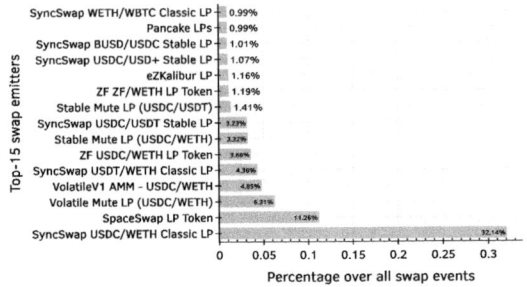

Fig. 8. Top 15 contracts emitting the most Swap events between April 1st, 2023 and March 24th, 2024, and their percentage over all Swap events emitted.

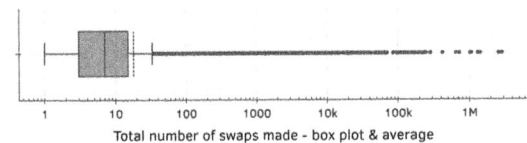

Fig. 9. Distribution of swaps per unique wallet addresses.

actual liquidity pool involved in the swap (e.g., SyncSwap and Koi) or a generic LP contract managing all the pools in the DEX (e.g., SpaceSwap and PancakeSwap). To understand which tokens were being traded in these generic LP contracts, we would have to process the transfer events emitted in the same transaction of these Swap events.

Figure 8 shows the top 15 contracts that emitted the most swaps even during the period under analysis. The largest emitter is, by a significant margin, the USDC/WETH pool on SyncSwap, which accounts for almost a third of all emitted Swap events. All combined swap events from SpaceSwap represent 11% of all swaps, followed by two USDC/WETH pools from other DEX.

Finally, we can use the "receivers" field to analyze swappers. In other words, this field provides the wallet address receiving the swapped token. Figure 9 displays the distribution of swaps made by unique wallet addresses.

We note that most users performed less than 50 swaps during the period under analysis. Concretely, the percentile 95% of this distribution is 42 swap events. However, the distribution has a significant skew to the right, with a few addresses generating a large number of swaps in the year examined. These large "traders" are usually routers and other protocols that interact with DEXs; thus, they represent many end-users. Examples include the top swappers, which are the *Mute.io router*, the *SpaceFi router*, and the *Odos V2 router*, respectively.

4 Future Directions

Among the data analysis presented in this paper, our ZKsync dataset can be applied to different studies. We list some of them below, where this dataset can be valuable.

MEV and Arbitrage. MEV and arbitrage have been extensively studied in L1 blockchains extensively [24,36,37,39,42]. However, only recently have new studies shifted their focus to L2s [6,14,15,40], including ZKsync Era. Our dataset can contribute to this type of research by enabling further analysis of MEV on ZKsync Era. For example, one type of MEV known as *backrunning* involves arbitrageurs ensuring their transactions are included immediately after a target transaction. This can be particularly useful in scenarios like liquidation-MEV, where arbitrageurs take advantage of opportunities that arise right after an oracle update [24,36,42]. Another form of arbitrage worth analyzing is CEX-DEX MEV, where arbitrageurs exploit price deviations between Centralized Exchange (CEX) and DEX platforms [18]. Additionally, studying cross-rollup MEV could provide insights into opportunities where arbitrageurs benefit from differences across two or more rollups [14].

Analysis of User Activity on Chain. Analyzing user activity in the ZKsync chain provides valuable insights into user behavior. This includes examining the transactions issued by users and their interactions with smart contracts. Such an analysis can also help identify airdrop farmers who create multiple accounts, known as Sybils, although this task can be challenging [12,26]. Another important area of analysis is measuring the impact of users in social media networks driving activities on the blockchain. For example, examining the recent boom in inscriptions in L2s chains can reveal how social networks can influence blockchain activity [23,28]. Additionally, since our dataset includes all event logs, it allows for the analysis of decentralized governance of protocols deployed on ZKsync Era. This involves studying proposals to amend smart contracts and their voting processes. By filtering data related to governance contracts, such as how each user voted and the distribution of these governance tokens among users, it can shed light on the implications of token concentration on decentralized governance, raising concerns about fairness [25,38].

Data Science Analytics. This dataset can also be valuable for users or non-researchers interested in exploring blockchain data. It offers an opportunity for those who wish to better understand blockchains. For example, data scientists can utilize this dataset to explore and analyze blockchain data on public platforms such as Kaggle. Data scientists widely use it to demonstrate their general skills in data analytics, machine learning, and data science. Therefore, this dataset can help data scientists acquire new skills, giving them a competitive edge in the market or improving their prospects of securing a job in a blockchain company.

We hope this dataset proves to be a valuable resource for research groups interested in conducting studies on L2s blockchains and ZKsync Era. We plan to publish our dataset and code in a GitHub repository to facilitate this.

5 Conclusion

At a high level, this paper addresses a critical concern within the scientific community: *the availability and accessibility of blockchain data*. Data-driven research is dependent on high-quality datasets to make meaningful findings. Although blockchain data are theoretically publicly available, practical challenges often prevent researchers, especially those without technical expertise, from obtaining and preprocessing them. In addition, the cost of using external services or deploying infrastructure to run archive nodes can be prohibitive.

To address these challenges, we have collected, pre-processed, and made available our ZKsync dataset to facilitate access for researchers. We also provide a detailed background on blockchains, including blocks, transactions, receipts, and logs, designed to help non-experts understand and utilize the data effectively. To illustrate the potential of this dataset, we offer example analyses and discuss future research directions.

We believe our contribution will be valuable to researchers studying blockchain L2 ecosystems, particularly those interested in ZKsync. This dataset also adds to the existing body of L2 research. It is designed for ease of use, using the Python library Polars to allow straightforward data processing on a local laptop.

Finally, to promote scientific reproducibility and to support further research, we have made our dataset publicly available on GitHub [1].

References

1. Data sets and scripts used to analyze the ZKsync Era blockchain (2024). https://github.com/matter-labs/zksync-data-dump
2. L1 <-> L2 Communication (2024). https://docs.zksync.io/zk-stack/concepts/l1_l2_communication
3. Reth Book (2024). https://reth.rs
4. System contracts/bootloader description (VM v1.4.0) (2024). https://github.com/code-423n4/2023-10-zksync/blob/main/docs/SmartcontractSection/Systemcontractsbootloaderdescription.md
5. Transaction Lifecycle (2024). https://docs.zksync.io/zk-stack/concepts/transaction-lifecycle#transaction-types
6. Bagourd, A., Francois, L.G.: Quantifying mev on layer 2 networks. arXiv preprint arXiv:2309.00629 (2023)
7. Bertoni, G., Daemen, J., Peeters, M., Van Assche, G.: Keccak sponge function family main document. Submission to NIST (Round 2) (2009)
8. bitcoin.org: Bitcoin Core (2024). https://bitcoin.org/en/bitcoin-core
9. bnbchain.org: BNB Smart Chain (2024). https://www.bnbchain.org/en/bnb-smart-chain
10. Buterin, V.: A rollup-centric ethereum roadmap (Oct 2020). https://ethereum-magicians.org/t/a-rollup-centric-ethereum-roadmap/4698
11. Day, A., Medvedev, E., AK, N., Price, W.: Introducing six new cryptocurrencies in bigquery public datasets—and how to analyze them. Google Cloud (2019)
12. Fan, S., Min, T., Wu, X., Cai, W.: Altruistic and profit-oriented: making sense of roles in web3 community from airdrop perspective. In: Proceedings of the 2023 CHI Conference on Human Factors in Computing Systems. CHI '23 (2023)
13. Gogol, K., Fritsch, R., Messias, J., Schlosser, M., Kraner, B., Tessone, C.: Liquid staking tokens in automated market makers (2024)
14. Gogol, K., Messias, J., Miori, D., Tessone, C., Livshits, B.: Cross-rollup mev: non-atomic arbitrage across l2 blockchains (2024)
15. Gogol, K., Messias, J., Miori, D., Tessone, C., Livshits, B.: Quantifying arbitrage in automated market makers: an empirical study of ethereum zk rollups. arXiv preprint arXiv:2403.16083 (2024)
16. Gogol, K., Messias, J., Schlosser, M., Kraner, B., Tessone, C.: Cross-border exchange of cbdcs using layer-2 blockchain. arXiv preprint arXiv:2312.16193 (2023)
17. Heimbach, L., Kiffer, L., Ferreira Torres, C., Wattenhofer, R.: Ethereum's proposer-builder separation: promises and realities. In: Proceedings of the 2023 ACM on Internet Measurement Conference. IMC '23 (2023)

18. Heimbach, L., Pahari, V., Schertenleib, E.: Non-atomic arbitrage in decentralized finance. In: 2024 IEEE Symposium on Security and Privacy (SP) (2024)
19. Johnsson, T.: Efficient compilation of lazy evaluation. In: Proceedings of the 1984 SIGPLAN Symposium on Compiler Construction (1984)
20. L2Beat: L2Beat: The state of the layer two ecosystem (2024). https://l2beat.com/scaling/summary?sort-by=total&sort-order=desc#layer2s
21. Matter Labs: Boojum Upgrade: zkSync Era's New High-performance Proof System for Radical Decentralization (2024). https://zksync.mirror.xyz/HJ2Pj45EJkRdt5Pau-ZXwkV2ctPx8qFL19STM5jdYhc
22. Messias, J., Alzayat, M., Chandrasekaran, B., Gummadi, K.P., Loiseau, P., Mislove, A.: Selfish & opaque transaction ordering in the bitcoin blockchain: the case for chain neutrality. In: Proceedings of the 21st ACM Internet Measurement Conference. IMC '21 (2021)
23. Messias, J., Gogol, K., Silva, M.I., Livshits, B.: The writing is on the wall: analyzing the boom of inscriptions and its impact on EVM-compatible blockchains. arXiv preprint arXiv:2405.15288 (2024)
24. Messias, J., Pahari, V., Chandrasekaran, B., Gummadi, K.P., Loiseau, P.: Dissecting bitcoin and ethereum transactions: on the lack of transaction contention and prioritization transparency in blockchains. In: Proceedings of the Financial Cryptography and Data Security (FC'23) (2023)
25. Messias, J., Pahari, V., Chandrasekaran, B., Gummadi, K.P., Loiseau, P.: Understanding blockchain governance: analyzing decentralized voting to amend defi smart contracts (2024)
26. Messias, J., Yaish, A., Livshits, B.: Airdrops: giving money away is harder than it seems. arXiv preprint arXiv:2312.02752 (2023)
27. Offchain Labs: A gentle introduction to Arbitrum (2024). https://docs.arbitrum.io/intro
28. Omena, J.J., Messias, J., Gouveia, F., Ventura, R.: Digital methods for blockchain research (2024). https://www.researchgate.net/publication/382511569_Digital_Methods_for_Blockchain_Research
29. Omkar Godbole: Layer 2 Blockchains Become Cheaper After Ethereum's Dencun Upgrade (2024). https://www.coindesk.com/markets/2024/03/14/layer-2-blockchains-become-cheaper-after-ethereums-dencun-upgrade
30. Optimism Foundation: Optimism (2024). https://www.optimism.io
31. Pandas: Pandas: Python data analysis library (2024). https://pandas.pydata.org
32. Paradigm: Paradigm Data Portal (2024). https://www.paradigm.xyz/oss/portal
33. Paradigm: Paradigm Data Portal (2024). https://github.com/paradigmxyz/paradigm-data-portal
34. Polars: Lazy / Eager API: Polars user guide (2024). https://docs.pola.rs/user-guide/concepts/lazy-vs-eager
35. Polars: Polars: Dataframes for the new era (2024). https://pola.rs
36. Qin, K., Zhou, L., Gervais, A.: Quantifying blockchain extractable value: how dark is the forest? In: 2022 IEEE Symposium on Security and Privacy (SP) (2022)
37. Qin, K., Zhou, L., Livshits, B., Gervais, A.: Attacking the defi ecosystem with flash loans for fun and profit. In: International Conference on Financial Cryptography and Data Security (2021)
38. Sharma, T., et al.: Unpacking how decentralized autonomous organizations (daos) work in practice. In: 2024 IEEE International Conference on Blockchain and Cryptocurrency (ICBC) (2024)

39. Torres, C.F., Camino, R., State, R.: Frontrunner jones and the raiders of the dark forest: an empirical study of frontrunning on the ethereum blockchain. In: 30th USENIX Security Symposium (USENIX Security 21) (2021)
40. Torres, C.F., Mamuti, A., Weintraub, B., Nita-Rotaru, C., Shinde, S.: Rolling in the shadows: analyzing the extraction of mev across layer-2 rollups. arXiv preprint arXiv:2405.00138 (2024)
41. Buterin, V., et al.: EIP-4844: Shard Blob Transactions (2022). https://github.com/ethereum/EIPs/blob/master/EIPS/eip-4844.md
42. Weintraub, B., Torres, C.F., Nita-Rotaru, C., State, R.: A flash (bot) in the pan: measuring maximal extractable value in private pools. In: Proceedings of the 22nd ACM Internet Measurement Conference (2022)

Early Observations of Based Rollups: A Case Study of Taiko

Jan Gorzny[1()], Phillip Kemper[2], and Martin Derka[3]

[1] Zircuit, Toronto, ON, Canada
jan@zircuit.com
[2] Zircuit, Munich, Germany
phillip@zircuit.com
[3] Zircuit, Waterloo, ON, Canada
martin@zircuit.com

Abstract. Rollups have become popular layer two networks for general purpose layer one blockchains that support smart contracts. In this work, we explore so-called *based rollups*: rollups which use the layer one network for sequencing. First, we explicate the benefits and potential pitfalls of this approach over centralized sequencers. Second, we use the Taiko rollup as a case study of early based rollups. In this case study, we analyze the cost and performance of Taiko and compare the findings to a similar-but-centralized rollup. Finally, we evaluate whether or not the purported properties of based sequencing are apparent in early systems based on the data collected in our case study. We find that while based rollups have promising properties, additional work is needed to make them competitive with centralized sequencers.

1 Introduction

Blockchains like Ethereum [1] have evolved to be dependable and stable and to support applications built on top of them, but not necessarily to maximize transaction throughput. To overcome this limitation, so-called *layer two* (L2) solutions [2] are built as applications on Ethereum, which is called a *layer one* (L1) in turn. Although several L2 designs exist, rollups have emerged as popular solution. As of 6 January 2025, there are 135 active rollups (or variants) which collectively hold more than $56 billion USD in cryptocurrencies [3].

Rollups aim to increase the transaction throughput of the L1 ecosystem. They do this by separating execution from consensus and performing state updates off-chain, posting verifying data and updates which are considered final after some conditions are met. The execution allows transactions to be ordered and blocks to be built for the L2 – namely, sequencing – in a way that allows blocks to be larger, produced more often, or both. This work studies rollups which use their L1 network to drive sequencing. These rollups are called *based rollups* by Drake, who defines them as follows [4]:

A rollup is said to be based, or L1-sequenced, when its sequencing is driven by the base L1. More concretely, a based rollup is one where the next L1 proposer may, in collaboration with L1 searchers and builders, permissionlessly include the next rollup block as part of the next L1 block.

Based rollups may benefit from improved cross-chain communication and message passing, inherit strong liveness guarantees from the underlying layer one, and are purported to have simpler designs. In this work, we investigate these claims and explicate the design of such a rollup by analysing the Taiko based zero-knowledge (ZK) rollup [5]. Using data from Ethereum and Taiko, we evaluate the cost and performance impact of implementing a based rollup over other designs.

Contributions. This paper makes the following contributions:

- We explicate the advantages and disadvantages of based sequencer rollup designs (Sect. 2).
- We report on the cost and performance of based sequencing by analyzing data obtained from the Taiko based rollup. We compare this to a non-based ZK rollup, Scroll [6], to illustrate the differences in performance that may arise as a result of based sequencing (Sect. 3).
- We evaluate the advantages of based rollups in the context of the data collected (Sect. 4). We provide the code and data collected for future research.

1.1 Related Work

Rollups (a.k.a *commit-chains* [7] or *validating bridges* [8]) have received a lot of research attention. A general introduction to rollups can be found in works like [2,9], and [10]. In [10], various topics like based sequencing are used to build a taxonomy that can compare and differentiate modern rollups. Others (Motepalli et al. [11], Mamageishvili and Schlegel [12]) have explored decentralized sequencers and shared sequencers. Both of these concepts change how a rollup's sequencer behaves, but a decentralized sequencer may not be a based one. Incentives for honest validators for optimistic rollups are studied in [13].

The costs and performance of rollups have also been studied. The authors of [14] and [15] have looked at the performance and cost savings of rollups in general and for zero-knowledge rollups like Taiko. The authors of [16] looked at how compression is used by rollups to reduce the cost of posting data on-chain, while the authors of [17] investigated strategies for efficient batch posting itself, and strategies for posting data as blobs (after EIP-4844 [18]) were studied in [19].

To the best of the authors' knowledge, no other works explore and evaluate the performance of based sequencers. We address this gap in order to confirm that the purported advantages of based sequencing are plausible and to measure the trade-offs that are necessary for these designs. Moreover, our work provides a dataset that others can use to analyze early implementations of a based sequencer and we establish research directions for these systems that should be resolved in order to support mature based rollups.

2 Based Sequencing

We describe based sequencing in this section. We focus on the specifics of how a rollup's sequencing is driven by the L1; there may be several ways that this can be achieved. The process of driving the rollup's sequencing is not precisely defined, and there may be many ways to implement this functionality. Buterin says that in based rollups, "L2 blocks are L1 transactions" [20] and based sequencers indeed work by proposing blocks to an Ethereum smart contract.

It is important to note that based sequencing is less about deriving a sequence of transactions to be ordered than the ability to build blocks. While this distinction may be useless in most blockchain environments, there are situations for which it is important. For example, some blockchains may not wish to allow permissionless block building (or at least not without additional requirements) but might want to have an ordering of transactions supplied by L1 (e.g., those implementing things like sequencer level security [21] or for cross-chain communication). However, the ability to merely order included transactions may be beneficial to that chain: as an argument for fairness or as a requirement for the exact conditions under which a transaction should be analyzed as malicious.

Based rollups are purported to have several advantageous traits that do not introduce additional trust assumptions, though they do not come for free. Table 1 shows the initial traits listed by Drake [4]. These imply others: for a positive example, permissionless L2 block proposal implies censorship resistance on the L2; for a negative example, the design may increase L2 transaction latency. Shortly after this definition was proposed, Buterin suggested that based sequencing may be "total anarchy" [22] as multiple L2 blocks could be proposed within the same L1 block, resulting in wasted gas and computation. This can be overcome by proposer-builder separation (PBS) (see e.g., [23]) for the underlying blockchain, with at most one L2 block per L1 block and delayed validity proofs. We explore the validity of these traits (as well as Buterin's anarchy concerns) in Sect. 3.2.

Table 1. Advantages (+) and disadvantages (−) of based rollups according to Drake [4], along with a short justification of the trait.

+/−	Trait	Short Justification
+	Liveness	L2 continues to function as long as the underlying L1 continues to function.
+	Decentralization	Permissionless inclusion of the next L2 block.
+	Simplicity	No need for escape hatches (see, e.g. [24]), additional consensus, or signature verification.
+	L1 economic alignment	MEV [25] extraction on based rollups is performed by actors building L2 blocks – namely, L1 actors – and therefore any extracted value stays within the L1.
+	Sovereignty	Based rollups can still issue a governance token and use it to make decisions about the network
−	No MEV income	Block builders (L1 actors) will not necessarily be motivated to maximize L2 fees
−	Constrained sequencing	Pre-confirmations [20] are hard and the actual ordering of transactions may not be enforced by the L1 actors building the blocks.

3 Case Study: Taiko

As of 6 January 2025, there are only a handful of based rollups in operation, including Taiko [5]. Taiko is a ZK rollup that describes itself as a "based contestable rollup", which we investigate as a case study. Taiko was chosen as it has the largest Total Value Locked (TVL) among based rollups at the time of writing ($295 million USD [3] on 6 January 2025), which indicates its popularity among blockchain users. The data was collected for the initial version of the Taiko based rollup, prior to their "Ontake" upgrade [26], which occurred at Taiko block height 538304 on 7 November 2024. As a result, the data may not accurately reflect the current state of Taiko or based rollups in general. Future based rollups may have different designs, satisfy additional properties, or refine the notion of a based rollup altogether. Nonetheless, this data provides insights into challenges of building based rolups and can help to shape future based rollup designs. In Sect. 3.1 we describe the architecture of Taiko. Then, in Sect. 3.2 we evaluate the distribution of L2 block proposers and related based rollup concerns. Finally, we compare Taiko to Scroll – a ZK rollup with a centralized sequencer – in Sect. 3.3.

3.1 Architecture

The Taiko rollup differs from other rollups in part because of its based design. As with other rollups, some parts of the system are on-chain while others operate off-chain. The system consists of smart contracts, a mempool, an execution engine, and a consensus client.

The smart contracts for Taiko implement the L1 sequencing, canonical bridging, and proof verification functionalities, among others. Taiko uses a smart contract[1] on Ethereum to propose L2 blocks. Bridging functionality implemented by Taiko is similar to that of other rollups. Proof verification is similar, though the rollup supports *tiers* of validity proofs: lower tiers include proofs generated by Trusted Execution Environments (TEEs) (see e.g., [27]), while higher tiers use zero-knowledge proof systems [10] to prove state transitions. Tiered proofs are a Taiko-specific design, and are not a defining feature of based rollups.

Since the submission of all L2 transactions to the L1 contract would negate the cost savings of using an L2, Taiko has an off-chain mempool client. The mempool is in the L2 execution engine, a modified fork of the Go-Ethereum[2] client. Deposit transactions, which bridge assets from L1 to the L2 (i.e., mint or unlock a representation of the L1 asset on L2), must still be submitted to the relevant bridging contract on Ethereum to be processed.

Actors who want to propose a block can run a *proposer*. The proposer service calls `txpool_content` to get pending transactions from the mempool and build blocks. In turn it calls the `proposeBlock` function which emits a `BlockProposed` event. The proposer must submit the parameters for the block, which include things like the proposer's signature and the transaction list. Arguments are passed as `calldata` or blobs [28]: data which is not accessible on the L1 beyond the function call, but is included in the state root for the L1 block that processes the transaction. Proposed blocks are *soft commitments* to the rollup's state. Taiko does not use EIP-4844 blobs for data availability.

---

[1] Proxy: 0x06a9Ab27c7e2255df1815E6CC0168d7755Feb19a
   Implementation: 0xBA1d90BCfA74163bFE09e8eF609b346507D83231.

[2] https://geth.ethereum.org/.

Taiko consensus clients listen for BlockProposed events emitted on the L1 and uses these to update the canonical L2 chain. These events create blocks that are merely proposed: such a block may still be determined valid or invalid. A proposed block will be invalidated if transactions included within it are not valid (has an invalid signature or nonce, not enough ETH for the fees, or some other common conditions). A blocks status can progress to proved if the assigned prover for the block provides a validity proof for the execution of the block (via a call to proveBlock which emits a TransitionProved event): a proof that, given the previous state root, the state transition function (i.e., Ethereum Virtual Machine execution), and the transaction list, the resulting block is one that is valid. In the current design, the prover submits a bond of tokens alongside the proof.

The Taiko rollup is not simply a based rollup, but a "based contestable rollup" [29]. In this design, a low-tier proof for a block which was previously submitted can be contested by anyone. This means that anyone can claim that the proof is invalid and request that a higher-tier proof is provided (the highest tier proofs cannot be contested). In such a case, a TransitionContested event is emitted and a bond is collected. When a higher tier proof is submitted, the honest actor receives a reward. This design borrows from optimistic rollups and is not necessary if all proofs are of the highest tier (zero-knowledge proofs).

Proved blocks may not make it into the final L2 blockchain. Proved blocks are those for which the state transition they outline is valid, but this may be a transition from an invalid L2 state. In particular, an ancestor of the L2 block may have been contested and removed from the L2 chain. Taiko uses the verified status to indicate blocks which have been proven and for whom there is a chain of blocks back to the Taiko genesis block. That is, verified blocks make up the final L2 chain. Batches of blocks are verified by calling the verifyBlocks function on the Taiko smart contract. Any uncontested blocks which are past their contestable period are assumed correct and can be verified by anyone. Verified blocks provide *hard commitments* for the rollup's state.

3.2 Analysis

In this section we report on observed interactions with the Taiko network on Ethereum. We are interested in determining how the system may differ when compared to a standard (non-based) rollup. Our data is collected[3] from the Ethereum blockchain from block 19773965 (May-01-2024 08:03:47 AM +UTC) to 21136529 (Nov-07-2024 03:00:23 PM +UTC), using Infura endpoints. This represents over 6 months of blocks (1362564 blocks) on Ethereum in 2024, starting when the Taiko L1 smart contract was deployed and ending when the relevant events were no longer observed (due to the Taiko Ontake upgrade). The data was collected by iterating over relevant L1 blocks and collecting transactions which emitted BlockProposed, TransitionProved, TransitionContested, or

---

[3] Source code: https://github.com/jgorzny/based-rollups.

BlockVerified events. Note that while the data we collect is from the time the Taiko contract is deployed, the first Taiko block is proposed on 25 May 2024. We counted the number of Externally Owned Accounts (EOAs) on Ethereum which made transactions that emitted key events, the frequency of these events, and which parts of the based rollups contribute to the on-chain costs of the network.

The charts in Fig. 1 illustrate various findings related to Taiko events. Figure 1a is a stacked bar chart of the number of transactions on each day that emitted a blockProposed event. Each color in the chart is a different EOA, though it is clear that the vast majority of transactions originate with a single address (dark blue). This address[4] is the TaikoBeat proposer operated by Taiko Labs, and is singlehandledly responsible for over $498145/538303 \approx 92.54\%$ of all block proposing events. There are 100 total addresses which submitted a block proposing transaction during the period of blocks studied. On average 3242.79 block proposing transactions were sent on a day, with the largest number being 5818 proposals in a single day. Figure 1b shows the number of EOAs who either proposed, proved, or verified a block each day in the studied period. On average there were 11.80, 12.02, and 7.15 proposers, provers, and block verifiers respectively. The maximum number of distinct proposing and proving EOAs was 43, with a maximum of 21 verifiers. Finally, Fig. 1c shows a scatter plot where the x-axis is L1 block numbers and the y-axis is the number of BlockProposed events in that L1 block, if that L1 block contains at least one L2 block proposal. This not only shows that most L1 blocks contain either 1 or 2 Taiko block proposal and it took some time for L1 blocks to frequently contain more than 2 L2 block proposals. The distribution of L2 block proposals in L1 is also shown in Fig. 1c. The vast majority (98.69%) of L1 blocks resulted in either 0 or 1 block being proposed.

3.3 Comparison

The Taiko based rollup therefore has a different architecture from other non-based rollups. There is an additional requirement of a mempool client and the role of the sequencer is implicit rather than explicit. The notion of submitting blocks (or batches) as soft-commitments from the sequencer is replaced by the requirement to call a proposeBlock. This means the call must record some data within a smart contract so that it can be checked later, which is not always the case for other soft-commitments. Other rollups posts L2 blocks as calldata (or as blobs) without explicitly writing state – simply calling a view function on a specified contract; this is impossible for Taiko, which needs to record the time it received the proposed block so that it can be eventually finalized. Moreover, a validity proof for an L2 block is no longer sufficient to consider it final on L1 – the block must also be verified. In a ZK rollup, this is handled by building a coordinator service behind the scenes that is responsible for ensuring that proofs are only generated for soft-commitments that are finalized on the L1.

---

[4] 0x000000633b68f5D8D3a86593ebB815b4663BCBe0.

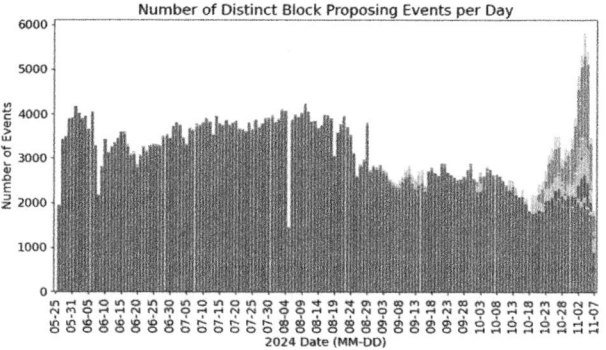

(a) A stacked bar chart showing the number of `BlockProposed` events emitted per day. Each color is a EOA who sent the transaction that resulted in the event.

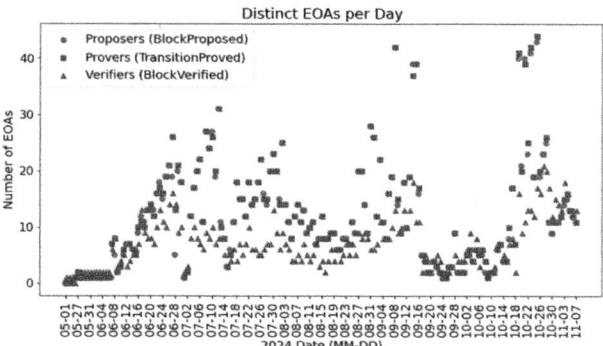

(b) A scatter plot showing the number of distinct EOAs that sent a transaction that emitted a key event for Taiko. Recall that only one `TransitionContested` was emitted (by a single EOA).

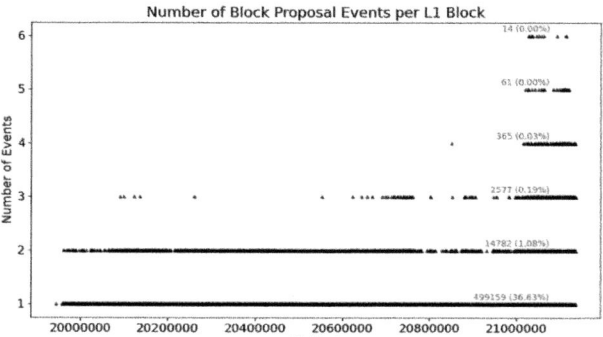

(c) A scatter plot showing the number of L2 blocks proposed per L1 block containing a block proposal; the red label shows the count for each non-zero y value. 845606 (62.06%) L1 blocks did not propose an L2 block.

Fig. 1. Various illustrations related to block proposal in Taiko.

Table 2. Transactions (TX) performing multiple rollup actions at once.

Rollup	Distinct TX	Duplicate TX	% Duplicate
Taiko	1076696	156318	14.52%
Scroll	308481	0	0.00%

This explicit on-chain verification step may also be more costly in a based rollup and may negatively affect the blockchain performance.

To evaluate this claim, we compare Taiko to Scroll. Scroll is a ZK rollup with a centralized sequencer; it is not a based rollup. Scroll was chosen as it is a ZK rollup which uses the same ZK proof system as Taiko, halo2 [30], in order to make as much of a direct comparison as possible. Scroll proves every block on its network and we describe the process briefly: transactions are put into blocks, which are put into chunks, which are then put into batches which are finally posted on L1. Each of these has an associated validity proof. First, the Scroll network commits a batch of L2 transactions on-chain which emits a `CommitBatch` event. This is similar to Taiko in that a proof is necessary to finalize the batch, which results in a `FinalizeBatch` event, but the batch may not be a single L2 block. The batch consists of part of a *chunk* to be proved, and may therefore contain data from multiple L2 blocks. This allows Scroll to maximize prover utilization (which needs a specific set of memory to prove a block regardless of whether it's full; small blocks can be virtually merged to use all this space). This also allows them to post batches only when necessary, rather than for every block, and may result in multiple blocks being contained in a single batch. Scroll can emit a `RevertBatch` if operator wishes to revert a batch; in the past, 55 batches were reverted to fix a bug in batch compression [31]; this occurred on 3 July 2024 and is the reason for the sharp drop of costs on that day.

Table 3 displays data regarding the distribution of the events for both Taiko and Scroll. We can see that almost every Taiko block proposed was proven. There is a slight discrepancy that arises from the fact that the final Scroll blocks proposed in the dataset were to be finalized outside of the block range studied. Similarly, block verification happens after blocks are proven, so the verification count is smaller than the proposed count as verification will come after the last block studied. There was a single transition contested event[5] and it is unclear why it occurred; it may have been a deliberate test or a legitimate bug. Taiko proposed 3.12 times as often as Scroll the number of batches that Scroll committed. In terms of blocks, Taiko produced 538,303 blocks while Scroll produced 5,609,661 L2 blocks; Taiko produced less than 10% as many as Scroll. Table 2 shows the total number of relevant L1 transactions for each rollup; Taiko had just short of 15% of transactions do more than one action at a time.

Figure 2 breaks down the daily L1 costs of the two rollups. Figure 2a shows the costs in units of gas times 10^9 for transactions that emitted key based sequencing

---

[5] Transaction: 7600471694620e19c3296a4e26fc753149cbcd9803f37747521aa3399261 ced8.

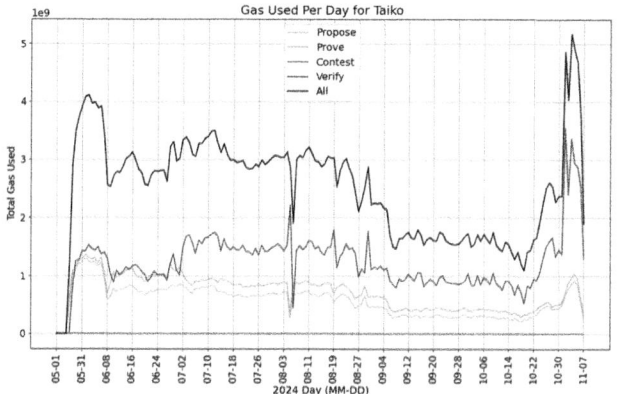

(a) A breakdown of daily L1 gas costs associated with Taiko.

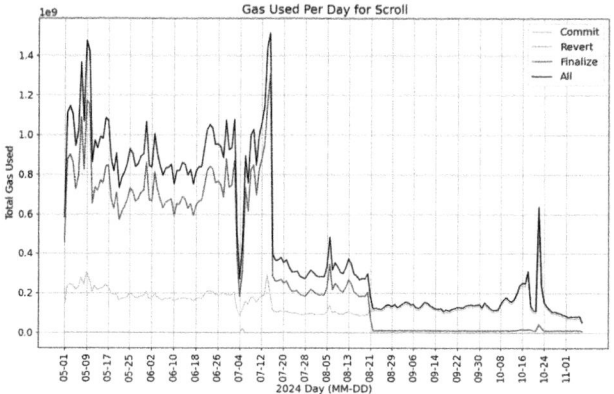

(b) A breakdown of daily L1 gas costs associated with Scroll.

Fig. 2. On-chain transaction costs for Taiko and Scroll.

events. Note that the spike near 31 October 2024 may be explained[6] by a contract upgrade ahead of the Ontake fork. Verification of proofs is the most expensive component, and block proposal and proving are similar in cost. Costs related to contested transactions are almost entirely zero given the infrequency of the event. Compared with the costs for Scroll in Fig. 2b, Taiko is nearly 5 times more expensive: the units on the y-axis is the same in both charts, but Scroll's peak daily amount is around $1.5 \cdot 10^9$ while Taiko's is over $5 \cdot 10^9$. The difference is also visualized in Fig. 3a, which shows the cumulative cost in units of gas required to operate each network for the studied block duration (this time in gas units times 10^{11}). From this figure, it's clear that Taiko's operating costs are worse than Scroll's even before the spike in daily costs near the end of the studied

---

[6] https://x.com/taikoxyz/status/1849703188678705365.

Table 3. Event counts for the studied period. Note that for Taiko, one more transition is proved than blocks are proposed, as the genesis block did not emit a `BlockProposed` event.

Taiko Event	Count	Scroll Event	Count
`BlockProposed`	538303	`CommitBatch`	172120
`TransitionContested`	1	`RevertBatch`	55
`TransitionProved`	538304	`FinalizeBatch`	136360
`BlockVerified`	53806		

period. Moreover, this is true despite the fact that Scroll committed batches between the time the Taiko contract was deployed and the first Taiko block was proposed (about 27 days). These costs might not be accurate: these transactions may perform other actions as well as calling the appropriate rollup functions, though calling non-rollup functions would likely not be desirable.

Figures 3b and 3c show the differences in block generation time for each chain. Each point is the average block generation time computed over the last 500 L2 blocks, starting with the first 500 during the studied period; units are in seconds. The red line on each is the average over the last 10 points (5000 blocks). Taiko's block generation time is much more varied than Scroll's, and Taiko blocks are often 20 or 30 seconds apart, though they are closer together near the end of the studied period. On the other hand, Scroll bocks are typically 3 seconds apart, and sometimes much less than that. Scroll's worst average block time is still better than Taiko's best average block time.

4 Discussion

In this section, we discuss the comparison between Taiko and Scroll and aim to to evaluate the claimed positive traits of based rollups (c.f. Table 1).

Performance. The results of Sect. 3.3 show that Taiko was nearly five times more expensive to operate and nearly ten times slower to produce blocks. The expense may come from the multiple steps required to prove blocks, but is more easily explained by the lack of batching and aggregation, as well as any additionally advantageous compression. It is not surprising that if most L1 blocks that proposed Taiko blocks only proposed one L2 block, the performance gains would not be as great as if batching transactions occurred. Moreover, this explains the delays in block generation as well. In short, based sequencing requires additional effort to be competitive with those which do not use the L1 to build blocks. It is worth noting that the Ontake update to Taiko did introduce batching to the system, but given the downsides of omitting this functionality, it might be worth considering that feature as essential for based rollups.

Liveness. The Taiko rollup appears to suggest that the liveness trait is valid. Although a single proposer is responsible for the majority of the L2 blocks proposed (c.f. Figure 1a), there are other block proposers who could continue to

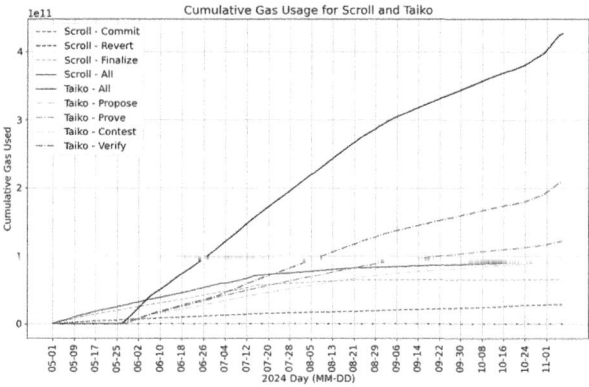

(a) Cumulative L1 gas costs for Taiko and Scroll.

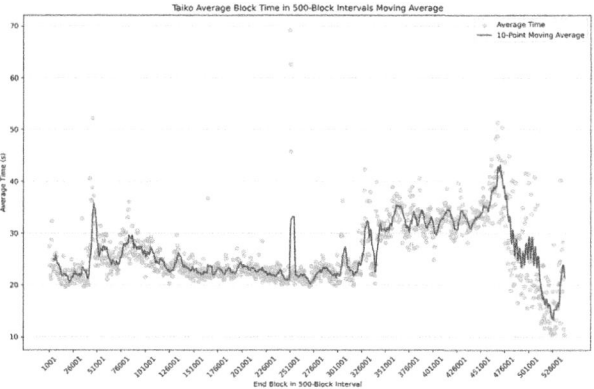

(b) Taiko's average blocktime.

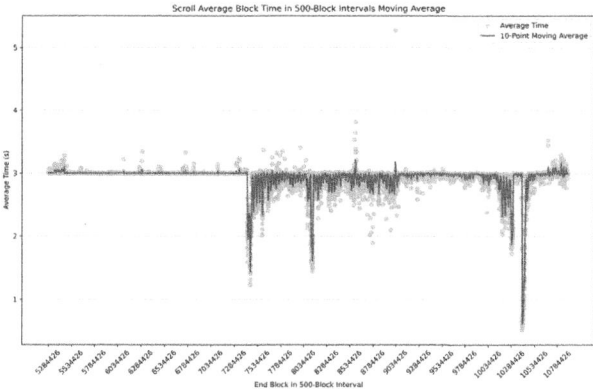

(c) Scroll's average blocktime.

Fig. 3. Cumulative gas costs for both networks (a) and average blocktimes for Taiko (b) and Scroll (c).

progress the L2 blockchain in the event that the `TaikoBeat` proposer is offline. However, the Taiko team still controls the ability to update the contracts which negatively affect this trait; barring any such issues, the data confirms that based rollups have strong liveness.

The Taiko chain does not have "total chaos" from too many L2 blocks proposed in a single L1 blocks; it was designed in such a way that this is not problematic. Although some L1 blocks had two or more L2 blocks proposed in them, the majority (98.69%) of L1 blocks did not propose any L2 block or proposed exactly one. In our investigation, no two L2 blocks proposed at the same block had the same L2 block number, so there appears to be no wasted effort. However, future work is necessary to check if two L2 blocks within the same L1 block actually shared transactions – this might still mean wasted blockspace and is not immediately apparent from the event log. It will also be important to revisit this concern for based rollups that allow batches of blocks to be posted in a single L1, as these batches increase the likelihood of wasted effort.

Decentralization. The data in Fig. 1b shows that based rollups have the potential to be decentralized. Although there is a number of proposers, they do not propose the majority of L2 blocks. This is similar to L1 blockchains with mining pools: a large number of users participate in the network but block production is nonetheless centralized to a smaller number of parties [32]. Unlike in these L1 networks, this may change more easily for the Taiko network. Based rollups do not necessitate a Proof-of-Stake (PoS) barrier to entry as no funds beyond those necessary to transact and the appropriate proving hardware are required. Taiko's current design includes an indirect PoS-like mechanic as provers must be bonded, though this may not be necessary when only the highest tier proofs are used. The current bond may be too expensive to attract additional network participants. Nonetheless, the trait appears plausible in mature rollups.

Simplicity. The engineering effort of a based rollup remains difficult to judge. Just like Ethereum itself, Taiko uses a consensus client and an execution client, and has smart contracts as well. The development and maintenance of these systems is non-trivial and even without the need for specific features like escape hatches, care is needed to ensure all requirements are implemented and can be evaluated [33]. This is made worse by the introduction of cryptoeconomic incentives which need to be carefully balanced, the choice of proof systems, and the inability to optimize particular functionality. It is unclear if based rollups are truly simpler than standard designs; such a verdict will need to be rendered only after there are mature feature-complete examples of both kinds of rollups.

L1 Economic Alignment and Sovereignty. Taiko appears to be aligned with Ethereum while maintaining sovereignty. The design of the rollup necessitates several Ethereum transactions to build L2 blocks, so those participating in Taiko's block building process must operate on and within the Ethereum ecosystem. Additionally, Taiko has a token (TKO) which it uses as a bond for block provers and governance; this will provide sovereignty and further aligns its participants with the Ethereum blockchain economically. These traits appear plausible, but a more rigorous definition of each and further study is necessary. It may be too early to determine the usefulness of the TKO token within the Taiko ecosystem.

4.1 Threats to Validity and Limitations

This work provides an initial comparison with Taiko and Scroll; however, several potential threats to validity must be considered. First, the comparison is not a direct one as there may be additional architectural differences between these rollups aside from their sequencer (as is evident by tiered proofs). Second, the data requires deeper analysis to ensure that duplicate transactions do not have their costs counted twice; ideally, a function-level analysis of gas cost would be used. Third, Taiko's subsequent upgrades and other based rollups may not suffer from the same problems as the version of Taiko studied. Future developers of based rollups should repeat this study with the most modern, optimized versions of these systems that exist. Critically, the Taiko Ontake update added critical features like block batching [26], which could drastically affect operating costs and is already present in Scroll. Finally, even if cost metrics can be directly compared, there are other factors – such as transaction latency – that may be omitted by such an analysis but important when choosing a rollup design.

5 Conclusion

In this work, we discussed the expected advantages and disadvantages of based rollup design before reporting on the design of a real-world based rollup, Taiko. Using Taiko as an example based rollup, we confirmed that there are few technological challenges prohibiting their development. However, there is work necessary to make them cost-effective, there is room to improve on the design, and these rollups appear decentralized but are largely operated by a single entity. Nonetheless, we believe based rollups are a feasible and promising layer two solution that will improve over time. Without optimization for features that are key to centralized sequencer-based designed, based rollups do appear likely to be competitive.

There are a number of interesting directions for future work. First, a more fine grained-evaluation of Taiko is possible: e.g., measure the finality and proof delay time, evaluate other (based) rollups, include the costs for data availability, or measure per-function gas usage. Second, there are likely a number of interesting questions about Taiko itself: e.g., if transitions may need to be contested, how many contesting actors are active over a given time period? Third, one could revisit the claimed properties of based rollups: e.g., are L1 actors really apathetic to maximizing based rollup block fees? A fine-grained evaluation of their purported simplicity and economic alignment is omitted from this work and should be conducted. As Buterin [34] suggests that rollups are a cultural extension of Ethereum, it is important that we understand and improve them.

Acknowledgements. The authors would like to thank the anonymous reviewers of CAAW 2025 for their numerous helpful and insightful comments.

References

1. Wood, G.: Ethereum: a secure decentralised generalised transaction ledger, 2014. Ethereum Project Yellow Paper, https://ethereum.github.io/yellowpaper/paper.pdf
2. Gudgeon, L., Moreno-Sanchez, P., Roos, S., McCorry, P., Gervais, A.: SoK: layer-two blockchain protocols. In: Bonneau, J., Heninger, N. (eds.) FC 2020. LNCS, vol. 12059, pp. 201–226. Springer, Cham (2020). https://doi.org/10.1007/978-3-030-51280-4_12
3. Kiepuszewski, B.: L2Beat value secured (2025). https://l2beat.com/scaling/tvs
4. Drake, J.: Based rollups—superpowers from L1 sequencing, March 2023. https://ethresear.ch/t/based-rollups-superpowers-from-l1-sequencing/15016/6. Accessed 2 Feb 2024
5. Taiko. taiko.xyz/. Accessed 2 Feb 2024
6. Scroll. https://scroll.io/. Accessed 12 Dec 2024
7. Khalil, R., Zamyatin, A., Felley, G., Moreno-Sanchez, P., Gervais, A.: Commit-chains: Secure, scalable off-chain payments. Cryptology ePrint Archive, Paper 2018/642 (2018). https://eprint.iacr.org/2018/642
8. McCorry, P., Buckland, C., Yee, B., Song, D.: SoK: validating bridges as a scaling solution for blockchains. Cryptology ePrint Archive, Paper 2021/1589 (2021). eprint.iacr.org/2021/1589
9. Thibault, L.T., Sarry, T., Hafid, A.S.: Blockchain scaling using rollups: a comprehensive survey. IEEE Access **10**, 93039–93054 (2022)
10. Gorzny, J., Derka, M.: A rollup comparison framework. *CoRR*, abs/2404.16150 (2024)
11. Motepalli, S., Freitas, L., Livshits, B.: Decentralized sequencers for rollups, SoK (2023)
12. Mamageishvili, A., Schlegel, J.C.: Shared sequencing and latency competition as a noisy contest. *CoRR*, abs/2310.02390 (2023)
13. Mamageishvili, A., Felten, E.W.: Incentive schemes for rollup validators. In: MARBLE, Lecture Notes in Operations Research, pp. 48–61. Springer (2023)
14. Onica, E., Georgica, M.: Can smart contracts become smart?: An overview of transaction impact on Ethereum DApp engineering. In: DICG@Middleware, pp. 31–36. ACM (2023)
15. Chaliasos, S., Reif, I., Torralba-Agell, A., Ernstberger, J., Kattis, A., Livshits, B.: Analyzing and benchmarking ZK-rollups. IACR Cryptol. ePrint Arch., p. 889 (2024)
16. Palakkal, R., Gorzny, J., Derka, M.: SoK: compression in rollups. In: ICBC, pp. 712–728. IEEE (2024)
17. Mamageishvili, A., Felten, E.W.: Efficient rollup batch posting strategy on base layer. In: FC Workshops, volume 13953 of Lecture Notes in Computer Science, pp. 355–366. Springer (2023)
18. Buterin, V., et al.: EIP-4844: shard blob transactions (2022). https://eips.ethereum.org/EIPS/eip-4844
19. Crapis, D., Felten, E.W., Mamageishvili, A.: EIP-4844 economics and rollup strategies. *CoRR*, abs/2310.01155 (2023)
20. Buterin, V.: Epochs and slots all the way down: ways to give ethereum users faster transaction confirmation times, June 2024. https://vitalik.eth.limo/general/2024/06/30/epochslot.html. Accessed 1 Jan 2025

21. Derka, M., Gorzny, J., Siqueira, D., Pellegrino, D., Guggenmos, M., Chen, Z.: Sequencer level security. *CoRR*, abs/2405.01819 (2024)
22. Buterin, V.: Epochs and slots all the way down: ways to give Ethereum users faster transaction confirmation times, January 2021. https://vitalik.eth.limo/general/2021/01/05/rollup.html
23. Heimbach, L., Kiffer, L., Ferreira Torres, C., Wattenhofer, R.: Ethereum's proposer-builder separation: promises and realities. In: IMC, pp. 406–420. ACM (2023)
24. Gorzny, J., Lin, P.-A., Derka, M.: Ideal properties of rollup escape hatches. In: DICG@Middleware, pp. 7–12. ACM (2022)
25. Daian, P., et al.: Flash boys 2.0: frontrunning in decentralized exchanges, miner extractable value, and consensus instability. In: SP, pp. 910–927. IEEE (2020)
26. Taiko mainnet upgrade and Ontake hardfork. https://taiko.mirror.xyz/OJA4SwCqHjF32Zz0GkNJvnHWlsRYzdJ6hcO9FXVOpLs. Accessed 17 Jan 2025
27. Wen, X., Feng, Q., Niu, J., Zhang, Y., Feng, C.: TeeRollup: efficient rollup design using heterogeneous TEE. *CoRR*, abs/2409.14647 (2024)
28. Lee, S.: 180 days after eip-4844: will blob sharing solve dilemma for small rollups? (2024)
29. Based booster rollup (BBR): a new major milestone in Taiko's roadmap, December 2023. https://taiko.mirror.xyz/Z4I5ZhreGkyfdaL5I9P0Rj0DNX4zaWFmcws-0CVMJ2A. Accessed 1 Oct 2024
30. Electric Coin Company. halo2: a zero-knowledge proof system. https://zcash.github.io/halo2/. Accessed: 6 Jan 2025
31. Incident report for scroll. https://status.scroll.io/incidents/44k6s4qg6kcs. Accessed 17 Jan 2025
32. Li, C., Palanisamy, B.: Comparison of decentralization in DPoS and PoW blockchains. In: Chen, Z., Cui, L., Palanisamy, B., Zhang, L.-J. (eds.) ICBC 2020. LNCS, vol. 12404, pp. 18–32. Springer, Cham (2020). https://doi.org/10.1007/978-3-030-59638-5_2
33. Gorzny, J., Derka, M.: Requirements engineering challenges for blockchain rollups. In: RE Workshops, pp. 340–347. IEEE (2024)
34. Buterin, V.: Layer 2s as cultural extensions of Ethereum, May 2024. https://vitalik.eth.limo/general/2024/05/29/l2culture.html. Accessed 6 Jan 2025

What Drives Liquidity on Decentralized Exchanges? Evidence from the Uniswap Protocol

Brian Zhu[1]($^{\boxtimes}$), Dingyue Liu[2], Xin Wan[2], Gordon Liao[3], Ciamac Moallemi[1], and Brad Bachu[2]

[1] Columbia University, New York, USA
bzz2101@columbia.edu, ciamac@gsb.columbia.edu
[2] Uniswap Labs, New York, USA
{kite.liu,xin,brad.bachu}@uniswap.org
[3] Circle Internet Financial, New York, USA
gordon@circle.com

Abstract. We study liquidity on decentralized exchanges (DEXs), identifying factors at the platform, blockchain, token pair, and liquidity pool levels with predictive power for market depth metrics. Using the *counterfactual v2 spread* metric, we decompose the contribution of each factor on market depth into two channels: total value locked (TVL) and concentration. We further explore how external liquidity from competing DEXs and private inventory on DEX aggregators influence market depth. We find that (i) gas prices, token price returns, and the market share of trading volume affect liquidity through concentration, (ii) internalization of order flow by private market makers affects TVL but not the overall market depth, and (iii) token price volatility, fee revenue, and markout affect liquidity through both channels.

1 Introduction

Liquidity plays a fundamental role in financial markets, serving as a critical determinant of market efficiency and stability. This is particularly evident in traditional finance (TradFi), where liquidity impacts execution prices, price discovery, and overall market robustness. Extensive research has explored how factors such as asset volatility and investor behavior shape liquidity in TradFi. However, the evolving nature of decentralized finance (DeFi) introduces dynamics for liquidity provision that remain under-explored.

Decentralized exchanges (DEX) introduce novel paradigms for liquidity provision and trading, utilizing *liquidity pools* and *pricing functions* as opposed to limit order books. Understanding the dynamics of liquidity in DEXs under this new paradigm is not only important for traders and investors, but also for the design and development of DEXs. While a substantial body of literature exists in TradFi regarding liquidity, there is a pressing need for more research on the idiosyncratic elements of liquidity provision in DEXs. This paper addresses this gap by investigating the forces that drive liquidity and market depth in DEXs, contributing to both academic discourse and practical applications in DeFi.

One recent development in DeFi has been the rise of liquidity aggregators, which combine liquidity from on- and off-chain sources to deliver better execution prices for trades. While research has shown that these services improve prices for traders, their impact on liquidity provision in AMMs is less studied. We answer this question by analyzing if and how these services affect on-chain liquidity.

We focus on liquidity dynamics within the Ethereum ecosystem, examining pools on the Uniswap v3 protocol deployed on the Ethereum Mainnet (L1) and Layer 2 (L2) networks. As the primary blockchain for decentralized applications, Ethereum is host to a variety of DEXs, with Uniswap standing out as the leading platform in trading volume, total value locked (TVL), and user adoption. While our analysis focuses on Uniswap v3, we show that our framework is applicable to a broader class of AMMs, including those used on Uniswap v2 and v4.

Our Contributions. The results of our analysis offer valuable insights into the determinants of liquidity in AMMs. The key contributions of this paper are:

1. **Identifying on-chain predictive factors for liquidity:** We identify factors on period t that forecast various market depth metrics on period $t+1$. We find that gas prices, token pair returns and volatilities, and in-pool fee revenue and markout have significant explanatory power on future market depth, consistent with prior theoretical results.
2. **Decomposing the contribution of each factor on liquidity into two channels:** With the *counterfactual v2 spread* metric, we decompose effective spreads into TVL and concentration components. This allows us to identify the channel(s) in which changes to market depth occur, whether through the *deployment* and/or *concentration* of liquidity.
3. **Understanding impacts of external liquidity:** We examine the impact of liquidity sources outside Uniswap v3 pools, focusing on competing DEX liquidity and off-chain liquidity used by aggregators. We find that a higher competitor market share negatively impacts liquidity, while more internalization by fillers has no significant impact on overall liquidity.

Related Literature. Our paper contributes to the literature on liquidity provision in DEXs. Some studies focus on incentives for/against liquidity providers (LPs). Lehar and Parlour [15] as well as Capponi and Jia [5] study equilibrium in liquidity pools, showing that volatility arbitrage risk causes LPs to exit pools. Capponi, Jia, and Zhu [7] analyze the phenomenon of just-in-time liquidity [23], showing that it may lead to shallower pools by taking fees away from and leaving toxic order flow to passive LPs. An important factor behind these incentives are the losses incurred by LPs. Two popular loss metrics are *impermanent loss* [12,13,17,18] and *loss-versus-rebalancing* [20,21], which compare the profitability of providing liquidity against holding and rebalancing, respectively.

Other studies focus on liquidity in AMMs that use *concentrated liquidity*, e.g. Uniswap v3. Lehar, Parlour, and Zoican [16] find that large (small) LPs prefer low-fee (high-fee) pools on Uniswap v3 and adjust their positions (in)frequently. Lyandres and Zaidelson [19] examine capital allocation on Uniswap v3, finding that market efficiency causally impacts capital efficiency. Cartea et al. [8] and Fan et al. [11] study strategies for liquidity provision on Uniswap v3.

We contribute to this literature by providing the first comprehensive empirical analysis regarding determinants of liquidity and market depth on DEXs. We consider the effects of multiple factors on liquidity simultaneously, with our sample spanning three years and across multiple blockchains.

Closest to our *counterfactual v2 spread (Cv2S)* metric for liquidity concentration is the *capital allocation efficiency (CAE)* metric of [19]. While CAE is dependent on the trades that occurred in the pool during the calibration period, Cv2S is a function of trade size and independent of other trades. Thus, two pools with the same "liquidity landscape" can have different CAE values, but always have the same Cv2S given trade size.

Our paper also contributes to the literature on informed trading taking place in DEXs. Capponi, Jia, and Yu [6] show that trades with higher priority fees contain more information and have a higher price impact. Klein et al. [14] analyze information contained in both trade and liquidity events on DEXs, finding evidence of heterogeneity in price impact across several dimensions. We contribute by showing that informed trading within a pool, proxied by markout, has a negative effect on market depth.

Another contribution of our paper is to the literature on liquidity in off-chain exchanges for cryptocurrencies, i.e. centralized exchanges (CEXs) and DEX aggregators. Brauneis et al. [4] study liquidity on CEXs, finding that returns and volume have predictive power on liquidity. Bachu, Wan, and Moallemi [3] provide empirical evidence of DEX aggregators improving prices for traders. Chitra et al. [9] analyze a model with theoretical implications that internalization of order flows by fillers negatively affects on-chain liquidity. We contribute by finding that in practice, there is no evidence of such an effect, which speaks positively to the coexistence of DEXs with order flow auction venues.[1]

2 Background

Automated Market Makers. AMMs use liquidity pools and algorithmic pricing functions to facilitate the on-chain exchange of tokens. When LPs deposit tokens into a pool, they receive pool tokens that indicate their stake of the pool and determine the amount they withdraw. Traders typically have to pay a fee proportional to the trade size; this fee is distributed pro-rata among LPs by their stake and incentivizes them to stay in the pool.

Many AMMs are constant function market makers (CFMMs), which requires post-trade pool reserves to be on the same level set of the pricing function as pre-trade reserves. For example, in a pool with X tokens X and Y tokens Y, a trade of Δ_X tokens X for Δ_Y tokens Y must satisfy the relation $F(X+\Delta_X, Y+\Delta_Y) = $

---

[1] Our finding does not necessarily contradict those of [9], since their assumption that filler inventory must be in-wallet does not always hold (cf. UniswapX, CoW Swap).

$F(X, Y)$, where $F : \mathbb{R}^2_+ \to \mathbb{R}$ is the pricing function. AMM protocols using this design include Uniswap v2, Curve, and Balancer.

The "concentrated liquidity" (CL) mechanism for AMMs [2], first pioneered by Uniswap v3, allows LPs to choose the price range in which their liquidity is active, with narrower ranges yielding higher "virtual" liquidity. This allows for higher capital efficiency, but also introduces new complexities for LPs in terms of managing risk and exposure, since out-of-range LP positions do not earn fees and poorly concentrated pools may increase trading costs.

DEX Aggregators. The success of AMMs has lead to a proliferation in DEXs, with there being over 100 DEXs at the time of writing. This growth has led to the fragmentation of liquidity across multiple DEXs. In response, protocols such as 1inch Fusion, CowSwap, and UniswapX have introduced new methods to handle order flow, leveraging liquidity from various on-chain sources and off-chain private market makers (PMMs), to optimize trading outcomes for users in a fragmented ecosystem.

DEX aggregators process order flow from their interfaces and allow specialized users, including PMMs, to determine the ordering and/or routing of trades to achieve better execution prices, most commonly implemented via order flow auctions (OFAs). These OFAs can have varying formats: for example, CowSwap uses batch auctions, whereas 1inch Fusion and UniswapX use Dutch auctions.

3 Data

We use publicly available Uniswap v3 data from May 5, 2021 to July 31, 2024. The liquidity pools in our sample, shown in Table 1, are selected as follows:

- Obtain the top 4 blockchains by average trading volume through the sample period. For each selected blockchain, obtain the top 100 pools by average trading volume through the sample period.
- Select the pools corresponding to the token pair and fee tier combinations appearing in all four top-100 lists.

3.1 Liquidity Metrics

Effective Spread. We compute the effective spread, which we define as the difference in quoted price between buying and selling a fixed amount of a given token in a liquidity pool, minus transaction fees. By using quoted prices rather than execution prices and subtracting out transaction fees, we ignore the impacts of MEV- and fee-related slippage (see [1] for example), which isolates the effect of liquidity on the trading costs. Effective spreads are a key measure of liquidity, representing the difference between buying and selling an asset in a market, with a smaller (larger) effective spread indicates a deeper (shallower) market.

Table 1. Liquidity Pools Included in Sample by Pair, Network, and Fee Tier.

Pair\Network	Ethereum	Arbitrum (L2)	Optimism (L2)	Polygon (L2)
CRV–WETH	30 bps	30 bps	30 bps	30 bps
DAI–WETH	30 bps	30 bps	30 bps	30 bps
LDO–WETH	30 bps	30 bps	30 bps	30 bps
LINK–WETH	30 bps	30 bps	30 bps	30 bps
USDC–WETH	5, 30 bps	5, 30 bps	5, 30 bps	5, 30 bps
WBTC–WETH	5, 30 bps	5, 30 bps	5, 30 bps	5, 30 bps
WETH–USDT	5, 30 bps	5, 30 bps	5, 30 bps	5, 30 bps

We acquire quoted prices from Uniswap v3 quoter contracts.[2] These contracts have functions to obtain quotes for buying or selling a token at historical blocks, allowing the user to specify blockchain, token pair, fee tier, and swap size. For a given trade size of Δ WETH, we compute the relative difference in quoted price between buying and selling Δ WETH minus twice the fee tier f. Using Uniswap v3's quoter contract, the ExactOutput function yields the ask price, denoted A, and the ExactInput function yields the bid price, denoted B. For each day in our sample period, we obtain quotes every six hours (for four samples per day), and take the spread for the day as the average of these measurements.

Formally, the normalized effective spread ("v3 spread"), in basis points attributed to market depth at day t on a given pool with fee tier f is

$$\text{v3S}_t^{pool} = 10^4 \times \left(\frac{1}{4} \sum_{i \in [4]} \frac{A_{t,i}^{pool} - B_{t,i}^{pool}}{\frac{1}{2}(A_{t,i}^{pool} + B_{t,i}^{pool})} - 2f \right)$$

where i indexes the in-day samples. Since quoted prices contain fees, we subtract $2f$ from the average and multiply by 10^4 to obtain basis points. For our selected pools, f is 0.0005 or 0.003, corresponding to 5 or 30 basis points, respectively.

Total Value Locked. Total value locked (TVL), the US dollar value of a pool's token reserves, is another important measure of liquidity in DEXs. In CFMMs, the TVL is a perfect signal of market depth as execution prices are computed directly based on the pool reserves. In AMMs using CL like Uniswap v3, however, TVL is a noisier signal as market depth also depends on how those reserves are concentrated around the pool's current tick. Since fee revenue and risk are shared pro-rata on the Uniswap protocol, TVL is also a benchmark that other pool metrics can be normalized against.

We compute TVL by aggregating mint (deposit), burn (withdrawal), and swap events on liquidity pools, keeping track of how token quantities in each pool vary over time. At the end of each day t, we sum the number of each token

---

[2] https://docs.uniswap.org/contracts/v3/reference/periphery/lens/Quoter.

in a liquidity pool weighted by the end-of-day token price in USD to arrive at the end-of-day TVL.

Summary Statistics. The summary statistics of our liquidity metrics are displayed in Table 2. We highlight the differences between liquidity in pools on L1 (Ethereum) and L2 networks. Effective spreads are lower, less dispersed, and more right-skewed on L1 pools relative to L2 pools. TVL is higher, less dispersed, and more left-skewed on L1 pools than L2 pools. Notably, both liquidity metrics are relatively normally distributed for L2 pools in our sample. Relevant data visualizations for these liquidity metrics are in the Online Appendix.

Table 2. Summary Statistics for Liquidity Metrics.

	log v3S (L1)	log TVL (L1)	log v3S (L2s)	log TVL (L2s)
N	11371	11371	27069	27069
Mean	−0.6944	17.976	2.6869	13.7407
S.D.	2.1329	1.9306	2.3198	1.9985
Skew	1.7493	−1.5520	0.1135	−0.1417
25%	−1.9277	17.5133	0.9339	12.3722
50%	−1.2828	18.3872	2.5252	13.7500
75%	−0.1236	19.5271	4.1776	15.2480

3.2 Independent Variables

The set of factors to regress our liquidity metrics is motivated by previous theoretical and empirical research on liquidity in DEXs, from which several factors consistently appear: gas price at the blockchain level, price returns and volatility at the token pair level, and adverse selection (informed trading) and fee revenue (noise trading) at the pool level. These are summarized in Table 3, and generally agree with each other on the direction effects of the variables on liquidity.

We enhance these studies by empirically testing theoretical predictions and verifying empirical findings in a setup with more variables to rule out confounding. Our counterfactual v2 spread metric also allows us to test implications for both Uniswap v2- and v3-like AMMs with only Uniswap v3 data. We thus select gas prices, returns, volatility, markout, and fee revenue as a baseline set of factors, with markout as a proxy for adverse selection. We compute these variables at a daily frequency, using publicly available data from Dune Analytics. We collect data on gas prices per transaction on each blockchain, token price data from centralized exchanges (CEXs), and data on liquidity and swap events occurring on each pool. More detailed descriptions of each variable follow.

Gas Prices. We compute the average gas price, in USD, of all transactions on a given chain for the current day t.

Table 3. Factors Affecting Liquidity Provision Studied by Previous Works.

Variable	Prediction/Finding (Setting)
gas price	[16,18]: ↗ gas price ⟹ ↘ rebalancing frequency (v3)
returns	[8]: returns have ambiguous effects on price ranges (v3)
volatility	[15]: ↗ volatility ⟹ ↘ pool size (v2) [5,8]: ↗ volatility ⟹ wider ranges (v3)
fee revenue	[5,7,15]: ↗ fee revenue ⟹ ↗ pool size (v2) [8]: ↗ fee revenue ⟹ narrower ranges (v3)
adverse selection	[5,7]: ↗ adverse selection ⟹ ↘ pool size (v2) [5]: ↗ adverse selection ⟹ narrower ranges (v3)

Log-Returns. Let $\{p_t\}$ be the price ratio of the token pair traded on a pool in our sample, in units of the other token per WETH and measured via CEX prices, at day t. Log-returns at time horizon h_r are then given by

$$\text{LogReturns}_t^{pair} = 100 \times \log\left(p_t / p_{t-h_r}\right).$$

Volatility. We compute the annualized volatility of the token price ratio during day t, using 15-minute intervals to obtain returns. This choice of time interval captures the fine-grained intra-day price variability while reducing the influence of microstructure noise present in shorter intervals.

Fee Revenue. The pro-rated fee revenue (or *pool APR*), computed by dividing total fees accrued to a pool from a day's swaps by the end-of-day pool TVL, is

$$\text{FeeRevenue}_t^{pool} = \frac{1}{\text{TVL}_t} \times \frac{f}{1+f} \sum_{\text{swaps } s \text{ on } pool \text{ in day } t} p_{\tau_s}^{TI}(s) \cdot q^{TI}(s)$$

where τ_s is the time of the swap and $p_{\tau_s}^{TI}(s)$ and $q^{TI}(s)$ are the dollar price and amount, respectively, of the token that swap s puts *into* the pool.[3]

Markout. Markouts capture the informativeness of trades on an exchange by comparing the price of a trade to a benchmark price sometime after the trade, in our case the pool's mid-price, which indicates how favorable to the trader the swap was in hindsight. Commonly used in traditional market microstructure, markouts have also been used as a proxy for LVR [16,21] in DEXs.

For each swap, we compare the swap price with the mid-price of the pool determined by the "current tick" at time $\tau_s + h_m$, where τ_s is the time of a swap s and h_m is the time horizon for computing markout. The resulting difference in

---

[3] As fees on Uniswap are determined by the token-in amount, and our swap event tracker includes fees in q^{TI}, we multiply the sum across swaps by $f/(1+f)$.

price is then volume-weighted. We aggregate markouts for all swaps in a given day and normalize by the end-of-day pool TVL:

$$\text{Markout}_t^{pool} = \frac{1}{\text{TVL}_t} \times \sum_{\text{swaps } s \text{ on } pool \text{ in day } t} D_s \cdot |q^{TI}(s)| \cdot \left(\left| \frac{q^{TO}(s)}{q^{TI}(s)} \right| - p_{\tau_s + h_m}^{pool} \right)$$

where $D_s = 1$ if the swapper is selling WETH and $D_s = -1$ otherwise (i.e. buying WETH), $q^{TO}(s)$ is the token-out amount for swap s, and $p_{\tau_s + h_m}^{pool}$ denotes the pool price, in units of the other token per WETH, at time h_m after the swap occurred. Under this definition, more positive (negative) values indicate better (worse) LP profitability and thus less (more) adverse selection costs from swappers.

4 Methodology

In AMMs with concentrated liquidity, market depth is not only influenced by the TVL in the pool, but is also by how concentrated that liquidity is across different price ranges. In this section, we introduce a novel method to measure concentration, which we use to distinguish between the effects of TVL and liquidity concentration on changes in effective spreads. This decomposition allows us to better understand the mechanics of liquidity provision in concentrated AMM pools and provide insights on LP behavior.

4.1 Decomposing Spread in Uniswap v3

The *counterfactual v2 spread (Cv2S)*, is computed by looking at the TVL in a v3 pool at some given time, counterfactually considering a v2 pool with the same TVL under no trading fees such that the spot price on the v2 pool aligns with the CEX price at that time, and computing the effective spread as described in Sect. 3 on the counterfactual pool. Note that this v2 pool is counterfactual and does not correspond to any actual pool on Uniswap v2 for the token pair. We align the counterfactual v2 pool's reserves with the CEX price to simulate the effect of arbitrageurs. A quick derivation (with details in Appendix A) shows that the counterfactual v2 spread for a trade size of Δ WETH can be expressed as a function of token prices and TVL:

$$\text{Cv2S}_t^{pool} = 10^4 \times \frac{4 p_t^{ETH}}{\text{TVL}_t^{pool}} \Delta.$$

The quotient between the actual v3 and counterfactual v2 spreads, which we call the *spread quotient (SQ)*, is defined as

$$\text{SQ} := \frac{\text{v3S}}{\text{Cv2S}},$$

is a proxy for how well-concentrated the pool is around its mid-price: as the spread quotient increases, the spread of the actual pool becomes higher relative to that of the counterfactual pool, meaning that liquidity is not well-concentrated in the actual pool; conversely, as the spread quotient decreases, the spread of the actual pool becomes lower, suggesting a more efficient concentration of liquidity. Taking logarithms of the above equation reveals that

$$\log \text{v3S} = \log \text{Cv2S} + \log \text{SQ}.$$

This motivates the following three regression models:

$$\log \text{v3S}_{t+1}^{pool} = \beta_0 + \beta_1 \log \text{GasPrice}_t^{chain} + \beta_2 \text{LogReturns}_t^{pair} + \beta_3 \text{Volatility}_t^{pair}$$
$$+ \beta_4 \log \text{FeeRevenue}_t^{pool} + \beta_5 \text{Markout}_t^{pool} + \gamma^{pool} + \delta_t + \varepsilon_{t+1}^{pool} \quad (1)$$

$$\log \text{Cv2S}_{t+1}^{pool} = \beta_0 + \beta_1 \log \text{GasPrice}_t^{chain} + \beta_2 \text{LogReturns}_t^{pair} + \beta_3 \text{Volatility}_t^{pair}$$
$$+ \beta_4 \log \text{FeeRevenue}_t^{pool} + \beta_5 \text{Markout}_t^{pool} + \gamma^{pool} + \delta_t + \varepsilon_{t+1}^{pool} \quad (2)$$

$$\log \text{SQ}_{t+1}^{pool} = \beta_0 + \beta_1 \log \text{GasPrice}_t^{chain} + \beta_2 \text{LogReturns}_t^{pair} + \beta_3 \text{Volatility}_t^{pair}$$
$$+ \beta_4 \log \text{FeeRevenue}_t^{pool} + \beta_5 \text{Markout}_t^{pool} + \gamma^{pool} + \delta_t + \varepsilon_{t+1}^{pool} \quad (3)$$

Due to skewed data, we take logarithms of the spread, GasPrice, and fee revenue. The terms γ^{pool} and δ_t represent pool-level and day-level fixed effects, respectively, while ε_{t+1}^{pool} is the error term. The pool fixed effects capture time-invariant characteristics specific to each pool, such as whether the pool is included in the default Uniswap interface or other platform-specific settings that remain consistent. Day fixed effects account for factors that affect all pools on a given date, such as regulatory news or shifts in overall market sentiment. Standard errors are clustered at the pool level to account for heteroscedasticity and autocorrelation within pools over time.

4.2 Results and Discussion

We estimate the regression models with a trade size of $\Delta = 1$ WETH to compute spreads, a return horizon h_r of 1 day, and a markout horizon h_m of 5 min.[4] Prior to estimation, we normalize each independent variable in the data matrix to have mean zero and standard deviation one, preserving the significance of the coefficients while allowing for interpretable effect sizes.[5] Our main results are

---

[4] The gas price and markout variable exhibits extreme values that could disproportionately influence the regression results. To address this, we exclude pool-days where the gas price markout exceeds 5 standard deviations from their respective means, removing 56 pool-days from the sample.

[5] For example, raw gas prices and markouts may have values that differ in orders of magnitude, so normalizing makes the coefficients easier to interpret in measuring the strength of the relationship between the independent and dependent variables, while keeping t-statistics the same.

generally robust to modifications in Δ, h_r and h_m; specifically, we also have considered $\Delta \in \{0.1, 10\}$, $h_r = 7$ days, and $h_m = 1$ h. See the Online Appendix for the regression results under robustness checks.

Our decomposition implies that for each control, the estimated coefficients from model (2) and (3) sum to the coefficient from estimating model (1), though their significance levels may vary:

$$\hat{\beta}_i^{\log \text{v3S}} = \hat{\beta}_i^{\log \text{Cv2S}} + \hat{\beta}_i^{\log \text{SQ}} \quad \forall i.$$

We also regress the log-TVL at time $t+1$ on the independent variables at time t for completeness. Since the counterfactual v2 spread is a function of price and TVL, and fixed effects by pool and day are included, the coefficients from this regression will equal to those from regression (2) times minus one:

$$\hat{\beta}_i^{\log \text{Cv2S}} = -\hat{\beta}_i^{\log \text{TVL}} \quad \forall i.$$

Table 4. Baseline Regression Model (1) with Decomposition (2) + (3)

	(1) log v3S	(2) log Cv2S	(3) log SQ	(4) log TVL
log GasPrice	0.213	0.085	0.128***	−0.085
	(0.132)	(0.126)	(0.048)	(0.126)
LogReturns	−0.033***	−0.009	−0.024***	0.009
	(0.008)	(0.006)	(0.005)	(0.006)
Volatility	0.401***	0.101**	0.300***	−0.101**
	(0.053)	(0.044)	(0.027)	(0.044)
log FeeRevenue	−0.928***	−0.237***	−0.690***	0.237***
	(0.117)	(0.074)	(0.086)	(0.074)
Markout	−0.086***	−0.169***	0.083***	0.169***
	(0.028)	(0.019)	(0.021)	(0.019)
Observations	38440	38440	38440	38440
N. of groups	40	40	40	40
R^2	0.313	0.078	0.435	0.078

Pool and day fixed effects are included; standard errors are clustered at the pool level.
Note: *p<0.1; **p<0.05; ***p<0.01

Table 4 presents the estimated effects of factors on each dependent variable specification. We omit β_0 estimates for brevity. All factors except for GasPrice significantly impact the overall effective spread. Specifically, v3 spreads are increasing in volatility and is decreasing in returns, fee revenue, and markout.

The estimated coefficients on volatility, fee revenue, and markout for regression (2) are significant, suggesting that these factors have predictive power on how TVL affects overall spreads. Higher fee revenue and better markouts against swappers indicate more profitability for LPs, incentivizing them to provide liquidity, thus reducing spreads. Since volatility is associated with LP losses (both impermanent loss and LVR), higher volatility lowers liquidity provision.

All factors are significant in regression (3), implying that they play an important role in liquidity concentration. Higher gas prices increase rebalancing costs, leading to "stale" positions that are not concentrated around current pool prices. More volatility and negative markout (indicating informed trading) lead to LPs widening their price ranges in order to, as explained in [5], create a more convex pricing function that reduces losses to informed traders and volatile prices. Conversely, more fee revenue means that LPs can increase their profits by targeting narrower price ranges with a larger concentration liquidity, according to [8]. Recall that putting a fixed amount of assets in a wider range lowers the amount of "virtual liquidity" (see [2]) in the AMM, resulting in lower spreads.

For returns, we note that in traditional markets, liquidity tends to dry up during market declines and periods of increased volatility [10,22]. This implies that higher returns should positively predict market depth, while higher volatility has a negative effect, which is consistent with our results, suggesting that this stylized fact also carries over to decentralized markets with WETH as numéraire.

5 Extension: External Liquidity

The success of AMMs has lead to the proliferation of DEXs, with there being over one hundred DEXs at the time of writing. The increase in competition between DEXs introduces challenges such as the fragmentation of liquidity across multiple liquidity pools and DEXs. In addition, DEX aggregators have created new methods for order routing, using liquidity from various on-chain sources and off-chain private market makers (PMMs). While these services improve trading outcomes [3], PMMs take away fees from on-chain LPs.

5.1 Measuring External Liquidity

To better understand how these external liquidity sources might affect on-chain liquidity provision, we introduce variables that (i) capture the volume of swaps taking place on other DEXs and (ii) filled by private liquidity due to aggregator routing. Using data from Dune Analytics, we track swap volume on other DEXs and routed through aggregators, isolating swaps filled completely by private liquidity by comparing transaction hashes with on-chain events. A simple heuristic to identify these types of swaps is to take all swaps emitting events to aggregator trackers that did not emit a swap event to on-chain data trackers.

Competitor Market Share. For a set $\mathcal{D}$ of DEXs (including the given DEX) and a chain-pair, we compute the fraction of trading volume for that chain-pair occurring outside of the given DEX on day t:[6]

$$\text{CompetitorShare}_t^{chain,pair} = 1 - \frac{v_t}{\sum_{D \in \mathcal{D}} v_t^D}$$

where v_t and v_t^D are the swap volumes on the given DEX and DEX D in USD, respectively, for a given chain-pair on day t.

Internalization Ratio. Given a set $\mathcal{D}$ of DEXs, a set $\mathcal{A}$ of aggregators, and a chain-pair, we compute the proportion of swap volume routed or internalized by private market makers active on $\mathcal{A}$, henceforth referred to as "private volume," to the total on-chain plus private volume for that chain-pair on day t:[7]

$$\text{Internalization}_t^{chain,pair} = \frac{\sum_{A \in \mathcal{A}} v_t^A}{\sum_{D \in \mathcal{D}} v_t^D + \sum_{A \in \mathcal{A}} v_t^A}$$

where v_t^A is the private volume on aggregator A and v_t^D is the swap volume on DEX D, both in USD, for a given chain-pair on day t.

Extended Regression Model. We take $\mathcal{D}$ as the 130 DEXs whose swap events are tracked on Dune Analytics and $\mathcal{A}$ as the 13 aggregators whose swap events are tracked on Dune Analytics. We add the competitor market share and internalization ratio variables to the baseline model and estimate the model with the dependent variable specifications in models (1)–(3):

$$\begin{aligned}
y_{t+1}^{pool} = {} & \beta_0 + \beta_1 \log \text{GasPrice}_t^{chain} + \beta_2 \text{LogReturns}_t^{pair} + \beta_3 \text{Volatility}_t^{pair} \\
& + \beta_4 \log \text{FeeRevenue}_t^{pool} + \beta_5 \text{Markout}_t^{pool} + \beta_6 \text{CompetitorShare}_t^{chain,pair} \\
& + \beta_7 \text{Internalization}_t^{chain,pair} + \gamma^{pool} + \delta_t + \varepsilon_{t+1}^{pool}
\end{aligned} \quad (4)$$

where $y \in \{\log \text{v3S}, \log \text{Cv2S}, \log \text{SQ}\}$.[8]

5.2 Results and Discussion

Table 5 displays the estimation results of each dependent variable using the extended model that includes the competitor trading volume share and internalization ratios. We find that a higher competitor share of the token pair predicts higher effective spreads, while there is no significant explanatory power from internalization. Interestingly, the channels in which competitor share and internalization affect market depth differ: the former affects liquidity via concentration while the latter affects liquidity through value locked.

---

[6] Typically, market share for DEXs is evaluated in terms of trading volume. As a single DEX can have several pools trading a pair on a chain, we require a platform-level metric to assess competition and trader's sentiments towards a given DEX.

[7] Since an aggregator could route trades to a variety of DEXs, we need $\mathcal{D}$ to include all DEX that the aggregators in $\mathcal{A}$ may route to.

[8] We performed robustness checks similar to those in footnote 4.

One possible explanation for this difference is that while providing liquidity privately and to competing DEXs are both alternative opportunities for LPs to earn fee revenue, providing liquidity privately is more discretionary, as PMMs can choose which orders to fill, while providing liquidity to a competing DEX requires the LP to take the opposite position of all trades routed to the DEX. The greater risk involved in this option incentivizes LPs to widen price ranges, following the same intuition as the discussion on volatility and markout. Conversely, the lesser risks involved in being a PMM mean that LPs choosing this option may not need to widen ranges on existing position, instead directly withdrawing liquidity from pools to serve as private liquidity.

Table 5. Model (4) with External Liquidity Variables

	(1) log v3S	(2) log Cv2S	(3) log SQ	(4) log TVL
log GasPrice	0.178	0.083	0.095**	−0.083
	(0.126)	(0.120)	(0.047)	(0.120)
LogReturns	−0.033***	−0.009	−0.024***	0.009
	(0.008)	(0.006)	(0.006)	(0.006)
Volatility	0.379***	0.089**	0.290***	−0.089**
	(0.052)	(0.045)	(0.026)	(0.045)
log FeeRevenue	−0.869***	−0.201**	−0.668***	0.201**
	(0.119)	(0.079)	(0.079)	(0.079)
Markout	−0.088***	−0.169***	0.081***	0.169***
	(0.026)	(0.019)	(0.020)	(0.019)
CompetitorShare	0.222***	0.088	0.134***	−0.088
	(0.065)	(0.056)	(0.031)	(0.056)
Internalization	0.062	0.113***	−0.051	−0.113***
	(0.082)	(0.027)	(0.070)	(0.027)
Observations	38440	38440	38440	38440
N. of groups	40	40	40	40
R^2	0.327	0.093	0.447	0.093

Pool and day fixed effects are included; standard errors are clustered at the pool level.
Note: *p<0.1; **p<0.05; ***p<0.01

6 Conclusion

This study provides a valuable understanding of what drives liquidity on DEXs, specifically within the Uniswap v3 protocol, having analyzed various factors and their explanatory power in predicting future market depth. We use the counterfactual v2 spread metric to decompose the drivers of overall effective spread, distinguishing between impacts through TVL and liquidity concentration. Our findings suggest that increased competition between DEXs and the presence of private liquidity sources are significant contributors to liquidity fragmentation on Uniswap v3, though they influence market depth via differing channels.

Our findings have significant implications for both LPs and DEX designers. Understanding these dynamics is essential for LPs looking to optimize liquidity provision strategies, and for DEX designers, these insights can guide the development of features that address the adverse effects of liquidity fragmentation. Our results on private liquidity are optimistic for the coexistence of DEX aggregators and on-chain liquidity, as internalization shows no significant effect on *overall* market depth.

Future research could explore more elements of competition and internalization in multi-DEX ecosystems, especially as aggregator services evolve. Further studies on how alternative blockchain environments and emerging Layer 2 solutions support affect liquidity provision can provide a broader perspective on the scalability and sustainability of DEXs in a rapidly growing DeFi landscape.

Acknowledgements and Disclosures. The fifth author was supported by the Briger Family Digital Finance Lab at Columbia Business School and is an advisor to fintech companies.

A Derivation of the Counterfactual v2 Spread

As a v2 pool between tokens X and Y aligned to CEX prices has equal values of each token, the pool reserves (X_t, Y_t) given TVL at time t should satisfy

$$(X_t^{pool}, Y_t^{pool}) = \left(\frac{\text{TVL}_t^{pool}}{2p_t^X}, \frac{\text{TVL}_t^{pool}}{2p_t^Y} \right)$$

where p_t^X and p_t^Y are the CEX prices of tokens X and Y, respectively. A swap buying Δ_X tokens X for Δ_Y tokens Y must satisfy $(X - \Delta_X)(Y + \Delta_Y) = XY$. Solving for Δ_Y and scaling by Δ_X yields the counterfactual ask price of

$$A_t^{pool} = \frac{\Delta_Y}{\Delta_X} = \frac{Y_t^{pool}}{X_t^{pool} - \Delta_X}.$$

A swap selling Δ_X tokens X for Δ_Y tokens Y must satisfy $(X + \Delta_X)(Y - \Delta_Y) = XY$. Solving for Δ_Y and scaling by Δ_X yields the counterfactual bid price of

$$B_t^{pool} = \frac{\Delta_Y}{\Delta_X} = \frac{Y_t^{pool}}{X_t^{pool} + \Delta_X}.$$

The counterfactual v2 spread for a trade size of Δ WETH is then

$$\text{Cv2S}_t^{pool} = 10^4 \times \frac{A_t^{pool} - B_t^{pool}}{\frac{1}{2}(A_t^{pool} + B_t^{pool})} = 10^4 \times \frac{4p_t^{ETH}}{\text{TVL}_t^{pool}} \Delta.$$

References

1. Adams, A., Chan, B.Y., Markovich, S., Wan, X.: Don't Let MEV Slip: The Costs of Swapping on the Uniswap Protocol. arXiv Preprint arXiv:2309.13648 (2024)
2. Adams, H., Zinsmeister, N., Salem, M., Keefer, R., Robinson, D.: Uniswap v3 core. Tech. rep, Uniswap Labs (2021)
3. Bachu, B., Wan, X., Moallemi, C.C.: Quantifying Price Improvement in Order Flow Auctions. arXiv Preprint arXiv:2405.00537 (2024)
4. Brauneis, A., Mestel, R., Riordan, R., Theissen, E.: How to measure the liquidity of cryptocurrency markets? J. Banking Finance **124**, 106041 (2021)
5. Capponi, A., Jia, R.: Liquidity provision on blockchain-based decentralized exchanges. Rev. Financial Stud. Forthcoming (2025)
6. Capponi, A., Jia, R., Yu, S.: Price discovery on decentralized exchanges. Available at SSRN 4236993 (2023)
7. Capponi, A., Jia, R., Zhu, B.: The Paradox of Just-in-Time Liquidity in Decentralized Exchanges: More Providers Can Lead to Less Liquidity. Available at SSRN 4648055 (2023)
8. Cartea, A., Drissi, F., Monga, M.: Decentralised finance and automated market making: predictable loss and optimal liquidity provision. SIAM J. Financial Math. **15**(3), 931–959 (2024)
9. Chitra, T., Kulkarni, K., Pai, M., Diamandis, T.: An Analysis of Intent-Based Markets. arXiv preprint arXiv:2403.02525 (2024)
10. Chordia, T., Roll, R., Subrahmanyam, A.: Market liquidity and trading activity. J. Finance **56**(2), 501–530 (2001)
11. Fan, Z., Marmolejo-Cossio, F., Moroz, D., Neuder, M., Rao, R., Parkes, D.C.: Strategic Liquidity Provision in Uniswap V3. In: 5th Conference on Advances in Financial Technologies, pp. 25:1–22 (2023)
12. Heimbach, L., Schertenleib, E., Wattenhofer, R.: Risks and returns of uniswap V3 liquidity providers. In: Proceedings of the 4th ACM Conference on Advances in Financial Technologies, pp. 89–101 (2022)
13. Kim, H.J., Lee, G.M., Lee, J., Kang, S., Chae, S.W., Park, J.S.: A comparison of impermanent loss for various CFMMs. In: 2024 IEEE International Conference on Blockchain (Blockchain), pp. 542–548 (2024)
14. Klein, O., Kozhan, R., Viswanath-Natraj, G., Wang, J.: Price Discovery in Cryptocurrencies: Trades versus Liquidity Provision. Available at SSRN 4642411 (2023)
15. Lehar, A., Parlour, C.A.: Decentralized exchange: the uniswap automated market maker. J. Finance **79**(6) (2024)
16. Lehar, A., Parlour, C.A., Zoican, M.: Fragmentation and Optimal Liquidity Supply on Decentralized Exchanges. Available at SSRN 4267429 (2024)
17. Li, T., Naik, S., Papanicolaou, A., Schoenleber, L.: Implied Impermanent Loss: A Cross-Sectional Analysis of Decentralized Liquidity Pools. Available at SSRN 4811111 (2024)
18. Li, T., Naik, S., Papanicolaou, A., Schoenleber, L.: Yield Farming for Liquidity Provision. Available at SSRN 4422213 (2024)
19. Lyandres, E., Zaidelson, A.: Does Market Efficiency Impact Capital Allocation Efficiency? The Case of Decentralized Exchanges. Available at SSRN 4853306 (2024)
20. Milionis, J., Moallemi, C.C., Roughgarden, T.: Automated Market Making and Arbitrage Profits in the Presence of Fees . arXiv Preprint arXiv:2305.14604 (2023)
21. Milionis, J., Moallemi, C.C., Roughgarden, T., Zhang, A.L.: Automated Market Making and Loss-Versus-Rebalancing. arXiv Preprint arXiv:2208.06046 (2022)

22. Pástor, L., Stambaugh, R.F.: Liquidity risk and expected stock returns. J. Polit. Econ. **111**(3), 642–685 (2003)
23. Wan, X., Adams, A.: Just-in-time Liquidity on the Uniswap Protocol. Available at SSRN 4382303 (2022)

Liquidity Fragmentation or Optimization? Analyzing Automated Market Makers Across Ethereum and Rollups

Krzysztof M. Gogol[1(✉)], Manvir Schneider[2], Claudio J. Tessone[1,3], and Benjamin Livshits[4]

[1] University of Zurich, Zurich, Switzerland
gogol@ifi.uzh.ch
[2] Cardano Foundation, Zurich, Switzerland
[3] UZH Blockchain Center, Zurich, Switzerland
[4] Imperial College London, London, UK

Abstract. Layer-2 (L2) blockchains inherit Ethereum's security guarantees while reducing gas fees. As a result, they are gaining traction among traders at Automated Market Makers (AMMs), sparking debate over whether they contribute to liquidity fragmentation of Ethereum. Our research suggests that such fragmentation is not currently occurring. However, it could emerge in the future—particularly if Liquidity Providers (LPs) recognize the higher returns available on L2s. Using Lagrangian optimization, we develop a model for optimal liquidity allocation across AMMs on Ethereum and its L2s, using staking as a benchmark. We show that, in equilibrium, AMM liquidity provision returns converge to this reference rate. Additionally, we measure the elasticity of trading volume with respect to Total Value Locked (TVL) in AMMs and find that, on well-established blockchains, an increase in TVL does not necessarily lead to higher trading volume. Finally, our empirical findings reveal that Ethereum's liquidity pools are oversubscribed compared to those on L2s and often yield lower returns than staking Ether. LPs could maximize their rewards by reallocating more than two-thirds of their liquidity to L2s and staking.

1 Introduction

Automated Market Makers (AMMs) [36], pioneered by Uniswap on Ethereum in 2018 [4], are the foundation of Decentralized Exchanges (DEXs). DEXs enable token exchanges without counterparty risk in an atomic blockchain transaction [14]. They were originally introduced to avoid the inefficiencies of the on-chain order book associated with high on-chain storage costs and security vulnerabilities [21]. At AMM-DEX, exchange rates are set by a conservation function and current token reserves in the AMM pool. Liquidity Providers (LPs) supply tokens, earning trading fees paid by traders. As a result, a higher trading volume results in increased fees, which are subsequently distributed among LPs. Furthermore, a higher Total Value Locked (TVL) in liquidity pools attracts traders by reducing price impact during swaps, a primary cost component incurred during swap transactions [3].

Nevertheless, it is not always the optimal strategy for LPs to allocate their liquidity to the AMM pools with the highest trading volume. The trading fees accrued from traders are distributed among LPs in proportion to their respective contributions to the pool's TVL. Therefore, it is the ratio of fees to TVL, often referred to as capital efficiency, that should be the primary consideration for LPs. LPs must also carefully select token pairs in the AMM pools. Volatile crypto-currency pairs lead to impermanent loss, reducing LP rewards [18]. Arbitrageurs equalizing token prices across AMM-DEXs, or with Centralized Exchanges (CEXs) amplify LPs' losses from market movement [25]. The Loss-Versus-Rebalancing (LVR) metric measures LP rewards relative to arbitrageurs [25]. Finally, should the rewards from liquidity provisions fall below those achieved by staking ETH, which is widely regarded the safest token allocation to yield rewards [13], the rationale behind the liquidity provision becomes questionable. The Loss-Versus-Staking metric compares LP returns to staking rewards [13].

The advent of rollups, a Layer-2 (L2) scaling solution [31], has shifted DeFi activities from Ethereum to its rollups. The success of rollups lies in their data integrity, which is secured by staked ETH, and the significant reduction in gas fees achieved by offloading computations off-chain [12,30]. After the Ethereum Dencun upgrade in March 2024, the swap fees on L2s have dropped below $0.01 per transaction. Consequently, the volume of swap transactions on rollups has surpassed that on the Ethereum mainnet, albeit with lower trading volumes. The reduced gas fees on rollups have facilitated transactions within the $1-$10 range, a previously unfeasible scenario on Ethereum. Furthermore, most rollups support the Ethereum Virtual Machine (EVM), allowing for the seamless deployment of AMM-DEXs originally designed for Ethereum onto rollups. Currently, DEXs such as Uniswap, Curve, and their forks have been deployed on rollups, enhancing the diversity of AMM pools accessible to LPs. As a result, LPs have more options to consider for providing liquidity, which serves as the starting point for this research.

Faster block production in rollups, along with cheaper gas fees, impacts the strategies of LPs in L2s. While Ethereum produces blocks every 12 s, rollups do it in 0.2 to 2 s depending on their implementation. The cheaper gas fees and faster block production allow LPs to adjust their strategies more often, which is especially vital for Concentrated Liquidity Market Makers (CLMM) such as Uniswap (v3) [2]. With more frequency LP-position rebalancing in CLMMs, LPs earn higher rewards compared to similar pools on Ethereum.

This study investigates liquidity provision to AMM pools on L2s and Ethereum. After developing the theoretical framework for optimal liquidity allocation within the same cryptocurrency pools, we analyze our results using empirical on-chain data. We show that providing liquidity to certain AMM pools on rollups is more profitable compared to Ethereum. Despite the fact that liquidity pools on Ethereum have higher trading volumes, they often become oversubscribed, diminishing the rewards for LPs.

Related Work. A comprehensive review of major AMM categories has been made available in [36] and expanded and updated in [29]. The empirical study of liquidity provisions to AMMs has primarily focused on the Ethereum blockchain, especially for Uniswap (v2) [19] and Uniswap (v3) [10,18,24,26,27]. These investigations emphasize impermanent loss as a key indicator for assessing LP profitability across different cryptocurrency pairs. Furthermore, Tiruviluamala et al. [33] proposed a framework to address impermanent loss, a major risk for LPs.

Alternative metrics for comparing LP profitability include LVR and LVS. Milionis et al. [25] compared LP rewards with arbitrage using loss-versus-rebalancing (LVR), while Fritsch and Canidio [11] extended its empirical analysis to more pools and showed that arbitrage profit increases on faster blockchains. Gogol et al. [13] introduced loss-versus-staking (LVS) as another comparative measure, evaluating LP returns against staking rewards. Yaish et al. [37] demonstrated the suboptimal behavior of LPs in DeFi lending pools.

Research on AMMs on L2s is nascent, focusing mostly on MEV and arbitrage. Torres et al. [34] reported on cycling arbitrage (MEV) within L2s, while Gogol et al. [15,16] examined non-atomic arbitrage involving cross-rollup and L2-CEX. In his pioneering work, Adams [2] observed that the liquidity concentration at Uniswap (v3) on Arbitrum and Optimism surpasses that on Ethereum by 75%, indicating that LPs often readjust their positions on L2s. Chemaya and Liu [7] estimated AMM traders preferences for blockchain security on two main L2 networks in comparison to Ethereum.

Contribution. This research analyzes both empirically and theoretically the liquidity provision for AMMs on L2s. We assess LP rewards on Uniswap (v3) within Ethereum and its optimistic rollups (Arbitrum, Base, Optimism), and ZK rollups (ZKsync). The contributions of this work are as follows:

- Using Lagrangian optimization, we find the optimal allocation of liquidity across staking and AMMs pools on Ethereum and its rollups, with the objective of maximizing LP rewards. We further show that in equilibrium, liquidity provisions to AMMs should provide returns equal to risk-free rate across all blockchains.
- We measure the elasticity of trading volume with respect to TVL at AMM pool and found that at the well established blockchains—Ethereum, Arbitrum and Optimism, contrary to expectations, an increase in TVL is not associated with an increase in trading volume. In contrast, emerging blockchains, Base and ZKsync, exhibit a positive elasticity value, indicating that the volume of trade is positively correlated with TVL on these chains.
- We empirically find that the current allocation of liquidity to WETH-USDC pools of Uniswap (v3) on Ethereum and rollups is not optimal for LPs. The pool on Ethereum tend to be overcapitalized and does not compensate LP for the missed opportunity to stake the entire capital. Specifically, over 66%

of Ethereum liquidity should be reallocated to rollups in order to maximize LP returns and to attain equilibrium with staking rates.

2 Background on Layer-2s

According to the blockchain scalability trilemma [28], blockchains can prioritize only two of three: decentralization, security, or scalability. Ethereum, the main platform for DeFi with the highest TVL, prioritizes decentralization and security. This led to network congestion, high gas fees, and throughput limited to 12 transactions per second (TPS). The Layer 1 (L1) and Layer 2 (L2) scaling solutions address blockchain scalability. L1 scaling involves the development of new blockchains with novel consensus mechanisms [23], sharding [35], and their own physical infrastructure. In contrast, in L2 scaling intensive computations are executed off-chain, with their results being recorded on the underlying L1 blockchain [12,30].

Rollup. Rollups [32], the non-custodial form of L2 scaling, act as blockchains. They generate blocks, execute transactions, and subsequently record compressed batched data on the L1. This approach ensures that the integrity of the rollup data is guaranteed by L1 security, such as staked ETH in the case of Ethereum's rollups. In order to maliciously modify the rollup state history, an attacker must compromise the security of the underlying L1 network.

Sequencer. A sequencer [5] is an integral component of rollup, tasked with executing and ordering transactions, forming blocks, and creating batches that are uploaded to the L1 chain. By bundling transactions together, rollups provide more gas-efficiency compared to the L1 network. To avoid additional trust assumptions in sequencer operators, rollups use optimistic or zero-knowledge proofs (ZKPs) to ensure the correctness and integrity of the data. Figure 1 illustrates the architecture of optymistic and ZK-rollups. Presently, major Ethereum optimistic rollups (e.g., Arbitrum, Optimism, Base) and ZK-rollups (e.g., ZKsync, StarkNet) rely on centralized sequencers and, in the case of ZK-rollup, centralized provers.

Optimistic Rollup. Optimistic rollups [22] operate on a trust-based system, assuming transactions are valid unless disputed. This approach simplifies the implementation of optimistic rollups, particularly in supporting the Ethereum Virtual Machine (EVM). Consequently, optimistic roll-ups were faster to launch EVM compatibility and attracted higher DeFi adoption. However, the optimistic fraud-proof mechanism can lead to delays in withdrawals. Currently, most optimistic rollups enforce a 7-day challenge period.

ZK-Rollup. In contrast, ZK-rollups [6] leverage ZKPs to validate the state on L1 immediately after a proof has been generated off-chain by *provers* and submitted to *verifiers*. Verifiers, smart contracts on L1, validate transactions aggregated by the sequencer and confirm their correctness. Consequently, rapid finality is ensured, albeit for increased computational costs. ZK-rollups also offer enhanced compression opportunities, e.g. by posting to L1 only ZKPs instead of all transaction data.

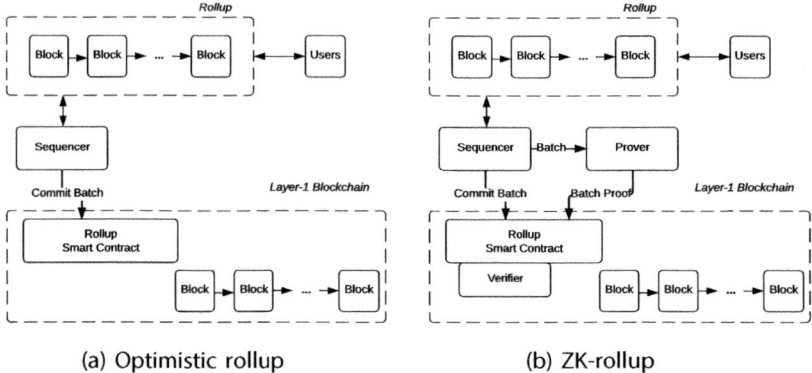

Fig. 1. High-level architecture of rollups

3 Model

Our model comprises n blockchains: Ethereum and its rollups. Each blockchain has an identical AMM deployed with the liquidity pool of the same two cryptocurrencies and the same configuration.

- Each liquidity pool i has a different TVL_i and trading volume Vol_i. The trading fees f are the same for each pool, and the total fees of the pool earned by LP are $fees_i := f \cdot Vol_i$.
- Each liquidity pool i consists of the same tokens and consequently has the same impermanent loss (IL).
- Blockchains vary in gas fees and block production times.

In our model, we also consider that LPs have the possibility to stake and earn the staking rewards r. We consider the staking rate r_s to be similar to the risk-free rate in traditional finance. Consequently, we assume that if liquidity pools do not provide higher rewards than the staking r_s, the LP reallocates her wealth to staking. Given that, within the Ethereum ecosystem, the volume of capital allocated to staking vastly exceeds that which is locked within liquidity pools [17], we assume that the staking rate remains unaffected by staked capital in our model.

3.1 Constant Product Market Maker

Liquidity provider aims to optimize her earnings, which are directly related to the capital w_i she contributes to the liquidity pool on blockchain i with total value locked TVL_i and total fees earned $fees_i$. The earnings for LP are calculated as follows:

$$\frac{w_i}{\text{TVL}_i + w_i} fees_i = \frac{w_i}{\text{TVL}_i + w_i} f \cdot \text{Vol}_i \quad (1)$$

Thus, the return rate of LP on fees for allocating w_i capital to the liquidity pool on blockchain i is:

$$r_i(w_i) = \frac{f \cdot \text{Vol}_i}{\text{TVL}_i + w_i} \quad (2)$$

Returns, as presented by DEX aggregators and the GUI of AMM-DEX, are $r_i(0)$. In order to calculate the LP return, impermanent loss (IL) must be deduced from $r_i(0)$.

3.2 Concentrated Liquidity Market Maker (CLMM)

Uniswap (v3) enables LPs to define the price range within which liquidity is supplied, thereby enhancing capital efficiency. Consequently, LPs accrue fees solely on the capital allocated to the specific tick where swaps occur. To compare the ETH-USDC pools on Uniswap (v3) across Ethereum and its rollups, each with its unique liquidity concentrations, we evaluate the profitability per unit of ambient (unbounded) liquidity and seek equilibrium conditions that equalize their returns.

Thus, the return of LP for allocating w_i capital (unbounded) to the pool on the blockchain i is the following:

$$r_i(w_i) = \frac{f \cdot \text{Vol}_i}{\text{TVL}_i^j + \frac{w_i}{m}}. \quad (3)$$

where TVL_i^j is the liquidity in the current tick j and m is the number of ticks

3.3 Optimal Allocation

Assume there is one LP. We denote by w_0 the amount of capital allocated to staking at the staking rate r_s and for $i = 1, \ldots, n$ we denote w_i as the capital allocated to liquidity pool i. We are looking for a vector $\mathbf{w} = (w_0, w_1, \ldots, w_n)$ that maximizes LP's earnings. We assume that the LP has total liquidity W to allocate to staking and AMM pools. By allocating w_0 to staking, the return from staking is $r_s w_0$.

Given an allocation vector $\mathbf{w}$, the total earnings for the LP are $r_s w_0 + \sum_{i=1}^{n} r_i(w_i) w_i$. The LP's objective is to maximize his earnings, that is, she faces the following optimization problem (using Eq. (2)):

$$\max_{\mathbf{w}=(w_0,\ldots,w_n)} r_s w_0 + \sum_{i=1}^{n} \frac{w_i}{\text{TVL}_i + w_i} f \cdot \text{Vol}_i \quad (4)$$

subject to $w_i \geq 0$ for each $i = 0, \ldots, n$ and $\sum_{i=0}^{n} w_i = W$.

Incorporating impermanent loss into the above model can easily be done by increasing the reference rate r_s with the rate of impermanent loss, as each liquidity pool incurs an equal impermanent loss.

Proposition 1. *The allocation vector* $\mathbf{w} = (w_0, \ldots, w_n)$ *with*

$$w_i = TVL_i(\sqrt{r_i(0)r_s^{-1}} - 1), \quad i = 1, \ldots, n \tag{5}$$

and $w_0 = W - \sum_{i=1}^{n} w_i$ *is the solution to* (4) *and maximizes LP's earnings.*

Proof. We define the Lagrangian $\mathcal{L}(\mathbf{w}, \lambda) = r_s w_0 + \sum_{i=1}^{n} \frac{f \cdot Vol_i}{TVL_i + w_i} w_i + \lambda (W - \sum_{i=0}^{n} w_i)$ where $w_i \geq 0$ and $\sum_{i=0}^{n} w_i = W$. Taking the derivatives with respect to w_0, w_i, and λ, and solving yields the optimal conditions (5). □

3.4 Convergence

Assume now that there are m independent and identical LPs that invest into the staking and AMMs consecutively. Each action of an LP changes the return rates of the AMMs. Based on these changes other LPs will take action accordingly. In particular, an allocation of capital to a pool increases its TVL and thereby decreases the rate of return, see Eq. (2). If LPs allocate their capital consecutively, the rate of return of each pool will decrease until it reaches r_s. Once each pool reaches r_s, the remaining LPs will invest into staking. Formally, we have the following convergence result. Let r_i^j be the rate of return for pool i, after $j - 1$ LPs have invested their capital. Note that after each investment by an LP, the respective pool's TVLs increase by that amount.

Proposition 2. *Assuming m LPs that consecutively invest into the staking and AMMs following* (5). *The rate of return from each pool converges to the staking rate* r_s. *In particular,* $r_i^m(0) \xrightarrow{m \to \infty} r_s$ *for all* $i = 1, \ldots, n$.

Proof. LPs and let the LPs invest consecutively. The rate of return can be simplified using Proposition 1. In particular, $r_i^j(w_i^j) = \sqrt{r_i^{j-1}(0)}\sqrt{r_s}$ Note that the latter is independent of w_i^j and the convergence result follows $j = m$. □

Example 1. We illustrate in Fig. 2 and Fig. 3 the convergence result from Proposition 2 for one AMM and $m = 8$ LPs. We assume a given wealth of $W = 10'000'000$ per LP, a staking rate of $r_s = 3.42\%$, a fee value $f = 1$, Vol = $400'000$ and TVL = $4'000'000$. The LPs sequentially allocate their funds to the AMM and/or to staking.

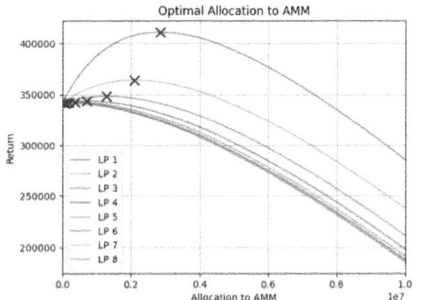
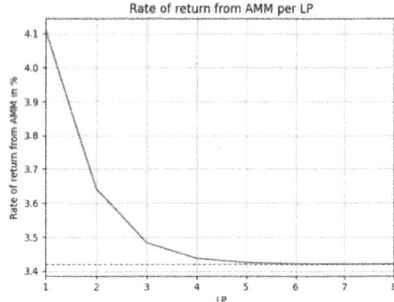

Fig. 2. Optimal allocation for each LP (sequential allocation).

Fig. 3. Rate of return of the AMM converges to the staking rate r_s

3.5 Modeling Volume Dynamics

We introduce a parameter for volume elasticity [20], denoted by ϵ_v. The elasticity parameter captures how sensitive trading activity is to changes in liquidity. The trading volume follows the functional form

$$\text{Vol} = k \cdot \text{TVL}^{\epsilon_v}, \tag{6}$$

where k is a scaling constant. This form is particularly motivated because deeper liquidity pools (i.e. pools with higher liquidity) reduce price impact and slippage, incentivizing larger trades.

- $\epsilon_v > 1$: Highly elastic volume, where trading activity increases significantly as liquidity grows.
- $\epsilon_v \leq 1$: Inelastic volume, where trading volume grows slower than liquidity.

Following the previously introduced notation, the LP's objective is to maximize their earnings:

$$\max_{\mathbf{w}=(w_0,\ldots,w_n)} r_s w_0 + \sum_{i=1}^{n} f \cdot k_i \cdot (\text{TVL}_i + w_i)^{\epsilon_v - 1} w_i \tag{7}$$

subject to $w_i \geq 0$ for each $i = 0, \ldots, n$ and $\sum_{i=0}^{n} w_i = W$. Note that we replaced Vol_i with (6), considering that the LP's contribution w_i to pool i must be added to TVL_i.

Proposition 3. *The allocation vector* $\mathbf{w} = (w_0, w_1, \ldots, w_n)$ *which solves*

$$w_i = \left(\frac{r_s}{fk_i(TVL_i + \epsilon_v w_i)}\right)^{\frac{1}{\epsilon_v - 2}} - TVL_i, \quad i = 1, \ldots, n, \tag{8}$$

and $w_0 = W - \sum_{i=1}^{n} w_i$, is the solution to the optimization problem (7) and maximizes LP's earnings. For w_i small with respect to TVL_i, the above equation can be approximated:

$$w_i \approx \left(\frac{r_s}{fk_i TVL_i}\right)^{\frac{1}{\epsilon_v - 2}} - TVL_i, \quad i = 1, \ldots, n. \tag{9}$$

Proof. The proof is included in Appendix A.

The optimal allocation can be numerically calculated using (8). An approximate result for small w_i is given in (9).

Convergence. Assume m identical independent LPs invest sequentially into staking and AMM pools. An allocation of capital to a pool increases its TVL and reduces the rate of return. The rate of return for pool i after $j-1$ LPs have invested is given by:

$$r_i^j(w_i^j) = f \cdot k_i \cdot (\text{TVL}_i^{j-1} + w_i^j)^{\epsilon_v - 1}. \tag{10}$$

Proposition 4. *For $\epsilon_v < 1$, the return from each pool converges to the staking rate r_s as $m \to \infty$. That is, $r_i^m(w_i^m) \to r_s$ as $m \to \infty$ for all $i = 1, \ldots, n$.*

Proof. As LPs invest sequentially, the TVL for each pool increases, which decreases the marginal return $r_i^j(w_i^j)$ in (10). When $r_i^j(w_i^j) \leq r_s$, no rational LP will add more liquidity to that pool, preferring staking instead. Thus, the return from all AMM pools stabilizes at r_s in the limit $m \to \infty$.

Note that if $\epsilon_v > 1$, increasing TVL increases the return instead of reducing it. As more LPs enter, trading volume scales more than liquidity, leading to increasing LP rewards rather than convergence to r_s. This creates a self-reinforcing effect, where AMM pools can keep attracting liquidity as returns remain high, contradicting the equilibrium assumption. This implies that LPs should always prefer AMM liquidity over staking when $\epsilon_v > 1$, as staking will always yield lower returns. For $\epsilon_v = 1$, the rates of return are constant for each pool.

4 Empirical Analysis

Data. For our empirical analysis, we focus on the WETH-USDC pools on Uniswap v3, as they exhibit the highest trading volume and TVL. Additionally, we always examine the WETH-USDC pool on Ethereum and across each L2 to ensure that all LPs are exposed to the same market risks. We collect on-chain data for every swap in these pools, covering the period from 2023 to the first half of 2024. The analysis includes Ethereum and its EVM-compatible L2s, specifically optimistic rollups such as Arbitrum, Optimism, and Base, as well as a ZK-rollups—ZKsync. For Arbitrum, we analyze pools with native USDC and bridged USDC.e against WETH. The Arbitrum pool with bridged USDC.e we

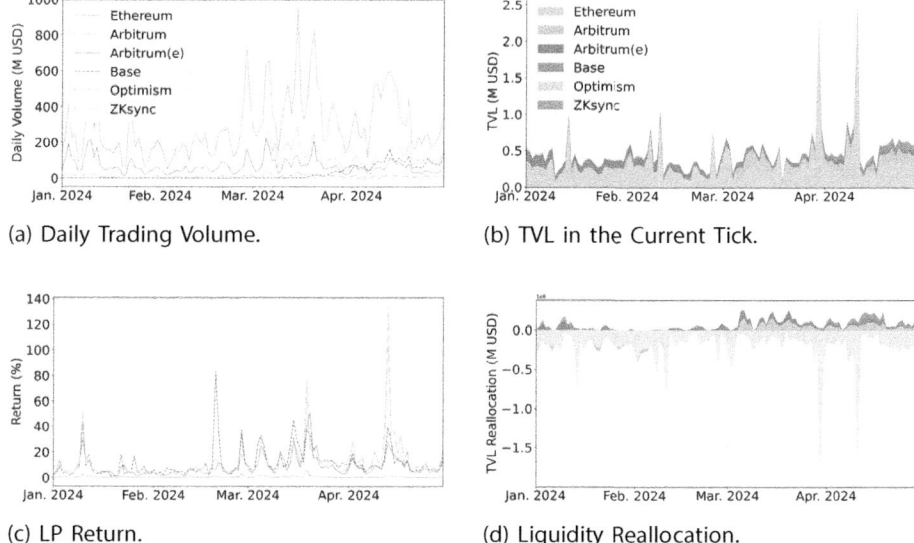

Fig. 4. Overview of WETH-USDC liquidity pools on Uniswap (v3) across Ethereum and its rollups: trading volume, TVL in the current tick and LP returns. The last chart illustrates the reallocation of liquidity required to attain equilibrium. Liquidity that is not allocated to any pool is directed towards staking.

further denote as Arbitrum (e). LP fee in these pools is 5bps, with the exception of ZKsync pool with 20bps. The trading volume in these pools is shown in Fig. 4a.

Methodology. For each day and each pool, we find the last swap and, based on the liquidity and current tick, we calculate TVL in the current tick, shown in Fig. 4b. Then, we calculate the returns of the AMM pool based on the TVL in the current tick using Eq. (3) and the optimal allocation using Eq. (5). We also assume that the LP provides liquidity in ticks around 12% of the current spot price and, based on the finding of Adams [2], the liquidity concentration is 75% higher on L2s compared to Ethereum. The annualized return of such LP position is depicted in Fig. 4c.

Empirical Calibration. To model the relationship between trading volume and TVL in liquidity pools, we use the function defined in Eq. (6). To estimate the parameters k and ϵ_v, we apply a logarithmic transformation to linearize the equation:

$$\log(\text{Vol}) = \log(k) + \epsilon_v \log(\text{TVL}), \quad (11)$$

which can be expressed as a linear regression model $y = a + bx$ where $y = \log(\text{Vol})$, $x = \log(\text{TVL})$, $a = \log(k)$, and $b = \epsilon_v$.

Table 1. Elasticity analysis across Ethereum and selected rollups. ϵ_v represents the elasticity coefficient, k the scaling constant, R^2 the goodness-of-fit, and SE denotes standard errors for ϵ_v and k.

Chain	Elasticity (ϵ_v)	Scaling constant (k)	R^2	SE(ϵ_v)	SE(k)
Ethereum	−0.121	3.05e+09	0.012	0.101	2.091
Arbitrum	−0.177	3.95e+09	0.039	0.118	2.348
Arbitrum (e)	−0.143	9.19e+08	0.010	0.128	2.488
Base	1.045	0.118	0.895	0.033	0.539
Optimism	-0.178	2.37e+08	0.026	0.100	1.757
ZKsync	0.654	4.701	0.556	0.054	0.746

4.1 Interpretation of Elasticity and Scaling Constant Results

Table 1 presents the estimated elasticity of volume with respect to virtual TVL and the scaling constant for six different chains. These metrics are derived from a log-log regression model that captures the relationship between TVL and trading volume. The key insights from the results are discussed below.

The elasticity of volume with respect to TVL for Ethereum is estimated to be −0.12. This suggests that, contrary to expectations, an increase in TVL on Ethereum is associated with a slight decrease in trading volume. However, the scaling constant indicates a high baseline volume relative to TVL, suggesting that Ethereum has a significant trading volume regardless of TVL changes. Both Arbitrum and Arbitrum (e) pools exhibit negative elasticity values. These results imply that an increase in TVL leads to a decrease in trading volume on these chains. The scaling constants indicate that Arbitrum has a higher baseline volume compared to Arbitrum (e). Optimism displays a negative elasticity, similar to Arbitrum. The scaling constant for Optimism indicates a lower baseline volume compared to Arbitrum and Ethereum. Yet, the R^2 values are for these chains remain low.

Base shows a positive elasticity value of 1.05, indicating that a 1% increase in TVL is associated with a 1.05% increase in trading volume. The scaling constant for Base is 0.12, which is significantly lower than other chains, suggesting that Base has a lower baseline trading volume. ZKsync also exhibits a positive elasticity value of 0.65, indicating that trading volume is positively correlated with TVL on this chain. The scaling constant for zkSync is 4.70, suggesting a relatively modest baseline volume compared to the other chains.

The elasticity results highlight the variability in the relationship between TVL and trading volume across different chains. While Base and ZKsync—new blockchains (launched in 2023) with new deployments of Uniswap (v3) show positive elasticities, suggesting that TVL growth drives volume, Ethereum, Arbitrum, and Optimism—well established and older chains - show negative elasticities with low R^2 values indicating that the relation between TVL and Vol-

Table 2. Calculations results for the new LP to the pools on Ethereum and its L2s on 30th April 2024: TVL in the current tick after the last swap of the day, the daily traded volume, and the annualized return of the pools. Further, the optimal allocation for the new LP assuming the staking rate of ETH equal to 3.47%. The last column presents the returns for the LP, based on the given allocations. There is no allocation into the pool on Ethereum, as the return is below staking rate.

Chain	TVL	Daily Volume	Return (%)	Allocation	LP Return (%)
Ethereum	219,361.63	344,883,212.09	3.03	–	–
Arbitrum	87,534.74	145,128,466.78	13.43	84,699.60	6.62
Arbitrum(e)	38,322.85	58,601,891.49	12.33	33,913.61	6.36
Base	68,627.34	142,939,078.94	17.16	83,973.61	7.38
Optimism	6,147.50	16,156,525.13	22.12	9,372.02	8.24
ZKsync	103.96	26,430.69	16.72	124.26	7.30

Fig. 5. The optimal redistribution of current liquidity among blockchains and with the staking rate to attain equilibrium as of 30th April. The source liquidity is the current tick within the Ethereum Uniswap (v3) WETH-USCD pool ($315k) and corresponding target pools are: Ethereum ($102k), Base ($83.9k), Arbitrum ($84.7k), Arbitrum(e) ($33.9k), Optimism, ($9.4k), and ZKsync ($0.8k).

ume cannot be easily established. This can be attributed to differences in user behavior, liquidity distribution, or (lack of) protocol incentives on these chains. Arbitrum and Optimism were launched in 2021, and Ethereum in 2015.

4.2 Interpretation of Optimal Allocation Results

Table 2 presents the calculated results for the new LP willing to allocate $212k liquidity among the pools on Ethereum and its L2s on 30th April 2024, assuming 3.47% staking rate of ETH. If the new LP would possess more liquidity, the additional liquidity should be allocated to staking. If the LP would possess less liquidity, it should be allocated to the pools with the highest rewards first. The first observation is that the AMM pool on Ethereum is oversubscribed with a return rate lower than the staking rate. Thus, the current LPs would yield higher returns by reallocating their capital to L2s, or to staking. Second, the highest return presents the pool on Optimism—22.12%, however, given the trading volume on Optimism, the highest capital allocation in optimal LP strategy is achieved for the pools on Arbitrum and BASE, approx. 80k USD. The returns of LP after allocating capital to the pools on L2s are presented in the last column of Table 2 and ranges between 6 and 8.5%, significantly lower compared to the current returns of 12 to 22%.

The optimal allocation formula can be is applied to identify the optimal allocation of current liquidity that is deployed to Uniswap (v3) pools across Ethereum and rollups. This is achieved by allowing the negative allocations and assuming a initial LP wealth of 0. Figure 4a illustrates the re-allocation of liquidity among pools to attain equilibrium. The results indicate that the present allocation of liquidity to Ethereum is excessively high and should be redistributed to pools on alternative chains and towards staking.

More detailed analysis is depicted in Fig. 5 for 30th April 2024. It presents that over 2/3 of current capital allocated to the current tick of the pool at Ethereum should be reallocated, mostly to pools on Arbitrum and Base. This corresponds to Fig. 4a depicting trading volumes, which are only 2–3 times higher at Ethereum than Arbitrum and Base, very low current LP returns for liquidity provision at Ethereum (below staking rated) as depicted in Fig. 4a.

5 Discussion

A key question arising from our analysis is why LPs do not reallocate their capital to AMMs on L2s or to staking. Since our methodology ensures that all selected pools share the same market risk exposure, LPs' reluctance toward L2s likely stems from security concerns, inertia, or a preference for Ethereum's infrastructure. Potential security concerns include risks associated with centralized sequencers, the upgradeability of L2 protocols, and bridging vulnerabilities. Similar risk-related preferences have been observed among AMM traders on L2s [7].

Cost of Bridging. The cost of transferring tokens between Ethereum and L2s is minimal—less than 1 basis point (0.01%) of the trade volume when intent-based interoperability protocols [8], such as Across Protocol [1], are used. For instance, in the case of a $100k transfer (as illustrated in Fig. 5), the cost would not exceed $5 per rollup, with transaction times ranging from just a few seconds to a maximum of 15 min [1]. Furthermore, gas fees on Ethereum and L2s do not pose a significant barrier to token transfers, as these costs remain low—below $2 on Ethereum and approximately $0.10 on L2s [9].

Time of Bridging. The time of transfer during which the tokens cannot earn LP fees lasts only seconds (up to 15 min), as bridges and intent-based interoperability protocols absorb the risk of L2 transaction not reaching the full finality on Ethereum (*hard finality*), but assume trust in the centralized sequencers and execute the transfers once the transaction in included L2 block by the sequencer (*soft finality*) [38]. Especially for optimistic rollups this approach reduces the finality time from 7 d of hard finality to 0.2–2.0s of soft finality.

Future Research. LP rewards should not only compensate for impermanent loss and the opportunity cost of not staking capital (loss-versus-staking) [13] but should also reflect the volatility of the traded assets. AMM pools with more volatile tokens should yield higher returns relative to staking than pools with less volatile pairs. This study focuses on the highly liquid WETH-USDC pool on Uniswap v3. Future research could expand the analysis to other pools, particularly those with lower liquidity or higher volatility (e.g., memecoin pools), where loss-versus-rebalancing (LVR) [25] and impermanent loss may significantly influence LP allocation decisions. A sensitivity analysis that incorporates variations in key parameters, such as TVL, trading volume, and stake rates, or an analysis of other relationships between TVL and trading volume, could provide further insight into the behavior of LP.

6 Conclusions

The question of whether L2 blockchains cause the liquidity fragmentation of Ethereum has been the subject of extensive debate. Our research indicates that such fragmentation is currently not occurring, but, it could develop in the future—particularly if LPs become aware of potentially higher returns available on L2s. Using Lagrangian optimization, we developed a model for the optimal liquidity provisions across AMMs on Ethereum and its L2s with staking as a reference rate. We showed that the returns of the AMM liquidity provision converge to the staking rate.

In addition, we modeled and measured the elasticity of trading volume with respect to TVL at the WETH-ETH pools at Uniswap (v3) across Ethereum and rollups. Our finding indicate that at the well established blockchains - Ethereum, Arbitrum and Optimism, an increase in TVL is not associated with an increase in trading volume. In contrast, emerging blockchains, Base and ZKsync, exhibit a positive elasticity value, indicating that the volume of trade is positively correlated with TVL on these chains.

Finally, we empirically compared profitability of liquidity provisions to WETH-USDC pools, and observed that the Ethereum pool, compared to corresponding pools on L2s, is oversubscribed and often yields lower returns than staking Ether. Using historical trading volumes and TVLs, we calculated the optimal liquidity allocation for the new LP as well as the optimal capital reallocation across Ethereum and L2s. Specifically, we found that more than 66% of the Ethereum liquidity could be reallocated to rollups to maximize LP returns and to achieve equilibrium with staking rates.

Acknowledgments. The authors express their gratitude to Johnnatan Messias, Malte Schlosser, Aviv Yaish and Xin Wan for their insights and feedback during the course of this research.

Portions of this research were conducted by the first and fourth authors during their tenure at Matter Labs. This research article is a work of scholarship and reflects the authors' own views and opinions. It does not necessarily reflect the views or opinions of any other person or organization, including the authors' employer. Readers should not rely on this article for making strategic or commercial decisions, and the authors are not responsible for any losses that may result from such use.

A Proof of Proposition 3

The Lagrangian function is given by:

$$\mathcal{L}(\mathbf{w}, \lambda) = r_s w_0 + \sum_{i=1}^{n} f k_i (\text{TVL}_i + w_i)^{\epsilon_v - 1} w_i + \lambda \left(W - \sum_{i=0}^{n} w_i \right).$$

Derivative w.r.t w_0:

$$\frac{\partial \mathcal{L}}{\partial w_0} = r_s - \lambda = 0.$$

Solving for λ:

$$\lambda = r_s.$$

For $i = 1, \ldots, n$:

$$\frac{\partial \mathcal{L}}{\partial w_i} = f k_i \left[(\text{TVL}_i + w_i)^{\epsilon_v - 1} + (\epsilon_v - 1)(\text{TVL}_i + w_i)^{\epsilon_v - 2} w_i \right] - \lambda = 0.$$

Substituting $\lambda = r_s$:

$$f k_i \left[(\text{TVL}_i + w_i)^{\epsilon_v - 1} + (\epsilon_v - 1)(\text{TVL}_i + w_i)^{\epsilon_v - 2} w_i \right] = r_s.$$

Factor out $(\text{TVL}_i + w_i)^{\epsilon_v - 2}$:

$$f k_i (\text{TVL}_i + w_i)^{\epsilon_v - 2} \left[(\text{TVL}_i + w_i) + (\epsilon_v - 1) w_i \right] = r_s.$$

Since

$$(\text{TVL}_i + w_i) + (\epsilon_v - 1) w_i = \text{TVL}_i + \epsilon_v w_i,$$

we rewrite the equation as:

$$f k_i (\text{TVL}_i + w_i)^{\epsilon_v - 2} (\text{TVL}_i + \epsilon_v w_i) = r_s.$$

Dividing both sides by $f k_i (\text{TVL}_i + \epsilon_v w_i)$, we get:

$$(\text{TVL}_i + w_i)^{\epsilon_v - 2} = \frac{r_s}{f k_i (\text{TVL}_i + \epsilon_v w_i)}.$$

Taking the power $\frac{1}{\epsilon_v - 2}$ on both sides:

$$\text{TVL}_i + w_i = \left(\frac{r_s}{f k_i (\text{TVL}_i + \epsilon_v w_i)} \right)^{\frac{1}{\epsilon_v - 2}}.$$

Solving for w_i:

$$w_i = \left(\frac{r_s}{fk_i(\text{TVL}_i + \epsilon_v w_i)}\right)^{\frac{1}{\epsilon_v - 2}} - \text{TVL}_i.$$

Finally, the budget constraint must hold:

$$W = w_0 + \sum_{i=1}^{n} w_i.$$

□

References

1. Across Protocol. https://across.to/, Accessed 5 February 2025
2. Adams, A.: Layer 2 be or Layer not 2 be: Scaling on Uniswap v3 (2024)
3. Adams, A., Chan, B.Y., Markovich, S., Wan, X.: The costs of swapping on the uniswap protocol. In: Financial Cryptography and Data Security (FC) (2024)
4. Adams, H., Zinsmeister, N., Robinson, D.: Uniswap v2 Core (2020)
5. Chaliasos, S., Firsov, D., Livshits, B.: Towards a Formal Foundation for Blockchain Rollups. arXiv preprint arXiv:2406.16219 (2024)
6. Chaliasos, S., Reif, I., Torralba-Agell, A., Ernstberger, J., Kattis, A., Livshits, B.: Analyzing and Benchmarking ZK-Rollups (2024)
7. Chemaya, N., Liu, D.: Estimating Investor Preferences for Blockchain Security. Available at SSRN 4119827 (2022)
8. Chitra, T., Kulkarni, K., Pai, M., Diamandis, T.: An Analysis of Intent-Based Markets. Available at arXiv arXiv:2403.02525 (2024)
9. CryptoStats: L2 Fees (2025). https://l2fees.info/, Accessed 5 February 2025
10. Fritsch, R.: Concentrated liquidity in automated market makers. In: the ACM CCS Workshop on Decentralized Finance and Security (FC-DeFi) (2021)
11. Fritsch, R., Canidio, A.: Measuring Arbitrage Losses and Profitability of AMM Liquidity (2024)
12. Gangwal, A., Gangavalli, H.R., Thirupathi, A.: A survey of layer-two blockchain protocols. J. Netw. Comput. Appli. **209** (2022)
13. Gogol, K., Fritsch, R., Schlosser, M., Messias, J., Kraner, B., Tessone, C.: Liquid staking tokens in automated market makers. In: The 5th International Conference on Mathematical Research for Blockchain Economy (Marble) (2024)
14. Gogol, K., Killer, C., Schlosser, M., Boeck, T., Stiller, B., Tessone, C.: SoK: Decentralized Finance (DeFi) - Fundamentals, Taxonomy and Risks. arXiv preprint arXiv:2404.11281 (2023)
15. Gogol, K., Messias, J., Miori, D., Tessone, C., Livshits, B.: Layer-2 Arbitrage: An Empirical Analysis of Swap Dynamics and Price Disparities on Rollups. arXiv preprint arXiv:2406.02172 (2024)
16. Gogol, K., Messias, J., Miori, D., Tessone, C., Livshits, B.: Quantifying arbitrage in automated market makers: an empirical study of ethereum ZK rollups. In: The 5th International Conference on Mathematical Research for Blockchain Economy (Marble) (2024)
17. Gogol, K., Velner, Y., Kraner, B., Tessone, C.: SoK: Liquid Staking Tokens (LSTs) and Emerging Trends in Restaking. arXiv preprint arXiv:2404.00644 (2023)

18. Heimbach, L., Schertenleib, E., Wattenhofer, R.: Risks and returns of uniswap V3 liquidity providers. In: the 4th ACM Conference on Advances in Financial Technologies (AFT) (2022)
19. Heimbach, L., Wang, Y., Wattenhofer, R.: Behavior of Liquidity Providers in Decentralized Exchanges. arXiv preprint arXiv:2105.13822v2 (2021)
20. Investopedia: What Is Elasticity in Finance (2025). https://www.investopedia.com/terms/e/elasticity.asp, Accessed 1 March 2025
21. Jensen, J., von Wachter, V., Ross, O.: An introduction to decentralized finance (DeFi). Complex Syst. Inform. Model. Q. (2021)
22. Kalodner, H., Goldfeder, S., Chen, X., Weinberg, S.M., Felten, E.W.: Arbitrum: scalable, private smart contracts. In: Proceedings of the 27th USENIX Conference on Security Symposium (2018)
23. Lashkari, B., Musilek, P.: A comprehensive review of blockchain consensus mechanisms. IEEE Access (2021)
24. Loesch, S., Hindman, N., Welch, N., Richardson, M.B.: Impermanent Loss in Uniswap v3. arXiv preprint arXiv:2111.09192 (2021)
25. Milionis, J., Moallemi, C.C., Roughgarden, T., Zhang, A.L.: Automated Market Making and Loss-Versus-Rebalancing. arXiv preprint arXiv:2208.06046v5 (2022)
26. Miori, D., Cucuringu, M.: DeFi: Modeling and Forecasting Trading Volume on Uniswap v3 Liquidity Pools. Available at SSRN 4445351 (2023)
27. Miori, D., Cucuringu, M.: Clustering uniswap v3 traders from their activity on multiple liquidity pools, via novel graph embeddings. Digital Finance, 1–31 (2024)
28. Monte, G.D., Pennino, D., Pizzonia, M.: Scaling blockchains without giving up decentralization and security. In: Proceedings of the Workshop on Cryptocurrencies and Blockchains for Distributed Systems (2020)
29. Rüetschi, M., Campajola, C., Tessone, C.J.: How do decentralized finance protocols compare to traditional financial products? a taxonomic approach. Ledger **9** (2024), review Article
30. Sguanci, C., Spatafora, R., Vergani, A.M.: Layer 2 blockchain scaling: a survey. arXiv preprint arXiv:2107.10881 (2021)
31. Thibault, L.T., Sarry, T., Hafid, A.S.: Blockchain scaling using rollups: a comprehensive survey. IEEE Access **10** (2022)
32. Thibault, L.T., Sarry, T., Hafid, A.S.: Blockchain scaling using rollups: a comprehensive survey. IEEE Access (2022)
33. Tiruviluamala, N., Port, A., Lewis, E.: A General Framework for Impermanent Loss in Automated Market Makers (2022)
34. Torres, C.F., Mamuti, A., Weintraub, B., Nita-Rotaru, C., Shinde, S.: Rolling in the Shadows: Analyzing the Extraction of MEV Across Layer-2 Rollups. arXiv preprint arXiv:2405.00138 (2024)
35. Wang, G., Shi, Z.J., Nixon, M., Han, S.: SoK: sharding on blockchain. In: Proceedings of the 1st ACM Conference on Advances in Financial Technologies (2019)
36. Xu, J., Paruch, K., Cousaert, S., Feng, Y.: SoK: decentralized exchanges (DEX) with automated market maker (AMM) protocols. ACM Computing Surv. **55**(11) (2021)
37. Yaish, A., Dotan, M., Qin, K., Zohar, A., Gervais, A.: Suboptimality in DeFi. Cryptology ePrint Archive, Paper 2023/892 (2023)
38. Yee, B., Song, D., McCorry, P., Buckland, C.: Shades of Finality and Layer 2 Scaling. arXiv preprint arXiv:2201.07920 (2022)

Quantifying Price Improvement in Order Flow Auctions

Brad Bachu[1(✉)], Xin Wan[1], and Ciamac C. Moallemi[2]

[1] Uniswap Labs, New York, USA
{brad.bachu,xin.wan}@uniswap.org
[2] Columbia University, New York, USA
ciamac@gsb.columbia.edu

Abstract. We introduce a methodology for empirically evaluating the outcomes of on-chain order flow auctions (OFAs), using price improvement as the key metric and attributing it to factors such as routing efficiency, gas optimization, and priority fee settings. The framework is agnostic to the underlying OFA mechanisms and applies to a broad range of tokens, including those not frequently traded or listed on centralized exchanges (CEXes), enabling comprehensive comparisons of OFA performance. This approach allows for real-world, on-chain evaluations of auction outcomes, providing users with insights into which OFAs perform best and how these improvements are achieved. As an example, we show how the methodology can be applied to 1Inch and Uniswap, demonstrating significant price improvements of 4–5 basis points above the Uniswap router, attributed to added liquidity in large swaps.

1 Introduction

Blockchain-based Automated Market Makers (AMMs) have achieved significant success, with Uniswap surpassing 2 trillion USD in transactions [13]. However, AMMs face challenges including fragmented liquidity and inefficiencies resulting in losses exceeding 540 million USD [17].

Order Flow Auctions (OFAs), such as 1inch Fusion [15], UniswapX [2], CowSwap [16], and MEV-Share [14] address these issues through batching, auctioning, matching orders and rebates. The general idea among all OFAs is that the profit from aforementioned inefficiencies (sometimes referred to as MEV) can be redistributed to the user by auctioning of the right to execute the order or transaction. However, empirical validation of their benefits remains challenging. Comparing prices to centralized exchanges (CEXes) is insufficient as many tokens trade only on DEXes. Cross-platform comparisons by block face selection bias—our dataset shows only 85 overlapping blocks between UniswapX and 1Inch Fusion out of 12,199 total blocks (Table 1). To enable meaningful comparisons, we propose viewing 'price improvement' relative to a consistent baseline. Our methodology decomposes price improvement into routing efficiency, gas optimization, and priority fee settings.

We demonstrate the use of the methodology on 1Inch and Uniswap on Ethereum mainnet [11] for WETH<>USDC over two months in 2023. [11][1]. We select these two as a starting point, primarily due to the similarity in OFA mechanism (Dutch auctions). In this scenario, we find that 1Inch and Uniswap provide similar improvements in trading experience.

Summary of our Contributions. In this paper, we make four main contributions:

- *Framework for Price Improvement.* We introduce a systematic approach to evaluate OFA performance through price improvement metrics, enabling consistent comparisons across different interfaces.
- *Methodology for Gas Cost Internalization.* Gas costs can account for over 90% of effective spread in small AMM trades [1]. Our framework internalizes these costs into trade prices, capturing greater variability than median benchmarks and correcting statistical bias in simulated transactions.
- *Price Improvement Attribution Model.* We attribute price improvements to controllable factors, providing actionable insights for OFA optimization.
- *Empirical Application.* Applied to Uniswap and 1Inch on Ethereum, we find that 4–5 basis points (bps) of improvements above the Uniswap router can be achieved, driven by liquidity and routing optimization.

To our knowledge, this is the first formal definition and framework for assessing price improvements in on-chain OFAs, providing granular insights into their effectiveness. Preliminary findings suggest that OFAs may outperform interfaces that rely solely on onchain data and liquidity sources.

Table 1. Overlap of blocks with transactions between WETH<>USDC during November and December of 2023.

	Uniswap Classic	Uniswap X	1Inch Aggregator	1Inch Fusion
Uniswap Classic	1800	38	9	16
Uniswap X	38	9498	43	85
1Inch Aggregator	9	43	1677	17
1Inch Fusion	16	85	17	2701

2 Literature Review

Execution quality in financial markets has been widely studied, with early work focusing on traditional equity markets. [6] reviews methods for measuring execution cost, including quoted, effective, and realized spreads, while [4] shows that

---

[1] While our framework handles batch auctions and rebate mechanisms, their empirical analysis is left for future work.

these costs can vary based on the measurement methodology. Similarly, [5] and [19] assess execution quality and costs across different US exchanges, highlighting the impact of market structure and policy changes on execution outcomes.

Additional studies have shown that execution quality is multi-dimensional. [7] emphasizes the importance of both cost and speed, while [9] explores the trade-off between these two factors. Intraday patterns further complicate execution quality, as [12] finds compensatory patterns between cost and speed in Nasdaq trades.

Price improvement, a key aspect of execution quality, is also shaped by factors such as payment for order flow and broker competition. [3] explores instances where orders are executed at prices better than quoted, while [18] introduces a theory in which price improvements vary with customer market power. [10] documents differences in price improvement across asset classes, particularly in markets where payment for order flow plays a role.

In the context of decentralized finance, [1] reports that effective spreads on Uniswap are comparable to those in traditional asset classes. However, this study does not account for cross-platform comparisons or the specific impact of gas costs. [20] and [8] further investigate liquidity strategies and execution costs in decentralized markets, but these studies stop short of offering a comprehensive comparison of OFA systems.

To our knowledge, no existing framework systematically compares execution quality across decentralized platforms, particularly when factoring in gas costs and price improvement. This paper bridges this gap by introducing a formal methodology to evaluate OFA performance across platforms and analyze execution quality, taking into account the unique mechanics of decentralized trading

3 Theoretical Framework

We aim to define 'price' and 'price improvement' consistently across OFA systems, where transaction costs (gas fees) are the primary differentiator. While some OFAs internalize gas fees, others require upfront user payment. Direct comparisons are complicated because gas fees may be denominated differently than input tokens, with unclear exchange rates for conversion. Ignoring gas fees leads to inaccurate price comparisons, as they can determine OFA performance differences.

We aim to define 'price' and 'price improvement' consistently across OFA systems, where transaction costs (gas fees) are the primary differentiator. While some OFAs internalize gas fees, others require upfront user payment. Direct comparisons are complicated because gas fees may be denominated differently than input tokens, with unclear exchange rates for conversion. Ignoring gas fees leads to inaccurate price comparisons, as they can determine OFA performance differences.

Our methodology applies to transactions where either input or output token is the gas token (ETH) or its wrapped version (WETH), covering approximately

90% of Ethereum DEX trades[2]. This standardization allows uniform price definitions across all OFAs, regardless of their gas fee handling. In Sect. 4, we demonstrate how to apply the formalism to Dutch auction based OFAs, and leave additional empirical studies for future work.

3.1 Price

Consider a user with pre-trade balance (a, b) and post-trade balance (a', b') of tokens A and B. We define the price p as

$$p = \frac{b' - b}{a - a'}, \qquad (1)$$

where the signs reflect the increase in Token B and decrease in Token A. When a user initiates a trade with fixed input i, the price depends on three controllable variables: output amount o (optimized via routing), gas usage g (varies with transaction complexity), and priority fee f (affects transaction ordering). We express these as vector $\boldsymbol{x} = (o, g, f)$, defining price as $p(\boldsymbol{x})$. For example, trading ETH for USDC with gas cost $g(b + f)$ (where b is the base fee) gives:

$$p = \frac{o}{i + g(b + f)}. \qquad (2)$$

The price calculation varies by OFA type:

- **Traditional**: Gas costs directly affect price through ETH balance changes
- **Gas-free**: Price reflects only token exchange ratios (via Permit2)
- **MEV-aware**: Price includes potential rebates.

See Appendix A for detailed examples of each case.

3.2 Price Improvement

We define *price improvement* (π) as the relative difference between the realized price p and a baseline counterfactual price p', where p' represents the price that would have been achieved under normal conditions without an Order Flow Auction (OFA). Formally:

$$\pi(p, p') = \frac{p - p'}{p'}. \qquad (3)$$

The counterfactual baseline p' serves as a neutral reference point, enabling us to evaluate execution quality across systems by comparing realized outcomes with the baseline.

---

[2] https://dune.com/queries/3675220.

3.3 Flexibility in Generating Counterfactual Prices

The baseline serves as a reference point, much like measuring altitude relative to sea level, ground level, or another benchmark: while the chosen reference point affects absolute measurements, it does not impede the ability to make meaningful relative comparisons across different systems (if chosen correctly).

Since price p is a function of output tokens o, gas fees g, and priority fees f, a counterfactual price p' can also be generated by counterfactual values o', g', and f'. Therefore, the counterfactual price p' can be expressed as $p' = p(o', g', f') = p(\boldsymbol{x}')$, where $\boldsymbol{x}' = (o', g', f')$ represents the primed (counterfactual) values for these variables. For more detailed information on how we generate the counterfactual variables $\boldsymbol{x}'$, refer to Sect. 4.

While alternative baselines, such as CEX prices, could be considered, they would restrict the analysis by limiting available tokens and reducing attribution to factors like gas costs or liquidity routing (see Sect. 3.5), as they do not provide $\boldsymbol{x}' = (o', g', f')$.

3.4 Price Improvements Across Time

Our primary definition of price improvement π compares realized prices against counterfactual prices at the settlement time t_0. However, it is also useful to evaluate price improvement across various time offsets Δt from t_0, allowing us to account for execution speed and timing differences among OFAs. This approach is conceptually similar to markout in traditional finance, where the performance of a trade is measured relative to its price at different time intervals post-execution.

Implicit in the realized price p is the settlement time t_0, $p = p(t_0)$, but a counterfactual price $p' = p'(t)$ can be generated at any time. Thus, we extend our definition of price improvement by including the time dimension as follows $\pi(p, t_0; p', t) = \frac{p(t_0) - p'(t)}{p'(t)}$.

Since t_0 is fixed historically, the only key differences arise from offsets $\Delta t = t - t_0$. To explore this, we shift the definition by $-t_0$, treating all times relative to the settlement time. This leads to the more practical definition: $\rho(p; p', \Delta t) = \frac{p - p'(\Delta t)}{p'(\Delta t)}$, where we have dropped t_0 for simplicity. When $\Delta t = 0$, we recover our original definition of price improvement $\rho(p; p', 0) = \pi(p, t_0; p', t_0)$. This process is depicted in Sect. 1.

Evaluating price improvement across different time offsets Δt provides several benefits:

1. Transaction Speed: It helps account for potential differences in transaction inclusion speed between the actual interface and the counterfactual interface, highlighting robustness issues related to execution speed.
2. Order Filling Mechanisms: Different trading interfaces have mechanisms that affect whether or how orders are filled. By analyzing multiple offsets, we can identify and adjust for any selection biases these mechanisms may introduce.

3. **Blockchain Conditions**: The blockchain environment can be unpredictable, with gas spikes or storage issues affecting outcomes. Evaluating a range of time offsets mitigates the impact of transient conditions, ensuring more accurate results.
4. **Transaction Ordering**: On platforms like Ethereum, transaction ordering can be adversarial. Comparing against multiple counterfactual orderings reveals sensitivity to transaction ordering strategies.
5. **Interpretation Flexibility**: Depending on the context, we can compare counterfactual prices at different points in time, such as at arrival or execution, allowing for flexible interpretations of price improvement.

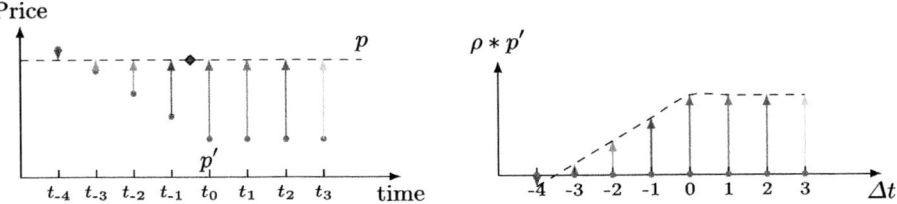

Fig. 1. On the left, we show the real transaction that occurred in the 0th block with price p, and the counterfactual transactions generated at the end of the given blocks with prices $p'(t)$. The arrows represent the differences between p and p' at different times, or the un-normalized price improvement: $\pi(p, t_0; p', t) * p'(t)$. On the right, we show the same un-normalized price improvements, however, with the x-axis now changed to relative time: $\rho(p; p', \Delta t) * p'(t)$.

3.5 PI Attribution

In our framework, price improvement π is conceptualized as an aggregated result of various controllable decisions, such as routing, gas usage, priority fee settings. To provide a more granular insight into how PI was achieved empirically, we decompose π into three economically significant components: routing optimization π^{routing}, gas optimization π^{gas}, and priority fee optimization π^{fee}

$$\pi = \pi^{\text{routing}} + \pi^{\text{gas}} + \pi^{\text{fee}}, \tag{4}$$

where π^{routing} captures the π through optimizing liquidity access, π^{gas} captures the π from reduced gas costs, and π^{fee} captures the π from lower priority fees.

Interface decision making impacts these PI components through several mechanisms:

1 **Route Optimization**: Interfaces optimize routing by selecting liquidity sources, which may include on-chain pools or off-chain sources. While more liquidity is generally better, it comes at the cost of additional gas usage. π^{routing} measures the PI achieved through including more liquidity in the route than the baseline.

2. **Gas Efficiency**: An optimal routing decision minimizes gas usage while maximizing liquidity access. π^{gas} quantifies the PI achieved through using less gas compared to the baseline.
3. **Priority Fee Setting**: Under EIP-1559, any positive priority fee is usually sufficient for inclusion, but some interfaces recommend higher priority fees for faster execution. π^{fee} measures the PI gained by minimizing the priority fee.

To attribute π, we Taylor expand the price function $p(\boldsymbol{x})$ about the baseline variables $\boldsymbol{x}'$,

$$\begin{aligned} p(\boldsymbol{x}) &= p(\boldsymbol{x}') \\ &+ \left.\frac{\partial p}{\partial o}\right|_{\boldsymbol{x}'}(o-o') + \left.\frac{\partial p}{\partial g}\right|_{\boldsymbol{x}'}(g-g') + \left.\frac{\partial p}{\partial f}\right|_{\boldsymbol{x}'}(f-f') \\ &+ R(\boldsymbol{x}, \boldsymbol{x}'), \end{aligned} \qquad (5)$$

where $R(\boldsymbol{x}, \boldsymbol{x}')$ represents the remainder term. Note that, in all the cases we consider, $p(\boldsymbol{x})$ is differentiable in the domain of interest. For example, considering the WETH/ETH out in Eq. 8, we have $\frac{\partial p}{\partial o} = \frac{1}{i}$, $\frac{\partial p}{\partial g} = \frac{-(b+f)}{i}$ and $\frac{\partial p}{\partial f} = \frac{-g}{i}$. Rearranging Eq. (5) gives us:

$$\begin{aligned} \pi &= \left.\frac{\partial p}{\partial o}\right|_{\boldsymbol{x}'}\frac{(o-o')}{p'} + \left.\frac{\partial p}{\partial g}\right|_{\boldsymbol{x}'}\frac{(g-g')}{p'} + \left.\frac{\partial p}{\partial f}\right|_{\boldsymbol{x}'}\frac{(f-f')}{p'} + \frac{R(\boldsymbol{x}, \boldsymbol{x}')}{p'} \\ &= \pi_0^{\text{routing}} \qquad\quad + \pi_0^{\text{gas}} \qquad\quad + \pi_0^{\text{fee}} \qquad\quad + \pi^{\text{rem.}}, \end{aligned} \qquad (6)$$

where the 0 subscript indicates leading order contributions. Note that every term here is a function of on-chain values $\boldsymbol{x} = (o, g, f)$ and simulated values $\boldsymbol{x}' = (o', g', f')$, and so is calculable. Of course, it is not guaranteed that remainder term $\pi^{\text{rem.}}$ is small, but we will find that for some cases, it is.

For OFAs where gas is internalized, the amount output token o that the user receives is post-fee. By using onchain data for g, b and f, we can calculate what the pre-fee output would have been, allowing us to attribute π in these cases.

4 Methodology

While our primary contribution is a theoretical framework for evaluating any OFA's price improvements, this section demonstrates its practical application to market leaders that utilize Dutch auctions, Uniswap and 1Inch, highlighting both implementation challenges and potential at scale.

4.1 Sample Interfaces

Uniswap and 1Inch interfaces each offer two execution paths. One provides traditional transactions, which are predetermined routes through public on-chain sources (Uniswap Classic and 1Inch Aggregator), whereas the other (UniswapX and 1Inch Fusion) provides intents and Dutch auction based settlement, where the liquidity can be derived from both private and public on-chain sources. The interfaces dynamically route orders to the path offering better execution. This introduces selection bias: UniswapX and Fusion trades appear to outperform because they are only chosen when advantageous. A comprehensive evaluation must therefore consider both execution paths together to understand true OFA performance in the context of overall routing decisions. These interfaces provide an ideal comparison because they share similar characteristics: Classic and Aggregator require direct gas payment in ETH, while UniswapX and Fusion internalize gas costs through specialized participants called solvers ot fillers. This parallel structure enables consistent application of our methodology while highlighting key differences in execution approaches.

4.2 Selection of Baseline

Our theory permits any baseline that can generate counterfactual values of output token, gas and priority fees. To illustrate the application of our framework, we select our baseline as a counterfactual simulated swap using the Uniswap Classic routing API at the end of the block in which the actual trade occurred, executed through three steps:

1. **Route Calculation**: Submit identical token pair and amount to the routing API, which finds optimal routes using blockchain state from surrounding blocks (n blocks before/after) for robustness
2. **Route Formation**: API assesses end-block state and pool liquidity (from The Graph), determines optimal route, and formats into calldata with gas estimates
3. **Simulation**: Execute calldata through Tenderly simulator with consistent priority fee (0.1 Gwei), obtaining gas consumption and output details

This choice is beneficial for several reasons:

1. **Assumption Test**: The price improvement (PI) of Uniswap Classic compared to itself should be zero, providing a crucial accuracy check of the baseline simulation at the end of the block.
2. **User Experience**: Provides realistic approximation of typical trading conditions, enabling meaningful comparisons between different OFAs.
3. **Token Coverage**: Uniswap's extensive pool coverage enables comprehensive analysis that can capture long-tail tokens and on-chain dynamics.
4. **Public Access**: Open API enables reproducible analysis by any third party.

The API accesses historical blockchain states, enabling simulations at different block times Sect. 3.4.

4.3 Data Collection

In this section, we describe the process of collecting the data necessary for our analysis. We focus on historical values for input amounts i, base fees per gas b, output amounts, gas used, and priority fees per gas, represented as $\boldsymbol{x} = (o, g, f)$. Counterfactual baseline values $\boldsymbol{x}' = (o', g', f')$ are generated via the Uniswap Classic routing API.

Our dataset includes all WETH-USDC trades from November and December 2023, which are sourced from Dune Analytics, and validated for Uniswap Labs from provided internal datasets. We collect transactions from Uniswap Classic and UniswapX by filtering interactions via the Uniswap Interface, and for 1Inch trades, we extract data using the `oneinch` table in Dune Analytics. To focus purely on execution quality, all interface fees are ignored (Table 2).

Table 2. Distribution of swaps and volumes across different settlement paths for 1Inch and Uniswap interfaces.

Interface	Path	Size	% Parent	Volume ($)	% Vol
1Inch	Aggregator	1687	36%	37,891,096	22%
	Fusion	2941	64%	134,221,271	78%
Uniswap	Classic	1809	16%	28,573,360	13%
	X	9607	84%	185,599,214	87%

To generate a baseline price p', we rely on API calls for historical transactions. For each block time t and input amount i, the API provides counterfactual estimates of the output token o' and gas used g'. We define a baseline function to generate counterfactual prices as $\mathcal{B}$ as $\mathcal{B} : (i, t) \rightarrow (o', g')$, with a consistent baseline priority fee per gas f' of 0.1 Gwei. For more details on counterfactual generation see Appendix A.

4.4 Baseline Gas Corrections

One key challenge in generating accurate counterfactual baselines is estimating gas usage g'. The gas estimated by simulations may not always match the actual gas used g in historical transactions. Figure 2 illustrates the difference between the simulated gas g' and the actual gas g for Uniswap Classic trades. Ideally, g' should closely match g.

Discrepancies arise due to factors like Just-In-Time (JIT) liquidity provision [20], where the actual gas used may be lower than estimated. Additionally, simulations are performed at the end of a block, while trades occur at various times within the block, leading to potential differences.

To correct for this (i.e., to address the systematic error), we apply a correction factor. By comparing g' to the actual gas g, we fit the adjustment factor (β_1) via regression: $g' \approx \beta_1 g$. We then adjust the estimate: $g' \leftarrow g'/\beta_1$. This adjustment (or calibration) reduces the gap between the simulated and actual gas usage, improving the reliability of the price improvement measurement by ensuring our estimates better reflect actual outcomes.

4.5 Uncertainty Analysis

In our analysis of price improvement π and its components $\pi_0^{\text{attribute}}$, we calculate an average value $\bar{\pi}$ weighted by the trade's USD value. This average is influenced by two sources of uncertainty: *statistical* uncertainty (which arises from variations in individual trades) and *systematic* uncertainty (which arises from potential biases in our gas estimates).

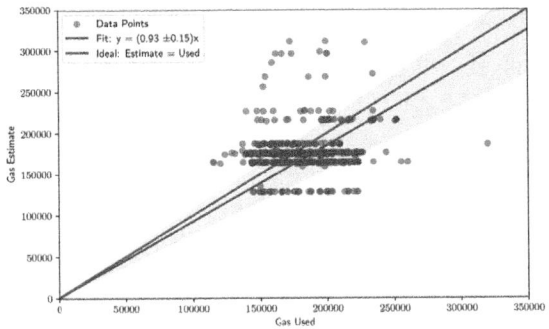

Fig. 2. Comparison between actual gas used g and estimated gas g' for Uniswap Classic transactions. The red line represents perfect gas estimation, and the green dashed line shows the corrected estimate with confidence bounds. (Color figure online)

Statistical uncertainty (σ_{stat}) is computed using the weighted standard error. For a trade i with price improvement $z_i \in \{\pi, \pi_0^{\text{attribute}}\}$ and weight w_i, we calculate:

$$\sigma_{\text{stat}}^2 = \frac{\sum_i w_i(\bar{z} - z_i)^2}{n \sum_j w_j}.$$

This gives us the uncertainty due to variability in the sample data.

Systematic uncertainty (σ_{sys}) of the gas estimation is computed by varying β_1 and calculating the bounds: $\sigma_{\text{sys}}^{\text{upper}} = \bar{z}(\beta_1 + \delta\beta_1) - \bar{z}(\beta_1)$ and $\sigma_{\text{sys}}^{\text{lower}} = \bar{z}(\beta_1) - \bar{z}(\beta_1 - \delta\beta_1)$. Note that this is an asymmetric uncertainty. Finally, we combine both sources of uncertainty into the total uncertainty for $\bar{z}$, given by $\bar{z} \pm \sqrt{\sigma_{\text{stat}}^2 + \sigma_{\text{sys}}^2}$.

4.6 Discussion and Additional Limitations

Although various factors introduce uncertainty, we find their impact to be minimal since, on average, since the price improvement of Uniswap Classic compared to itself is zero in Fig. 3. This validation suggests that while these factors exist, they do not significantly affect the average value. Several factors introduce uncertainty in both gas usage estimates g' and output token estimates o':

1. **Simulation changes**: Updates to the simulation algorithm may cause discrepancies in gas and output estimates.
2. **Intra-block effects**: Simulating at the end of the block overlooks intra-block dynamics, such as liquidity shifts and ticks crossed, which can influence gas usage and output accuracy.
3. **Self-impact**: Transactions interacting with the same liquidity pool may degrade counterfactual results due to self-induced effects, similar to front-running, impacting output token amounts.
4. **Data-integrity**: Un-validated data for 1Inch may introduce biases from indexing delays or missing transactions.

5 Results

Our analysis reveals that auction-based platforms like UniswapX and 1Inch Fusion can achieve substantial price improvements, in this case, primarily through enhanced liquidity access. Uniswap Classic shows no price improvement relative to itself, confirming the accuracy of our framework, while small correction terms validate the use of first-order approximations for most systems. Larger correction terms for auction-enhanced platforms like UniswapX suggest the need to account for higher-order effects.

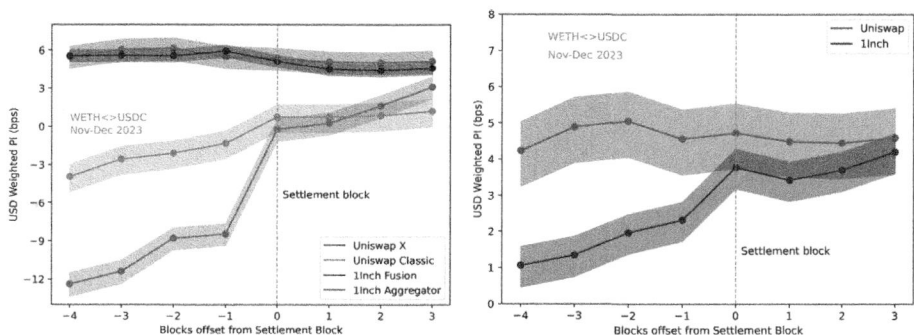

Fig. 3. USD-weighted price improvement trajectory ρ comparing Uniswap Classic, Uniswap X, 1Inch Ag- gregator, and 1Inch Fusion across time (in units of blocks) relative to settlement. The left panel shows settlement-path level decomposition, validating our methodology through Uniswap Classic's zero improvement at settlement, while the rightpanel presents interface-level aggregation revealing systematic differences in execution quality. Shaded areas indicate $\pm 1\sigma$ intervals, accounting for both statistical and systematic uncertainties

Figure 3 shows the USD-weighted price improvements across platforms at different time offsets from the settlement block. As expected, Uniswap Classic exhibits zero price improvement at settlement, confirming our methodology's accuracy in capturing where improvements exist. Both Uniswap-X and 1Inch Fusion, the Dutch auction components, show equivalent price improvements averaging 5–6 basis points. On the right, the combined result for all interface trades (which accounts for the selection bias), shows that the difference in overall performance is a result of the interfaces' traditional routing execution.

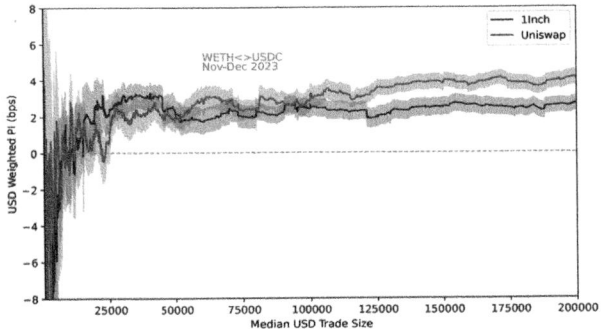

Fig. 4. Price Improvement (PI) analysis across trade sizes for Uniswap and 1Inch interfaces. The rolling USD-weighted PI demonstrates how execution quality varies with trade size, revealing distinct patterns for each interface. Larger trades show more consistent improvements, while smaller trades exhibit higher variability. Shaded areas indicate $\pm 1\sigma$ intervals, combining statistical and systematic uncertainties.

Price improvement is further analyzed by trade size in Fig. 4. While smaller trades exhibit more volatility, larger trades stabilize with consistent positive price improvement. UniswapX reaches nearly 4 basis points for trades around $200k, outperforming 1Inch Fusion as trade size increases.

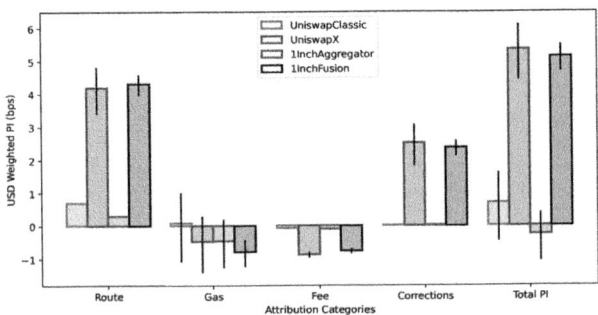

Fig. 5. Decomposition of USD-weighted price improvements across settlement paths, showing relative contributions from routing efficiency, gas optimization, and priority fee settings. The breakdown reveals that routing efficiency dominates price improvements, particularly in auction-based systems (UniswapX and 1Inch Fusion), while gas optimization plays a secondary but significant role.

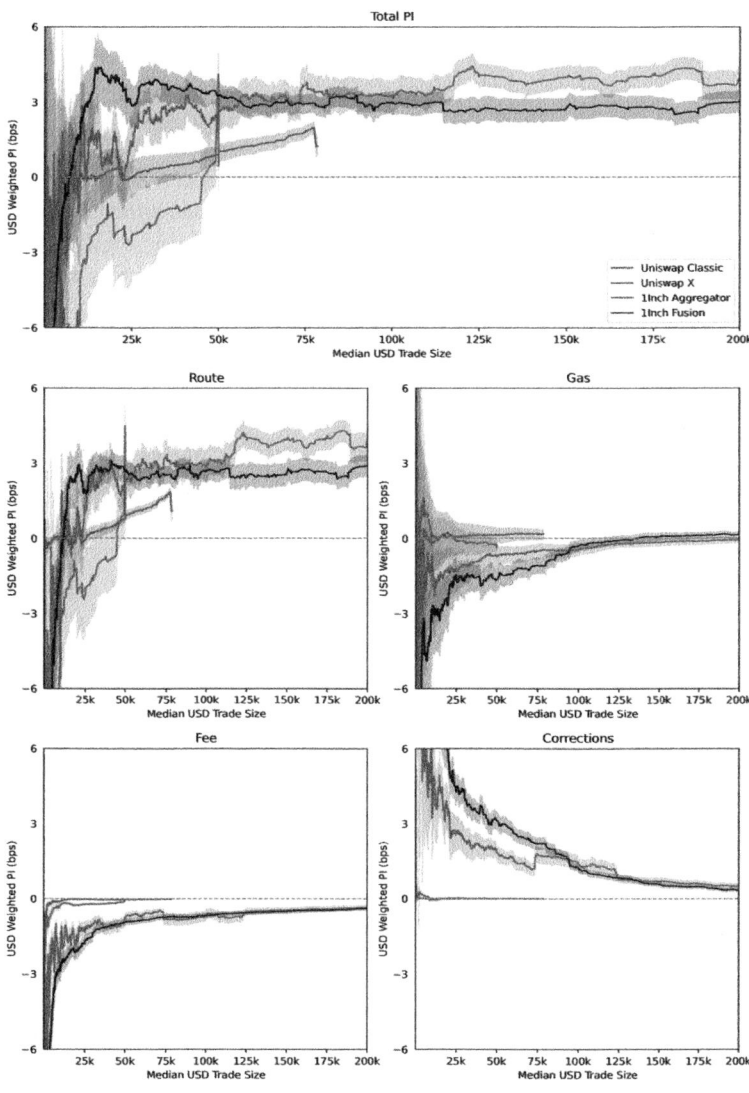

Fig. 6. Component-wise analysis of price improvement contributions across trade sizes for all settlement paths (Uniswap Classic, 1Inch Aggregator, Uniswap-X, and 1Inch Fusion). The breakdown demonstrates how different mechanisms dominate at different trade sizes, with routing efficiency becoming increasingly important for larger trades while gas optimization effects remain relatively constant. Shaded regions represent $\pm 1\sigma$ combined statistical and systematic uncertainties.

To investigate the differences, Fig. 5 and Fig. 6 provide a breakdown of price improvement into key attributes: routing efficiency, gas optimization, and priority fee settings. Routing efficiency is the dominant factor, with smaller contributions from gas and priority fees. Gas overheads (0.5-1 basis points) are observed in both UniswapX and 1Inch Fusion, though they do not outweigh the routing benefits.

To validate the approximation, we examine correction terms. For Uniswap Classic and 1Inch Aggregator, these corrections are negligible, confirming the accuracy of the first-order approximation. For UniswapX and 1Inch Fusion, larger correction terms indicate non-linear effects, particularly from gas optimization and priority fees, which can be understood by explicitly extending Eq. (6). While first-order terms capture much of the system's behavior, these corrections highlight the complexity of auction-based platforms. Note that, the differences between Uniswap Classic and 1Inch Aggreagator arise primarily from the routes, whereas the differences between Uniswap-X and 1Inch Fusion arise primarily due to the filler networks.

6 Outlook

This work provides a framework for analyzing price improvement in OFAs, with extensions to better understand transaction costs and their impact on trading outcomes. The applications of this methodology to batched auctions (COW Swap) and rebate systems (MEV Share, MEV Blocker) is left for future work. Extensions can include comparisons between fillers using private and public on-chain liquidity sources, the impact of different benchmarks to validate ordering assumptions, and investigating performance differences between OFA types.

Acknowledgements and Disclosures. Ciamac Moallemi was supported by the Briger Family Digital Finance Lab at Columbia Business School and is an advisor to fintech companies.

A Price Details

Realized and counterfactual prices depend on if gas is/not internalized and if the input token is/not WETH. **Realized prices:** For traditional transactions where gas is not internalized, we have two cases,

$$p = \begin{cases} \frac{o-g(b+f)}{i}, & \text{when token out address = WETH/ETH} \\ \frac{o}{i+g(b+f)}, & \text{when token in address = WETH/ETH} \end{cases} . \quad (7)$$

For modern OFAs using Permit2 signatures[3] enable gas-free user experiences, $p = \frac{o}{i}$. For systems involving MEV rebates, the price is similar to traditional transactions but adjusted for the rebate. **Counterfactual prices:** As mentioned before, the baseline function generates quotes $\mathcal{B}(i) \to (o', g')$. When the API is

---

[3] https://blog.uniswap.org/permit2-and-universal-router.

given an input i, it can generate a token out amount estimate o', and gas use estimate g'. When the gas is not internalized, we compute p' as

$$p' = \begin{cases} \frac{o' - g'(b+f')}{i}, & \text{when token out address} = \text{WETH/ETH} \\ \frac{o'}{i + g'(b+f')}, & \text{when token in address} = \text{WETH/ETH} \end{cases} \quad (8)$$

When gas is internalized, we compute a token in amount gas adjusted $i' = i - g'(b+f')$, we define the following $\mathcal{B}(i') = (o'', g'')$, and

$$p' = \begin{cases} \frac{o' - g'(b+f')}{i}, & \text{when token out address} = \text{WETH/ETH} \\ \frac{o''}{i' + g'(b+f')}, & \text{when token in address} = \text{WETH/ETH} \end{cases} \quad (9)$$

Note that the denominator is just i, but we have written it in a way that allows us to estimate the amount of input token that you have available to route i', and the amount that you must pay in gas $g'(b+f')$. The amount of token that you have available to route is then used to generate the token out amount estimate o''.

References

1. Adams, A., Chan, B.Y., Markovich, S., Wan, X.: The costs of swapping on the uniswap protocol. arXiv preprint arXiv:2309.13648 (2023)
2. Adams, H.: Introducing the uniswapx protocol (2023). https://blog.uniswap.org/uniswapx-protocol
3. Angel, J.: Who gets price improvement on the nyse (1994)
4. Bessembinder, H.: Issues in assessing trade execution costs. J. Finan. Markets **6**(3), 233–257 (2003)
5. Bessembinder, H.: Trade execution costs and market quality after decimalization. J. Finan. Quant. Anal. **38**(4), 747–777 (2003)
6. Bessembinder, H., Venkataraman, K.: Bid-ask spreads: measuring trade execution costs in financial markets. In: Encyclopedia of Quantitative Finance, pp. 184–190 (2010)
7. Boehmer, E.: Dimensions of execution quality: recent evidence for us equity markets. J. Financ. Econ. **78**(3), 553–582 (2005)
8. Capponi, A., Jia, R., Zhu, B.: The paradox of just-in-time liquidity in decentralized exchanges: more providers can sometimes mean less liquidity. Available at SSRN (2023)
9. Engle, R.F., Ferstenberg, R., Russell, J.R.: Measuring and modeling execution cost and risk (2006)
10. Ernst, T., Spatt, C.S.: Payment for order flow and asset choice. Technical report, National Bureau of Economic Research (2022)
11. Flashbots: Orderflow.art. https://orderflow.art/frontends
12. Garvey, R., Wu, F.: Intraday time and order execution quality dimensions. J. Financ. Markets **12**(2), 203–228 (2009)
13. Uniswap Labs (2024). https://x.com/Uniswap/status/1776218671058239621
14. Miller, B.: MEV-share: programmably private orderflow to share MEV with users (2023). https://collective.flashbots.net/t/mev-share-programmably-private-orderflow-to-share-mev-with-users/1264

15. 1inch Network: The 1inch network releases a major upgrade, fusion (2022). https://blog.1inch.io/the-1inch-network-releases-a-major-upgrade-fusion/
16. CoW Protocol: General FAQ. https://swap.cow.fi/#/faq
17. Qin, K., Zhou, L., Gervais, A.: Quantifying blockchain extractable value: how dark is the forest? In: 2022 IEEE Symposium on Security and Privacy (SP), pp. 198–214. IEEE (2022)
18. Rhodes-Kropf, M.: Price improvement in dealership markets. J. Bus. **78**(4), 1137–1172 (2005)
19. Wah, E., Feldman, S., Chung, F., Bishop, A., Aisen, D., Exchange, I.: A comparison of execution quality across us stock exchanges. In: Global Algorithmic Capital Markets: High Frequency Trading, Dark Pools, and Regulatory Challenges, pp. 91–146 (2017)
20. Wan, X., Adams, A.: Just-in-time liquidity on the uniswap protocol. Available at SSRN 4382303 (2022)

Short Paper: Atomic Execution is Not Enough for Arbitrage Profit Extraction in Shared Sequencers

Maria Inês Silva[2,3](✉) [iD] and Benjamin Livshits[1] [iD]

[1] Imperial College London, London, UK
[2] NOVA Information Management School, Lisbon, Portugal
misilva73@gmail.com
[3] Matter Labs, Berlin, Germany

Abstract. There has been a growing interest in shared sequencing solutions, in which transactions for multiple rollups are processed together. Their proponents argue that these solutions allow for better composability and can potentially increase sequencer revenue by enhancing MEV extraction. However, little research has been done on these claims, raising the question of understanding the actual impact of shared sequencing on arbitrage profits, the most common MEV strategy in rollups. To address this, we develop a model to assess arbitrage profits under atomic execution across two Constant Product Market Marker liquidity pools and demonstrate that switching to atomic execution does not always improve profits. We also discuss some scenarios where atomicity may lead to losses, offering insights into why atomic execution may not be enough to convince arbitrageurs and rollups to adopt shared sequencing.

Keywords: Sequencers · Atomic Execution · Arbitrage · MEV · Rollups

1 Introduction

Decentralized Finance (DeFi) has been essential to the growth of the Ethereum ecosystem, attracting many users and successful applications. Recently, it has expanded to Layer-2 (L2) scaling solutions like rollups, where trading volumes are rising, with some rollups now experiencing more daily activity than Ethereum itself [4]. With this growth in adoption comes more opportunities for Maximal-Extractable Value (MEV)—a collection of techniques for extracting value from transaction inclusion and reordering [3]. One of the most prevalent forms of MEV on rollups is arbitrage, in which arbitrageurs exploit price differences between centralized exchanges and/or Decentralized Exchanges (DEXs) [14,15].

A relevant consideration for MEV in rollups is *sequencer design*. The sequencer is the operator responsible for receiving and scheduling user transactions for processing, and most rollups currently use an independent centralized sequencer [8]. Recent proposals have introduced an alternative—shared

---

Some of this work was performed while the authors were at Matter Labs.

sequencers. Shared sequencing schemes propose to process transactions for multiple rollups together, allowing for better composability between rollups. Despite being a recent topic, Astria [1] already has a solution in production, while Radius [11], NodeKit [9], and Expresso Systems [12] are in the test phase. However, we have not yet seen significant adoption from rollups.

Proponents of shared sequencing argue that it can enhance MEV extraction in cross-rollup arbitrage, thus adding a potential for increased revenue for rollups. Arbitrageurs can already execute cross-rollup arbitrage by submitting independent transactions to each rollup. However, this strategy involves additional liquidity and currency risk costs.

In this context, shared sequencing offers two relevant properties for arbitrageurs: *atomic execution* and *atomic bridging*. Atomic execution allows an arbitrageur to bundle two swaps (one for each rollup) and have the guarantee that if one of the swaps reverts, the other will also revert. This property requires control over block-building on the rollups running full nodes of the rollups to guarantee execution validity. Atomic bridging goes further by allowing for bridge operations between rollups, eliminating the need for liquidity across different chains. An arbitrageur can take a flash loan on one rollup, swap tokens, bridge them to another rollup for the second swap, and then bridge the tokens back to repay the loan. Yet, this property is significantly more challenging to achieve and requires additional trust assumptions on the shared sequencing infrastructure.

With the added complexities of implementing atomic bridging, in this work, we aim to understand how arbitrage profits can be impacted by a shared sequencing solution that only provides atomic execution. Even though this property seems intuitively beneficial for arbitrageurs, we argue this is not always true. In fact, atomic execution is insufficient to consistently improve MEV extraction for arbitrageurs and therefore to increase revenue for sequencers.

Concretely, we build a model to assess the difference in terms of the expected arbitrage profit of switching to a shared sequencing regime with atomic execution. Here, we consider a cross-rollup arbitrage between two Constant Product Market Maker (CPMM) liquidity pools and compute the expected profit obtained by the arbitrageur given key parameters such as the prices in the pools and the probabilities of failure of the swaps. Then, we analyze how this difference in expected profit changes with these parameters and conclude that an arbitrageur does not always benefit from atomic execution. We also discuss and provide some intuition as to why atomic execution leads to losses in some particular cases.

These results are consistent with previous work from Mamageishvili and Schlegel [6], in which they consider how atomic execution impacts arbitrageurs' latency competition and their incentives to invest in latency. Interestingly, they observe that in a regime where transaction order and inclusion is determined through bidding, the revenue of shared sequencing is not always higher than that of separate sequencing and depends on the transaction ordering rule applied and the arbitrage value potentially realized.

2 Modelling Arbitrage Extraction

Before describing the model to estimate the impact of atomic execution for cross-rollup arbitrage, we must define some concepts and variables.

2.1 Preliminaries

We begin by assuming that an arbitrageur identifies an opportunity to arbitrage the pools of the X-Y token pair in two different rollups, A and B. The arbitrage opportunity is identified at the end of the last sequenced block of each rollup. At this time, the X-Y pool in rollup A has a price of P_A and token reserves of (x_A, y_A), while the same pool in rollup B has a price of P_B and token reserves of (x_B, y_B). Note that we are considering prices denominated in token Y. In other words, $P_A = y_A/x_A$ and $P_B = y_B/x_B$. Without loss of generality, let's assume that $P_A > P_B$.

We further assume that the arbitrageur maintains liquidity on both rollups, which is kept in the target tokens X and Y. Concretely, the arbitrageur's liquidity is $L^X = L_A^X + L_B^X$ (for token X) and $L^Y = L_A^Y + L_B^Y$ (for token Y). We can value the total liquidity of the arbitrageur in units of token Y using an external price P_{ext}, and thus, $L = L^Y + L^X \cdot P_{\text{ext}}$. Note that P_{ext} is a theoretical price representing how the arbitrageur values its liquidity. It can be thought of as the price coming from an external source (e.g. an exchange or an oracle) or the price the arbitrage experiences when they settle their liquidity in a future time.

In practice, arbitrageurs do not maintain their liquidity in different tokens, preferring to hedge currency risk by only holding stable tokens such as USDC. In our case, this would mean maintaining liquidity in the stable token and converting back and forth between the target tokens (X and Y) and the stable token. However, looking at the impact on liquidity for the target tokens allows for a simpler model while distilling the key aspects of how atomicity impacts arbitrage profit extraction across different scenarios.

In this setup, the arbitrageur will perform two swaps (one in each rollup) to extract this arbitrage opportunity:

- Swap S_B in rollup B: Pay Δy_B units of token Y and receive Δx_B units of token X in rollup B.
- Swap S_A in rollup A: Pay Δx_A units of token X and receive Δy_A units of token Y.

We define $\mathcal{F}_{S_A}$ and $\mathcal{F}_{S_B}$ as the random variables representing whether the swaps S_A and S_B (respectively) fail. These variables take the value 1 if the swap fails and 0 if the swap is successful. Here, we assume that the failure probabilities for each rollup are independent.

It is important to note that we are ignoring transaction costs in our model. This assumption allows us to avoid converting these costs (usually denominated in ETH) to the target token Y, simplifying the analysis. On the other hand, given the current state of rollups, we expect transaction costs to be low enough not to change the conclusions substantially.

2.2 Profit Variables

Given the arbitrage opportunity defined above, the profit an arbitrageur will extract is simply the difference in liquidity resulting from the swaps S_A and S_B, which ultimately depends on the trade sizes (Δx_A, Δx_B, Δy_A, and Δy_B) and the failure outcomes ($\mathcal{F}_{S_A}$ and $\mathcal{F}_{S_B}$).

Under the non-atomic sequencing regime, one swap can fail while the other does not. Therefore, the difference in liquidity for each target token after the arbitrage is defined as:

$$\Delta L^X_{\text{non-atomic}} = \Delta x_B \cdot (1 - \mathcal{F}_{S_B}) - \Delta x_A \cdot (1 - \mathcal{F}_{S_A}) \tag{1}$$

and

$$\Delta L^Y_{\text{non-atomic}} = \Delta y_A \cdot (1 - \mathcal{F}_{S_A}) - \Delta y_B \cdot (1 - \mathcal{F}_{S_B}) \tag{2}$$

On the other hand, under the atomic execution regime, if one of the swaps reverts, the other swap will also revert. Thus, under this regime:

$$\Delta L^X_{\text{atomic}} = \begin{cases} \Delta x_B - \Delta x_A & \text{if } \mathcal{F}_{S_A} = \mathcal{F}_{S_B} = 0 \\ 0 & \text{otherwise} \end{cases} \tag{3}$$

and

$$\Delta L^Y_{\text{atomic}} = \begin{cases} \Delta y_A - \Delta y_B & \text{if } \mathcal{F}_{S_A} = \mathcal{F}_{S_B} = 0 \\ 0 & \text{otherwise} \end{cases} \tag{4}$$

Using the external price P_{ext}, we can define the overall profit under each sequencing regime as:

$$\text{Profit}_{i \in \{\text{non-atomic, atomic}\}} = \Delta L^Y_i + \Delta L^X_i \cdot P_{\text{ext}} \tag{5}$$

Now, we only need to derive the optimal trade sizes Δx_A, Δx_B, Δy_A, and Δy_B, which we do in the following subsection.

2.3 Trade Sizes

To derive the trade sizes of the two swaps, we assume that both pools are CPMMs, charge the same trading fee f, and that the arbitrageur will execute the optimal trade (i.e., sizing their trade to extract the maximal value from the two target pools). We will further assume that, from the time the arbitrage opportunity is identified to the time the arbitrage trade is executed, no uninformed traders will submit further transactions that shift the prices in affected pools.

In the swap S_B, the arbitrageur sends Δy_B units of token Y to the pool and pays a fee of f. Here, we consider that the DEX is processing fees outside of the pool reserves, which means that when a trader wishes to swap a given amount of tokens and pay Δy, only part of this payment goes to the pool reserve. Concretely, $(1-f) \cdot \Delta y$ is added to the pool reserves, while $f \cdot \Delta y$ is paid to Liquidity Providers (LPs). This is the case of Uniswap V3 pools, for instance.

We can derive how many X tokens the arbitrageur receives in a trade of Δy_B by using the property of CPMM pools in which the product of the two token reserves must always be a constant:

$$x_B \cdot y_B = [x_B - \Delta x_B][y_B + (1-f)\Delta y_B] \iff \Delta x_B = \frac{x_B(1-f)\Delta y_B}{y_B + (1-f)\Delta y_B} \quad (6)$$

If the arbitrageur executes this trade, the price after the trade will be:

$$P_B^{\text{end}} = \frac{y_B + (1-f)\Delta y_B}{x_B - \Delta x_B} = \frac{y_B + (1-f)\Delta y_B}{x_B - \frac{x_B(1-f)\Delta y_B}{y_B+(1-f)\Delta y_B}} = \frac{[y_B + (1-f)\Delta y_B]^2}{x_B \cdot y_B} \quad (7)$$

Using similar logic for the swap S_A, the arbitrageur pays Δx_A units of token X and receives the following units of token Y:

$$\Delta y_A = \frac{y_A(1-f)\Delta x_A}{x_A + (1-f)\Delta x_A} \quad (8)$$

And, at the end of the trade, the price of the pool will be:

$$P_A^{\text{end}} = \frac{x_A \cdot y_A}{[x_A + (1-f)\Delta x_A]^2} \quad (9)$$

When the arbitrageur executes the optimal trade, they will pay in rollup A the same units of X tokens they received in rollup B, which means that $\Delta x_A = \Delta x_B$. With this equality and Eqs. 6 and 8, we can describe the trade sizes Δx_A, Δx_B, and Δy_A based on the optimal initial size Δy_B.

As for Δy_B, the optimal trade occurs when the prices (excluding fees) in both pools at the end of the trade are equal, i.e., $(1-f)^2 P_A^{\text{end}} = P_B^{\text{end}}$. We can use this to derive Δy_B:

$$(1-f)^2 P_A^{\text{end}} = P_B^{\text{end}} \iff \Delta y_B = \frac{(1-f)\sqrt{x_A \cdot y_A \cdot x_B \cdot y_B} - x_A \cdot y_B}{(1-f)x_A + (1-f)^2 x_B} \quad (10)$$

3 Atomicity Profit Conditions

Based on the model developed in Sect. 2, the impact on arbitrage profits of moving from a non-atomic regime to an atomic regime depends on the combined outcome of the random variables $\mathcal{F}_{S_A}$ and $\mathcal{F}_{S_B}$, which represent whether each swap fails. Recall that they take the value 1 if the swap fails and 0 otherwise.

There are four possible combined outcomes for these two variables. For each, we can describe the difference in arbitrage profits between the atomic and non-atomic regimes (i.e., $\text{Profit}_{\text{diff}} := \text{Profit}_{\text{atomic}} - \text{Profit}_{\text{non-atomic}}$):

- $\mathcal{F}_{S_A} = 0 \cap \mathcal{F}_{S_B} = 0$. In this outcome, both swaps execute, and thus, the difference in arbitrage profits between the two regimes is zero.

- $\mathcal{F}_{S_A} = 1 \cap \mathcal{F}_{S_B} = 1$. In this outcome, both swaps fail. Thus, the difference in arbitrage profits between the two regimes is again zero.
- $\mathcal{F}_{S_A} = 1 \cap \mathcal{F}_{S_B} = 0$. In this outcome, swap S_A fails, but swap S_B executes. Here, there is a difference since, in the atomic regime, both swaps would be reverted. Therefore, $\text{Profit}_{\text{diff}} = 0 - (\Delta x_B P_{\text{ext}} - \Delta y_B) = \Delta y_B - \Delta x_B P_{\text{ext}}$
- $\mathcal{F}_{S_A} = 0 \cap \mathcal{F}_{S_B} = 1$. In this outcome, swap S_A executes, while swap S_B fails. Again, there is a difference in this combined outcome since, in the atomic regime, both swaps would be reverted. Therefore, $\text{Profit}_{\text{diff}} = 0 - (\Delta y_A - \Delta x_A P_{\text{ext}}) = \Delta x_A P_{\text{ext}} - \Delta y_A$

Now, if we define f_A and f_B as the probability of swaps S_A and S_B failing, respectively, we can describe the expected value of the profit difference as follows:

$$\mathbb{E}[\text{Profit}_{\text{diff}}] =$$
$$= (\Delta y_B - \Delta x_B P_{\text{ext}}) \cdot P[\mathcal{F}_{S_A} = 1 \cap \mathcal{F}_{S_B} = 0] +$$
$$\quad (\Delta x_A P_{\text{ext}} - \Delta y_A) \cdot P[\mathcal{F}_{S_A} = 0 \cap \mathcal{F}_{S_B} = 1]$$
$$= (\Delta y_B - \Delta x_B P_{\text{ext}}) \cdot f_A \cdot (1 - f_B) + (\Delta x_B P_{\text{ext}} - \Delta y_A) \cdot (1 - f_A) \cdot f_B$$
$$= f_A(\Delta y_B - \Delta x_B P_{\text{ext}}) + f_B(\Delta x_A P_{\text{ext}} - \Delta y_A) + f_A f_B(\Delta y_A - \Delta y_B) \quad (11)$$

Interestingly, we can rewrite Eq. 11 in terms of the price paid by the arbitrageur in each swap, namely, $P_A^* = \Delta y_A / \Delta x_A$ and $P_B^* = \Delta y_B / \Delta x_B$. Note that here we are using again the fact that $\Delta x_A = \Delta x_B$:

$$\mathbb{E}[\text{Profit}_{\text{diff}}] = \Delta x_B \big[f_A(P_B^* - P_{\text{ext}}) + f_B(P_{\text{ext}} - P_A^*) + f_A f_B(P_A^* - P_B^*) \big] \quad (12)$$

Equation 12 highlights that the expected gain that an arbitrageur will experience when switching from a non-atomic regime to an atomic regime ultimately depends on a few key parameters.

1. We have the trade size Δx_B. Recall from Sect. 2 that the trade size is determined by the state of the pools in each rollup, namely, the token reserves, the price difference, and the trading fee. In general, the larger the pools' reserves and the price difference, the larger the optimal trade sizes. Since $\Delta x_B > 0$, the pools' state does not control whether the difference is negative or positive on average. Instead, it has a multiplicative effect on the expected profit difference, controlling the size of this difference.
2. We have the external price P_{ext} and its relative position to the prices experienced by the arbitrageur in their optimal trade, P_A^* and P_B^*. These prices are always between the initial price of the pool before the arbitrage and the end price after the arbitrage is executed (i.e., $P_A > P_A^* > P_A^{\text{end}}$ and $P_B < P_B^* < P_B^{\text{end}}$).
3. There are the failure probabilities f_A and f_B, which we will analyze together with the external price. Figure 1 provides an example for each of the three possible configurations of the relative position of P_{ext} and P_A^* and P_B^*, and the full range of failure probabilities f_A and f_B.

We should highlight that this formula does not depend on the exact design of the Automated Market Maker (AMM). To ease the implementation of the entire simulation, we assumed it was a CPMM as it made the derivation of the optimal trade sizes simpler. However, this formula would also hold for more complex designs such as Uniswap v3.

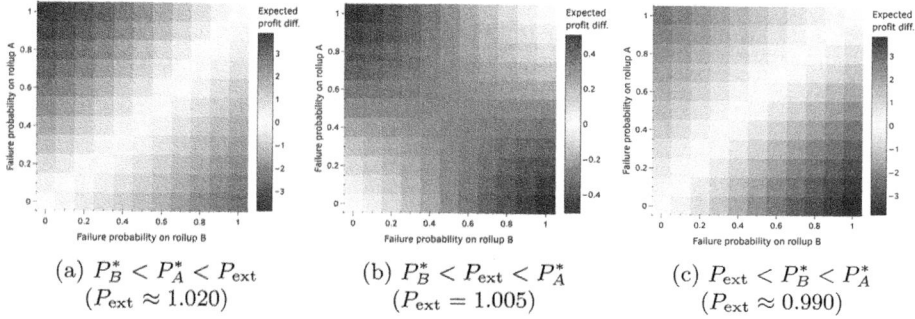

(a) $P_B^* < P_A^* < P_\text{ext}$
($P_\text{ext} \approx 1.020$)

(b) $P_B^* < P_\text{ext} < P_A^*$
($P_\text{ext} = 1.005$)

(c) $P_\text{ext} < P_B^* < P_A^*$
($P_\text{ext} \approx 0.990$)

Fig. 1. Expected value of the difference in arbitrage profits between the atomic and non-atomic regimes for varying failure probabilities and relative external prices. Pool states are kept unchanged: $f = 0.05\%$, $P_A = 1.01$, $P_B = 1$, and $y_A = y_B = 100{,}000$.

When the external price is *larger* than both pool prices (Fig. 1(a)), the expected profit difference can be positive or negative, depending on the failure probabilities. If failures are more likely on rollup B, the difference is positive, meaning that the arbitrageur will profit on average by switching to the atomic regime. However, if failures are more likely on rollup A, the difference is negative, and switching is no longer profitable.

Intuitively, this relationship makes sense. When the external price has a larger difference to the price on rollup B than the price differences in the two rollups, it would be better to only execute the swap on rollup B than to arbitrage it against rollup A. Therefore, having swap S_A failing and swap S_B executing leads to a net gain for the arbitrageur when valued against this external price (which means that atomicity is worse for the arbitrageur).

On the other hand, when the external price is *smaller* than both pool prices (Fig. 1(c)), the relationship is inverted. In this case, the rationale is similar, and switching to an atomic regime is only advantageous when failures are more likely on rollup A since simply swaping on rollup A generates more profit than arbitraging it against rollup B.

Finally, there is the case where the external price is between the two pool prices (Fig. 1(b)). Interestingly, the expected profit difference is always negative in this case, independently of the failure probabilities. Similarly to the previous cases, when we value liquidity using an external price, and one of the swaps fails and the other executes, we are, in a way, arbitraging the pool that did not fail against the external price. When the external is between the prices in each pool, having only one swap failing is always better than having both reverting, as we would collect some additional profit from arbitraging the pool that did not fail against the external price.

Focusing on the failing probabilities, there is a special case we can analyze. If the two failure probabilities are equal (i.e., $f_A = f_B$), the expected profit difference is always negative, meaning that, on average, the arbitrageur should *stick with the status quo* without atomicity. This result comes directly from Eq. 12:

$$\mathbb{E}[\text{Profit}_{\text{diff}}] =$$
$$= \Delta x_B \left[f_A(P_B^* - P_{\text{ext}}) + f_A(P_{\text{ext}} - P_A^*) + f_A^2(P_A^* - P_B^*) \right] =$$
$$= \Delta x_B \left[f_A(P_B^* - P_A^*) + f_A^2(P_A^* - P_B^*) \right] =$$
$$= \Delta x_B \cdot f_A \cdot (1 - f_A) \cdot (P_B^* - P_A^*) < 0 \qquad (13)$$

4 Related Work

The seminal work from Daian et al. [3] laid the groundwork for understanding MEV by demonstrating how block producers could exploit transaction ordering on Ethereum to capture arbitrage and frontrunning profits. Since then, multiple empirical studies have examined MEV on Ethereum by uncovering common strategies and measuring their prevalence and impact [10,13].

Recent work has extended the analysis into the Layer-2 domain. For instance, Ha et al. [5,14] and Torres et al. [2] present different measurements of MEV across popular rollups and other Layer-2 s, revealing the most common strategies, their volume, and the corresponding profit. Complementarily, Gogol et al. [4] examines arbitrage across different rollups and identifies many untapped arbitrage opportunities resulting from the non-atomic nature of cross-rollup transactions. Finally, Öz et al. [15] systematically analyzes non-atomic cross-chain arbitrage strategies across multiple L2s. It reveals that liquidity fragmentation across heterogeneous blockchain networks creates substantial arbitrage opportunities while also highlighting the inherent challenges posed by non-atomic execution.

Beyond empirical analyses, McMenamin [7] categorizes MEV extraction methods across multiple domains and outlines proposals for shared sequencers coordinating transaction ordering across chains. In addition, Mamageishvili and Schlegel [6] models the economic incentives under different sequencing regimes. Their results suggest that while a unified sequencer could facilitate atomic cross-chain arbitrage, it may also intensify latency competition and not necessarily increase overall sequencer revenue compared to independent rollup-specific sequencers.

5 Conclusions

Our work studies cross-rollup arbitrage in the context of a shared sequencing system offering atomic execution, a feature that ensures either all or none of a sequence of arbitrage transactions across multiple rollups are executed. Here, we investigate whether atomic execution is sufficient to significantly boost arbitrage profits and, in turn, sequencer revenue.

Our results reveal that arbitrage profits do not always improve under atomic execution, and thus, this feature alone is not enough to convince both arbitrageurs and rollup operators to switch to this new approach. When considering a case where an arbitrageur exploits an opportunity between two CPMM pools and values the final profit using an external price, we find that whether switching from non-atomic to atomic execution is net positive for the arbitrageur depends on the failure probabilities of the swaps in each rollup and the relative difference of the external price to the pool prices.

This work could be extended in multiple ways. Firstly, we assume that the arbitrageur maintains their liquidity in the tokens being arbitraged. However, arbitrageurs may keep liquidity in a stable token and convert it on demand to address volatility; our model could be extended to account for this conversion. Secondly, we do not consider transaction costs. Although it is currently low and likely to remain such for rollups, adding this cost would be another possible extension to the model. Thirdly, and more importantly, one could explore how prevalent the scenarios in which atomic execution is not beneficial to an arbitrageur are. This would require a detailed empirical analysis of various pools across different deployed rollups and varying time periods.

References

1. Astria: The Shared Sequencer Network (2024). https://www.astria.org/blog/astria-the-shared-sequencer-network
2. Bagourd, A., Francois, L.G.: Quantifying MEV On Layer 2 Networks (2023). https://doi.org/10.48550/arXiv.2309.00629. http://arxiv.org/abs/2309.00629. arXiv:2309.00629
3. Daian, P., et al.: Flash boys 2.0: frontrunning in decentralized exchanges, miner extractable value, and consensus instability. In: 2020 IEEE Symposium on Security and Privacy (SP), pp. 910–927 (2020). https://doi.org/10.1109/SP40000.2020.00040. https://ieeexplore.ieee.org/abstract/document/9152675. ISSN: 2375-1207
4. Gogol, K., Messias, J., Miori, D., Tessone, C., Livshits, B.: Layer-2 Arbitrage: An Empirical Analysis of Swap Dynamics and Price Disparities on Rollups (2024). https://doi.org/10.48550/arXiv.2406.02172. http://arxiv.org/abs/2406.02172. arXiv:2406.02172
5. Ha, Vlachou, Kilbourn, De Michellis: FlashBabies - MEV on L2 (2021)
6. Mamageishvili, A., Schlegel, J.C.: Shared Sequencing and Latency Competition as a Noisy Contest (2023). http://arxiv.org/abs/2310.02390. arXiv:2310.02390
7. McMenamin, C.: SoK: Cross-Domain MEV (2023). http://arxiv.org/abs/2308.04159. arXiv:2308.04159

8. Motepalli, S., Freitas, L., Livshits, B.: SoK: Decentralized Sequencers for Rollups (2023). https://doi.org/10.48550/arXiv.2310.03616. http://arxiv.org/abs/2310.03616. arXiv:2310.03616
9. NodeKit: The Composable Network: Unifying Chains with Javelin, the first Superbuilder (2024). https://nodekit-tinywins.vercel.app/posts/the-composable-network
10. Qin, K., Zhou, L., Gervais, A.: Quantifying blockchain extractable value: how dark is the forest? In: 2022 IEEE Symposium on Security and Privacy (SP), pp. 198–214 (2022). https://doi.org/10.1109/SP46214.2022.9833734. https://ieeexplore.ieee.org/abstract/document/9833734. ISSN: 2375-1207
11. Radius: Radius: Trustless Shared Sequencing Layer (2023). https://medium.com/@radius_xyz/radius-trustless-shared-sequencing-layer-b293dfa75db
12. Espresso Systems: The Espresso Sequencer (2023). https://hackmd.io/@EspressoSystems/EspressoSequencer
13. Torres, C.F., Camino, R., State, R.: Frontrunner Jones and the Raiders of the Dark Forest: An Empirical Study of Frontrunning on the Ethereum Blockchain, pp. 1343–1359 (2021). ISBN 978-1-939133-24-3. https://www.usenix.org/conference/usenixsecurity21/presentation/torres
14. Torres, C.F., Mamuti, A., Weintraub, B., Nita-Rotaru, C., Shinde, S.: Rolling in the Shadows: Analyzing the Extraction of MEV Across Layer-2 Rollups (2024). http://arxiv.org/abs/2405.00138. arXiv:2405.00138
15. Öz, B., Torres, C.F., Gebele, J., Rezabek, F., Mazorra, B., Matthes, F.: Pandora's Box: Cross-Chain Arbitrages in the Realm of Blockchain Interoperability (2025). https://doi.org/10.48550/arXiv.2501.17335. http://arxiv.org/abs/2501.17335. arXiv:2501.17335

Revisiting Bitcoin's Merkle Tree Security: Practical Implications and an Attack on Core Chain

Yogev Bar-On[✉]

Tel Aviv University, Tel Aviv, Israel
baronyogev@gmail.com

Abstract. This paper revisits a flaw in the Merkle tree construction underlying Bitcoin's light client security model. Although Bitcoin was innovative in introducing Proof of Work and simple payment verification (SPV), a design shortcoming in its Merkle tree structure can be exploited to prove the inclusion of a malicious or nonexistent transaction in a block. We investigate how this fault remains not only theoretical but can compromise the security of real-world systems. In particular, we examine Core Chain (an EVM-compatible blockchain using delegated Proof of Work from Bitcoin miners), which relies on a Bitcoin light client for consensus. We show that an attacker can exploit the Merkle tree flaw to forge proofs of mining power delegation. By removing all mining power from legitimate validators, the entire consensus process can be disrupted. Furthermore, we outline potential mitigations and best practices for light-client developers, and emphasize why those do not suffice, and necessary changes within Bitcoin itself are required to eliminate this vulnerability.

Keywords: Blockchain · Security · Bitcoin · Merkle Tree · Light Client

1 Introduction

Bitcoin [15] introduced the first decentralized and permissionless cryptocurrency system, leveraging Proof of Work (PoW) to secure the network. Its key innovation lies in a protocol that allows participants to agree on a global state without central authorities. One of the fundamental ideas presented in the Bitcoin whitepaper is the concept of a *Simple Payment Verification* (SPV) client - often referred to as a *light client*. By verifying the work in block headers while using cryptographic Merkle proofs to check the inclusion of specific transactions, light clients can verify the inclusion of transactions in the Bitcoin network using a constant amount of external information and no trust.

Despite its remarkable design, Bitcoin has certain known but often understated shortcomings. Among these is a subtlety in the Merkle tree construction used to compute a block's Merkle root. In principle, to compute the Merkle root, each transaction is hashed at the leaves of the Merkle tree, and internal nodes are generated by concatenating and hashing their child nodes. However, Bitcoin does not strictly enforce that the leaves' data format (transaction structure) differs from the internal nodes. As a result, it is possible to interpret the value of an internal node as if it were a leaf, a valid 64-byte transaction, enabling malicious "inclusion" [13].

Although this issue has been publicly disclosed, there remains limited awareness of its real-world implications and many practical implementations may still be at risk. In this work, we demonstrate how the Core Chain consensus mechanism can be exploited, **risking more than \$500M** at the time of reporting [7], to illustrate that the vulnerability persists in certain systems, highlighting the need for a more thorough examination of the Merkle tree construction at the Bitcoin protocol level.

Core Chain uses special form of a Proof of Stake (PoS) for its consensus mechanism. In a standard PoS system, validators lock up funds ("stake") to receive voting power in the network. The validators can then use their voting power to participate in the chain's consensus and prevent censorship. When the validators act correctly, they receive rewards, which incentivize them to participate honestly. Otherwise, if the validators act incorrectly or maliciously, their locked up funds are taken away from them in a process called "slashing".

Core Chain extends this protocol with *Delegated Proof of Work*. The network allows validators to increase their voting power by delegating (assigning) mined Bitcoin blocks to their Core Chain's address. This is a form of *restaking*, a mechanism in which you can use the same resources to secure more than one application. Core Chain uses a Bitcoin SPV client to verify the delegation, making it a high value target for an attacker that looks to disrupt the network.

Responsible Disclosure. After discovering this vulnerability within the Core Chain delegated PoW mechanism, we conducted responsible disclosure through the Immunefi bug bounty platform [1]. Both Immunefi and the Core team later agreed to allow the publication of the findings. All findings are up to the date of reporting the issue on March 2024.

1.1 Our Contributions

In this work, we make the following contributions:

- We review the Merkle tree flaw in Bitcoin's design in a practical setting, and clarify why it allows adversaries to prove the inclusion of non-existent or manipulated transactions.
- We show a novel attack on the *Core Chain* blockchain that exploits this design. We show how an attacker can exploit Core Chain's reliance on Bitcoin's light client to remove everyone's voting power from the system, by carefully forging Merkle proofs of non-existent transactions.
- We revisit possible mitigations for the issue and discuss where they fail in practice, arguing in favor of a Bitcoin fork.

1.2 Related Works

The SPV client security issue emerging from the Bitcoin Merkle tree design was discussed in prior works and online discussions [2,5,13,16], previously affecting Bitcoin Core (assigned CVE-2017-12842 [4], not to be confused with Core Chain) and Keep Network [17].

Additionally, a different vulnerability with the Bitcoin Merkle tree design was previously found and patched at the protocol level (assigned CVE-2012-2459 [3]). This issue was due to padding the block with extra transactions in case the number of transactions was odd, making the real block indistinguishable from the padded block.

Our attack on Core Chain is a form of exploiting restaking mechanisms. Another perspective on the subject is how the delegated PoW affects the economics of the network and whether this can be exploited as well (for example, with enough similar networks, a small portion of the compute power on the Bitcoin network could provide unproportionate aggregate voting power across the other networks). The theory of economic security of restaking networks has been explored in [6,11,12].

1.3 Outline

We begin by reviewing Bitcoin's Merkle tree design and its flaw in the next section. In Sect. 3, we then show our attack on Core Chain that exploits this design flaw. We conclude in Sect. 4, where we discuss mitigations and next steps for the community.

2 Bitcoin's Design Flaw

The primary function of a light client (SPV client) in Bitcoin is to verify that a given transaction is included in a specific block *without* downloading the entire block. This is achieved using block headers and Merkle proofs [14].

2.1 What Is a Light Client?

A *light client* (or SPV client) differs from a full node in that it does not store or validate all transactions. Instead, it:

- **Downloads block headers:** The client obtains each block header, which includes the Merkle root of transactions and the nonce used in Proof of Work.
- **Verifies Proof of Work:** The client checks that the header hash is below the network's target, thereby confirming that miners expended computational effort.
- **Receives Merkle proofs:** For any transaction of interest, the client obtains a Merkle proof (the path in the Merkle tree from the leaf to the root).

By hashing the transaction with the intermediate nodes in the proof, the client can reconstruct the Merkle root and compare it against the root included in the verified block header. If they match, the transaction is deemed part of that block.

2.2 Why the Merkle Tree Design Is Faulty

In a *typical* Merkle tree, the leaves represent atomic data items (e.g., transactions), and each internal node is a hash of its children:

$$\text{parent} = \text{Hash}(\text{child1} \mathbin{\|} \text{child2}).$$

To provide a proof of inclusion for a leaf, you must provide the internal nodes adjacent to the path from the leaf to the root, as illustrated in Fig. 1.

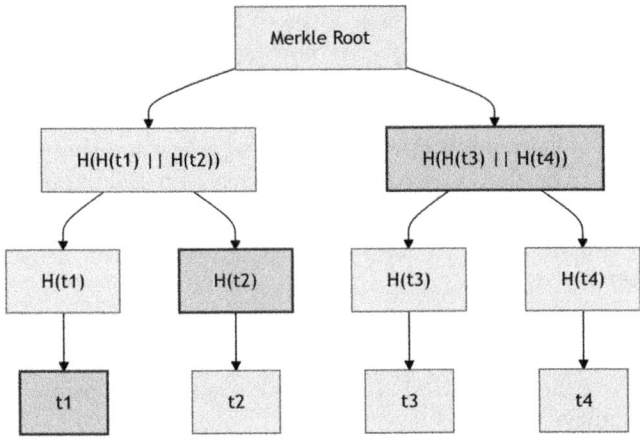

Fig. 1. A simplified Merkle tree representing four transactions (H represents a hash function). The shaded nodes are used as the proof for transaction $t1$.

In Bitcoin, the leaves are specifically the double-SHA256 hash of each transaction's serialized bytes. As we progress up the tree, the internal nodes are likewise double-SHA256 hashes of their children. Crucially, in *secure* Merkle tree usage, leaves are *distinguishable* from internal nodes: an internal node is, semantically, the hash of two children, while a leaf is the hash of a transaction.

64-Byte Transactions Are Valid. However, Bitcoin does not *enforce* a difference in data format. A node that is a concatenation of hashes of two children can itself be interpreted as if it were a 64-byte "transaction", if the resulting data meets certain conditions.

Bitcoin sets no absolute minimum size for a transaction aside from a handful of rules that do not preclude a carefully crafted 64-byte object from being *interpreted* as a transaction. For instance, a valid Bitcoin transaction must contain:

- A 4-byte version field
- An input count and output count
- Each input (with a previous output reference, script length, script, sequence)

- Each output (with a value, script length, script)
- A 4-byte lock time

While many typical transactions are much larger, there is no built-in rule disallowing a transaction from being 64 bytes if these fields appear well-formed. Consequently, if internal node data can be massaged to *look* like 64 bytes of a transaction, it might slip past naive checks in an SPV client's Merkle verification code.

Since the Merkle root is computed over the entire tree, an attacker can craft a scenario in which:

- **They pick/create two real transactions** whose hashes line up in such a way that concatenating them forms a 64-byte blob that decodes as a valid transaction.
- **They demonstrate a Merkle path** that claims this 64-byte entity is included as a leaf, thus forging a transaction's inclusion that never actually appeared as an original leaf in the block.

Figure 2 illustrates how a valid proof can be crafted for an internal node, to prove its inclusion as an actual 64-byte transaction.

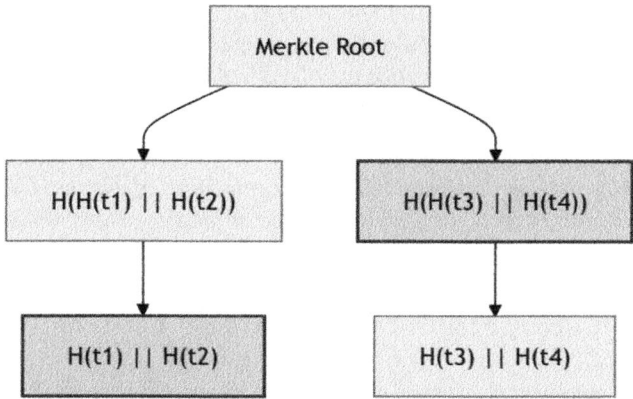

Fig. 2. Fake, but indistinguishable, view for the same Merkle tree from Fig. 1. The shaded nodes are used as the proof for the (originally) internal node $H(t1) \parallel H(t2)$.

3 Attack on Core Chain

In this section, we focus on *Core Chain* [8] as a real-world example of an unsafe SPV-based design. Core Chain is an EVM-compatible blockchain that uses *delegated Proof of Work* from Bitcoin miners, combined with Proof of Stake, to determine validator voting power.

Accurately computing voting power is essential for the correct execution of the network. The security of the funds being held on the network is determined by how hard it is to disrupt transaction processing and consensus on transaction inclusion. By having the wrong voting power, legitimate validators cannot enforce the correct behavior of the network, and other, perhaps malicious validators, can remove transactions, stop the network, and in the worst cases change the history of the chain and remove funds from wallets.

Our analysis shows how we can leverage the Bitcoin Merkle tree issue to cause the network to compute the voting powers incorrectly.

3.1 Core Chain Overview

Core Chain is a blockchain project advertising a *Satoshi Plus* consensus algorithm aimed at combining:

1. **Staking CORE**: Locking the native token of the chain.
2. **Mining Bitcoin**: Bitcoin miners can delegate the blocks they mine to validators in Core Chain, to increase their effective stake in the network.

To delegate a mined block to a Core validator, the Bitcoin miner includes a coinbase transaction (the first transaction in the block) that specifies the *Core validator address* in the op_return transaction field. A predefined amount of blocks is defined as an *epoch*, and the more blocks delegated to a single validator address in a single epoch, the more voting power this validator has.

To see this, let the set of validators be V. A validator $v \in V$ on Core Chain will have a total voting power computed as follows:

Definition 1 (Voting Power). *Let C_v be the amount of native tokens staked for a validator $v \in V$, and let M_v be the amount of blocks delegated to it in the current Bitcoin epoch, as configured by the chain. The validator has a total voting power of [10]:*

$$p_v = \rho M_v \sum_{u \in V} C_u + C_v \sum_{u \in V} M_u, \tag{1}$$

where ρ is a constant factor (configured by Core Chain) that determines how much voting power each delegated Bitcoin block provides.

We can see from this definition a useful artifact that we will make use of later:

Fact 1. *If all mining powers can be nullified ($M_v = 0$ for all $v \in V$), then **nobody has voting power**, even if they stake the native cryptocurrency CORE.*

3.2 SPV Verification on Core Chain

Core Chain must provide a secure way to verify block delegation from Bitcoin. Since these two chains operating independently, with the Bitcoin protocol even being unaware of the existence of Core Chain, this is tricky.

To do this, Core Chain uses an SPV client. By only storing Bitcoin headers on-chain instead of the transactions themselves, Core Chain avoids the massive storage overhead of full Bitcoin blocks. Instead, the system expects a Merkle proof that the coinbase transaction that delegates voting power to a validator, is indeed included in a Bitcoin block in the current epoch.

Our attack allows an attacker to forge Merkle proof for non-extant transactions, providing them with a way to delegate Bitcoin blocks to non-legitimate validators. To do this, the attacker needs to craft a special valid transaction and make sure it is included as the first transaction after the coinbase transaction in the Bitcoin block.

When crafting this transaction, the attacker must make sure that its hash concatenated with the real coinbase transaction hash is a possible serialization of another, non-existant transaction:

$$\text{Hash}(\text{coinbase\_tx} \,\|\, \text{crafted\_tx}) = \text{Valid transaction serialization}.$$

To understand how to craft such transaction, we first need to understand how a Bitcoin transaction is deserialized by the Core Chain smart contract. Bitcoin transactions are serialized the following way:

- 4 bytes: `version`
- >1 bytes: `input count`
- Each input includes:
  - 32 bytes: previous output hash
  - 4 bytes: previous output index
  - >1 bytes: script length
  - (variable size) script
  - 4 bytes: sequence
- >1 bytes: `output count`
- Each input includes:
  - 8 bytes: Value
  - >1 bytes: script length
  - (variable size) script
- 4 bytes: `locktime`

The Bug. The bug in Core Chain that allows our attack is that there is minimal verification for the serialized transaction. If the transaction fails more complex verifications, the block is simply delegated to no one instead of raising an error.

Mainly, the verification is only that the lengths match the amount of data expected [9]. Specifically, we must provide at least one input and one output. By carefully setting input count, output count, and scripts length, we can produce a valid 64-byte structure that Core Chain accepts, without needing the content to make sense. This means we only need to control a few key bytes in the serialized transaction: we can use a single input with a script length of 0 and a single output with a script length of 4 as a possible solution. We can verify that the resulted transaction length is indeed 64:

- [Total: 4] 4 bytes: `version`
- [Total: 5] 1 byte: `input count`
- [Total: 5] A single input:
  - [Total: 37] 32 bytes: previous output hash
  - [Total: 41] 4 bytes: previous output index
  - [Total: 42] 1 byte: script length
  - [Total: 42] 0 bytes: script
  - [Total: 46] 4 bytes: sequence
- [Total: 47] 1 byte: `output count`
- [Total: 47] A single output:
  - [Total: 55] 8 bytes: Value
  - [Total: 56] 1 bytes: script length
  - [Total: 60] 4 bytes: script
- [Total: 64] 4 bytes: `locktime`

This solution requires the attacker to control only 4 bytes (32 bits) in the serialized transaction; the input length, output length, and input and output script lengths. Thus, one out of ~4B randomly crafted transactions would work for the exploit, easily enumerated by a computer.

Thus, the complete flow will be as following:

1. Randomly generate a valid Bitcoin transaction (e.g. by randomizing the `locktime`).
2. Compute the resulted serialized transaction, by hashing the crafted transaction and concatenating to the hash of the predicted coinbase transaction.
3. Repeat until the resulted hash has a single input with an empty script and a single output with 4 bytes of script.
4. Send the crafted transaction to Bitcoin, for it to be included as the first non-coinbase transaction.
5. Send the 64-byte hash as a coinbase transaction to Core Chain, delegating the block to no one.

Outcome. The net effect of the exploit is to create a "fake coinbase transaction" that delegates voting power to no real validator. Repeating this for all blocks in the epoch will nullify the delegated proof of work from all validators, which as we saw in Eq. (1), means no validator will have any voting power.

Its important to note that the attack requires the attacker to accurately predict the contents of the coinbase transaction, which can be tricky - but it is not random and thus not cryptographically secure. Over a long period of time, it is within reason that an attacker will successfully execute this attack.

4 Discussion

A number of mitigations for the Bitcoin Merkle design issue have been proposed in prior work [13], many of which avoid modifying Bitcoin itself. One mitigation is to simply verify the transaction is serialized to more than 64 bytes in length.

Given that valid 64-byte Bitcoin transactions are extremely rare under standard checks, a light client can safely assume fraud when encountering such data.

Another possible mitigation is to additionally include a proof for the rightmost transaction. If the number of transactions is not a power of two, the rightmost transaction is duplicated in the Merkle tree, thereby revealing the tree's actual depth. Yet, its hard to guarantee that the tree is never a perfect power-of-two without a protocol-level restriction.

While such non-forking solutions address immediate threats at the SPV client layer, they do not eradicate the underlying design flaw from the Bitcoin protocol. In principle, a future soft-fork or hard-fork could insert explicit markers or length constraints, ensuring that internal nodes can never be misconstrued as leaf nodes. However, any modification to Bitcoin's consensus layer is inherently contentious, and the ecosystem has historically been conservative about protocol changes.

Despite the hardships, we encourage to consider a fork as the only viable solution. As the ecosystem grows with newer projects allocating large capital, we cannot trust developers to be aware of all of Bitcoin's faults and mitigate them. This is true for Bitcoin in particular, since it is considered the most mature and secure blockchain by many, as evident by this specific vulnerability being found in multiple applications.

4.1 Conclusions

In this paper, we revisited a known but under-acknowledged flaw in Bitcoin's Merkle tree structure, showing how it can be leveraged to craft invalid transaction proofs in SPV contexts. By studying the real-world example of Core Chain, an EVM-compatible blockchain that delegates validator power based on Bitcoin blocks, we demonstrated a tangible exploit: forging coinbase inclusion to nullify all legitimate validator power.

The broader lesson is that cryptographic building blocks, while powerful, require careful attention to data formatting and structural constraints. As the industry continues to build multi-chain ecosystems, vigilance is needed to ensure that mistakes are fixed (especially in mature and trusted blockchains like Bitcoin), and do not threaten large-scale capital.

References

1. Immunefi. https://immunefi.com/
2. Merkle tree vulnerabilities. Bitcoin Optech. https://bitcoinops.org/en/topics/merkle-tree-vulnerabilities/. Accessed 02 Jan 2025
3. CVE-2012-2459. National Vulnerability Database (NVD) (2012). https://nvd.nist.gov/vuln/detail/CVE-2012-2459
4. CVE-2017-12842. National Vulnerability Database (NVD) (2017). https://nvd.nist.gov/vuln/detail/CVE-2017-12842
5. Weaknesses in bitcoin's merkle root construction. Bitcoin Dev Mailing List (2019). https://gnusha.org/pi/bitcoindev/CAFp6fsGtEm9p-ZQF-XqfqyQGzZK7BS2SNp2z680QBsJiFDraEA@mail.gmail.com/2-BitcoinMerkle.pdf. Accessed 02 Jan 2025

6. Chitra, T., Pai, M.: How much should you pay for restaking security? arXiv preprint arXiv:2408.00928 (2024)
7. CoinMarketCap: Core dao (core) price, market cap, and info (2025). https://coinmarketcap.com/currencies/core-dao/. Accessed 02 Jan 2025
8. CoreDAO: Core whitepaper. https://whitepaper.coredao.org/. Accessed 02 Jan 2025
9. CoreDAO: btcpowermirror github repository (2023). https://github.com/coredao-org/btcpowermirror/tree/0c9db0d9189a6cc8c4e519220945984a4d401d7d, commit 367adc3d
10. CoreDAO: Core genesis contracts github repository (2024). https://github.com/coredao-org/core-genesis-contract/tree/367adc3d9779cab7b27bc4922b16c00cdf42c859, commit 367adc3d
11. Dong, X., et al.: Remote staking with economic safety. arXiv preprint arXiv:2408.01896 (2024)
12. Durvasula, N., Roughgarden, T.: Robust restaking networks. arXiv preprint arXiv:2407.21785 (2024)
13. Lerner, S.D.: Leaf node weakness in bitcoin merkle tree design (2018). https://bitslog.com/2018/06/09/leaf-node-weakness-in-bitcoin-merkle-tree-design/. Accessed 02 Jan 2025
14. Merkle, R.C.: A digital signature based on a conventional encryption function. In: Conference on the Theory and Application of Cryptographic Techniques, pp. 369–378. Springer (1987)
15. Nakamoto, S.: Bitcoin: a peer-to-peer electronic cash system. Satoshi Nakamoto (2008)
16. Todd, P.: Trusted merkle tree depth for safe tx inclusion proofs without a soft fork. Bitcoin Dev Mailing List (2018). https://gnusha.org/pi/bitcoindev/20180607171311.6qdjohfuuy3ufriv@petertodd.org/. Accessed 02 Jan 2025
17. Łukasz Zimnoch: Spv merkle proof malleability allows the maintainer to prove invalid transactions. GitHub Advisory Database (2024). https://github.com/advisories/GHSA-wg2x-rv86-mmpx. Accessed 02 Jan 2025

A Quantitative Notion of Economic Security for Smart Contract Compositions

Emily Priyadarshini[1] and Massimo Bartoletti[2] (✉)

[1] IISER Pune, Pune, India
[2] University of Cagliari, Cagliari, Italy
bart@unica.it

Abstract. Decentralized applications are often composed of multiple interconnected smart contracts. This is especially evident in DeFi, where protocols are heavily intertwined and rely on a variety of basic building blocks such as tokens, decentralized exchanges and lending protocols. A crucial security challenge in this setting arises when adversaries target individual components to cause systemic economic losses. Existing security notions focus on determining the existence of these attacks, but fail to quantify the effect of manipulating individual components on the overall economic security of the system. In this paper, we introduce a quantitative security notion that measures how an attack on a single component can amplify economic losses of the overall system. We study the fundamental properties of this notion and apply it to assess the security of key compositions. In particular, we analyse under-collateralized loan attacks in systems made of lending protocols and decentralized exchanges.

1 Introduction

Developing decentralized applications nowadays involves suitably designing, assembling and customizing a multitude of smart contracts, resulting in complex interactions and dependencies. In particular, recent DeFi applications are highly interconnected compositions of smart contracts of various kinds, including tokens, derivatives, decentralized exchanges (DEX), and lending protocols [15,16].

This complexity poses significant security risks, as adversaries targeting one of the components may compromise the security of the overall application. Note that, for this to happen, the attacked component does not even need to have a proper vulnerability to exploit. For example, in an application composed of a lending protocol and a DEX serving as a price oracle, adversaries could target the DEX in order to artificially inflate the price of an asset that they have previously deposited to the lending pool. This manipulation would allow adversaries to borrow other assets with an insufficient collateral, circumventing the intended economic mechanism of the lending protocol [1,5,12,20,21].

The first step to address these risks is to formally define when a system of smart contracts is secure. In recent years, a few security notions have emerged, starting from Babel, Daian, Kelkar and Juels' "Clockwork finance" [3]. Broadly, these definitions try to characterise the economic security of smart contract systems based on the extent of economic damage that adversaries can inflict on them. In this context, adversaries are typically assumed to have the powers of consensus nodes. Namely, they can reorder, drop or insert transactions in blocks. Accordingly, the economic damage on a system S can be quantified in terms of the Maximal Extractable Value (MEV) that adversaries can extract from S by leveraging these powers [10]. To provide a more concrete formulation of the existing notions, consider a set of contracts Δ to be deployed in a system S. We denote by $S \mid \Delta$ the system composed of S and Δ. The security criterion in [3] requires that $\mathrm{MEV}(S \mid \Delta) \leq (1+\varepsilon)\,\mathrm{MEV}(S)$: namely, the MEV extractable from $S \mid \Delta$ does not exceed the MEV extractable from S by more than a factor of ε. This notion does not capture our intuition of assessing the security of Δ in terms of the economic losses that Δ could incur due to adversaries interacting with the context S. For example, an airdrop contract Δ that gives away tokens would be deemed insecure, while in reality its interactions with S are irrelevant.

In a different security setting, a similar intuition was the basis of Goguen and Meseguer' non-interference [11], which was originally formulated as follows:

"One group of users, using a certain set of commands, is noninterfering with another group of users if what the first group does with those commands has no effect on what the second group of users can see".

In the setting of smart contract compositions, this notion can be reinterpreted by requiring that adversaries interacting with S do not inflict economic damage to Δ. The notion of *MEV non-interference* introduced by [6] is based on this idea, using MEV as a measure of economic damage. The approaches in [14,24] are also based on the idea of non-interference, but replacing MEV with an explicit tagging of contract variables as high-level or low-level variables.

A common aspect of these approaches to economic non-interference is their *qualitative* nature: namely, these definitions classify a composition as either secure or insecure, in a binary fashion. While a qualitative evaluation is sufficient when a composition is deemed secure, in that case that it is not, it does not provide any meaningful estimate of the *degree* of interference. For example, in the insecure composition between a lending protocol and a DEX mentioned above, a quantitative measure could provide insights into the extent to which the system state (e.g., the liquidity reserves in the DEX) and the contract parameters (e.g., the collateralization threshold) contribute to increasing the economic loss.

Contributions. This paper introduces a quantitative notion of economic security for smart contract compositions. Our *MEV interference*, which we denote by $\mathcal{I}(S \leadsto \Delta)$, measures the increase of economic loss of contracts Δ that adversaries can achieve by manipulating the context S. We apply our notion to assess the security of some notable contract compositions, including a bet on a token price, and a lending protocol relying on a DEX as a price oracle. We prove some fundamental properties of our notion: more specifically, $\mathcal{I}(S \leadsto \Delta)$ increases when S is extended with contracts that are not in the dependencies of Δ (Theorem 1); $\mathcal{I}(S \leadsto \Delta)$ does not depend on the token balances of users except adversaries (Theorem 2); $\mathcal{I}(S \leadsto \Delta)$ is preserved when extending S with contracts Γ that

Table 1. Summary of notation.

A, B	User accounts	$\mathcal{A}, \mathcal{B}$	Sets of [user|contract] accounts
C, D	Contract accounts	$\mathcal{C}, \mathcal{D}$	Sets of contract accounts
T, T'	Token types	$\$1_T$	Price of T
X, X'	Transaction names	A : C.f(args)	Transaction
S, S'	Blockchain states	$\$_\mathcal{C}(S)$	Wealth of contracts $\mathcal{C}$ in S
W, W'	Wallet states	$deps(\mathcal{C})$	Dependencies of contracts $\mathcal{C}$
Γ, Δ	Contract states	$\dagger\Gamma$	Contract accounts in Γ

enjoy some specific independency conditions with respect to Δ (Theorem 3) (Table 1).

2 Smart Contracts Model

We consider a contract model inspired by account-based platforms such as Ethereum. The basic building blocks of our model are a set $\mathbb{T}$ of *token types* (T, T', ...), representing crypto-assets (e.g., ETH), and a set $\mathbb{A}$ of *accounts*. We partition accounts into *user accounts* A, B, ... $\in \mathbb{A}_u$ (representing the so-called *externally owned accounts* in Ethereum) and *contract accounts* C, D, ... $\in \mathbb{A}_c$.

The state of a user account is a map $w \in \mathbb{T} \to \mathbb{N}$ from token types to non-negative integers, representing a *wallet* of tokens. The state of a contract account is a pair (w, σ), where w is a wallet and σ is a key-value map, representing the contract storage. A *blockchain state* S is a map from accounts to their states. We write an account state in square brackets, wherein we denote by n : T a balance of n units of token T in the wallet, and by $\mathtt{x} = v$, the association of value v to the storage variable x. For example, C[1 : T, owner = A] represents a state where the contract C stores 1 unit of T, and the variable owner contains the address A. We write a blockchain state as the composition of its account states, using the symbol | as a separator. For example, $S = $ A[1 : T, 2 : ETH] | C[1 : T, owner = A] is a state composed by a user account and a contract account.

Contracts are made up of a finite set of *functions*, which can be called by *transactions* sent by users. A function can: (i) receive parameters and tokens from the caller, (ii) transfer tokens to user accounts (including the caller), (iii) update the contract state, (iv) call other functions (possibly of other contracts, and possibly transferring tokens along with the call), (v) return values to the caller. Functions can only manipulate tokens as described above: in particular, they cannot mint or burn tokens, or drain tokens from other accounts. Transactions X, X', ... are calls to contract functions, written A : C.f(args), where A is the user signing the transaction, C is the called contract, f is the called function, and args is the list of actual parameters. Parameters can also include transfers of tokens T from A to C, written A **pays** n : T. Invalid transactions are reverted (i.e., they do not update the blockchain state). We remark that our security definition and results do not rely on a particular language for functions: we just assume a deterministic transition relation $\to$ between blockchain states, where state transitions are triggered by transactions. To write examples, however, we will instantiate this abstract model using a contract language inspired by Solidity.

We assume that a contract D can call a function of a contract C only if C was deployed before D. Formally, defining $C \prec D$ (read: "C *is called by* D") when some function in D calls some function in C, we require that the transitive and reflexive closure $\sqsubseteq$ of $\prec$ is a partial order. We define the *dependencies* of a contract C as $deps(C) = \{C' \mid C' \sqsubseteq C\}$, and extend this notion to *sets* of contracts $\mathcal{C}$. We assume that blockchain states S enjoy the following conditions: (i) S contains all its dependencies, i.e. if C is a contract in S, then also the contracts $deps(C)$ are in S; (ii) S contains *finite tokens*. All states mentioned in our results are assumed to enjoy these well-formedness assumption.[1] We write $S = W \mid \Gamma$ for a blockchain state S composed of user wallets W and contract states Γ. We can deconstruct wallets, writing $S = W \mid W' \mid \Gamma$ when the accounts in W and W' are disjoint, as well as contract states, writing $S = W \mid \Gamma \mid \Delta$. We denote by $\dagger \Gamma$ the set of contract accounts in Γ, i.e. $\dagger \Gamma = \text{dom}\,\Gamma$. For example, $\dagger(C[\cdots] \mid D[\cdots]) = \{C, D\}$. Given $X = A : C.f(\text{args})$, we write $callee(X)$ for the target contract C.

3 Threat Model

To define economic security of smart contract compositions, following [3] we consider the Maximal Extractable Value (MEV) that can be extracted when new contracts $\mathcal{C}$ are deployed in a blockchain state $S = W \mid \Gamma$, leading to a new state $S \mid \Gamma \mid \Delta$ where Δ contains the initial state of the new contracts $\mathcal{C}$. Since our goal is measuring the loss of the new contracts Δ caused by attacking their dependencies Γ, rather than considering the overall MEV of $S \mid \Delta$, we isolate the MEV extractable from Δ and compare it to the MEV that could be extracted from Δ *without* exploiting the dependencies Γ. To this purpose, we leverage the adversary model and the notion of *local MEV* introduced in [6].

We start by designating a finite subset $\mathbb{M}$ of user accounts as adversaries. We assume that adversaries have full control of the selection and ordering of transactions—a standard assumption in definitions of MEV [3]. Then, to measure the economic loss of a set of contracts $\mathcal{C}$, we consider the wealth of $\mathcal{C}$ in a blockchain state before and after the attack. The wealth of $\mathcal{C}$ in S, written $\$_\mathcal{C}(S)$, is given by the amount of tokens in each contract $C \in \mathcal{C}$ in S weighted by their prices. Recalling that a contract state is a pair (w, σ) whose first element is a wallet, and denoting by $\$1_T$ the price of a token type T, the wealth of a single contract state $C[w, \sigma]$ is given by $\sum_T w(T) \cdot \$1_T$, i.e. the summation, for all token types T, of the number of tokens T in the wallet of C, times the price of T.[2] By extending this to the set $\mathcal{C}$, we obtain the following general definition of wealth:

$$\$_\mathcal{C}(S) = \sum_{C \in \mathcal{C}, T} \mathit{fst}(\Gamma(C))(T) \cdot \$1_T \qquad (1)$$

---

[1] Note that well-formedness rules out some problematic features like reentrancy, which instead is present in Ethereum. However, reentrancy can always be removed by using suitable programming patterns, so we do not consider this as a limitation.

[2] Here we implicitly assume that the prices of *native* crypto-assets are constant, since they do not depend on the blockchain state. We discuss this assumption in Sect. 6.

Building on the definition of wealth, we now revisit the notion of local MEV introduced in [6]. The local MEV extractable by a set of contracts $\mathcal{C}$ in a blockchain state S, denoted by $\text{MEV}(S, \mathcal{C})$, is the maximum loss that adversaries can inflict to $\mathcal{C}$ by performing an arbitrary sequence of transactions crafted using their knowledge. By denoting with $\kappa(\mathcal{M})$ the set of transactions craftable by $\mathcal{M}$, this amounts to the maximum loss $\$_{\mathcal{C}}(S) - \$_{\mathcal{C}}(S')$ over all possible states S' reachable through a sequence $\vec{X}$ of transactions in $\kappa(\mathcal{M})$. In symbols:

$$\text{MEV}(S, \mathcal{C}) = \max \left\{ \$_{\mathcal{C}}(S) - \$_{\mathcal{C}}(S') \,\middle|\, \vec{X} \in \kappa(\mathcal{M})^*,\ S \xrightarrow{\vec{X}} S' \right\} \quad (2)$$

In $\text{MEV}(S, \mathcal{C})$, adversaries are allowed to call any contract in S, including the dependencies of $\mathcal{C}$ not defined in $\mathcal{C}$ itself. This follows from the fact that $\kappa(\mathcal{M})$ does not pose any restriction on the callee of the transactions craftable by $\mathcal{M}$. To estimate the MEV extractable from Δ *without* exploiting the dependencies Γ, we introduce an additional parameter $\mathcal{D}$ to local MEV, representing the set of contracts callable by $\mathcal{M}$. We denote by $\kappa_{\mathcal{D}}(\mathcal{M}) = \{X \in \kappa(\mathcal{M}) \mid \textit{callee}(X) \in \mathcal{D}\}$ the set of transactions craftable by $\mathcal{M}$ and targeting contracts in $\mathcal{D}$. We define:

$$\text{MEV}_{\mathcal{D}}(S, \mathcal{C}) = \max \left\{ \$_{\mathcal{C}}(S) - \$_{\mathcal{C}}(S') \,\middle|\, \vec{X} \in \kappa_{\mathcal{D}}(\mathcal{M})^*,\ S \xrightarrow{\vec{X}} S' \right\} \quad (3)$$

Note that by the finite token assumption in Sect. 2, the wealth is always finite, and so also the local MEV.

4 A Quantitative Notion of Economic Security

In this section we introduce our notion of quantitative security for smart contract compositions, and study its theoretical properties. In Sect. 5 we will apply it to analyse some archetypal compositions and attacks.

Let S be a blockchain state, formed by users' wallets W and contract states Γ, where we want to deploy new contracts with an initial state Δ. Note that, by the well-formedness assumption introduced in Sect. 2, the dependencies of Δ must be included in $\Gamma \mid \Delta$, i.e. any function call made by a contract in Δ must target some contracts in Γ or in Δ. We want to measure the security of the composition $S \mid \Delta$ by analysing the additional loss that an adversary can inflict to the contracts in Δ by manipulating the dependencies Γ. To this purpose, our definition will compare:

- $\text{MEV}(S \mid \Delta, \dagger\Delta)$, the maximal loss of the contracts in Δ, where adversaries are able to send transactions to *any* contract in $S \mid \Delta$;
- $\text{MEV}_{\dagger\Delta}(S \mid \Delta, \dagger\Delta)$, the maximal loss of the contracts in Δ, where adversaries can *only* send transactions to contracts in Δ. Note that interactions between Δ and Γ are still possible, as contracts in Δ can invoke functions of contracts in Γ (*"contract dependencies"*), and adversaries can extract tokens from Γ to play them in calls to contracts in Δ (*"token dependencies"*).

Listing 1.1. A simple airdrop contract.

```
contract Airdrop {
  fund(pay x:T) { }  // any user can deposit x:T to the contract
  withdraw(x) {      // any user can withdraw any amount x:T
    require(balance(T)>=x); // check that the contract has at least x:T
    transfer(sender,x:T);   // transfer x:T to the caller
  }
}
```

Listing 1.2. A simple airdrop contract with fees.

```
contract AirdropFee {
  fund(pay x:T) { }  // any user can deposit x:T to the contract
  withdraw(x) {      // any user can withdraw any amount x:T (minus fee)
    require(balance(T)>=x);
    fee = floor((FeeManager.getFee() * x) / 100); // integer division
    transfer(sender, x-fee:T);
    transfer(FeeManager.getOwner(), fee:T);
  }
}
contract FeeManager {
  constructor() { owner=sender; feeRate=1; }
  getOwner() { return owner; }
  getFee()   { return feeRate; }
  setFee(r)  { require (r>=0 && r<=100); feeRate=r; }
}
```

Our security notion, called *MEV interference*, measures how leveraging the dependencies in S can amplify the loss caused to Δ. We denote with $\mathcal{I}(S \leadsto \Delta)$ the MEV interference caused by a blockchain state S to Δ.

Definition 1 (MEV interference). *For a blockchain state S and a contract state Δ, we quantify the MEV interference caused by S on Δ as:*

$$\mathcal{I}(S \leadsto \Delta) = \begin{cases} 1 - \dfrac{\mathrm{MEV}_{\dagger \Delta}(S \mid \Delta, \dagger \Delta)}{\mathrm{MEV}(S \mid \Delta, \dagger \Delta)} & \text{if } \mathrm{MEV}(S \mid \Delta, \dagger \Delta) \neq 0 \\ 0 & \text{otherwise} \end{cases}$$

Our notion is consistent with the notion of MEV non-interference in [6], which classifies S and Δ as non-interferent if $\mathrm{MEV}_{\dagger \Delta}(S \mid \Delta, \dagger \Delta) = \mathrm{MEV}(S \mid \Delta, \dagger \Delta)$. Namely, $\mathcal{I}(S \leadsto \Delta) = 0$ iff S and Δ are non-interferent according to [6].

Example 1 (Any/Airdrop). Consider an instance $\Delta = \texttt{Airdrop}[n : \texttt{T}]$ of the airdrop contract in Listing 1.1, to be deployed in an arbitrary blockchain state S. Note that $\mathrm{MEV}(S \mid \Delta, \{\texttt{Airdrop}\}) = n \cdot \$1_\texttt{T}$, since the adversary can craft a transaction $\texttt{M} : \texttt{Airdrop.withdraw}(n)$ to extract all the tokens from the contract. The restricted $\mathrm{MEV}_{\{\texttt{Airdrop}\}}(S \mid \Delta, \{\texttt{Airdrop}\})$ is equal to the unrestricted one, since the adversary just needs to interact with Airdrop. Therefore, if $n > 0$:

$$\mathcal{I}(S \leadsto \Delta) = 1 - \dfrac{\mathrm{MEV}_{\{\texttt{Airdrop}\}}(S \mid \Delta, \{\texttt{Airdrop}\})}{\mathrm{MEV}(S \mid \Delta, \{\texttt{Airdrop}\})} = 0$$

The same holds if $n = 0$. This is consistent with our intuition, since the adversary does not need to exploit the dependencies in S to extract MEV from Δ. ◇

Example 2 (FeeManager/Airdrop). Consider a variant of the airdrop contract, where each withdrawal requires the user to pay a proportional fee (Listing 1.2). To obtain the fee rate, the AirdropFee contract calls the FeeManager contract. Assume that we want to deploy $\Delta = \mathtt{AirdropFee}[n : \mathtt{T}]$ in a blockchain state S containing $\mathtt{FeeManager}[\mathtt{feeRate} = r]$. The unrestricted MEV is $n \cdot \$1_\mathtt{T}$, since an adversary can set the fee to 0 by calling FeeManager.setFee(0) and then withdraw the full balance of $n : \mathtt{T}$ from AirdropFee. Instead, the restricted MEV only amounts to $(n - \lfloor r \cdot n / 100 \rfloor) \cdot \$1_\mathtt{T}$, since the adversary cannot call FeeManager to manipulate the fee rate. Therefore, if $n > 0$:

$$\mathcal{I}(S \leadsto \Delta) = 1 - \frac{n - \lfloor r \cdot n / 100 \rfloor}{n} \leq \frac{r}{100}$$

This is coherent with our intuition: the closer the fee rate is to 100, the greater the difference between restricted and unrestricted MEV, and so the possibility for the attacker to inflict more damage to the contract. ◇

We now study the theoretical properties of MEV interference. Because of space constraints, we relegate the proofs of our statements to a technical report on ArXiV. Lemma 1 establishes a few basic properties of MEV interference: its value is zero when the context S has no contracts and when Δ is empty; furthermore, the interference is always comprised between 0 and 1.

Lemma 1. *(i)* $\mathcal{I}(S \leadsto \emptyset) = 0$; *(ii)* $\mathcal{I}(W \mid \emptyset \leadsto \Delta) = 0$; *(iii)* $0 \leq \mathcal{I}(S \leadsto \Delta) \leq 1$.

Note that $\mathcal{I}(S \leadsto \Delta)$ ranges from a minumum 0, representing the case where the context S is not useful to extract MEV from Δ, to a maximum 1, corresponding to the case where the economic loss that can be inflicted to Δ is purely due to the interactions of the adversary with S. Enclosing MEV interference into an interval is a design choice, which we illustrate with an example. Let S be a state with an airdrop contract releasing $1 : \mathtt{T}$, where we want to deploy a new contract Δ that, upon the payment of $1 : \mathtt{T}$, releases all its balance of $n : \mathtt{ETH}$. Assume that the adversary has no tokens T, so that she needs to extract $1 : \mathtt{T}$ from the airdrop in order to extract MEV from Δ. If we measured the interference from S to Δ as the difference between unrestricted and restricted MEV, i.e.:

$$\mathcal{I}(S \leadsto \Delta) \stackrel{?}{=} \mathrm{MEV}(S \mid \Delta, \dagger\Delta) - \mathrm{MEV}_{\dagger\Delta}(S \mid \Delta, \dagger\Delta)$$

then we would obtain that $\mathcal{I}(S \leadsto \Delta) = n \cdot \$1_{\mathtt{ETH}}$, i.e. the interference would be proportional to the ETH balance in Δ. We do not find this measure particularly insightful: after all, what we observe is just that *all* the MEV extractable from Δ is due to the interaction with the context S. In general, under these conditions, our intuition is that the interference should take its maximum value.

Lemma 2 states that when the newly deployed contracts Δ have no wealth (i.e., when $\$_{\dagger\Delta}(\Delta) = 0$), then they have no MEV interference with the context.

Lemma 2. *If* $\$_{\dagger\Delta}(\Delta) = 0$, *then* $\mathfrak{I}(S \rightsquigarrow \Delta) = 0$.

Of course, if Δ has zero wealth, no loss can be inflicted to Δ, regardless of any potential manipulation of its dependencies in S. This also underscores a fundamental aspect of our definition—namely, that it measures what happens in *specific* contract states, rather than in *arbitrary* reachable states of a given contract. For this reason, our intuition is to have $\mathfrak{I}(S \rightsquigarrow \Delta) = 0$ whenever Δ has zero wealth, while not ruling out the possibility of having $\mathfrak{I}(S' \rightsquigarrow \Delta') > 0$ in a state Δ' where the contracts have been funded.

Theorem 1 says that widening a blockchain state S potentially increases MEV interference to newly deployed contracts Δ. Formally, this amounts to showing that $\mathfrak{I}$ is monotonic w.r.t. the operation of adding contracts Γ to the context, i.e. $\mathfrak{I}(S \rightsquigarrow \Delta) \leq \mathfrak{I}(S \mid \Gamma \rightsquigarrow \Delta)$. Note that by the well-formedness assumption, the statement implicitly assumes that Δ has no dependencies in Γ.

Theorem 1. $\mathfrak{I}(S \rightsquigarrow \Delta) \leq \mathfrak{I}(S \mid \Gamma \rightsquigarrow \Delta)$

For illustration, consider a state S where we want to deploy new contracts Δ, with an interference estimated as $\mathfrak{I}(S \rightsquigarrow \Delta)$. Assume now that the deployment of Δ is front-run by that of another set of contracts Γ. Of course Δ cannot have dependencies in Γ, since otherwise it would not be possible to deploy Δ in S (as this would violate the well-formedness assumption). Now, the interference $\mathfrak{I}(S \mid \Gamma \rightsquigarrow \Delta)$ could either be equal to $\mathfrak{I}(S \rightsquigarrow \Delta)$, or possibly increase when the adversary can drain tokens from Γ to inflict more loss to Δ. Theorem 1 states that, in any case, the interference should not decrease.

The following example shows a case where the inequality given by Theorem 1 is strict. This is because, even if Δ has no *contract* dependencies in Γ, the adversary may exploit their *token* dependencies, i.e. extract tokens from Γ and leverage them to extract more tokens from Δ.

Example 3. Let $S = \text{M}[0 : \text{T}]$ be a state where the adversary has no tokens, and there are no contracts. Consider a contract Doubler with a function that, upon receiving as input $n : \text{T}$, returns to the sender $2n : \text{T}$, and let $\Delta = \text{Doubler}[2 : \text{T}]$. By Lemma 1, S does not interfere with Δ. Instead, adding $\Gamma = \text{Airdrop}[1 : \text{T}]$ to S yields $\mathfrak{I}(S \mid \Gamma \rightsquigarrow \Delta) = 1$, since $\text{MEV}_{\{\text{Doubler}\}}(S \mid \Gamma \mid \Delta, \{\text{Doubler}\}) = 0$ while $\text{MEV}(S \mid \Gamma \mid \Delta, \{\text{Doubler}\}) = 2 \cdot \$1_\text{T}$. This increase is caused by the ability of M to leverage the token dependencies between the newly deployed Airdrop contract to extract more MEV from Doubler than previously possible. ◇

The previous example also shows that wealthier adversaries not always cause greater interference. Indeed, if $S = \text{M}[1 : \text{T}]$, then M does not need to exploit the Airdrop to extract MEV from the Doubler contract, since she has enough tokens in her wallet. Of course there are also cases where wealthier adversary can cause more MEV interference: we will see this in Example 5, where a sufficiently wealthy M can win a bet by producing a price fluctuation in an AMM.

Theorem 2 shows that users' wallets are irrelevant to the evaluation of MEV interference. Namely, $\mathfrak{I}(S \rightsquigarrow \Delta)$ is preserved when removing from S all the wallets except those of adversaries. Recall that a wallet state W is a map from accounts to wallets. Then, in a state $S = W \mid \Gamma$, we just need to consider the restriction of W to the domain $\mathcal{M}$.

Theorem 2. *If* $\operatorname{dom} W_{\mathcal{M}} = \mathcal{M}$, *then* $\mathfrak{I}(W_{\mathcal{M}} \mid W \mid \Gamma \rightsquigarrow \Delta) = \mathfrak{I}(W_{\mathcal{M}} \mid \Gamma \rightsquigarrow \Delta)$.

Here the intuition is that the adversary does not have any control of the tokens in users' wallets, and therefore these tokens play no role in the extraction of MEV from Δ. This assumption highlights a simplification in our attacker model, namely that the mempool of users' transactions is not known by the adversary. Formally, this assumption is visible in the definition of MEV in (3), where the set $\kappa_{\mathcal{D}}(\mathcal{M})$ of transactions craftable by the adversary does not take the mempool as a parameter. Were mempool transactions playable by the adversary, then their success would also depend on the users' wallet, and consequently the MEV interference would possibly depend on them. We discuss this in Sect. 6.

Theorem 3 provides sufficient conditions under which an adversary $\mathcal{M}$ gains no advantage by front-running the newly deployed contracts Δ with malicious contracts $\Gamma_{\mathcal{M}}$. Condition (i) requires the contracts in $deps(\Delta)$ to be *sender-agnostic*, i.e. their functions are unaware of the identity of the sender, only being able to use it as a recipient of token transfers. Condition (ii) requires that the contracts in $deps(\Delta)$ are *token independent* with those in the other contracts (not in $deps(\Delta)$) which could be possibly exploited by $\mathcal{M}$. Note that since Definition 1 assumes that states are well-formed, Theorem 3 implicitly assumes that contracts in Δ do not call contracts in $\Gamma_{\mathcal{M}}$. Before stating Theorem 3, we formalise sender-agnosticism and token independence.

Definition 2 (Sender-agnosticism). *A contract* C *is* sender-agnostic *if, for all states S and for all transitions that involve an (external or internal) call to* C, *replacing the caller's address* a *with any other address* b *results in the same post-transition state, up to the substitution of* a *with* b.

In practice, the effect of calling a function of a sender-agnostic contract C can be decomposed into: (i) updating the states of contracts (either directly or through internal calls); (ii) transferring tokens between users and contracts; (iii) transferring tokens to the sender of the call to C. Any call to C with the same arguments and origin, but distinct sender, has exactly the same effect, except for item (iii), where tokens are transferred to the new sender.

Token independence relies on two auxiliary notions: the token types that can be received by contracts Γ from other contracts in S, denoted by $in_S(\Gamma)$, and those that can be sent from Γ to other contracts, written $out_S(\Gamma)$.

Definition 3 (Token independence). *Let $S = W \mid \Gamma$, and let $\Delta \preceq \Gamma$ be a subset of the contract states in Γ. We define:*

- $in_S(\Delta)$ *as the set of token types* T *for which there exists a state S' reachable from S through a sequence of steps, containing a transaction that causes an inflow of tokens* T *from outside Δ to one of the contracts in Δ.*

Listing 1.3. An exchange contract.

```
contract Exchange {
  constructor(pay x:tout_, tin_, rate_) { // receive x:tout_ from sender
    require rate_>0 && tin_!=tout_;
    rate=rate_; tout=tout_; tin=tin_; owner=sender;
  }
  getTokens() { return (tin,tout); }
  getRate(tout) { return rate; } // 1:tin for getRate(tout):tout
  setRate(r) { require sender==owner; rate=r; } // sender can update rate

  swap(pay x:tin) {              // sender sells x units of token tin
    y = x*getRate(tout);         // units of token tout sold to sender
    require balance(tout)>=y;    // Exchange has enough tout tokens
    transfer(sender, y:tout);    // send y units of token tout to sender
  }
}
```

- $out_S(\Delta)$ as the set of token types T for which there exists a state S' reachable from S through a sequence of steps, containing a transaction that causes an outflow of tokens T from Δ to one of the contracts outside Δ.

Let now $\Delta_0 \preceq \Gamma$ and $\Delta_1 \preceq \Gamma$. We say that Δ_0 and Δ_1 are token independent in $S = W \mid \Gamma$ when $in_S(\Delta_0) \cap out_S(\Delta_1) = \emptyset = in_S(\Delta_1) \cap out_S(\Delta_0)$.

Theorem 3. $\mathfrak{I}(S \leadsto \Delta) = \mathfrak{I}(S \mid \Gamma_M \leadsto \Delta)$ holds if (i) the contracts in $deps(\Delta)$ are sender-agnostic, and (ii) $deps(\Delta)$ and $deps(S \mid \Gamma_M) \setminus deps(\Delta)$ are token independent in $S \mid \Gamma_M \mid \Delta$.

Note that $\mathfrak{I}(S \leadsto \Delta)$ is zero when the contract dependencies and the token dependencies of Δ in S are irrelevant to the ability of inflicting a loss to Δ. E.g., consider an arbitrary state S where we want to deploy an airdrop contract Δ (see Listing 1.1). In this scenario, the adversary cannot gain any advantage from the contracts in S, since she can extract the full MEV from the airdrop by interacting with Δ, only. Therefore, the MEV interference from S to Δ is zero.

5 Use Cases

We now illustrate MEV interference through a set of use cases. For simplicity, we assume the values in these use cases are real numbers and that all computations are performed using exact arithmetic. We note that adapting our results to smart contract platforms, that, like Ethereum, operate on integers, requires several modifications, such as applying flooring to arithmetic operations and replacing equalities with inequalities. We refer to the full technical report on ArXiV for details.

Example 4 (Airdrop/Exchange). Consider an instance of the Exchange contract in Listing 1.3, to be deployed in a blockchain state S containing an instance of the Airdrop contract in Listing 1.1. More specifically, let:

$$S = \texttt{M}[n_M : T] \mid \texttt{Airdrop}[n_A : T]$$
$$\Delta = \texttt{Exchange}[n_E : \texttt{ETH}, \texttt{tin} = T, \texttt{tout} = \texttt{ETH}, \texttt{rate} = r, \texttt{owner} = A]$$

The Exchange contract allows any user to swap tokens of type tin with tokens of type tout (in the instance, T and ETH, respectively), at an exchange rate of 1 unit of tin for rate units of tout. For simplicity, assume that $\$1_\text{T} = \$1_\text{ETH} = 1$. We evaluate the MEV interference from S to Δ. When the exchange rate is favourable, i.e. $r > 1$, the adversary M can extract MEV from Δ by exchanging T for ETH. This is possible as far as Exchange has enough ETH balance. The MEV can be further increased by draining n_A : T from Airdrop, and swapping these tokens through the Exchange. More precisely, we have:

$$\text{MEV}_{\{\text{Exchange}\}}(S \mid \Delta, \{\text{Exchange}\}) = \begin{cases} n_\text{M} \cdot r & \text{if } n_\text{M} < n_\text{E}/r \\ n_\text{E} & \text{otherwise} \end{cases}$$

$$\text{MEV}(S \mid \Delta, \{\text{Exchange}\}) = \begin{cases} (n_\text{M} + n_\text{A}) \cdot r & \text{if } n_\text{M} < n_\text{E}/r - n_\text{A} \\ n_\text{E} & \text{otherwise} \end{cases}$$

Therefore, the MEV interference from S on Δ is given by:

$$\mathcal{I}(S \rightsquigarrow \Delta) = \begin{cases} n_\text{A}/(n_\text{M}+n_\text{A}) & \text{if } n_\text{M} < n_\text{E}/r - n_\text{A} \\ 1 - n_\text{M} \cdot r/n_\text{E} & \text{if } n_\text{E}/r - n_\text{A} \leq n_\text{M} < n_\text{E}/r \\ 0 & \text{otherwise} \end{cases}$$

When M is sufficiently rich, she can drain the Exchange without invoking the Airdrop. Instead, when M's wealth is limited, she is able to inflict a greater loss of Exchange by leveraging the Airdrop. So, the interference caused to Exchange in this case has a dual dependence on the adversary's and the Airdrop's wealth. Furthermore, the interference is inversely proportional to M's wealth, i.e. richer adversaries have less need to exploit the context, resulting in lower interference from S to Δ. This is coherent with our intuition, since we would expect a poorer adversary to benefit more from exploiting the Airdrop than a richer one. ⋄

Example 5 (AMM/Bet). The Bet contract in Listing 1.4 allows a player to bet on the exchange rate between a token and ETH. It is parameterized over an oracle that is queried for the token price. To enter the bet, the player must match the initial pot set upon deployment. Before the deadline, the player can win a fraction potShare of the pot if the oracle exchange rate exceeds or equals potShare times the rate. The remaining fraction is taken by the owner. Consider an instance of Bet using the AMM in Listing 1.5 as a price oracle:

$$S = \text{M}[m : \text{ETH}] \mid \text{AMM}[r_0 : \text{ETH}, r_1 : \text{T}] \mid \text{block.num} = d - k \mid \cdots$$
$$\Delta = \text{Bet}[b : \text{ETH}, \text{owner} = \text{A}, \text{tok} = \text{T}, \text{rate} = r, \text{deadline} = d]$$

When M is allowed to leverage Bet's dependency, she can manipulate the AMM to influence the internal exchange rate. If M has sufficient funds to enter the bet, she can fire the following sequence of transactions, where, in the swap transaction, $x = m - b \geq 0$ is the number of ETH units sent to the AMM and $y = xr_1/r_0+x$ is the number of T units received (we omit M's wallet for brevity):

$S \mid \Delta \xrightarrow{\text{M:Bet.bet(M pays } b\text{:ETH},p)}$ $\text{AMM}[r_0 : \text{ETH}, r_1 : T] \mid \text{Bet}[2b : \text{ETH}, \text{potShare} = p, \cdots] \mid \cdots$

$\xrightarrow{\text{M:AMM.swap(M pays } x\text{:ETH},0)}$ $\text{AMM}[r_0 + x : \text{ETH}, r_1 - y : T] \mid \text{Bet}[2b : \text{ETH}, \cdots] \mid \cdots$

$\xrightarrow{\text{M:Bet.win()}}$ $\text{AMM}[r_0 + x : \text{ETH}, r_1 - y : T] \mid \text{Bet}[2b - 2bp : \text{ETH}, \cdots] \mid \cdots$

$\xrightarrow{\text{M:AMM.swap(M pays } y\text{:T},0)}$ $\text{AMM}[r_0 : \text{ETH}, r_1 : T] \mid \text{Bet}[2b - 2bp : \text{ETH}, \cdots] \mid \cdots$

The bet value that maximizes the loss caused to Bet depends on M's wealth, and is given by $p = {r_0+x}/{r(r_1-y)}$. Assuming M enters the bet only for $p \geq 1/2$ (since a smaller proportion makes the bet irrational for her), by Eq. (2) we have:

$$\text{MEV}(S \mid \Delta, \{\text{Bet}\}) = \left(2(r_0+m-b)^2/rr_0r_1 - 1\right) b$$

If M can only interact with Bet, she is limited to settle on a lower bet value:

$$\text{MEV}_{\{\text{Bet}\}}(S \mid \Delta, \{\text{Bet}\}) = \begin{cases} 2br_0/rr_1 - b - 1 & \text{if } r_0/rr_1 \geq 1/2 \\ 0 & \text{otherwise} \end{cases}$$

Accordingly, MEV interference is estimated through Definition 1 as follows:

$$\mathcal{I}(S \rightsquigarrow \Delta) = \begin{cases} 1 - \frac{2br_0^2 - rr_0r_1(b+1)}{2b(r_0+m-b)^2 - brr_0r_1} & \text{if } r_0/rr_1 \geq 1/2 \\ 1 & \text{otherwise} \end{cases}$$

We observe maximum interference when M exploits the Bet by manipulating the AMM, which would be impossible by interacting exclusively with Bet. Furthermore, the interference value is proportional to the adversarial wealth, as one would anticipate. By contrast, even if M was able to empty a portion of the Bet by fair play, she can always increase this loss by manipulating the AMM (provided she owns adequate funds). Note that in the composition between Bet and Exchange, the MEV interference is zero, as the adversary cannot manipulate the exchange rate (unless she is the Exchange owner). ◇

Example 6 (AMM/Lending Pool). The contract LP in Listing 1.6 implements a simplified lending protocol, where users can deposit and borrow tokens. Borrowing requires users to have a sufficient *collateralization* [5,13]. This value, defined as the ratio between the value of their deposits and that of their debits, is a measure of the borrowing capacity (full versions of lending protocols include a function that allows liquidators to repay loans of under-collateralized borrowers in exchange for part of their collateral). The contract LP is parameterized over an oracle that is queried for the token prices. Below we analyze a well-known attack where the underlying oracle is an AMM, which is manipulated by an adversary to increase her borrowing capacity [1,5,12,20,21].

More specifically, consider the following instance, where $\$1_{\text{ETH}} = 1 = \$1_T$, the AMM is balanced, and the adversary M has not deposited or borrowed tokens yet:

$$S = \text{M}[n : \text{ETH}] \mid \text{AMM}[r : \text{ETH}, r : T] \quad \Delta = \text{LP}[a : \text{ETH}, b : T, \text{Cmin} = C_{min}, \cdots]$$

Listing 1.4. A Bet contract.

```
contract Bet_oracle {
  constructor(pay x:ETH, tok_, deadline_, rate_) {
    require tok_!=ETH && oracle.getTokens()==(ETH,tok_);
    tok=tok_; deadline=deadline_; rate=rate_; owner=sender;
  }
  bet(pay x:ETH, p_) { // sender gives x:ETH to Bet and chooses potShare
    require player==null && x==balance(ETH) && p_>=0 && p_<=1;
    potShare = p_; player=sender;
  }
  win() { // only callable by player before the deadline
    require block.num<=deadline && sender==player;
    if (oracle.getRate(ETH)>=potShare*rate)
      transfer(player, potShare*balance(ETH):ETH);
  }
  close() { // after the deadline, transfer the ETH balance to the owner
    require block.num>deadline;
    transfer(owner, balance(ETH):ETH);
  }
}
```

Listing 1.5. A constant-product AMM contract.

```
contract AMM {
  constructor(pay x0:T0, pay x1:T1) { require x0>0 && x1>0; }

  getTokens() { return (T0,T1); }   // token pair

  getRate(tout) { // 1:tin for getRate(tout):tout
    if (tout==T0) { tin=T1 } else { tin=T0 };
    return balance(tout)/balance(tin);
  }
  swap(pay x:tin, ymin) { // sell x:tin to buy at least ymin:tout
    if (tin==T0) { tout=T1 } else { tout=T0 };
    y = x*getRate(tout);           // units of token tout sold to sender
    require ymin<=y<balance(tout); // the AMM has enough tout tokens
    transfer(sender, y:tout); // send y units of token tout to sender
  }
}
```

If M can interact with the AMM, she has the following attack strategy: deposit $(n - x)$: ETH to the LP, and use the remaining x : ETH to inflate the price of T in the AMM. This allows M to increase the amount of T she can borrow, since the LP now uses an artificially inflated price to determine her borrowing capacity.

To implement this strategy, M fires the following sequence of transactions, where we denote by y the amount of T units that M receives from the swap, and with t the amount of T units that M manages to borrow from the LP (below, we omit M's wallet, and the parts of the state that do not change upon a transition):

$S \mid \Delta \xrightarrow{\text{M:LP.deposit(M pays } (n-x)\text{:ETH)}} \text{AMM}[r : \text{ETH}, r : \text{T}] \mid \text{LP}[a + n - x : \text{ETH}, b : \text{T}, \cdots] \mid \cdots$

$\xrightarrow{\text{M:AMM.swap(M pays } x\text{:ETH,0)}} \text{AMM}[r + x : \text{ETH}, r - y : \text{T}] \mid \cdots$

$\xrightarrow{\text{M:LP.borrow}(t,\text{T})} \cdots \mid \text{LP}[a + n - x : \text{ETH}, b - t : \text{T}, \cdots] \mid \cdots$

$\xrightarrow{\text{M:AMM.swap(M pays } y\text{:T,0)}} \text{AMM}[r : \text{ETH}, r : \text{T}] \mid \cdots$

Listing 1.6. A Lending Pool contract (simplified).

```
contract LP_oracle {
  constructor(Cmin_) { Cmin = Cmin_; }  // collateralization threshold
  collateral(a) {  // return a's collateralization
    val_minted = 0;
    for c in minted: val_minted += minted[t][a] * oracle.getRate(t);
    val_debts = 0;
    for c in debts: val_debts += debt[t][a] * oracle.getRate(t);
    return val_minted / val_debts;
  }
  deposit(a pays x:t) {  // a deposits x units of token t in the LP
    minted[t][a] += x;   // record the deposited units in the minted map
  }
  borrow(a sig, x, t) {  // a borrows x units of token t in the LP
    require balance(t)>=x;
    debts[t][a] += x;    // record the borrowed units in the debts map
    require collateral(a)>=Cmin;  // a is over-collateralized
    transfer(a, x:t);
  }
}
```

The amount that M can borrow (as a function of x) is $t = (n-x)(r+x)^2 / C_{min}(r-y)^2$. Its maximum is obtained for $x = 4n - r/5$ when M benefits from the manipulation (i.e., when $4n \geq r$), and for $x = 0$ otherwise.

Assuming that the LP has sufficient funds, the unrestricted MEV is given by:

$$\text{MEV}(S \mid \Delta, \{\text{LP}\}) = \frac{(n-x)(r+x)^2}{C_{min}(r-y)^2} + x - n$$

$$= \begin{cases} \left(\frac{n+r}{5}\right)\left(\frac{1}{C_{min}}\right)\left(\frac{4(n+r)}{5r}\right)^4 - 1\right) & \text{if } 4n \geq r \\ n\left(\frac{1}{C_{min}} - 1\right) & \text{otherwise} \end{cases}$$

On the contrary, if M was restricted to interact with the LP only, she suffers a reduced borrowing allowance. By Equation (3) we have:

$$\text{MEV}_{\{\text{LP}\}}(S \mid \Delta, \{\text{LP}\}) = n\left(\frac{1}{C_{min}} - 1\right)$$

Accordingly, MEV interference is estimated through Definition 1 as follows:

$$\mathcal{I}(S \rightsquigarrow \Delta) = \begin{cases} 1 - \frac{5^5 r^4 n (1-C_{min})}{(n+r)(4^4(n+r)^4 - (5r)^4 C_{min})} & \text{if } 4n \geq r \\ 0 & \text{otherwise} \end{cases}$$

In accordance with our expectations, the interference is indeed proportional to the attack capital n of the adversary. Naturally, adversaries with higher manipulation capital experience an increased borrowing capacity. Moreover, the degree of interference is influenced by the AMM reserves since the profitability of the attack rests on the cost of manipulating and de-manipulating the AMM. ◇

6 Conclusions

We have proposed a notion of economic security for smart contract compositions, which quantifies the potential economic loss an adversary can inflict on a contract by targeting its dependencies. Below, we discuss some limitations of our approach and directions for future work.

Limitations. To keep our theory manageable, we have made a few simplifying assumptions in our model. A first assumption is that the prices of native crypto-assets are constant. Consequently, the amount of MEV interference is not affected by fluctuations of these prices (while they could depend on the prices provided by DEXes, like in Examples 5 and 6). Handling price updates would require to extend blockchain states with a function mapping tokens to their prices. Another assumption is that the local MEV in Eq. (3) does not allow adversaries to exploit their knowledge of pending users' transactions (the public *mempool*). The rationale underlying this choice is that, in our vision, MEV interference should be the basis for a static analysis of smart contracts, where dynamic data such as the mempool transactions are not known. Assuming an over-approximation of users' transactions, we could extend our MEV interference by making the mempool a parameter of local MEV, similarly to what done for the theory of MEV in [7].

Future Work. While some tools exist for detecting price manipulation attacks in DeFi protocols [18,22,23], and others for estimating MEV opportunities [3,4], there remains a gap in addressing general economic attacks on smart contract compositions. A common analysis technique underlying the detection of price manipulation attacks—also employed by some of the tools mentioned above—is *taint analysis*, which aims at identifying potential data flows from low-level to high-level data. In the DeFi setting, this typically corresponds to flows from to functions that influence token prices to functions that transfer tokens. While this technique could potentially be generalised to analyse *qualitative* MEV non-interference, capturing our notion of *quantitative* interference seems to require more advanced techniques. Some inspiration could be drawn from static analysis techniques for information-theoretic interference [2,9,17,19]. We plan to explore this research line in future work. Our blockchain model represents crypto-assets as token types with primitive transfer operations and built-in linearity guarantees preventing asset creation or destruction. In practice, several blockchains including Ethereum do not have native support for custom tokens, but rather require to implement them as smart contracts exposing standard interfaces. This opens the door for attackers to exploit potential discrepancies between these implementations and the standards, possibly leading to MEV [8]. Applying our MEV interference analysis to such compositions is left as future work.

Acknowledgments. Work partially supported by project SERICS (PE00000014) under the MUR National Recovery and Resilience Plan (NRRP) funded by the European Union – NextGenerationEU, and by PRIN 2022 NRRP project DeLiCE (F53D23009130001).

References

1. Arora, S., Li, Y., Feng, Y., Xu, J.: SecPLF: secure protocols for loanable funds against oracle manipulation attacks. In: ACM Asia Conference on Computer and Communications Security (ASIA CCS). ACM (2024). https://doi.org/10.1145/3634737.3637681
2. Assaf, M., Naumann, D.A., Signoles, J., Totel, E., Tronel, F.: Hypercollecting semantics and its application to static analysis of information flow. In: ACM SIGPLAN Symposium on Principles of Programming Languages (POPL), pp. 874–887. ACM (2017). https://doi.org/10.1145/3009837.3009889
3. Babel, K., Daian, P., Kelkar, M., Juels, A.: Clockwork finance: automated analysis of economic security in smart contracts. In: IEEE Symposium on Security and Privacy, pp. 622–639. IEEE Computer Society (2023). https://doi.org/10.1109/SP46215.2023.00036
4. Babel, K., Javaheripi, M., Ji, Y., Kelkar, M., Koushanfar, F., Juels, A.: Lanturn: measuring economic security of smart contracts through adaptive learning. In: ACM SIGSAC Conference on Computer and Communications Security (CCS), pp. 1212–1226. ACM (2023). https://doi.org/10.1145/3576915.3623204
5. Bartoletti, M., Chiang, J.H., Lafuente, A.L.: SoK: lending pools in decentralized finance. In: Bernhard, M., et al. (eds.) FC 2021. LNCS, vol. 12676, pp. 553–578. Springer, Heidelberg (2021). https://doi.org/10.1007/978-3-662-63958-0_40
6. Bartoletti, M., Marchesin, R., Zunino, R.: DeFi composability as MEV non-interference. In: Clark, J., Shi, E. (eds.) FC 2024. LNCS, vol. 14745, pp. 369–387. Springer, Cham (2025). https://doi.org/10.1007/978-3-031-78679-2_20
7. Bartoletti, M., Zunino, R.: A theoretical basis for MEV. In: Financial Cryptography and Data Security. LNCS, Springer, Cham (2025). To appear
8. Chen, T., et al.: Tokenscope: automatically detecting inconsistent behaviors of cryptocurrency tokens in Ethereum. In: ACM SIGSAC Conference on Computer and Communications Security (CCS), pp. 1503–1520. ACM (2019). https://doi.org/10.1145/3319535.3345664
9. Clark, D., Hunt, S., Malacaria, P.: A static analysis for quantifying information flow in a simple imperative language. J. Comput. Secur. **15**(3), 321–371 (2007). https://doi.org/10.3233/JCS-2007-15302
10. Daian, P., et al.: Flash boys 2.0: frontrunning in decentralized exchanges, miner extractable value, and consensus instability. In: IEEE Symposium on Security and Privacy, pp. 910–927. IEEE (2020). https://doi.org/10.1109/SP40000.2020.00040
11. Goguen, J.A., Meseguer, J.: Security policies and security models. In: IEEE Symposium on Security and Privacy, pp. 11–20. IEEE Computer Society (1982). https://doi.org/10.1109/SP.1982.10014
12. Gudgeon, L., Pérez, D., Harz, D., Livshits, B., Gervais, A.: The decentralized financial crisis. In: Crypto Valley Conference on Blockchain Technology (CVCBT), pp. 1–15. IEEE (2020). https://doi.org/10.1109/CVCBT50464.2020.00005
13. Gudgeon, L., Werner, S., Perez, D., Knottenbelt, W.J.: DeFi protocols for loanable funds: interest rates, liquidity and market efficiency. In: ACM Conference on Advances in Financial Technologies (AFT), pp. 92–112 (2020). https://doi.org/10.1145/3419614.3423254
14. Guesmi, S., Piazza, C., Rossi, S.: Noninterference analysis for smart contracts: would you bet on it? In: Distributed Ledger Technology Workshop (DLT). CEUR Workshop Proceedings, vol. 3791. CEUR-WS.org (2024)

15. Kitzler, S., Victor, F., Saggese, P., Haslhofer, B.: A systematic investigation of DeFi compositions in Ethereum. In: Matsuo, S., et al. (eds.) FC 2022. LNCS, vol. 13412, pp. 272–279. Springer, Cham (2022). https://doi.org/10.1007/978-3-031-32415-4_18
16. Kitzler, S., Victor, F., Saggese, P., Haslhofer, B.: Disentangling Decentralized Finance (DeFi) compositions. ACM Trans. Web **17**(2), 10:1–10:26 (2023). https://doi.org/10.1145/3532857
17. Klebanov, V.: Precise quantitative information flow analysis - a symbolic approach. Theoret. Comput. Sci. **538**, 124–139 (2014). https://doi.org/10.1016/j.tcs.2014.04.022
18. Kong, Q., Chen, J., Wang, Y., Jiang, Z., Zheng, Z.: DeFiTainter: detecting price manipulation vulnerabilities in DeFi protocols. In: ACM SIGSOFT International Symposium on Software Testing and Analysis, pp. 1144–1156 (2023). https://doi.org/10.1145/3597926.3598124
19. Köpf, B., Rybalchenko, A.: Automation of quantitative information-flow analysis. In: Bernardo, M., de Vink, E., Di Pierro, A., Wiklicky, H. (eds.) SFM 2013. LNCS, vol. 7938, pp. 1–28. Springer, Heidelberg (2013). https://doi.org/10.1007/978-3-642-38874-3_1
20. Mackinga, T., Nadahalli, T., Wattenhofer, R.: TWAP oracle attacks: easier done than said? In: IEEE International Conference on Blockchain and Cryptocurrency (ICBC), pp. 1–8. IEEE (2022). https://doi.org/10.1109/ICBC54727.2022.9805499
21. Qin, K., Zhou, L., Livshits, B., Gervais, A.: Attacking the DeFi ecosystem with flash loans for fun and profit. In: Borisov, N., Diaz, C. (eds.) FC 2021. LNCS, vol. 12674, pp. 3–32. Springer, Heidelberg (2021). https://doi.org/10.1007/978-3-662-64322-8_1
22. Wu, K.W.: Strengthening DeFi security: a static analysis approach to flash loan vulnerabilities. CoRR abs/2411.01230 (2025). https://doi.org/10.48550/arXiv.2411.01230
23. Wu, S., et al.: DeFiRanger: detecting price manipulation attacks on DeFi applications. CoRR abs/2104.15068 (2021). https://arxiv.org/abs/2104.15068
24. Yao, S., Ni, H., Myers, A.C., Cecchetti, E.: SCIF: a language for compositional smart contract security. CoRR abs/2407.01204 (2024). https://arxiv.org/abs/2407.01204

Hollow Victory: How Malicious Proposers Exploit Validator Incentives in Optimistic Rollup Dispute Games

Suhyeon Lee[1,2]

[1] Tokamak Network, Singapore, Singapore
suhyeon@tokamak.network
[2] Korea University, Seoul, South Korea
orion-alpha@korea.ac.kr

Abstract. Blockchain systems, such as Ethereum, are increasingly adopting layer-2 scaling solutions to improve transaction throughput and reduce fees. One popular layer-2 approach is the Optimistic Rollup, which relies security on a mechanism known as a dispute game for block proposals. In these systems, validators can challenge blocks that they believe contain errors, and a successful challenge results in the transfer of a portion of the proposer's deposit as a reward. In this paper, we reveal a structural vulnerability in the mechanism: validators may not be awarded a proper profit despite winning a dispute challenge. We develop a formal game-theoretic model of the dispute game and analyze several scenarios, including cases where the proposer controls some validators and cases where a secondary auction mechanism is deployed to induce additional participation. Our analysis demonstrates that under current designs, the competitive pressure from validators may be insufficient to deter malicious behavior. We find that increased validator competition, paradoxically driven by higher rewards or participation, can allow a malicious proposer to significantly lower their net loss by capturing value through mechanisms like auctions. To address this, we propose countermeasures such as an escrowed reward mechanism and a commit-reveal protocol. Our findings provide critical insights into enhancing the economic security of layer-2 scaling solutions in blockchain networks.

Keywords: Ethereum · Game Theory · Optimistic Rollup · Security · Smart Contract

1 Introduction

Blockchain technology, and Ethereum in particular, has witnessed rapid growth in recent years. However, scalability and high transaction fees remain critical challenges. To address these issues, various layer-2 scaling solutions have been proposed, among which *Optimistic Rollups* have gained significant attention. Optimistic Rollups enable off-chain computation while relying on an on-chain dispute resolution mechanism to ensure correctness. In these systems, block proposals are accepted optimistically, and validators are empowered to challenge any block they believe to be incorrect through a process known as a *dispute game*.

In a typical dispute game, a block proposer stakes a deposit and submits a block. Validators then monitor the block and, if they detect an error, submit a challenge. This challenge is called a fraud proof[1]. If the challenge is successful, the whole or a fraction of the proposer's deposit is confiscated and awarded to the challenger. Ideally, this mechanism is meant to deter malicious behavior by imposing significant economic penalties on a proposer who submits an incorrect block. Conversely, if the validator loses the challenge, their deposit for the challenge will be forfeited and granted to the block proposer. However, if the incentive mechanism is not carefully calibrated, a malicious proposer might be able to limit his losses to only a small challenge fee even when many validators participate in challenging the block. It results in undermining the intended economic deterrence.

In this paper, we model the dispute game using game-theoretic methods and analyze several attack scenarios with focusing on the malicious block proposer under a fraud proof challenge. We consider a case where the malicious proposer controls a subset of validators as well as cases in which a secondary auction is deployed to induce additional validator competition to get the dispute winner prize. Our analysis reveals that, under current incentive structures, the liveness of the dispute game may be insufficient to motivate them, thereby leaving the system vulnerable to strategic exploitation.

Our contributions are as follows:

- We develop a game-theoretic model of the dispute game in Optimistic Rollups, capturing the interactions between a malicious block proposer and validators under various challenge scenarios.
- We identify a critical vulnerability: malicious proposers can strategically minimize their own financial losses after being challenged, while simultaneously exploiting validator competition in a way that can diminish the net profitability for challengers, weakening the overall security model.
- We propose countermeasures, including an escrowed (deferred) reward mechanism and a commit-reveal protocol to rebalance the incentive structure and enhance the economic security of Optimistic Rollups.

The rest of the paper is organized as follows: Sect. 2 reviews related work on dispute games and incentive mechanisms in layer-2 solutions. In Sect. 3, we present our formal model of the Optimistic Rollup dispute game. Section 4 details the strategies a malicious proposer employ and introduces our proposed auction mechanism. Section 5 provides a game-theoretic analysis of the auction mechanism, including conditions under which validators are incentivized to participate.

---

[1] It is also referred to as a fault proof by Optimism, one of the leading optimistic rollup teams. However, the term fraud proof appears to be more widely accepted among optimistic rollups. Therefore, throughout this paper, we will use the term fraud proof.

Section 6 proposes two countermeasures to solve this structural vulnerability. Finally, Sect. 7 discusses potential solutions and future research directions, and concludes the paper.

2 Related Works

A variety of recent research has focused on understanding the economics and security of layer-2 scaling solutions. In this section, we review them particularly in the context of optimistic rollups.

Economic and Incentive Analysis in Rollups. Early works in the economic analysis of rollups have focused on establishing robust security guarantees through well-aligned incentive mechanisms. Tas *et al.* [14] propose a framework for *accountable safety* in rollups, which emphasizes the need for designs that hold participants economically accountable for misbehavior. Li [8] further explores the security of optimistic blockchain mechanisms, highlighting the importance of ensuring that validator incentives are strong enough to deter malicious actions. In a similar vein, Mamageishvili and Felten [10] analyze incentive schemes for rollup validators, discussing strategies under the attention test.

Data Availability Cost Optimization. Given that Optimistic Rollups are designed as a layer-2 scaling solution, minimizing the costs associated with data availability is a critical concern. Several studies have tackled this problem from different angles. Palakkal *et al.* [12] provide a systematization of compression techniques in rollups, outlining methods inefficiency in some rollups' practice. Mamageishvili and Felten [9] propose efficient rollup batch posting strategies on the base layer using call data, while Crapis *et al.* [4] offer an in-depth analysis of EIP-4844 economics and rollup strategies including blob cost sharing. Complementary empirical investigations by Heimbach and Milionis [5], Huang *et al.* [6], and Park *et al.* [13] further document the inefficiencies in current DA cost structures and examine their impact on rollup transaction dynamics and consensus security. Lee [7] investigates blob sharing as a potential remedy for the dilemma faced by small rollups in the post-EIP-4844 era.

Fraud Proof and Dispute Resolution Protocols. Prior research on fraud proofs in Optimistic Rollups has primarily focused on ensuring rapid dispute resolution and robust liveness. For example, BoLD [1] and Dave [11] propose protocols that optimize the dispute game to achieve low delays and cost-efficient on-chain verification, while Berger *et al.* [3] analyze economic censorship dynamics to guarantee that disputes are resolved even under adversarial conditions. While previous studies focus on ensuring the liveness of the dispute game, this paper present study concentrates on a different vulnerability: even when dispute games proceed smoothly, the existing incentive structure may fail to adequately reward honest validators, thereby allowing a malicious block proposer to strategically minimize his costs.

3 Dispute Game Model for Optimistic Rollups

In this section, we present a formal model of the dispute game used in optimistic rollups. We define the game in the style of a game-theoretic construct, denoted by $\mathcal{G}$, and specify the participants, assumptions, rules, and reward mechanisms.

3.1 Participants and Deposits

We consider two types of participants in the dispute game:

- **Proposer:** Denoted by P, the proposer is responsible for submitting a proposed block.
- **Validators:** Denoted by the set $\mathcal{V} = \{v_1, v_2, \ldots, v_n\}$, the validators (or challengers) participate in the dispute game to verify that a state transition is incorrect.

Each participant is required to hold a minimum deposit to obtain participation rights:

- The proposer holds a deposit D_P.
- Each validator v_i holds a deposit D_V, where we assume the same minimum deposit D_V for all validators.

3.2 Rules of the Dispute Game

The dispute game $\mathcal{G}$ is triggered when one of more validators submit a challenge to a block by proposer P. The key rules are as follows:

1. **Verification of State Transitions:** A dispute is resolved by verifying the correctness of the state transition. This is achieved either:
   (a) via the opponent's timeout, or
   (b) through the execution of a bisection protocol on a dispute game contract, wherein the virtual machine (VM) executes the disputed state transition steps.
2. **Collateral for Dispute:** Upon initiation of the dispute game, both parties are required to post an additional collateral deposit D_g, where

$$0 < D_g < D_{\max}.$$

This additional deposit is intended to further incentivize honest participation in the dispute resolution process.

3.3 Reward and Penalty Policy

The reward policy of the dispute game is designed to penalize a malicious proposer and reward the challenger(s) as follows:

- If the proposer P loses the dispute game, the challenger(s) may claim a portion of the deposits. Specifically, the winning party is entitled to claim:

$$\alpha \cdot D_P + D_g,$$

where α is a reward parameter. In most real-world rollups, the majority of systems states nearly all or most of the rewards are given to challengers, implying a value close to 1 (100%). Only one of the leading optimistic rollup teams, Arbitrum's document mentions only 1% of the confiscated asset will be certainly rewarded to the dispute game winner [2]. Still, its DAO can reward more of the confiscated asset to the winner. Therefore,

$$0 < \alpha \leq 1.$$

- The deposits that are not forfeited are allocated to a communal fund (e.g., managed by a DAO) to support the overall system.

3.4 Additional Assumptions

For the purpose of our analysis, we assume:

1. **Sequential and Parallel Occurrence:** The dispute game can occur in multiple rounds sequentially; furthermore, different instances of the dispute game may run in parallel.
2. **Timeouts:** Timeouts are set generously so that the proposer cannot deliberately force a timeout by delaying responses. The creation time of each dispute game, denoted by t_i, is sufficiently long to preclude strategic timeouts.

This model captures the strategic interaction between the proposer and validators under the assumptions of minimum deposits and additional collateral requirements. In our subsequent analysis, we use game-theoretic frameworks to examine the incentive imbalances that may arise, particularly focusing on how the profit for a validator as a dispute game winner can be limited nearly to zero.

4 Strategy of Malicious Block Proposer

In this section, we illustrate the various strategies that a malicious proposer may employ to minimize his cost in the dispute game. We consider three scenarios and then describe an auction mechanism that the malicious proposer can trigger to force additional validator participation. In our analysis, a malicious proposer is denoted by P and the set of validators by $\mathcal{V}$.

4.1 Scenario Descriptions

We consider the following three scenarios. The first scenario assumes the malicious proposer controls at least one validator. On the other hand, the left two scenarios do not assume the proposer-controlled validator. The difference between the scenario 2 and 3 is that the number of submitted challenges before the malicious proposer responds to any challenge. The scenario 3's feasibility will be analyzed in the next section.

Scenario 1 (Proposer-Controlled Validator Accounts). In this baseline scenario, the malicious proposer P controls a subset $\mathcal{V}_P \subset \mathcal{V}$ of validator accounts. When a block B is proposed and a valid challenge is submitted by some validator $v_i \in \mathcal{V} \setminus \mathcal{V}_P$, P can immediately counter by initiating a dispute game through one of his controlled validators $v_j \in \mathcal{V}_P$. Under the reward mechanism (where a winning party receives $\alpha \cdot D_P + D_g$ and $\alpha \in (0, 1]$), the net cost for P is limited to:
$$\text{Cost}_P = (1 - \alpha) \cdot D_P,$$
since the controlled validator wins the challenge and the attacker absorbs only the shortfall.

Scenario 2 (Multiple Challenges Exist). Suppose that multiple validators submit valid challenges against B. In this situation, P may reduce his effective cost by deploying an auction contract. The auction mechanism is designed to order the challenges: validators who have not yet challenged are induced to bid. Since a validator's alternative is to obtain a reward of zero (if they do not participate), the auction forces competitive bidding. In equilibrium, validators will bid amounts that reflect their full valuation, roughly given by
$$v = \alpha \cdot D_P + D_g.$$
Thus, if P loses the resulting auction-based challenge, his cost will be at least the winning bid, which in a competitive setting is driven upward by the participation of many validators.

Scenario 3 (Single Challenge Initially Submitted). In the case where only a single challenge is initially submitted, P may still deploy the auction contract to attract additional challenges. Even though one challenge exists, the auction mechanism creates a framework in which validators are incentivized to bid—since non-participation yields zero reward. The competitive pressure in the auction will then increase the cost borne by P if a challenger wins the dispute game. In both Scenarios 2 and 3, the key idea is that by forcing additional validator participation via an auction, P's effective cost is raised beyond the minimal challenge fee.

4.2 Auction Contract Construction

To explain the scenario in which multiple or a single initial challenge is submitted (Scenarios 2 and 3), we propose an auction-based mechanism that integrates directly with the dispute game. The auction contract is designed to foster competition between validators, thereby minimizing the malicious proposer's loss. In essence, if a valid challenge has already been submitted, the malicious proposer can trigger this auction contract to invite further challenges. As an on-chain smart contract, the auction contract ensures that the auction winner (validator) will win the dispute game first. Otherwise, the auction operator's (malicious

Algorithm 1. Dispute Game Auction Contract

1: **Input:** disputeId, auction duration T_{auction}
2: **Initialize:**
3:     auctionStart $\leftarrow$ current timestamp (or block number)
4:     Bids $\leftarrow \varnothing$
5:     Malicious proposer deposits E (equal to the promised reward)
6: **procedure** SUBMITBID(validator, bidAmount)
7:     **if** current time $<$ auctionStart $+ T_{\text{auction}}$ **then**
8:        Verify dispute game instance exists for disputeId
9:        Append (validator, $bidAmount$) to Bids
10:     **end if**
11: **end procedure**
12: **procedure** FINALIZEAUCTION
13:     **if** current time $\geq$ auctionStart $+ T_{\text{auction}}$ **then**
14:        Let b_{max} and b_{second} be the highest and second-highest bids in Bids
15:        Winner $\leftarrow$ validator associated with b_{max}
16:        Grant Winner the exclusive right to initiate the dispute game at cost b_{second}
17:     **end if**
18: **end procedure**
19: **procedure** RESOLVEDISPUTE(outcome)
20:     **if** outcome $=$ first win for the winning validator **then**
21:        Refund excess deposit to Winner
22:     **else**
23:        Transfer b_{second} from Winner's deposit to malicious proposer
24:     **end if**
25: **end procedure**

---

proposer) deposit in the auction contract will be confiscated and given to the auction winner.

Our design leverages only minimal EVM functionalities—such as reading block timestamps/number, basic list manipulations, and conditional checks—which makes it well-suited for implementation in a standard smart contract environment. The pseudocode (presented in Algorithm 1) outlines the essential steps:

We now describe the detailed steps of our proposed auction mechanism, which is designed to force additional validator participation and increase the economic cost for a malicious block proposer. The mechanism proceeds as follows:

Auction Initialization: When at least one valid challenge is detected, the auction contract is deployed. At this point, the malicious block proposer transfers, as a deposit, an amount corresponding to the reward promised by the dispute game setting. This initialization triggers the fixed bidding period during which the auction will accept bids.

Bid Submission: Validators who have not yet submitted a challenge are invited to participate in the auction. Prior to bidding, each validator must initiate a dispute game for the challenged block. This step is essential as it enables the auction contract to verify the existence of a corresponding dispute game contract and ensures that all contractual conditions are met. If a validator's valuation (which reflects the full reward) exceeds the current highest bid, they submit their bid along with the necessary deposit.

Auction Finalization: Once a pre-defined number of blocks have passed (or the auction duration has elapsed), the auction period terminates. At this point, the auction contract finalizes the bidding process using a Vickrey (second-price) auction mechanism, whereby the highest bidder wins but pays the amount of the second-highest bid. The winning validator is granted the exclusive guarantee to finish the dispute game challenge first.

Dispute Resolution and Cost Recovery: The dispute game then proceeds, and the system monitors all submitted challenges. Once it is verified—by querying the status of all dispute games—that the winning validator's dispute game is the first to conclude, the auction contract triggers the cost-recovery process. Specifically, the winning validator's deposit is used to transfer the winning bid amount to the malicious block proposer, while any remaining difference (if the winning bid is less than the full deposit) is refunded to the winning validator.

In summary, this auction contract serves as a critical component of our overall strategy. It transforms the challenge submission process into a competitive auction, where the equilibrium bid is driven by each validator's valuation.

5 Analysis on the Dispute Game Auction

In our dispute game auction, each validator faces a fixed participation cost $c > 0$ (accounting for gas fees, contract invocation, etc.). The reward available if a validator wins a dispute is given by

$$R = \alpha D_P + D_g,$$

where D_P is the forfeitable deposit of the malicious proposer, D_g is the additional collateral for the dispute game process, and $\alpha \in (0, 1]$ is a reward parameter. In practice, since the protocol is uniform, validators' valuations are very similar. To capture this slight heterogeneity, we assume that each validator's valuation is drawn from the interval $[R - \mu, R]$, where $\mu > 0$. Under these assumptions, the potential surplus a validator can obtain by winning the auction comes solely from the dispersion μ.

5.1 Expected Payoffs and Participation Conditions in a Second-Price Auction

Assume that n validators participate in a second-price (Vickrey) auction created by the malicious block proposer. Since the valuations are nearly identical, each validator's true valuation is $v_i \in [R - \mu, R]$. By a change of variable, let

$$X_i = v_i - (R - \mu),$$

so that X_i is uniformly distributed on $[0, \mu]$. It is well known that in a second-price auction with n independent draws from $U[0, \mu]$, the expected maximum is

$$E[X_{(1)}] = \frac{n}{n+1}\mu,$$

and the expected second-highest value is

$$E[X_{(2)}] = \frac{n-1}{n+1}\mu.$$

Thus, the expected surplus (i.e., the difference between the highest and second-highest bid) is

$$E[X_{(1)} - X_{(2)}] = \frac{\mu}{n+1}.$$

Since each validator pays a fixed cost c upon participation regardless of winning or losing, the net gain for a winning validator is

$$\pi_{\text{win, validator}} = \frac{\mu}{n+1} - c.$$

A validator who loses simply incurs a loss of c. Therefore, a validator's decision to participate (as opposed to abstaining and receiving a payoff of zero) is individually rational if the expected surplus exceeds the cost:

$$\frac{\mu}{n+1} - c > 0 \iff \mu > c(n+1).$$

We formalize this result as follows.

Theorem 1. *Let n risk-neutral, symmetric validators have valuations drawn independently from the interval $[R - \mu, R]$, with $\mu > 0$ representing the small dispersion in valuations. In a second-price auction in which each validator incurs a fixed participation cost $c > 0$, the expected surplus for the winning validator is*

$$E[\Delta] = \frac{\mu}{n+1}.$$

Thus, a validator has a positive incentive to participate if and only if

$$\mu > c(n+1).$$

Proof. Define $X_i = v_i - (R - \mu)$ so that $X_i \sim U[0, \mu]$. In a second-price auction with n bidders, the expected highest value is $E[X_{(1)}] = \frac{n}{n+1}\mu$ and the expected second-highest value is $E[X_{(2)}] = \frac{n-1}{n+1}\mu$. The expected surplus for the winner is therefore

$$E[X_{(1)} - X_{(2)}] = \frac{n}{n+1}\mu - \frac{n-1}{n+1}\mu = \frac{\mu}{n+1}.$$

Because each participating validator pays the fixed cost c, a validator who wins obtains a net payoff of $\frac{\mu}{n+1} - c$ while one who loses obtains $-c$. Thus, participation is beneficial compared to abstention (which yields 0) if and only if

$$\frac{\mu}{n+1} - c > 0 \iff \mu > c(n+1).$$

□

Next, consider the situation where k validators have already participated in the auction. For an additional validator joining, the auction becomes one among $k+1$ bidders. In this case, the condition for participation is modified to

$$\frac{\mu}{k+2} > c \iff \mu > c(k+2).$$

This corollary illustrates that as more validators join, the incremental benefit for an additional validator decreases, but participation remains attractive as long as the dispersion μ is sufficiently large relative to the total cost incurred by all bidders.

Corollary 1. *If k validators have already participated in the auction, an additional validator will have a positive incentive to join if and only if*

$$\mu > c(k+2).$$

5.2 Application to the Secondary Auction in a Single-Challenge Scenario

In realistic deployments of optimistic rollups, it is often observed that only a single dispute challenge is initially submitted. Without further intervention, additional validators may refrain from joining because the early mover appears to secure the reward, leaving later participants with a guaranteed loss of the fixed cost c. To overcome this free-riding behavior, we propose the deployment of a secondary auction contract that is triggered once the first challenge is registered. This contract compels additional validators to decide whether to participate in the auction.

Under the secondary auction, an additional validator now considers joining an auction with k current participants. As shown above, the participation condition is given by

$$\mu > c(k+2).$$

For instance, if initially only one challenge exists (i.e., $k = 1$), then an extra validator will join if and only if

$$\mu > 3c.$$

If this condition is satisfied, the secondary auction effectively transforms the environment into one with multiple bidders, thereby enabling competitive bidding. As more validators join, the competitive pressure increases, and the equilibrium outcome will impose a cost on the malicious proposer that approximates the winning bid. In turn, the malicious proposer must incur a cost that reflects the aggregate competitive surplus, rather than merely a minimal challenge fee.

In practice, even if the valuations are nearly identical (i.e., all validators have valuations in $[R - \mu, R]$ with a small μ), the auction mechanism's ability to induce additional participation depends critically on the relation between μ and the fixed cost c. If μ is sufficiently large relative to c (specifically, if $\mu > c(k+2)$ for the given number k of current participants), then additional validators are incentivized to join the auction. This, in turn, increases the cost imposed on the malicious proposer when the final dispute is resolved.

Based on the analysis of the validators' profit, we can calculate the net profit of the malicious proposer with this strategy as the below corollary. It indicates, ironically, when the reward parameter for validators α increases and the number of validators join the dispute challenges increases, the loss of the malicious proposer decreases.

Corollary 2. *Assuming the malicious proposer forfeits both D_P and D_G upon losing the dispute, and the auction operates ideally according to the Vickrey mechanism with n participating validators whose valuations are drawn from $[R-\mu, R]$ where $R = \alpha D_P + D_G$, the expected net loss of the malicious proposer is given by:*

$$\text{Expected Net Loss} = (1-\alpha)D_P + \frac{2\mu}{n+1}.$$

Proof. Let π_{proposer} be the expected net profit. The proposer receives the expected second-highest bid, $E[v_{(2)}]$, from the auction winner, while forfeiting deposits D_P and D_G. From the analysis of the second-price auction with valuations $v_i \sim U[R-\mu, R]$, where $R = \alpha D_P + D_G$:

$$E[v_{(2)}] = R - \frac{2\mu}{n+1}$$

The expected net profit is the revenue minus the costs:

$$\pi_{\text{proposer}} = E[v_{(2)}] - (D_P + D_G)$$

Substituting $E[v_{(2)}]$ and R:

$$\pi_{\text{proposer}} = \left((\alpha D_P + D_G) - \frac{2\mu}{n+1}\right) - (D_P + D_G)$$

$$= (\alpha - 1)D_P - \frac{2\mu}{n+1}$$

Since $\alpha \leq 1$ and $\mu > 0$, $\pi_{\text{proposer}} \leq 0$. The expected net loss is $-\pi_{\text{proposer}}$:

$$\text{Expected Net Loss} = (1-\alpha)D_P + \frac{2\mu}{n+1}.$$

In summary, our analysis under a second-price auction framework with slight valuation heterogeneity demonstrates that validators are incentivized to participate when the potential gain from winning outweighs the participation cost relative to the number of participants (n). Moreover, our findings reveal that a malicious proposer can strategically reduce their net loss by employing this auction. Increased competition, driven by either a higher validator reward parameter (α) approaching 1 or a larger number of participating validators (n), allows the proposer to recoup a greater portion of their forfeited deposit through the auction proceeds (specifically, the second-highest bid which approaches the full reward R as n increases or μ decreases). Consequently, this increased competition leads to a decrease in the proposer's overall net loss, approaching the theoretical minimum loss of $(1-\alpha)D_P$ as $n \to \infty$ or $\mu \to 0$.

6 Potential Solutions

In this section, we propose two solutions to mitigate the structural vulnerability which deincentivizes optimistic rollup validators.

6.1 Escrowed Reward Mechanism

The first approach addresses the vulnerability arising from early challenge exploitation by modifying the reward distribution mechanism. Rather than immediately allocating the prize to the first valid challenge—as many existing protocols do—this mechanism locks the reward in escrow as soon as a valid dispute challenge is raised. As shown in Algorithm 2, the reward remains locked until *all* challenges pertaining to the block are finalized. This delay in reward allocation prevents a malicious proposer from benefiting by simply finalizing the belately triggered challenge first, ensuring that the final reward distribution reflects the order and promptness of validators.

Algorithm 2. Escrowed Reward Mechanism for Dispute

1: **Input:** disputeStart, disputeDuration
2: **Initialize:**
3:     rewardsLocked ← false, rewardPool ← 0
4:     challengerDeposits ← empty mapping
5: **procedure** INITIATECHALLENGE(challenger, depositAmount)
6:     **if** currentTime < disputeStart + disputeDuration **then**
7:         challengerDeposits[challenger] ← challengerDeposits[challenger] + depositAmount
8:         **if** rewardsLocked is false **then**
9:             rewardsLocked ← true
10:            rewardPool ← current contract balance
11:         **end if**
12:     **end if**
13: **end procedure**
14: **procedure** FINALIZEDISPUTE
15:     **if** currentTime ≥ disputeStart + disputeDuration **then**
16:         winningChallenger ← SELECTWINNINGCHALLENGER
17:         Transfer rewardPool to winningChallenger
18:         rewardsLocked ← false
19:     **end if**
20: **end procedure**
21: **procedure** SELECTWINNINGCHALLENGER ▷ Determine winning challenger based on predefined criteria
22:     **return** chosen challenger address
23: **end procedure**

Mechanism Details:

- **Escrow of Rewards:** Regardless of the order in which challenges are initiated, the entire reward (i.e., the forfeited deposits) is held in escrow until the dispute resolution period for the block ends.
- **Final Distribution:** Once the dispute window closes, the reward is distributed to the winning challenger. If multiple challenges are valid, the reward is apportioned or allocated according to a predefined rule.

Trade-Offs. This mechanism effectively prevents a malicious proposer from pre-empting the dispute process by quickly triggering a challenge using controlled validator accounts. However, a potential downside is the introduction of Miner Extractable Value (MEV) opportunities. An attacker might monitor the mempool for early challenge transactions and submit parallel challenges via MEV-boost techniques to capture a larger portion of the reward. Mitigating this risk may require validators to use private mempools or other techniques to hide their challenge submissions.

6.2 Commit-Reveal Protocol for Challenge Decisions

The second approach presented in Algorithm 3 introduces a commit-reveal scheme that obscures validators' intentions to challenge a block. Instead of immediately broadcasting a challenge, validators submit a commitment during a designated epoch and then reveal their decision after a short delay.

Mechanism Details:

- **Commit Phase:** In each epoch, validators submit a hash of their decision (e.g., `challenge` or `not challenge`), the block number, and a nonce, all signed with their private key. This commit prevents others from knowing the validator's decision in advance. Especially, nonce ensures that other validators cannot deduce the challenge status from the hash value.
- **Reveal Phase:** After the commit phase, validators reveal their decision and associated data. The smart contract verifies that the reveal matches the commitment.
- This process prevents a "follow-the-leader" attack where a malicious actor could monitor challenge submissions and mimic or preempt them.

Trade-Offs. By using a commit-reveal protocol, the challenge decision of each validator is concealed until all commitments are made. This prevents any validator from strategically adjusting their decision based on others' actions (i.e., challenge follow-up attacks). In addition, if multiple valid challenges exist in the same block, the reward can be distributed fairly. However, this approach introduces extra overhead in the form of additional Layer-1 transactions for both commit and reveal phases. To mitigate increased transaction fees, one might consider extending the epoch duration, aggregating commits off-chain, or leveraging data blob solutions. On the other hand, while the commit phase obscures

Algorithm 3. Commit-Reveal Dispute Mechanism

1: **Data:** Mapping Commits (validator → (*commitHash, revealed, decision, blockNumber*)), commitDeadline, revealDeadline
2: **procedure** COMMITCHALLENGE(validator, commitHash)
3:    **if** currentTime < commitDeadline **then**
4:       Commits[validator] ← (*commitHash, false, _, _*)
5:    **end if**
6: **end procedure**
7: **procedure** REVEALCHALLENGE(validator, decision, blockNumber, nonce)
8:    **if** currentTime ≥ commitDeadline and currentTime < revealDeadline **then**
9:       **if** hash(*decision, blockNumber, nonce, validator*) = Commits[validator].commitHash **then**
10:          Update Commits[validator] to (_, *true, decision, blockNumber*)
11:       **end if**
12:    **end if**
13: **end procedure**
14: **procedure** PROCESSCHALLENGES
15:    **if** currentTime ≥ revealDeadline **then**
16:       Process valid challenges and distribute rewards.
17:    **end if**
18: **end procedure**

the specific timing and content of the challenge, the act of committing itself might signal an intent to challenge a particular block. To mitigate this issue, we can consider periodical attention tests using this commitment-based challenges.

In summary, both proposed solutions aim to eliminate the possibility for a malicious proposer to exploit the current dispute game incentives: The *Escrowed Reward Mechanism* ensures that rewards are only distributed after the dispute game for a given block has fully resolved, thereby removing the advantage of being the first to challenge. However, it may introduce MEV risks. The *Commit-Reveal Protocol* obscures validators' decisions during the dispute phase, preventing strategic follow-up challenges. The main trade-off here is the increased overhead due to additional transactions.

7 Discussion and Concluding Remarks

This work identified a critical incentive misalignment in Optimistic Rollup dispute games where validators may lack sufficient economic motivation to challenge invalid blocks due to potentially negligible net rewards. This vulnerability undermines the core security assumption relying on rational challengers.

We demonstrated how a malicious proposer can exploit this weakness, not only by leveraging controlled validators but also by strategically deploying secondary mechanisms like auctions. Such auctions, while seemingly fostering participation, can paradoxically allow the proposer to minimize their own financial penalties by capturing value from the induced validator competition. Our game-theoretic analysis revealed that increased validator engagement, whether through higher reward rates or more participants, can counterintuitively benefit the malicious actor by increasing the portion of the forfeited stake they recoup. This highlights the nuanced and sometimes non-monotonic relationship between participation incentives and overall system security. While our model provides a formal framework for understanding these dynamics, we acknowledge that real-world scenarios involve greater heterogeneity in validator valuations, costs, and risk preferences. Nonetheless, the core vulnerability stemming from the potential gap between gross rewards and net validator profits remains a significant concern.

To mitigate these risks, we proposed countermeasures focusing on decoupling reward timing from challenge finalization (escrowed reward) and obscuring validator challenge intentions (commit-reveal protocol). These solutions aim to restore robust validator incentives, though they introduce their own trade-offs regarding potential MEV opportunities and increased transactional overhead, respectively. Further research is needed to refine these mechanisms and potentially explore hybrid approaches or privacy-enhancing techniques.

Acknowledgement. I would like to thank Junwoo Choi of Samsung SDS and Hojung Yang of Korea University for their assessment of the initial idea. I am also grateful to HyukSang Jo of Tokamak Network for his support clarifying the dispute game contract and its operation.

References

1. Alvarez, M.M., et al.: Bold: fast and cheap dispute resolution. arXiv preprint arXiv:2404.10491 (2024)
2. Arbitrum: Bold economics of disputes (2025). https://docs.arbitrum.io/how-arbitrum-works/bold/bold-economics-of-disputes. Accessed 07 Mar 2025
3. Berger, B., Felten, E.W., Mamageishvili, A., Sudakov, B.: Economic censorship games in fraud proofs. Presented at Financial Cryptography 2025 (2025, to appear)
4. Crapis, D., Felten, E.W., Mamageishvili, A.: EIP-4844 economics and rollup strategies. In: Budurushi, J., et al. (eds.) Financial Cryptography and Data Security. FC 2024 International Workshops, pp. 135–149. Springer, Cham (2025)
5. Heimbach, L., Milionis, J.: The early days of the ethereum blob fee market and lessons learnt. In: Proceedings of Financial Cryptography 2025, presented at Financial Cryptography 2025 (2025, to appear)
6. Huang, Y., Wang, S., Huang, Y., Tang, J.: Two sides of the same coin: large-scale measurements of builder and rollup after EIP-4844. arXiv preprint arXiv:2411.03892 (2024)
7. Lee, S.: 180 days after EIP-4844: will blob sharing solve dilemma for small rollups? In: Proceedings of the DICG Workshop, in Association with the 45th IEEE International Conference on Distributed Computing Systems (ICDCS 2025), Glasgow, UK (2025, to appear)
8. Li, J.: On the security of optimistic blockchain mechanisms. Available at SSRN 4499357 (2023)
9. Mamageishvili, A., Felten, E.W.: Efficient rollup batch posting strategy on base layer. In: International Conference on Financial Cryptography and Data Security, pp. 355–366. Springer (2023)

10. Mamageishvili, A., Felten, E.W.: Incentive schemes for rollup validators. In: The International Conference on Mathematical Research for Blockchain Economy, pp. 48–61. Springer (2023)
11. Nehab, D., de Paula, G.C., Teixeira, A.: Dave: a decentralized, secure, and lively fraud-proof algorithm. arXiv preprint arXiv:2411.05463 (2024)
12. Palakkal, R., Gorzny, J., Derka, M.: SoK: compression in rollups. In: 2024 IEEE International Conference on Blockchain and Cryptocurrency (ICBC), pp. 712–728 (2024). https://doi.org/10.1109/ICBC59979.2024.10634469
13. Park, S., et al.: Impact of EIP-4844 on ethereum: consensus security, ethereum usage, rollup transaction dynamics, and blob gas fee markets. arXiv preprint arXiv:2405.03183 (2024)
14. Tas, E.N., Adler, J., Al-Bassam, M., Khoffi, I., Tse, D., Vaziri, N.: Accountable safety for rollups. arXiv preprint arXiv:2210.15017 (2022)

A Formalization of Signum's Consensus

Fausto Spoto[✉][iD]

Dipartimento di Informatica, Università di Verona, Verona, Italy
fausto.spoto@univr.it

Abstract. Bitcoin's proof of work consensus consumes energy and requires dedicated, expensive hardware. Therefore, alternatives have been proposed, including proof of stake and proof of space. The latter mines with disk space instead of CPU power. Signum is the only implemented proof of space blockchain with smart contracts, and runs since ten years. But its relatively simple consensus algorithm lacks any formalization. This paper formalizes Signum's consensus and uses that formalization to show that Signum is free from block-grinding attacks and is largely protected from challenge-grinding attacks. Moreover, this paper proposes a new protection for Signum against newborn attacks.

1 Introduction

A blockchain is a list of *blocks*, each reporting the hash of a previous block, satisfying some consistency or *consensus* rules. Blocks hold *transactions*, whose exact nature is not relevant here: they are requests to update the state of a global abstract machine (a ledger of payments as in Bitcoin [2,15]) or a sort of global memory where data structures are allocated and modified (as in Ethereum [3]). By using hashes as machine-independent pointers, blockchains can be distributed in a network of peers. This is desirable since data gets safely duplicated and no special peer determines the history by itself. However, peers expand the blockchain, independently from other peers, hence the blockchain becomes a tree rather than a list. A notion of chain quality incentivizes peers to append blocks to the highest-quality chain (the *best* chain). Therefore, a peer could replace its current best chain with another, even better chain, a so called *history change*.

As presented above, peers are free to generate new blocks at maximal speed, flood the network with new blocks and make the emergence of a best chain difficult. This is an efficiency and security issue: frequent history changes allow *double spending* and network forks. The actual genious of Nakamoto [15] was to (largely) solve this issue with a consensus rule requiring blocks to answer a *challenge* contained in their previous block. Namely, the hash of each block must be smaller than a *difficulty* value computed from the previous blocks, directly bound to the quality of the chain. Therefore, who creates (*mines*) a new block runs a *proof of work* algorithm that rotates (*grinds*) many alternative values for a block field (*nonce*), until the hash of the block is smaller than the difficulty. This hardens the creation of new blocks, makes it impossible to create blocks at arbitrary speed and introduces an incentive to expanding the best chain only, rather than creating alternative histories by mining on multiple chains. The difficulty changes overtime, to account for change in the total hashing power of the network. As shown in [9], this stabilizes the block creation rate and supports network consistency (all honest peers converge to the same chain, eventually).

Proof of work is a brute-force algorithm, because of the non-correlation property of hash functions. Therefore, it consumes energy (as much as a medium-sized country, for Bitcoin); moreover, it is not egalitarian, being worthwhile only in countries where electricity is cheap; furthermore, it is more efficient over dedicated, expensive hardware (such as ASICs), against the promise of a democratic and open network. Therefore, the current trend is towards *proof of stake*. Its different flavors share the common idea that mining is limited to a (static or dynamic, exclusive or delegatable) set of peers (*validators*), that *stake* a collateral in exchange of mining rights. Many criticize proof of stake for being centralized and undemocratic (*rich becomes richer*). Moreover, it suffers from what we call a *start-up issue*: as long as the cryptocurrency of a newborn blockchain has still no value, validators have no incentive to work and be updated. Moreover, validators get punished (*slashed*) if they misbehave, which might be perceived as unfair if that happens because a peer is not maintained up to date.

A further alternative is *proof of space* [4,8], where miners must dedicate a large chunk of disk memory for answering challenges. Its energy consumption is negligeable and no special hardware helps for mining, currently: the technology is both cheap and democratic. Moreover, proof of space allows one to capitalize on unused memory, for free, while proof of work has always an inherent electricity cost. For fairness, proof of space protocols should only allow to generate answers of quality directly proportional to the allocated space, or otherwise they are said to suffer from a time/memory tradeoff. As a drawback, cheap answers introduce new *nothing-at-stake* security attacks [16], that are instead anti-economic with proof of work, since computing power can only be dedicated to one mining task:

Block grinding: Miners might find it profitable (*rational*) to mine many alternative new blocks, each holding different transactions, finally selecting the block that leads to better answers to subsequent challenges.

Challenge grinding: Miners might find it profitable to provide suboptimal answers to the current challenge if this leads to subsequent challenges for which they have much better answers.

Mining on multiple chains: Miners might find it profitable to mine multiple chains simultaneously (not only the best one).

These attacks increase the risk of double spending and make it convenient to mine through space *and* work, thus neutralizing the benefits of proof of space.

Another nothing-at-stake problem, that has not received great attention up to now, is the *newborn attack* [23]: a miner that has allocated a large space for mining for a blockchain network N could use the same space, unchanged, for mining for a newborn, small network N'. If the total space used by the peers of N' is initially relatively small, it could be possible for the miner to hijack the history of N', effectively taking its control.

Most formalizations of proof of space [4,8,18] are based on challenges against graphs of high pebbling complexity, but no actual blockchain has ever been built that way: only SpaceMint [16] exists which is not a real blockchain but a minimal non-maintained prototype of the theoretical consensus protocol only. Namely, a real graph pebbling blockchain has never been implemented because: (1) the protocol includes an *initialization phase*, run for each new prover (miner) that joins the blockchain, that complicates the protocol itself and requires to spend cryptocurrency *before* starting mining; (2) answers to challenges (*proofs*), included in blockchain, are relatively large [1]: kilobytes or even megabytes for proofs created in the initialization phase.

An alternative is Permacoin [13], based on proof of retrievability rather than graph pebbling, still in the family of the proof of space algorithms [18]. But neither Permacoin has been implemented: only a prototypical and minimal implementation of only its consensus algorithm exists, discontinued in 2014. Neither SpaceMint nor Permacoin have been shown to support smart contracts.

Our target of analysis has been Signum [20], instead, since we wanted a fully-fledged implementation, which gives practical relevance to our work. Signum (previously Burstcoin) is actually deployed and runs continously since 2014. It provides smart contracts on top of its consensus algorithms. Signum is not based on graph pebbling: instead, each miner precomputes a large *plot file* of hashes, that is not shared nor stored in blockchain. A peer that wants to mine the next block derives a challenge from the current blockchain head and challenges a miner for an answer, called *deadline*, *ie.*, a small (less than 200 bytes) data structure, that can be very quickly derived from the plot, with a quality measure (its *waiting time*) proportional, on average, to the size of the plot. Signum's protocol is attractive since it has no initialization phase (each miner creates its plot file independently and off-line) and its answers are very small. In principle, Signum can be mined as described above (proof of space) but also by recomputing the plot file on-the-fly, at each challenge, without any disk allocation (proof of work). Because of that, Signum's mining is sometimes called *proof of capacity*. However, the proof of work version of Signum remains theoretical and there is no evidence that Signum has ever been mined like that. This is because plots use an expensive hashing algorithm (shabal256) and are very big, so that their recomputation takes longer than the block creation rate. Specialized hardware might change the situation in the future but, from its inception in 2014 to the present day, Signum seems to have been only mined with proof of space.

The actual drawback of Signum is that the underlying theory has never been formalized nor defined up to now. Moroever, [16] warned about a potential block-grinding attack. Without a formalization, it is impossible to judge if it is real.

Therefore, this paper provides the following contributions about Signum:

- a formalization of its algorithm, recostructed and interpolated from a very informal and partial description [22] and its poorly commented code [21];
- a proof that block-grinding attacks are impossible, against a previous hint [16];
- a proof that challenge-grinding attacks are limited;

Table 1. Notations and contextual information used in our formalization and their specific instantiations used in [22], when available.

notation	meaning	in [22]
⋈	concatenation of sequences	
#scoops	number of scoops contained in a nonce	4096
$h_{deadline}$	hashing function for computing nonces, plots and deadlines	shabal256
$h_{generation}$	hashing function for computing the generations of challenges	shabal256
h_{block}	hashing function for computing the hash of the blocks	sha256
κ	threshold to the number of bytes fed to $h_{deadline}$ in Algorithm 1	4096
beat	target block creation time interval (ms)	240000
$\sigma_{genesis}$	generation signature for the genesis block	
τ_{now}	current time (ms from Unix epoch)	
oblivion	acceleration reaction to changes of mining power (0 to 1)	

- a new protection against newborn attacks.

These results are relevant since they show that Signum's consensus is actually supported by a formal theory and protected from a large class of attacks.

The rest of this paper is organized as follows. Section 2 formalizes the structure of the plot files. Section 3 defines the challenges that the consensus algorithm must solve, and their answers (deadlines). Section 4 presents Signum's mining algorithm. Section 5 studies grinding attacks in Signum and proposes a new solution against newborn attacks. Section 6 presents related work. Section 7 concludes. Proofs are reported in appendix. Table 1 collects notations used throughout the paper. It also reports specific choices made in [22] (rightmost column), but this paper remains parametric *wrt.* them. For instance, for genericity, our formalization uses three hashing functions, that might actually coincide.

2 Nonces and Plots

This section formalizes the notions of nonce and plot and their algorithmic construction. Namely, Signum requires miners to hold one or more plots (sets of nonces) on disk. Their initialization is performed only once and offline, hence it is not part of the mining protocol.

The following definitions are used to deal with bytes and hashing.

Definition 1 (Concatenation operator ⋈). *Sequences (for instance, of bytes) are concatenated by ⋈. The same ⋈ is used to concatenate a sequence to an element or an element to a sequence.*

The following byte representation of natural numbers is used in [22]. It is the standard representation in most computers nowadays.

Definition 2 (nat2be and be2nat). *The operators nat2be and be2nat transform natural numbers into their big-endian byte representation, and vice versa.*

We recall that the big-endian representation of a natural number is its binary representation, split in bytes, with the most significant byte placed first.

Definition 3 (Hashing function). *A hashing function h of size > 0 is a total map $h : byte^* \to byte^{size}$, where $byte^*$ is a sequence of bytes, of arbitrary length, and $byte^{size}$ is a sequence of size bytes, called a* hash *for h. If h is a hashing function, then $size(h)$ is its size.*

A *scoop* is a pair of hashes. A *nonce* is a natural *progressive number* p, and a list of $\#scoops > 0$ scoops. Their definitions are parametric *wrt.* a hashing function $h_{deadline}$ used for their creation.

Definition 4 (Scoop, Nonce). *The sets of scoops and nonces are*

$$\text{Scoops} = \{\langle h_1, h_2\rangle \mid h_1, h_2 \text{ are hashes for } h_{deadline}\},$$
$$\text{Nonces} = \{\langle p, scoops\rangle \mid p \in \mathbb{N} \text{ and } scoops \in \text{Scoops}^{\#scoops}\}.$$

In the above definition, angular brackets stand for tuples (in this specific case, they stand for pairs). When definitions are given in terms of tuples, they silently introduce selection functions for the tuple elements. For instance, if *nonce* $\in$ Nonces, then *nonce.p* and *nonce.scoops* are its elements.

A *prolog* is the identifier of the creator of nonces and plots (for instance, its public key). For now, it is just a sequence of bytes. Section 5 will give structure to prologs and see how they can be useful.

Definition 5 (Prolog). *The set of prologs is* $\text{Prologs} = \{\pi \mid \pi \in bytes^*\}$.

Algorithm 1 constructs a nonce, given its progressive number and a prolog. It uses a constant $\kappa > 0$ (Table 1) to limit its computational cost, to avoid hashing very large chunks of data. This algorithm derives a sequence of hashes (steps 1 and 2) and constructs a *final* hash from all of them (step 3) that uses to modify the original sequence of hashes (step 4). Then it shuffles the sequence (step 5), which intuitively guarantees that, in order to compute a given scoop of the nonce (*i.e.* a pair of consecutive hashes), the algorithm must be thoroughly executed.

Algorithm 1 $(nonce(p, \pi))$ *Given $p \in \mathbb{N}$ and $\pi \in$* Prologs, *we define*

$$nonce(p, \pi) = \langle p, \langle h_0, h_1\rangle \bowtie \cdots \bowtie \langle h_{2 \cdot \#scoops - 2}, h_{2 \cdot \#scoops - 1}\rangle\rangle \in \text{Nonces},$$

where the hashes $h_0, \ldots, h_{2 \cdot \#scoops - 1}$ are constructed as follows[1].

1. *Let $seed = \pi \bowtie nat2be(p)$.*
2. *For each i from $2 \cdot \#scoops - 1$ to 0, let*[2]

$$h_i = h_{deadline}\left(\text{first } \kappa \text{ bytes } of((\bowtie_{i<j<2 \cdot \#scoops} h_j) \bowtie seed)\right).$$

---

[1] Step. 5 and the threshold κ have been added after the publication of [16], in response to some of their criticisms. See Sect. 5.

[2] In [22], it is said to take the *last* κ bytes, that would be meaningless since then the lowest h_i's would coincide. An inspection of their code shows that they actually take the *first* κ bytes. They probably use *last* here in the sense of *more recently computed*.

3. Let $h_{final} = h_{deadline}((\bowtie_{0 \leq j < 2 \cdot \#scoops} h_j) \bowtie seed)$.
4. For each i from 0 to $2 \cdot \#scoops - 1$, reassign h_i to $h_i \oplus h_{final}$.
5. For each odd i from 1 to $2 \cdot \#scoops - 1$, swap h_i with $h_{2 \cdot \#scoops - i}$.

Step 4 makes each h_i dependent on the others, so that one must compute them all in order to compute each of them. This is strengthened by the use of the xor, that limits the risk of hash collisions. Step 5 makes each scoop dependent on one h_i with $i \geq \#scoops$, so that smaller scoops are not easier to compute than the others. This avoids a potential time/memory tradeoff (see Sect. 5).

A *plot* is a set of nonces constructed with Algorithm 1, for a finite non-empty set of progressive numbers P and for a given prolog π, recorded in the plot.

Definition 6 (Plot). *The set of plots is defined as*

$$\mathsf{Plots} = \left\{ \langle \pi, nonces \rangle \,\middle|\, \begin{array}{l} \pi \in \mathsf{Prologs},\ \varnothing \neq P \subset \mathbb{N}\ \text{is finite} \\ \text{and}\ nonces = \{nonce(p, \pi) \mid p \in P\} \end{array} \right\}.$$

The computations of $nonce(p, \pi)$ and $nonce(p', \pi)$, for $p \neq p'$, are completely independent. Therefore, Definition 6 implies that the construction of a plot can be optimized on multicore hardware.

3 Challenges and Deadlines

A *challenge* specifies a puzzle that must be solved in order to mine a new block. In Signum, challenges become a query that can be asked to each nonce of a plot, resulting in an answer called *deadline*.

Definition 7 (Challenge). *The set of challenges is*

$$\mathsf{Challenges} = \left\{ \langle scoopNumber, \sigma \rangle \,\middle|\, \begin{array}{l} 0 \leq scoopNumber < \#scoops \\ \text{and}\ \sigma\ \text{is a hash for}\ h_{generation} \end{array} \right\}.$$

The σ component of a challenge is said to be its generation signature. *In the following, generation signature will be used as a synonym of hash for $h_{generation}$.*

Given a challenge and a nonce, the latter has a value that specifies how well the nonce answers the challenge.

Definition 8 ($value(nonce, challenge)$). *Let $nonce \in$ Nonces and challenge $\in$ Challenges. The value of nonce wrt. challenge, ie., $value(nonce, challenge)$, is $h_{deadline}(nonce.scoops[challenge.scoopNumber] \bowtie challenge.\sigma)$.*

The answer to a challenge could actually be a nonce n, whose quality is its value. But nonces are quite big (around 262 kbytes under the assumptions in the rightmost column of Table 1). Since answers are stored in blockchain, [22] introduces *deadlines*, a much smaller representation of the value of n, carrying the information needed to reconstruct n and verify that it actually answers the challenge.

Definition 9 (Deadline). *The set of* deadlines *is*

$$\text{Deadlines} = \left\{ \langle p, \pi, value, challenge \rangle \;\middle|\; \begin{array}{l} \pi \in \text{Prologs},\; p \in \mathbb{N}, \\ value \text{ is a hash for } h_{deadline} \\ and\ challenge \in \text{Challenges} \end{array} \right\}.$$

Deadlines are totally ordered by increasing value.

Intuitively, the value of a deadline expresses how many milliseconds must be waited until the deadline expires and a new block can be mined. However, if the mining power of the network increases, the minimal value of the deadlines generated by the network tends to decrease and the block creation rate would not be fixed to *beat* (Tab. 1), on average. This explains why the deadlines' value is modulated *wrt.* an *acceleration*[3], which is the inverse of Bitcoin's difficulty.

Definition 10 (Deadline's waiting time). *Given* $\delta \in$ Deadlines *and an* acceleration $\alpha \in \mathbb{N}$ *such that* $\alpha > 0$, *the* waiting time *for* δ *wrt.* α *is*[4]

$$waitingTime(\delta, \alpha) = \frac{be2nat(\delta.value)}{\alpha}.$$

Definition 11 finally shows how a nonce answers a challenge with a deadline.

Definition 11 ($\delta(nonce, \pi, challenge)$). *Given* $nonce \in$ Nonces, $\pi \in$ Prologs *and* $challenge \in$ Challenges, *the* deadline computed from $nonce$ for π and $challenge$ is $\delta(nonce, \pi, challenge) = \langle nonce.p, \pi, value(nonce, challenge), challenge \rangle$.

Definition 11 extends to plots. Remember that plots are non-empty (Definition 6) and embed the identifier of their creator π; and that deadlines are ordered by their value.

Definition 12 ($deadline(plot, challenge)$). *Given* $plot \in$ Plots *and* $challenge \in$ Challenges, *the* deadline computed from $plot$ for $challenge$ is[5]

$$\delta(plot, challenge) = \min_{nonce \in plot.nonces} \delta(nonce, plot.\pi, challenge).$$

A deadline is valid when the nonce built from its progressive and prolog has the same value as the deadline *wrt.* its challenge.

Definition 13 (Deadline's validity). *Given* $\delta \in$ Deadlines, *it is* valid *if and only if* $\delta.value = value(nonce(\delta.p, \delta.\pi), \delta.challenge)$.

---

[3] In [22] the term *base target* is used for it, but we think that *acceleration* is clearer.
[4] In [22], the divisor is actually $2^{size(h_{deadline})-8} \cdot \alpha$, to avoid using very large values for α. This is theoretically irrelevant and we prefer our simpler presentation.
[5] If more nonces of the plot lead to deadlines with the same minimal value, we assume that Definition 12 chooses one, according to some policy that is irrelevant here.

4 Blockchain Construction

The blocks of the blockchain contain information used for consensus, called *trunk* by borrowing this terminology from [6]; other information such as the previous block hash; and extra information that is irrelevant here, such as a list of transactions, that are not formalized below since they are not used by Signum's consensus. Blocks can be genesis and non-genesis. Both contain their time of creation and their acceleration. Genesis blocks have no trunk nor parent; their height is implicitly 0. Challenges c are generated in sequence: there is an initial constant challenge for the genesis block, while the challenge of non-genesis blocks b is generated from their trunk. In particular, c is *not* computed from the transactions in b, in order to avoid block-grinding attacks (Sect. 5). A deadline that answers c is recorded in the trunk of the sons of b.

Definition 14 (Trunk, Block). *The sets of* trunks *and* blocks *are*

$$\text{Trunks} = \{\langle height, \delta \rangle \mid height \in \mathbb{N} \text{ and } \delta \in \text{Deadlines}\},$$
$$\text{GenesisBlocks} = \{\langle \tau, \alpha \rangle \mid \tau \in \mathbb{N}, \ \alpha \in \mathbb{N} \text{ and } \alpha > 0\},$$
$$\text{NonGenesisBlocks} = \left\{ \left\langle \begin{array}{c} \tau, \alpha, power, \\ weightedBeat, trunk, \\ previousBlockHash \end{array} \right\rangle \middle/ \begin{array}{l} \tau, \alpha \in \mathbb{N}, \ \alpha > 0, \\ power, weightedBeat \in \mathbb{N}, \\ trunk \in \text{Trunks}, \\ previousBlockHash \text{ is a} \\ \text{hash for } h_{block} \end{array} \right\},$$
$$\text{Blocks} = \text{GenesisBlocks} \cup \text{NonGenesisBlocks}.$$

If b is a block, then $b.\tau$ is its creation time (milliseconds from the Unix epoch) and $b.\alpha$ is its acceleration. If b is a non-genesis block, then $b.power$ expresses how much space has been used to build the path to b, starting from the genesis block; it will be used to select the *best chain* for mining b's sons. The value of $b.weightedBeat$ is the average block creation rate in the path to b; it weighs the last blocks more. It will be compared to *beat* (Table 1) to understand if the acceleration must be increased or decreased in b's sons. The value of $b.previousBlockHash$ is the hash of the previous block in the path to b. If b is a genesis block, we abuse notation and assume that $b.power = b.weightedBeat = 0$.

Definition 15 (Block's height). *Let* $b \in $ Blocks. *The* height *of* b, *written* $height(b)$, *is* 0 *if* $b \in $ GenesisBlocks, *and* $b.trunk.height$ *if* $b \in $ NonGenesisBlocks.

Definition 16 shows how the first challenge is defined, for genesis blocks. It is a constant that only depends on contextual values (Table 1).

Definition 16 (*initialChallenge*). *The* initial challenge *is*[6] *initialChallenge* $=$ $\langle 0, \sigma_{genesis} \rangle$, *where* $\sigma_{genesis}$ *is a constant generation signature used for the genesis of the blockchain (see Table 1).*

---

[6] In [22] the scoop number is derived from $\sigma_{genesis}$; we simplify it to 0, without loss of generality.

Definition 17 shows how a challenge is derived from the trunk of a non-genesis block.

Definition 17 ($challenge_{next}(trunk)$). *Let $trunk \in$ Trunks. The next challenge for trunk is $challenge_{next}(trunk) = \langle be2nat(h_{generation}(\sigma \bowtie nat2be(trunk.height + 1))) \bmod \#scoops, \sigma \rangle$, where $\sigma = h_{generation}(trunk.\delta.challenge.\sigma \bowtie trunk.\delta.\pi)$.*

The construction of the generation signature σ for the next challenge, in Definition 17, has puzzled us for some time, since [22] appends a *previous block generator* to the previous block's generation signature $trunk.\delta.challenge.\sigma$. That concept, however, is defined nowhere. We had to dive in the source code of Signum to understand that it is actually an identifier (more concretely, the public key) of the creator of the deadline for the previous block (see https://github.com/signum-network/signum-node/blob/main/src/brs/GeneratorImpl.java, in the constructor of `GeneratorStateImpl`). Our prolog of the previous deadline generalizes that information, hence Definition 17 appends $trunk.\delta.\pi$ to define σ.

Later, it will be handy to determine the next challenge for a block. Note that it only uses the trunk inside the block.

Definition 18 *Let $b \in$ Blocks. Its next challenge is*

$$challenge_{next}(b) = \begin{cases} initialChallenge & \text{if } b \in \text{GenesisBlocks} \\ challenge_{next}(b.trunk) & \text{if } b \in \text{NonGenesisBlocks.} \end{cases}$$

Definition 19 shows how the information inside a block is used to construct that inside its sons. It is actually our proposal, since there is no information in [22] about this. The computation of the next weighted beat gives more or less weight to the previous weighted beat, depending on a constant *oblivion* ($0 \leq oblivion \leq 1$) that expresses how quickly the acceleration reacts to changes in mining power. The computation of the next power uses the same formula as Bitcoin [9,24], adapted to our context: the ratio between the maximal (hence worse) deadline's value $2^{8 \cdot size(h_{deadline})}$ and the actual deadline's value expresses how much space has been used to compute the deadline.

Definition 19 (Next functions). *Let $b \in$ Blocks and $\delta \in$ Deadlines. We define*

$$\tau_{next}(b,\delta) = b.\tau + waitingTime(\delta, b.\alpha),$$

$$weightedBeat_{next}(b,\delta) = \frac{waitingTime(\delta, b.\alpha) \cdot oblivion}{+b.weightedBeat \cdot (1 - oblivion)},$$

$$\alpha_{next}(b,\delta) = \frac{b.\alpha \cdot weightedBeat_{next}(b,\delta)}{beat},$$

$$power_{next}(b,\delta) = b.power + \frac{2^{8 \cdot size(h_{deadline})}}{be2nat(\delta.value) + 1}.$$

Definition 20 shows how a next block is constructed, once its deadline has been chosen.

Definition 20 (Next block). *Let $b \in$ Blocks and $\delta \in$ Deadlines. We define $block_{next}(b, \delta) \in$ NonGenesisBlocks as*

$$block_{next}(b, \delta) = \left\langle \begin{array}{c} \tau_{next}(b, \delta), \alpha_{next}(b, \delta), power_{next}(b, \delta), \\ weightedBeat_{next}(b, \delta), \langle height(b) + 1, \delta \rangle, h_{block}(b) \end{array} \right\rangle,$$

where $h_{block}(b)$ is the application of h_{block} to the byte representation of b.

A blockchain is a set of blocks, linked through their *previousBlockHash* field. It must contain exactly one genesis block; there is no hash collision among its blocks; and all its blocks must satisfy the *consensus rules*.

Definition 21 (Blockchain, Consensus). *A blockchain is a set $B \subseteq$ Blocks such that:*

1. *there is exactly one $b \in B \cap$ GenesisBlocks, written as $genesis(B)$;*
2. *for each hash h of h_{block}, there is at most one $b \in B$ such that $h_{block}(b) = h$, written as $block(B, h)$;*
3. *for each $b \in B$, the predicate $consensus(B, b)$ holds, where*
   - *if $b \in$ GenesisBlocks, then $consensus(B, b)$ is just the consensus rule:*
     (a) b is not created in the future: $b.\tau \leq \tau_{now}$;
   - *if $b \in$ NonGenesisBlocks, then $consensus(B, b)$ is the logical conjunction of all the following consensus rules:*
     (a) b is not created in the future: $b.\tau \leq \tau_{now}$;
     (b) the deadline of b (that is, $b.trunk.\delta$) is valid (Definition 13);
     (c) there are no dangling pointers: $p = block(B, b.previousBlockHash)$ exists;
     (d) b's deadline answers the challenge of p (Definition 18): $challenge_{next}(p) = b.trunk.\delta.challenge$
     (e) b is p's next block wrt. b's deadline (Definition 20): $b = block_{next}(p, b.trunk.\delta)$.

The above consensus rules, reconstructed and interpolated from [21,22], do not constrain the prologs of the deadlines: each block can have an arbitrary prolog. Section 5 will show why it is useful to restrain prologs with extra consensus rules.

Definition 22 (Blockchain network). *A blockchain network is a network of peers (computers), each connected to the other peers, each holding its own vision of the blockchain, all for the same genesis block. Each peer holds a plot (Definition 6) on disk, starts with a blockchain that only holds the genesis block and runs, concurrently, the* block mining *algorithm and the* block mined *algorithm.*

Definition 22 simplifies the picture very much: it assumes that peers are fully connected, never disconnect and never need to synchronize. In practice, peers do not hold plots but rely on (one or more) external services (miners) that hold the plots. The goal here is to keep the picture as simple as possible and concentrate on the properties of Signum's consensus only: Definition 22 does not pretend to describe a real blockchain implementation in detail.

Definition 22 defines the block mining algorithm. It is an infinite loop that looks for the most powerful block p in blockchain (step 1), derives a challenge c from p (step 2), uses a plot to compute a best deadline δ for c (step 3), computes the next block b' for δ (step 4) and waits for δ to expire (step 5). Then it adds b' in blockchain (step 6), whispers b' to all peers (step 7) and restarts.

Algorithm 2 (Block mining) *The block mining algorithm of a peer P, holding blockchain B, is the following infinite loop:*

1. *identify a most powerful[7] block p in B;*
2. *compute $c = challenge_{next}(p)$ (Definition 18);*
3. *compute $\delta' = \delta(plot, c)$ (Definition 12), where plot if the plot of P;*
4. *compute $b' = block_{next}(p, \delta')$ (Definition 20);*
5. *wait until $b'.\tau \leq \tau_{now}$;*
6. *add b' to B;*
7. *whisper b' to the peers connected to P;*
8. *go back to step 1.*

The block mined algorithm receives a block whispered from some connected peer (step 1), checks its validity (step 2) and adds it to the blockchain.

Algorithm 3 (Block mined) *The block mined algorithm of a peer P, holding blockchain B, is the following infinite loop:*

1. *wait for a block b whispered from some connected peer P';*
2. *if $B \cup \{b\}$ is a blockchain, add b to B;*
3. *go back to step 1.*

In practice, step 2 of Algorithm 3 could only allow the addition of b if it looks *powerful enough*, in order to avoid keeping useless blocks. This is not relevant here. Moreover, if the whispered block b at step 2 of Algorithm 3 is more powerful than b' at step 5 of Algorithm 2, a rational peer would interrupt waiting at step 5 of Algorithm 2, discard b' and restart Algorithm 2 from step 1, since the whispered b is better than the block b' that it is being mined, hence it is wiser to stop waiting and start mining on top of b. These are optimizations and are not considered here.

Peers check the validity of blocks coming from outside (step 2 of Algorithm 3), since they do not trust their connected peers. Instead, they do not check the validity of the blocks that they mine themselves (step 6 of Algorithm 2), since they are valid by construction. Namely, Prop. 1 guarantees that B remains a blockchain in every peer. The hypothesis on no hash collision is standard. Namely, all existing blockchains make that hypothesis and they would all collapse otherwise, because they all identify blocks by their hash.

Proposition 1. *If no hash collision occurs at step 6 of Algorithm 2, then the set B of blocks in each peer is a blockchain.*

---

[7] In theory, more *most powerful blocks* might exist in blockchain, although this is highly unlikely; in that case, step 1 will choose any of them.

5 Prolog Structure, Protection Against Attacks

This section uses the formalization of the previous sections to extend the framework in [22] and understand if nothing-at-stake attacks might work for Signum.

The peers of Definition 22 have two functions: to find new deadlines and to package new blocks with such deadlines. In practice, two machines perform each of them: one (the actual miner) finds deadlines by using plots: it must have a large disk space; the other (the actual peer) receives deadlines, packages and whispers new blocks: it must have a good network connection. Such machines will work for a blockchain network with a given chain identifier [2]. Therefore, we propose to use, as prologs, the byte representation of the following triple:

$$\langle chainIdentifier, publicKeyOfPeer, publicKeyOfMiner \rangle$$

(in [22], prologs are just *publicKeyOfMiner*). Moreover, we add two new consensus rules to Definition 21. Informally, one requires that the chain identifier of the blockchain is $b.trunk.\delta.\pi.chainIdentifier$; and the other requires that the signature of b is verified with $b.trunk.\delta.\pi.publicKeyOfPeer$. This has many advantages:

- the public keys of peer and miner can be used to remunerate them for their contribution, in an application-specific way;
- the creator of a plot must specify the public key of the peer: hence that plot can only be used to create deadlines for that given peer and miners become dedicated to that given peer, instead of working, with the same plot, for many peers. This creates a sort of miner fidelization and allows peers to compete by offering different remuneration schemes to miners;
- the creator of a plot must specify the chain identifier of the blockchain. Therefore, it becomes impossible to use the same plot for mining two blockchain networks at the same time. This protects against newborn attacks.

Note that this structure for the prologs entails that deadlines are around 170 bytes (assuming hashes, signatures and chain identifier to be 32 bytes each).

In [16], Burstcoin was criticized because the validation of a deadline (Definition 13) requires to run Algorithm 1 that, they say, requires hashing $8 \cdot 10^6 \cdot 32 = 256000000$ bytes. It must be stated that such hashing can actually be computed in a few milliseconds nowadays, with a minimal energy cost. Moreover, it is largely dominated by that for verifying the transactions in a block, in particular for Signum that allows smart contracts. Therefore, this time for deadline validation seems largely acceptable to us. In any case, step 2 of Algorithm 1 currently uses a threshold κ, that was possibly missing when [16] was written. Considering κ and the specific values and hashing used in [22] (rightmost column of Tab. 1), step 2 hashes at most κ bytes and is iterated $2 \cdot \#scoops$ times, that is, it hashes at most 33554432 bytes. Step 3 hashes $32 \cdot 2 \cdot 4096$ bytes plus the size of *seed*, which is reasonably at most 200 bytes. That is, it hashes 262344 bytes. In total, Algorithm 1 hashes 33816776 bytes, around 8 times less than what was reported in [16].

In Appendix B of [16], a potential block-grinding attack was hinted for Burstcoin, since, in [22], the next challenge of a previous block used its undefined *previous block generator*: "this seems possible to be grinded, by trying different sets of transactions to include in a block" [16]. As discussed just after our Definition 17, that notion is just the prolog $trunk.\delta.\pi$ of the deadline of the trunk in the previous block. Consequently, it cannot be grinded.

Proposition 2. *Signum is protected against block-grinding attacks.*

Proof. The next challenge of a block depends on the trunk of the block only (Definition 17). In particular, it does not depend on any other component of the block, such as the set of transactions that the miner decides to include in it. □

Without this formalization, it was impossible to exclude that attack.

We furthermore observe that Signum has some protection against challenge-grinding attacks. The challenge for the a block is actually uniquely determined by the trunk of its previous block (rule (d) of Definition 21 and Definition 18) but a peer might select suboptimal deadlines at step 3 of Algorithm 2 (*i.e.*, not the minimal one of Definition 12), hoping that such a sacrifice will lead to subsequent challenges for which it can find very good deadlines. But Proposition 3 shows that that choice does not pay off: deadlines do not affect the sequence of challenges, only the plots do.

Proposition 3. *Let B be a blockchain, $plot \in$ Plots, $b_0, \ldots, b_n$ and $b'_0, \ldots, b'_n$ be two sequences of blocks in B, rooted at the same $b_0 = b'_0$, mined by using plot only (possibly with suboptimal choices of the deadlines), that is,*

$$b_i.trunk.\delta = \delta(nonce_i, plot.\pi, challenge_{next}(b_{i-1}))$$
$$b'_i.trunk.\delta = \delta(nonce'_i, plot.\pi, challenge_{next}(b'_{i-1}))$$

for suitable $nonce_i, nonce'_i \in plot.nonces$, for every $1 \leq i \leq n$. Then it holds $challenge_{next}(b_j) = challenge_{next}(b'_j)$ for every $0 \leq j \leq n$.

Proposition 4. *Signum is largely protected against challenge-grinding attacks.*

Proof. By Proposition 3, the sequence of challenges depends only on the sequence of prologs used for mining, that is always the same by using a given plot. Therefore, a challenge-grinding attack in Signum would require a peer to use more plots, whose prologs have different keys, all in control of the peer, and grind among the plots. However, the number of plots is limited by the space allocated to the algorithm and the same set of plots would end up being used at each mining step, since they are too expensive to generate on the fly during grinding. This highly limits the benefits of grinding. □

For additional protection against challenge-grinding attacks, it is always possible to use one of the techniques presented in [16] (see Sect. 6).

Signum does not seem to have any protection against mining on different chains instead. The only possibility here seems to use the penalty transactions used in [16] and challenges that are not built from the trunk of the previous block but from that of a predecessor block deeper in the chain (see Sect. 6).

Appendix B of [16] shows that the original definition of Burstcoin had a time/memory tradeoff: it was possible to store only each h_{final} instead of each full nonce (see step. 3 of Algorithm 1) and reconstruct the smaller scoops on demand. The resulting (mining power)/(space used) ratio was proportionally higher than by storing the full nonces, "at the price of having to compute a modest number of extra hashes" [16]. We agree with the attack but not with the *modest number*: the discussion in [16] confuses plots with nonces and does not recognize that that modest number must be computed for all nonces in the plot, which are easily too many, considering the cost of the shabal256 hashing algorithm (Table 1). In any case, the developers of Signum have modified Algorithm 1 with the addition of step 5, in order to cope with this time/memory tradeoff. With that extra step, each scoop contains a h_i with $i \geq \#scoops$, so that at least half of all h_i's must be kept in memory in order to compute any scoop. Therefore, this specific time/memory tradeoff does not occur anymore. Of course, proving that the addition of step 5 is enough to ban *all* time/memory tradeoffs remains an open question, a daunting task that goes well beyond the scope of this paper.

6 Related Work

Proof of work was originally meant as protection against email spam [7]: senders must perform some work to have their emails accepted by recipients. Ethereum started with proof of work [3] and later moved to proof of stake. The latter can be seen as a Byzantine consensus algorithm, as pioneered by Tendermint [12]. Most current blockchains use some form of proof of stake nowadays.

Traditional properties of consensus algorithms are *consistency* (all honest peers eventually converge to the same blockchain), *liveness* (a transaction submitted to the network gets included in blockchain after a *reasonable* time) and *order-fairness* (peers include transactions in blockchain in their arrival order). This paper does not discuss them because Signum's consensus behaves exactly as Bitcoin's proof of work *wrt.* these properties. Namely, step 1 of Algorithm 2 guarantees that honest peers select the same chain (if whispering is working); while liveness and order-fairness hold for honest peers but not if a dishonest peer holds a large part of the total mining power (as in the 51% attack). Note that order-fairness is more easily lost in other consensus algorithms, such as Byzantine consensus algorithms, where validators can decide the history independently from their mining power. Solutions, in that context, are reported in [11].

The theory of proof of space was independently developed in two seminal papers [4,8], both based on directed acyclic graphs (DAGs) of high pebbling complexity. Pebbling, here, is a directed hash decoration of the nodes of the DAG, as in a Merkle tree. A prover must hold such a (big) DAG and its pebbling on disk, in order to answer, efficiently, challenges with proofs that should convince a verifier that the prover is actually holding data on disk. While [8] requires space to remain allocated between challenges (proof of *persistent* space), [4] requires one to allocate space only when answering challenges (proof of *transient* space or *proof of secure erasure*, as [8] calls it). Both solutions have an initialization phase, when the verifier performs a deep challenge of the prover and stores the resulting (big) proof in blockchain, followed by an execution phase, when the verifier challenges the prover for each new block. Also [18] uses pebbling for stacked expander graphs, to get simpler, more efficient, provably space-hard solutions. It works for both proof of transient space and proof of persistent space. It includes a nice review on proof of space and related techniques: memory-hard functions, proof of secure erasure, provable data possession, proof of retrievability.

Time/memory tradeoffs are studied in [19]. They occur if a prover can store only a part of the data on disk, with a less than proportional degradation of mining power. A good proof of space algorithm makes it difficult to recover the missing part when answering challenges. For graph pebbling, the initialization phase prevents most cheating (that is, keeping incomplete data on disk). In [19], the size of the portion of the file not kept on disk is related to the consequent time complexity degradation for computing the missing part. Ideally, the full file and pebbling must be kept on disk for having no time complexity explosion, but they show that this is not the case in existing solutions and provide sufficient conditions for the initialization phase, that guarantee the ideal result.

The use of graph pebbling seems to dominate the literature on proof of space, but [1] proposes an alternative theory, that supports the Chia network [5,6]: a proof of sequential work on top of a proof of space, based on challenges about the inversion of a random function, for which time/memory tradeoffs have been solved. However, this is not a pure proof of space. Another alternative is the proof of retrievability in [10]: the verifier sends, initially, a large file to the prover (miner) that later challenges, repeatedly, to see if it still keeps the file on disk. Its apparent simplicity is jeopardized by the difficulty of sharing big files among *all* (present and future) peers, for *all* (past, present and future) miners.

We are only aware of one implementation of graph-pebbling proof of space: SpaceMint [16], previously Spacecoin [17]. It is not a blockchain but a discontinued prototype of only the consensus protocol of [8]. Nevertheless, [16] exposes problems and solutions related to the actual game theory and implementation of proof of space. For instance, it uses the verifier's public key as an input parameter for pebbling, to discourage the use of mining pools, often seen negatively [14]. Furthermore, it provides solutions for nothing-at-stake problems. Against block grinding, it makes challenges independent from the transactions in the blocks, by splitting the blockchain in a proofs blockchain and in a transactions blockchain: only the first is used for mining, and the two are connected with the miner's signature. Against challenge grinding, it lets past blocks influence the quality of short sequences of future blocks only. A similar but more drastic solution in [6] uses the same challenge for several consecutive blocks, since it is unlikely that it will be good for all of them. Against mining on multiple chains, [16] proposes to spot such behavior and impose a penalty transaction to the culprit. Experiments in [16] include an estimation of the size of Spacemint's proofs: in the initialization phase, they are between two and three megabytes; in the execution phase, they can be optimized to around 100 kilobytes. Proofs must be persistently stored in blockchain (for each new miner, in the first case, and for each new block, in the second), which makes the blockchain's size much larger than in Bitcoin, and requires miners to hold cryptocurrency even before starting mining.

Signum [20], previously Burstcoin, has been launched in 2014, with possibly the first ever language for smart contracts, and is still active. Appendix B of [16] reports a formalization of an old version of Algorithm 1.

Newborn attacks are considered in [23]. Their solution is to split the space for mining on many chains, with an incentive to allocate, for each chain, a space proportional to the market value of that chain.

7 Conclusion

In the context of proof of space consensus, Signum's advantage is its simplicity, the small size of its proofs (deadlines, around 200 bytes) and the absence of an initialization phase and transactions. Moreover, it is the only fully implemented and deployed solution and supports smart contracts. Signum has recently added a layer of proof of commitment, that amplifies the fees for miners that staked more crypto. This seems just a way to sustain the value of their cyprotcurrency and is irrelevant *wrt.* the underlying proof of space algorithm described in this paper. There are, of course, drawbacks in Signum's algorithm. First of all, it is theoretically possible to mine new blocks in a proof of work style, although this is not been observed in practice up to now. More generally, there are drawbacks of proof of space that still need to be investigated: waste of storage, SSD degradation and even storage farm centralization.

Our formalization of Signum's consensus is valuable because it sheds light on a blockchain network that runs since ten years but was missing any formal definition. Moreover, it allowed us to understand that Signum is free from block-grinding attacks and is largely protected from challenge-grinding attacks.

Acknowledgments. We thank the developers of Signum and K. Pietrzak for discussing some theoretical aspects of Signum.

A Proofs

Proof of Proposition 1 at page 11
Let us prove it by induction on the number of blocks added to B in Algorithms 2 and 3. The thesis is true when the peer starts, by Definition 22. Algorithm 3 keeps B as a blockchain, since it explicitly checks it (step 2 of Algorithm 3). It remains to show that, if B is a blockchain at the beginning of step 6 of Algorithm 2, then $B \cup \{b'\}$ is a blockchain at its end. By Definition 20, it is $b' \in$ NonGenesisBlocks. Therefore, property 1 of Definition 21 remains true. By the assumption on no hash collision, property 2 remains true. It remains to prove that property 3 remains true as well. Let $b \in B \cup \{b'\}$.

- If $b \in$ GenesisBlocks, it is $b \neq b'$ and then $b \in B$; since τ_{now} cannot decrease with the time, by inductive hypothesis the property $b.\tau \leq \tau_{now}$ was true at the start of step 6 of Algorithm 2 and is still true at its end.

- If $b \in \mathsf{NonGenesisBlocks}$ and $b \in B$, by inductive hypothesis all consensus rules held when b was added to B and they must still hold now, since τ_{now} only increases with the time and since no block is ever removed from B (nor replaced in B, since there is no hash collision).
- If $b \in \mathsf{NonGenesisBlocks}$ and $b \notin B$, it must be $b = b'$. Let us prove that each consensus rule in Definition 21 holds.

    (a) This rule holds by step 5 of Algorithm 2 and by the fact that τ_{now} cannot decrease from step 5 to step 6;

    (b) It is

    $$b.trunk.\delta = b'.trunk.\delta$$

    $$(\text{step 4 of Algorithm 2 and Definition 20}) = \delta'$$
    $$(\text{step 3 of Algorithm 2}) = \delta(plot, c)$$
    $$(\text{Definition 12}) = \delta(nonce, plot.\pi, c)$$

    for some $nonce \in plot.nonces$. The deadline $\Delta = \delta(nonce, plot.\pi, c)$ is valid (Definition 13) since, by Definition 11:

    $$\Delta.value = value(nonce, c)$$
    $$= value(nonce, \Delta.challenge)$$
    $$(\text{Definition 6}) = value(nonce(nonce.p, plot.\pi), \Delta.challenge)$$
    $$(\text{Definition 11}) = value(nonce(\Delta.p, \Delta.\pi), \Delta.challenge).$$

    (c) It is

    $$b.previousBlockHash = b'.previousBlockHash$$
    $$(\text{step. 4 of Algorithm 2}) = block_{next}(p, \delta').previousBlockHash$$
    $$= h_{block}(p),$$

    where p is the most powerful block in B (by step. 1 of Algorithm 2). Therefore, $block(B, b.previousBlockHash)$ exists and coincides with the block p selected at step 1 of Algorithm 2. This fact is used in the subsequent points of this proof.

    (d) By step 2 of Algorithm 2, it is

    $$challenge_{next}(p) = c$$
    $$(\text{Defs. 12 and 11}) = \delta(plot, c).challenge$$
    $$(\text{step 3 of Algorithm 2}) = \delta'.challenge$$
    $$(\text{step 4 of Algorithm 2 and Definition 20}) = b'.trunk.\delta.challenge$$
    $$= b.trunk.\delta.challenge.$$

    (e) It is

    $$b = b'$$
    $$(\text{step. 4 of Algorithm 2}) = block_{next}(p, \delta')$$
    $$(\text{Definition 20}) = block_{next}(p, b.trunk.\delta).$$

    □

Proof of Proposition 3 at page 13
Let us proceed by induction on n. If $n = 0$, the thesis holds since $b_0 = b'_0$. Let $n > 0$ and assume that the thesis holds for $n - 1$. Let us prove it for n. By inductive hypothesis, it is enough to prove that $challenge_{next}(b_n) = challenge_{next}(b'_n)$. Since $n > 0$, by consensus rule (e) of Definition 21 and by Definition 20, it is $b_n \in \mathsf{NonGenesisBlocks}$. Therefore, by Definition 18, it is

$$challenge_{next}(b_n) = challenge_{next}(b_n.trunk)$$
$$(Definition\ 17) = \langle be2nat(h_{generation}(\sigma \bowtie nat2be(b_n.trunk.height + 1)))$$
$$\mod \#scoops, \sigma \rangle$$

$$\begin{pmatrix} \text{consensus} \\ \text{rule } (e) \\ \text{of Definition 21,} \\ \text{and Definition 20} \end{pmatrix} = \langle be2nat(h_{generation}(\sigma \bowtie nat2be(b_0.trunk.height + n + 1)))$$
$$\mod \#scoops, \sigma \rangle$$

and similarly

$$challenge_{next}(b'_n) = \langle be2nat(h_{generation}(\sigma' \bowtie nat2be(b_0.trunk.height + n + 1)))$$
$$\mod \#scoops, \sigma' \rangle$$

where

$$\sigma = h_{generation}(b_n.trunk.\delta.challenge.\sigma \bowtie b_n.trunk.\delta.\pi)$$

$$\begin{pmatrix} b_n \text{ has been mined} \\ \text{by using } plot, \\ \text{and Definition 11} \end{pmatrix} = h_{generation}(b_n.trunk.\delta.challenge.\sigma \bowtie plot.\pi)$$

$$\begin{pmatrix} \text{consensus rule } (d) \\ \text{of Definition 21} \end{pmatrix} = h_{generation}(challenge_{next}(b_{n-1}).\sigma \bowtie plot.\pi)$$

$$\begin{pmatrix} \text{inductive} \\ \text{hypothesis} \end{pmatrix} = h_{generation}(challenge_{next}(b'_{n-1}).\sigma \bowtie plot.\pi)$$

$$\begin{pmatrix} \text{consensus rule } (d) \\ \text{of Definition 21} \end{pmatrix} = h_{generation}(b'_n.trunk.\delta.challenge.\sigma \bowtie plot.\pi)$$

$$\begin{pmatrix} b'_n \text{ has been mined} \\ \text{by using } plot, \\ \text{and Definition 11} \end{pmatrix} = h_{generation}(b'_n.trunk.\delta.challenge.\sigma \bowtie b'_n.trunk.\delta.\pi)$$

$$= \sigma'.$$

It follows that $challenge_{next}(b_n) = challenge_{next}(b'_n)$. □

References

1. Abusalah, H., Alwen, J., Cohen, B., Khilko, D., Pietrzak, K., Reyzin, L.: Beyond Hellman's time-memory trade-offs with applications to proofs of space. In: Takagi, T., Peyrin, T. (eds.) Proc. Advances in Cryptology, the 23rd International Conference on the Theory and Applications of Cryptology and Information Security (ASIACRYPT'17), part II, volume 10625 of Lecture Notes in Computer Science, pp. 357–379. Springer, Hong Kong, China (2017)
2. Antonopoulos, A.M.: Mastering Bitcoin: Programming the Open Blockchain. Oreilly & Associates Inc, 2nd edition (June 2017)
3. Antonopoulos, A.M., Wood, G.: Mastering Ethereum: Building Smart Contracts and Dapps, 1st edition. Oreilly & Associates Inc. (November 2018)
4. Ateniese, G., Bonacina, I., Faonio, A., Galesi, N.: Proofs of space: when space is of the essence. In: Abdalla, M., De Prisco, R. (eds.) Proc. the 9th International Conference on Security and Cryptography for Networks (SCN'14), volume 8642 of Lecture Notes in Computer Science, pp. 538–557. Springer, Amalfi, Italy (2014)
5. Chia Network. https://www.chia.net. Accessed 26 August 2024
6. Cohen, B., Pietrzak, K.: The Chia Network Blockchain (2019). https://www.chia.net/wp-content/uploads/2022/07/ChiaGreenPaper.pdf. Accessed 2 September 2024
7. Dwork, C., Naor, M.: Pricing via Processing or Combatting Junk Mail. In: Brickell, E.F. (ed.) Proc. the 12th Annual International Cryptology Conference on Advances in Cryptology (CRYPTO'92), volume 740 of Lecture Notes in Computer Science, pp. 139–147. Springer, Santa Barbara, California, USA (1992)
8. Dziembowski, S., Faust, S., Kolmogorov, V., Pietrzak, K.: Proofs of space. In: Gennaro, R., Robshaw, M. (eds.) Proc. Advances in Cryptology (CRYPTO 2015) - 35th Annual Cryptology Conference, part II, volume 9216 of Lecture Notes in Computer Science, pp. 585–605. Springer, Santa Barbara, CA, USA (2015)
9. Garay, J., Kiayias, A., Leonardos, N.: The bitcoin backbone protocol with chains of variable difficulty. In: Katz, J., Shacham, H. (eds.) Proc. the 37th International Cryptology Conference (CRYPTO'17), Part I, volume 10401 of Lecture Notes in Computer Science, pp. 291–323. Springer, Santa Barbara, CA, USA (2017)
10. Juels, A., Kaliski, B.S., Jr.: Pors: proofs of retrievability for large files. In: Ning, P., De Capitani, S., di Vimercati, and Syverson. P. F., (eds.) Proc. the 2007 ACM Conference on Computer and Communications Security (CCS 2007), pp. 584–597. ACM, Alexandria, Virginia, USA (2007)
11. Kelkar, M., Zhang, F., Goldfeder, S., Juels, A.: Order-fairness for byzantine consensus. In: Micciancio, D., Ristenpart, T. (eds.) Proc. the 40th International Cryptology Conference (CRYPTO'20), volume 12172 of Lecture Notes in Computer Science, pp. 451–480. Springer, Santa Barbara, CA, USA (2020)
12. Kwon, J.: Tendermint: consensus without Mining (2014). https://www.weusecoins.com/assets/pdf/library/Tendermint%20Consensus%20without%20Mining.pdf. Accessed 26 August 2024
13. Miller, A., Juels, A., Shi, E., Parno, B., Katz, J.: Permacoin: repurposing bitcoin work for data preservation. In: Proceedings of the IEEE Symposium on Security and Privacy (SP 2014), Berkeley, CA, USA, pp. 475–490. IEEE Computer Society (May 2014)
14. Miller, A., Kosba, A.E., Katz, J., Shi, E.: Nonoutsourceable scratch-off puzzles to discourage bitcoin mining coalitions. In: Ray, I., Li, N., Kruegel, C. (eds.) Proc. the 22nd ACM SIGSAC Conference on Computer and Communications Security, pp. 680–691. ACM, Denver, CO, USA (2015)

15. Nakamoto, S.: Bitcoin: A Peer-to-Peer Electronic Cash System (October 2008). https://bitcoin.org/bitcoin.pdf. Accessed 26 August 2024
16. Park, S., Kwon, A., Fuchsbauer, G., Gaži, P., Alwen, J., Pietrzak, K.: SpaceMint: a cryptocurrency based on proofs of space. In: Meiklejohn, S., Sako, K. (eds.) FC 2018. LNCS, vol. 10957, pp. 480–499. Springer, Heidelberg (2018). https://doi.org/10.1007/978-3-662-58387-6_26
17. Park, S., Pietrzak, K., Alwen, J., Fuchsbauer, G., Gazi, P.: Spacecoin: A Cryptocurrency Based on Proofs of Space. IACR Cryptology ePrint Archive (2015). https://eprint.iacr.org/2015/528.pdf. Accessed 26 August 2024
18. Ren, L., Devadas, S.: Proof of space from stacked expanders. In: Hirt, M., Smith, A. (eds.) TCC 2016. LNCS, vol. 9985, pp. 262–285. Springer, Heidelberg (2016). https://doi.org/10.1007/978-3-662-53641-4_11
19. Reyzin, L.: Proofs of Space with Maximal Hardness. IACR Cryptol. ePrint Arch. p. 1530 (2023)
20. Signum Community Website and Documentation Project. https://wiki.signum.network. Accessed on August 26, 2024
21. Signum Node Source Code. https://github.com/signum-network/signum-node. Accessed 27 August 2024
22. Signum Plotting and Mining Technical Information. https://wiki.signum.network/signum-plotting-technical-information/index.htm. Accessed 26 August 2024
23. Tang, S., et al.: Towards a multi-chain future of proof-of-space. In: Chen, S., Choo, K.-K.R., Fu, X., Lou, W., Mohaisen, A. (eds.) Proc. the 15th EAI International Conference on Security and Privacy in Communication Networks (SecureComm'19), part I, volume 304 of Lecture Notes of the Institute for Computer Sciences, Social Informatics and Telecommunications Engineering, pp. 23–38. Springer, Orlando, FL, USA (2019)
24. Walker, G.: Longest Chain – The Chain of Blocks Nodes Adopt as Their Blockchain (2024). https://learnmeabitcoin.com/technical/blockchain/longest-chain/. Accessed 12 September 2024

Monero's Decentralized P2P Exchanges: Functionality, Adoption, and Privacy Risks

Yannik Kopyciok[1(✉)] , Friedhelm Victor[3] , and Stefan Schmid[1,2]

[1] TU Berlin, 10587 Berlin, Germany
{kopyciok,stefan.schmid}@tu-berlin.de
[2] Weizenbaum Institute, 10623 Berlin, Germany
[3] TRM Labs, San Francisco, USA
friedhelm@trmlabs.com

Abstract. Privacy-focused cryptocurrencies like Monero remain popular, despite increasing regulatory scrutiny that has led to their delisting from major centralized exchanges. The latter also explains the recent popularity of decentralized exchanges (DEXs) with no centralized ownership structures. These platforms typically leverage peer-to-peer (P2P) networks, promising secure and anonymous asset trading. However, questions of liability remain, and the academic literature lacks comprehensive insights into the functionality, trading activity, and privacy claims of these P2P platforms.

In this paper, we provide an early systematization of the current landscape of decentralized peer-to-peer exchanges within the Monero ecosystem. We examine several recently developed DEX platforms, analyzing their popularity, functionality, architectural choices, and potential weaknesses. We further identify and report on a privacy vulnerability in the recently popularized Haveno exchange, demonstrating that certain Haveno trades could be detected, allowing transactions to be linked across the Monero and Bitcoin blockchains. We hope that our findings can nourish the discussion in the research community about more secure designs, and provide insights for regulators.

Keywords: Decentralized Exchanges · Cryptocurrency · Privacy

1 Introduction

Centralized cryptocurrency exchanges have processed nearly three trillion dollars in trading volume in December 2024[1], enabling the exchange of fiat and cryptoassets. The vast majority of these exchanges operate within regulatory constraints. For example, in most jurisdictions, financial institutions are required to implement Know Your Customer (KYC) procedures to verify user identities, and monitor transactions for suspicious activity such as money laundering or various types of illicit monetary flows. The Financial Action Task Force's (FATF), an

---

[1] https://www.theblock.co/data/crypto-markets/spot.

intergovernmental organization developing policies to combat money laundering and terrorist financing, has proposed a "Travel Rule", recommending that countries adopt a *de minimis* threshold of 1,000 USD/EUR for virtual asset transfers, above which Virtual Asset Service Providers (VASPs) must collect and share detailed information about the originators and beneficiaries of these transactions [9]. In the European Union, the Markets in Crypto-Assets Regulation (MiCA) [8], which fully came into force on December 30, 2024, establishes comprehensive rules for cryptoasset issuance and services, including mandatory authorization and supervision of crypto-asset service providers.

Privacy-focused cryptocurrencies, with Monero (XMR) as the most prominent in 2024, appear to be at odds with prevailing regulations. Their privacy-enhancing technologies can render transaction monitoring largely ineffective. Although the reason is often not stated explicitly, it is likely that regulations have led to the delisting of Monero from most popular centralized exchanges: OKX Korea and UpBit (2019) followed FATF guidelines, while Bittrex (2021) and Huobi (2022) cited transparency concerns. Binance (2024) removed XMR over compliance conflicts, and Kraken phased out XMR in the European Economic Area at the end of 2024. While there exist very large DEXs on smart-contract supporting blockchains like Ethereum, Binance Smart Chain and Solana, Monero does not supported them. The combination of regulatory pressure and the disappearance of exchanges has pushed users toward decentralized exchanges (DEXs) and peer-to-peer (P2P) trading platforms supporting Monero. However, popular P2P platforms with centralized operators, such as LocalBitcoins (2023) and LocalMonero (2024), have already shut down.

In response, a new wave of decentralized P2P trading platforms has emerged, each exploring different architectural models to facilitate Monero trading. These platforms differ in network design, trade execution, dispute resolution, and governance but share the common goal of minimizing centralized control. As these platforms gain traction, questions arise regarding their functionality, and privacy. How exactly do they operate? Do they still rely on centralized components? And what can be observed regarding their privacy guarantees?

Contributions: In this paper, we provide a systematization of the landscape of P2P decentralized exchanges in the Monero ecosystem (cf Sect. 3), covering Haveno, Bisq, BasicSwapDEX, and the COMIT protocol, used e.g. by UnstoppableSwap. For each exchange, we study their functionality, describe the network architecture, the trade protocol, fees, dispute resolution, governance and operational details and potentially remaining centralized components which can also pose privacy risks. In Sect. 4, we examine Haveno in more detail, and unveil a privacy weakness that allows discovering Haveno-related Monero transactions, and in some instances their trade counterpart on transparent blockchains, for example on the Bitcoin blockchain. Finally, we discuss our findings in Sect. 5, focusing on what centralized network components remain, including the aspect of arbitrators and governance structures. We hope that our findings contribute to the ongoing research discussion on more secure designs while also serving as a foundation for addressing regulatory concerns surrounding these P2P exchanges.

2 Background and Related Work

In this section, we outline relevant background knowledge and related works. Decentralized exchanges provide an alternative to centralized trading platforms by enabling cryptocurrency transactions without intermediaries. While most research on DEXs has focused on automated market maker (AMM)-based exchanges such as Uniswap [1,2,26], P2P DEXs rely on direct interactions between users without the need for smart contracts. In contrast to centralized P2P trading platforms like LocalMonero, which operated under a centralized website, their decentralization extends to the operations, frequently featuring a standalone application, without a centralized website that needs to be accessed. P2P exchange systems differ significantly in their trade execution, governance models, and degree of decentralization. Bisq is one such P2P exchange that facilitates non-custodial trading on the Bitcoin blockchain that has been studied extensively by Hickey and Harrigan [14,15]. They found that its reliance on on-chain transactions makes it susceptible to blockchain analysis techniques such as address clustering, which has been used to trace Bisq trading activity and governance participation through its BSQ token. Haveno, a fork of Bisq designed for Monero, inherits much of Bisq's architecture but operates within Monero's privacy framework, aiming to solve some of Bisq's privacy issues.

Critical to decentralized trade execution are atomic swaps, which allow two parties to exchange assets without trusting an intermediary. Hash Time-Locked Contracts (HTLCs) were initially proposed for this purpose and remain a common mechanism in swap implementations, as seen in the COMIT protocol [18]. However, HTLCs rely on scripting capabilities unavailable in Monero and similar privacy-focused cryptocurrencies. To address this, recent advancements in cryptographic primitives such as adaptor signatures [23] and swap mechanisms that do not rely on locking mechanisms [17] have extended atomic swap compatibility to non-scriptable blockchains. These methods may allow for additional privacy-preserving exchange protocols to emerge in the near future.

Monero is designed to obfuscate transaction details using stealth addresses, Ring Confidential Transactions (RingCT), and decoy-based input selection. Unlike transparent blockchains such as Bitcoin or Ethereum, Monero transactions do not publicly reveal sender, receiver, or transferred amounts. However, research has shown that Monero is not entirely immune to analysis. The output merging (or co-spend) heuristic remains a key method for linking Monero transactions, as inputs controlled by the same entity can sometimes be identified when spent together in a single transaction [20]. Cross-chain analyses have also allowed for the deanonmization of input rings [16]. Furthermore, while prior research on Monero's privacy has largely focused on protocol-level weaknesses, more recent efforts have explored application-level vulnerabilities [12]. Cross-chain transactions remain a underexplored risk, as interactions between Monero and transparent blockchains may inadvertently weaken its privacy guarantees [10].

Cross-chain swap platforms supporting Monero have also been analyzed in terms of their privacy implications. ShapeShift, an early example of an off-chain swap service, was studied by Yousaf et al., who traced transactions revealing user behaviors [27]. More recently, similar analyses have been conducted on Evonax, where trading flows have been obtained [5,6]. As decentralized Monero exchanges like Haveno grow in adoption, it becomes increasingly important to investigate whether they exhibit privacy weaknesses.

3 Monero's P2P DEX Landscape

This section presents a systematization of prominent decentralized P2P exchanges along various dimensions. We will present key insights in the areas of: network architecture highlighting the P2P infrastructure and potential centralized components, trade protocol implementations including the implemented swap mechanisms, fee structure, and dispute resolution frameworks, operational prerequisites to participate on the DEX, and governance structures that regulate protocol modifications and ecosystem development. We study Haveno, Bisq, BasicSwapDEX, and COMIT as used by UnstoppableSwap. After detailing the exchanges, we summarize our findings in Table 1 at the end of this section.

To start, we briefly want to assess popularity of these exchanges. We can only assess historical trade activity for Bisq and Haveno, whereas for BasicSwapDEX and COMIT only a list of offers is obtainable at any given point in time. Figure 1 compares Bisq's with Haveno's Monero trading volume over the past 8 months, when Haveno started seeing usage. On both platforms, BTC is the preferred cryptoasset to trade with Monero. While Bisq is still leading in terms of trading volume, Haveno is quickly rising in popularity, and offers more Monero trading options besides cryptocurrencies, which are not displayed in the chart.

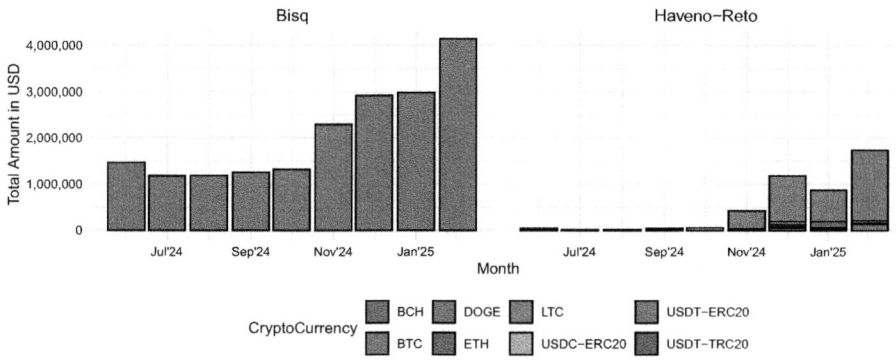

Fig. 1. Bisq and Haveno-Reto XMR trading volume against various cryptocurrencies. Bisq only supports XMR/BTC, and has significantly higher volume, but Haveno-Reto (Retoswap), is quickly growing and has approached nearly USD 2 Million in February 2025. While Haveno-Reto supports other XMR Trading Pairs, BTC is the most popular.

3.1 Haveno

Haveno [13] is an open source project, forked in 2023 from the Bisq [3] exchange project. Haveno implements a P2P exchange platform based on Tor and Monero and offers a platform to exchange various crypto- and fiat-currencies with Monero as its base currency. No custom or colored token is involved and trades are purely built on Monero's multi-signature wallet implementation.

Network Architecture: Haveno's core P2P components [13, docs/deployment-guide.md] include seed nodes, arbitrator nodes, price nodes, and client nodes. Seed nodes serve as the network backbone, managing state, onboarding new clients, and having their onion addresses hardcoded into binaries. They control seed node management, trade fees, and arbitrator privileges. Arbitrator nodes can register as arbitrators through an authentication mechanism, granting them special privileges. Price nodes run an HTTP service to collect and distribute price data but are not essential for core P2P functionality. Client nodes are regular peers with no special privileges or resource obligations.

Both seed and arbitrator nodes require a local Monero node for security and robustness. All communication occurs via Tor, covering trade interactions from offer creation to execution. Haveno implements a decentralized order book, where offers remain available as long as both the maker and arbitrator are online.

Trade Protocol: The Haveno trade protocol [13, docs/trade_protocol/trade-protocol.md] makes use of 2/3 multi-signature wallets where the three involved parties are the arbitrator, the entity wanting to buy XMR (taker), and the entity wanting to sell XMR (maker). During the process of a trade, up to five transactions are created where two of them are penalty transactions in case a party deviates from the protocol. If a taker accepts an offer, the tradable funds and a security deposit from both parties are sent to the multi-signature wallet. After this, the trade must be completed within 24 h. The taker pays the maker with the respective other coin or fiat currency outside of the Haveno application. The transaction is neither invoked by the Haveno application nor is it monitored. Once the funds are confirmed as received by the maker inside Haveno, the security deposit is refunded to the maker and the taker receives the paid funds plus its own security deposit. **Trade fee:** Haveno's code base has the option to enable trade fees but no major fork is applying them at the moment of writing. Therefore, only transactional fees on the respective chains have to be paid. **Dispute Resolution:** Haveno offers a chat function that can be used to directly communicate between maker and taker. If an issue is not solvable between the two peers, the arbitrator can be summoned. As the arbitrator is in control of one of the signatures needed for the 2/3 multi-signature wallets, he will assess the dispute and handle accordingly.

Governance: The Haveno network is dependent on an entity running the initial seed nodes and arbitrators providing arbitrator nodes. Haveno states that they "do not endorse any networks at this time" [13]. A live mainnet fork of the Haveno repository is currently in active use. It is the earliest and most notable instance named RetoSwap [22], a.k.a. Haveno-Reto, which has been operational since May 14, 2024.

Operational Details: Using the Haveno exchange requires only a desktop application and a small amount of Monero for the security deposit. While running a local Monero node is recommended for privacy, it is not required to participate.

3.2 Bisq

Bisq [3], the precursor to Haveno, shares a similar architecture but uses Bitcoin as its base currency, with Monero as an external payment method. It operates without a central authority, relying on a peer-to-peer network and multi-signature escrow for security. A future update, Bisq2 [4] plans for new trade protocols including atomic swaps, further enhancing flexibility and interoperability.

Network Architecture: The network architecture shares the same key components as the Haveno network with a key difference in their governance structure.

Trade Protocol: Bisq's trade protocol [3, Introduction;Security deposit] is based on Bitcoin's 2/2 multi-signature wallets where both seller and buyer control their respective private keys. To initiate a trade, both parties contribute security deposits to the multi-signature wallet, with the seller additionally depositing the agreed-upon Bitcoin amount. The buyer has a designated timeframe to transfer the payment via the specified method. Upon the seller confirming receipt, funds are released from the multi-signature wallet to both parties according to the trade terms. **Trade fee:** In addition to the transactional fees paid on each blockchain, a small trade fee [3, Trading fees] applies which can be either paid in the colored Bitcoin token BSQ or directly in BTC. **Dispute Resolution:** Bisq provides an integrated chat for peers to communicate if complications arise [3, Dispute Resolution in Bisq 1]. In disputed cases, a mediator can be requested to assess potential resolutions. For severe cases where one party disappears or is uncooperative, Bisq implements a pre-signed time-locked delayed payout transaction that activates after a predetermined period based on the payment method. This transaction directs all funds to designated "donation addresses" managed by the Bisq DAO. The cooperating party can then request arbitration, where an arbitrator investigates the case and reimburses the appropriate amount from their personal funds, later requesting compensation from the Bisq DAO.

Governance: Bisq is governed by a DAO [3, Introduction to the DAO] built on the Bitcoin blockchain. The DAO applies monthly voting cycles to determine revenue distribution, strategic decision-making, and ensuring honesty in high-trust roles. High-trust roles in Bisq involve responsibilities critical to the network, including domain ownership and operating key infrastructure such as seed and arbitrator nodes. These individuals must lock up funds which can be withdrawn by the community in case of misconduct. The high-trust roles do not own any part of Bisq but thereby have a certain incentive to keep the network alive and act in the will of the community.

Operational Details: Participating on the Bisq exchange requires only a desktop application. A user will need an initial small amount of Bitcoin for the security deposit but it is not required to operate a local node.

3.3 BasicSwap

BasicSwap (BSX) is a community-driven and open source DEX project developed within the Particl ecosystem [21]. Particl consists of multiple privacy-focused decentralized applications, with BasicSwap and a decentralized marketplace as its most prominent products. The ecosystem is built upon its own Particl blockchain implementation, which supports the PART cryptocurrency. Similar to Monero, PART applies privacy-enhancing cryptographic techniques including stealth addresses and ring signatures. A distinctive component of Particl's infrastructure is the SecureMessaging (SMSG) network [21, Under the Hood], an end-to-end encrypted peer-to-peer message mixnet inspired by the BitMessage protocol [25].

Network Architecture: BasicSwap leverages the SMSG network as its underlying P2P network. SMSG functions as a decentralized storage network where each node maintains a temporary copy of every end-to-end encrypted message broadcast within the last 48 h. Every BSX client operates a SMSG node serving the broader Particl P2P infrastructure that supports all Particl decentralized applications. A front-end is hosted locally with every running BSX client. Within this interface, users can interact with posted trade offers. The trade offers are broadcast using the SMSG network, enabling each peer to maintain its own copy of the decentralized order book without relying on centralized matching services. The DEX trading functionality is implemented through atomic swap protocols, with the SMSG network handling the necessary communication required to execute these trustless swaps. **Trade Protocol:** BasicSwap deploys two atomic swap protocols. If both coins support Bitcoin-style scripting, Hash Time-Locked Contracts (HTLCs) [7] can be used, enforcing swaps through on-chain scripts with shared secret hashes and timelocks. If a coin like Monero lacks these capabilities, swaps rely on adaptor signatures [11], where private key shares and one-time verifiably encrypted signatures ensure atomicity. Users create and accept offers via BSX's graphical interface, choosing which coins to trade and which swap protocol to use when the involved coins support both. The application then automates the swap process, handling secrets, keys, and transaction ID sharing via the SMSG network. **Trade Fee:** No additional trade fees apply, only network transaction fees. **Dispute Resolution:** Both protocols ensure swaps either complete or refund both parties without third-party intervention.

Governance: The Particl network applies a DAO structure [21, DAO and Network Treasury], details on how the DAO governs BSX is not provided but as trades do not include any fee related to the DAO or another third-party. Financial incentives and involvement in the project appear to be independent from Particl based on community participation rather than direct revenue generation.

Operational Details: Running blockchain nodes for multiple cryptocurrencies is needed and creates substantial resource requirement. Although Bitcoin synchronization can be accelerated using snapshots and Monero can utilize remote RPC endpoints, the initial setup remains time-consuming. Concurrent node operation demands significant computation, storage, and network resources, potentially deterring casual and test users. These known constraints are scheduled to be addressed as the DEX progresses beyond its current beta phase.

3.4 COMIT and UnstoppableSwap

UnstoppableSwap [24] emerged as a successor to the plain COMIT protocol adding a graphical interface to perform cross-chain atomic swaps between Monero and Bitcoin. COMIT is a CLI tool developed in accordance to the whitepaper by Hoenisch and del Pino [18].

Network Architecture: UnstoppableSwap implements a maker-taker model for facilitating atomic swaps. Makers run an Automated Swap Backend (ASB) [24, docs/pages/becoming_a_maker/overview.mdx] that provides Monero liquidity to the network. The ASB communicates directly with both the Bitcoin and Monero blockchains through intermediary services: monero-wallet-rpc for Monero and electrs for Bitcoin. While makers typically maintain persistent online presence to service swap requests, takers only connect to the network when initiating trades. Although running dedicated Bitcoin and Monero nodes is recommended for enhanced security and reliability, makers can alternatively configure their ASB to use remote blockchain services. Two discovery mechanisms [24, docs/pages/usage/market_maker_discovery.mdx] are implemented. When starting the UnstoppableSwap application a public registry is visible which is community-maintained and lists available makers. A second discovery mechanism is based on the libp2p rendezvous protocol [19]. This protocol enables decentralized peer discovery through rendezvous points, dedicated servers that facilitate connections between network participants. Makers register their services under these rendezvous points, and takers can query them to discover available swap providers. While community volunteers maintain several public rendezvous points, anyone can host their own. Users who already know a specific maker's network address, could directly open peer-to-peer connections.

Trade Protocol: The trade protocol facilitates atomic swaps as described by Hoenisch and del Pino [18] enabling cross-chain atomic swaps between Bitcoin and Monero. The atomic swaps make use of adaptor signatures where the key mechanism is public keys on both chains sharing the same secret key.

In the graphical interface takers are lead through four stages: locking the Bitcoin in a 2/2 multi-signature wallet, the maker locking the Monero, followed by the maker redeeming the Bitcoin and revealing the secret needed for the last step of redeeming the Monero. **Trade fees:** Fees are not applied as an additional amount but are included in the exchange rate. When setting up the ASB, a price ticker URL is configured that updates exchange rates based on the current market rate, by default provided by the centralized exchange Kraken. Makers can add a spread to this rate acting as a trade fee. A trade fee going to a third party is not considered. **Dispute Resolution:** A four step [24, docs/pages/usage/refund_punish.mdx] safety mechanism is implemented into the trade protocol: cancel, refund, punish, and cooperative redeem. If the maker is not redeeming the Bitcoin, either party can invoke a Bitcoin cancel transaction. This cancels the swap, and the taker must publish a refund transaction to return the BTC to the specified refund address. If no refund is published, the maker can punish the taker and redeem the Bitcoin. Monero becomes refundable once the swap enters the canceled state. In a punish scenario, the maker may still allow the taker to redeem the Monero, but is not obligated to.

Operational Details: As a taker, no additional setup besides installing the graphical interface or even only the CLI is needed. Makers are recommended to run local nodes for security and robustness but setting up local nodes is not enforced.

3.5 Comparative Analysis

Table 1 highlights key differences among Monero-focused DEXs. Haveno and Bisq use multi-signature trades with arbitrators, while BasicSwap and COMIT rely on atomic swaps. Haveno and Bisq have centralized seed nodes, whereas BasicSwap and COMIT are fully decentralized. Bisq charges fees, while Haveno remains fee-free for now. COMIT is limited to BTC-to-XMR swaps.

Table 1. Comparative Analysis of Monero's Decentralized P2P Exchanges

	Haveno	Bisq	BasicSwap	COMIT
Governance	–	DAO	–	–
Key Trade Mechanism	2/3 Multi-Sig.[†]	2/2 Multi-Sig.	Atomic Swap	Atomic Swap
Trade Settlement	P2P + arbitrator	P2P + mediator	P2P	P2P
Trade Fee	Not yet	Yes	No	No
Centralized Components	Seed/arbitrator nodes, (Sect. 3.1)	Seed/arbitrator nodes (Sect. 3.2)	No	No
Network Communication	Tor	Tor	SMSG	libp2p, optionally via Tor
Supported Assets	XMR ↔ *	BTC ↔ *	**	BTC → XMR

*Universal compatibility, including XMR.
***BTC, XMR, DASH, LTC, FIRO, PIVX, DCR, WOW, PART.
[†]Arbitrator controls the third signature.

4 Haveno Vulnerability and Cross-Chain Observability

During our analysis we recognized different potential weaknesses a DEX might be prone to. If the network architecture includes centralized components, it offers a central point of failure potentially bringing the whole network to a collapse. Centralized components raise legal concerns if critical infrastructure is controlled by a single entity, potentially qualifying as a financial service. Trade protocols also introduce risks beyond security vulnerabilities; their design may create detectable on-chain patterns, undermining privacy guarantees through blockchain analysis. On-chain observability greatly depends on the underlying cryptocurrency. While Bitcoin provides full transparency regarding wallet addresses and transaction amounts, Monero inherently obscures such information, though timing, transaction structure, and fees are still observable. Each structural characteristic gains in importance when observed in a specific arrangement including temporal observations. For trades involving fiat currencies, while the fiat transactions remain hidden for public observers, they maintain full visibility to the participating financial institutions.

The P2P network is usually used to communicate details before, during, and after trades, mostly only between the involved parties. Nonetheless, messages broadcast to the network can provide orientation for the activity of the application. Furthermore, it adds a time metric if offers, takes, and successful or unsuccessful trades are broadcast to the network.

4.1 Haveno Data Observability

Haveno offers multiple distinct features that can be publicly observed within the application, the P2P network, and the Monero blockchain. We will first derive an observable on-chain pattern from the trade protocol and continue to combine the blockchain information with application data. As the Monero blockchain hides most transaction details, trades involving another currency operating on a public ledger like Bitcoin will play a key part to identify both trade partners.

Trade Protocol Analysis: According to the trade protocol, a trade includes three transactions. Two lock transactions as security deposits and one spend transaction as payout. Both security deposits are invoked once a trade is taken and broadcast to the network by the arbitrator. The trade protocol allows the taker 24 h to send the external funds to the seller and once the maker confirms this, the trade concludes with the payout. On-chain, this means that within 24 h after the lock transactions, one output of each lock will be a ring member for the spend transaction as visualized in Fig. 2. Both lock transactions will have two outputs, and the spend transaction will have two outputs and two inputs. It is possible that the two security deposit transactions are split and written to two blocks if the network delays a transaction or a block reached its limit. But as the arbitrator verifies the trade details and transactions before broadcasting everything, most lock transactions are written to a single block. Finally, Haveno transactions use an increased fee structure. Although the fee is one of the standard fees commonly used by third party Monero applications, the high nature still rules out a majority of transactions that use the lower standard fee. See Fig. 2 for an illustration of the on-chain pattern.

Trade Statistics: Haveno offers historical trade statistics. The amounts involved in a trade are obfuscated by $\pm 5\%$ setting the frame for potential transactions on the Bitcoin blockchain too large to draw relevant conclusions. However, during the obfuscation the exchange rate stays accurate. Therefore, by reversing

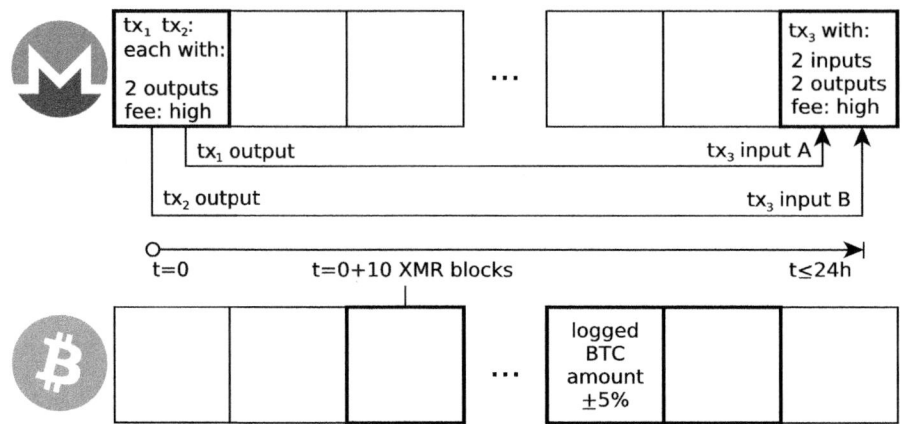

Fig. 2. On-Chain Pattern for a standard Haveno trade without a dispute. The two outputs created in the first two transaction are referenced in the final transaction within 24 h. Within this time window, a counterpart needs to exist on the other trading currency, in this case Bitcoin. Haveno by default uses the same high fee for both transactions, obfuscates the reported trade amount, but broadcasts the completion of the trade immediately via the P2P network.

the heuristic, we can extract every Bitcoin transaction that fits into the range of the obfuscation time window. As the Haveno interface allows the XMR to include a decimal number with a maximum of four digits after the point the number of potential Bitcoin transactions is already greatly reduced.

TradeLogger: A second obfuscation in the trade statistics happens on the trade timestamp. The timestamp is shifted by some time between zero and 24 h. However, the Haveno application immediately broadcasts the trade to the statistics once the trade is successfully completed. There might be delays in the network which unintentionally obfuscate the timestamp but typically, this notification in the network gives us the time when a trade has been completed. Combined with our trade protocol, this gives us roughly the timestamp of the XMR spend transaction, the payout. Therefore, we can narrow down external transactions from a 24 h window to the time frame we get of the observed on-chain pattern.

4.2 Results

To test our findings, we logged Haveno trades for two weeks and executed five test trades within the observation period. For all five transactions, we successfully identified all XMR transactions. Furthermore, our analysis correctly isolated a subset of BTC transactions including the real BTC payment transaction.

Datasets: For our evaluation we collected three datasets:

- Monero mainnet blockchain transactions from 2025-01-21 until 2025-02-03
- Bitcoin mainnet blockchain transactions from 2025-01-21 until 2025-02-03
- RetoSwap Trade Statistics
- RetoSwap trades logged from 2025-01-22 until 2025-02-03

The data includes 344 trades logged during this period, 66 of which used Bitcoin as the exchange currency. Our analysis will focus on these Bitcoin trades.

Monero Blockchain Analytics: To match our logged trades we started with scanning the Monero blockchain for potential swaps. As described, a swap includes two lock transactions and a single spend transaction. As the spend transaction provides the link to the lock transactions, we searched the chain in reverse starting with every possible spend transaction. For each possible spend transaction, we collect the transaction ID and all ring members of both inputs. The lock transactions must have been made within 24 h before this block and to take into account the possibility that the lock transactions are split, we allow the lock transactions to be in neighboring blocks.

Within the given time frame of 14 days, we find 671 potential swaps that fit with the observable Monero pattern. For comparison, within these 14 days (block 3,330,482 to 3,339,845), 371,206 transactions are written on the Monero blockchain with 14,666 matching the structural characteristics of a spend transaction. Only for 671 transaction, we can match potential corresponding locks and include them as potential swaps.

Haveno Trade Matching: We continue by combining the found swaps with the trades logged from the RetoSwap application. The spend transaction from the potential swap should be in a block that was mined around the time the trade was broadcast. We therefore match potential swaps when the spend was mined within ten minutes after or one minute before the trade was logged to account for network delays. We thereby found for 65 of the logged Bitcoin trades 98 potential swaps. Multiple swaps for a single trade are expected and not ultimately decide the matching accuracy as it mainly influences the time frame we will consider Bitcoin blocks for each swap.

Bitcoin Blockchain Analytics: As the amount of BTC and XMR is obfuscated, we first include a BTC transaction when it is within the possible range. Afterwards, we use the exchange rate to calculate the amount of XMR. If the resulting XMR amount is a real number with equal or less than four digits after the decimal point, we include the Bitcoin transaction as a possible transaction.

Matches: Taking all possible Bitcoin transactions into account, we match one Monero swap pattern to on average 933 Bitcoin transactions. But the majority of Bitcoin transactions relate to an XMR amount with four digits after the decimal point. We can reduce the set of possible transactions to a realistic subset by assuming traders usually trade even amounts. Matching amounts divisible by 1, 0.5, 0.25, or 0.1 reduces the candidate set to a size suitable for manual inspection. Using this subset, we find transactions for 50 trades, matching each to an average of 2.5 Bitcoin transactions, with a median of one transaction per swap.

5 Discussion

Our analysis of decentralized exchanges revealed several key differences. We observed varying network and governance structures across platforms, alongside considerable diversity in available trade protocols. These protocols facilitate varying cryptocurrency compatibility and potentially introduce vulnerabilities in cross-chain transaction privacy.

Central Network Components: Haveno's and Bisq's network architecture requires seed node infrastructure to be deployed before arbitrator nodes can register, and arbitrators have to be registered and online for peers to start trading. These components create potential centralization vectors. The disruption of seed nodes could render the network inoperative, while compromised arbitrator nodes would block trading functionality. Multiple seed and arbitrator nodes can and should exist to keep the network live 24/7 and simultaneously create a form of decentralization within the seed and arbitrator node infrastructure. Nonetheless, not every node and therefore not every peer is equal within the network, therefore challenging the claim that there is no central authority. If the seed nodes are taken off the grid, the network cannot exist. For BasicSwap, the integration with Particl provides robustness by eliminating centralized points of failure but it also creates some dependence and could present scalability challenges as the ecosystem grows. Decentralized applications within the ecosystem share a security model where threats targeted at either the Particl blockchain or the SMSG network would potentially impact all applications. However, this shared security model also means improvements and a growing network will benefit all applications. The P2P network architecture implemented in the COMIT protocol mitigates single points of failure through its distributed and lightweight design. Trading and communication is peer to peer. Only to discover makers centralized services are beneficial. The network has two distinct node types but each peer remains equal. Everybody can deploy an Automated Backend Server and act as a maker, and everyone can take the role of a taker.

Arbitrator Involvement: The integration of arbitrators and third-party mediators in certain DEX implementations presents significant implications for transaction security and privacy. Whereas BasicSwap and COMIT implement direct atomic swaps between two participants, Haveno and Bisq incorporate arbitration mechanisms that necessitate third-party involvement. The arbitrator has to be online for a peer to register the offer, to execute the trade, and for dispute resolution. A major difference between Haveno and Bisq is the involvement in the multi-signature wallet. Haveno's arbitrators have a third signature, giving them not sole control but still the power to align with either party and release the funds from the wallet. Bisq implements a more decentralized and objective approach where the arbitrator acts more as a mediator, objectively supporting the dispute resolution without actually giving them any power. Bisq's arbitrators seem to only provide infrastructure governed by the DAO, Haveno's trade protocol could be interpreted as giving the arbitrator actual access to the funds. Nonetheless, both scenarios might raise the question if some kind of financial service is provided by a single entity. This raises the regulatory question of whether arbitrators are facilitators of cryptocurrency exchanges. Furthermore, as the arbitrator is in possession of the third signature, the arbitrator necessarily requires access to Monero transaction details, challenging the claim of true anonymous peer to peer interaction. The arbitrator will only in dispute cases see the involved Bitcoin addresses but as he has access to the full transaction details including an accurate Bitcoin amount, a blockchain analysis could easily reveal the transaction in question. This raises serious privacy concerns if an arbitrator is not acting in good will and would require putting trust in a third-party.

Governance: Governance structures across the examined platforms reveal contrasting approaches to decentralized decision-making, with varying degrees of transparency and stakeholder participation that directly impact platform resilience and ultimately trust. Bisq and BasicSwap apply a DAO structure outlining treasury, infrastructure, and voting mechanisms. Whereas for Bisq the DAO has to decide on directly relevant issues regarding the DEX like fee structure and node management, BSX DAO is more aligned with the general Particl ecosystem and development as no specific infrastructure for BSX is needed and no trade fees apply. Haveno states that a live network is neither maintained nor endorsed. RetoSwap is supposed to be an independent structure running its own live network. Nonetheless, it appears that besides running the live network and hosting another website, the project and its repository appears identically.

Haveno: Haveno has been discussed in greater detail as it evolved to one of the most prominent exchanges in the context of Monero. While strong promises claim privacy with every transaction and independence from any central authority, the current implementation raises uncertainty. Our analysis showed detectable on-chain patterns and weaknesses in the platform that can be exploited to match transactions across chains. These vulnerabilities may be addressed through standardized fee structures that enhance transaction anonymity within larger transaction volumes. While trade statistics provide valuable metrics for users, their network propagation should be obfuscated through mechanisms such as aggregated daily updates to preserve trade privacy. A more complicated matter is within the missing governance structure. In contrast to the COMIT network, a Haveno network is not functional without an initial setup. Two peers cannot boot respective nodes and trade. Therefore, a decentralized transparent process regarding the decentralized critical infrastructure is necessary to make it really independent from central control. Bisq is an interesting example as it deploys the same architecture with a more transparent governing structure. Nonetheless, even with an existing clear governance, the described involvement of a third party is concerning especially with the motive of using Monero as a privacy first alternative.

6 Conclusion

In this paper, we have provided a systematization of the landscape of P2P decentralized exchanges in the Monero ecosystem, covering Haveno, Bisq, Basic-

SwapDEX, and the COMIT protocol, used e.g. by UnstoppableSwap. Our analysis reveals significant gaps between the decentralization and privacy promises of Monero-focused DEXs and their actual implementations. While these platforms offer alternatives to increasingly regulated centralized exchanges, they exhibit varying degrees of decentralization and privacy.

Haveno and Bisq rely on centralized components such as seed and arbitrator nodes, which introduce resilience and regulatory concerns. Additionally, we demonstrate that Haveno trades leave detectable on-chain footprints, allowing some degree of cross-chain transaction linking. Truly decentralized alternatives like COMIT eliminate these risks but sacrifice user experience and liquidity.

Governance structures range from well-defined decentralized autonomous organizations to loosely structured community-driven projects, raising questions about long-term sustainability and legal implications. Future work could explore mitigation strategies for privacy weaknesses in DEXs and evaluate emerging cross-chain trading techniques that aim to preserve Monero's anonymity. Our findings contribute to the discussion on secure DEX designs and provide a foundation for assessing regulatory concerns surrounding P2P cryptocurrency exchanges.

Acknowledgement. Partially funded by German Research Foundation (DFG), project ReNO (SPP 2378), 2023–2027.

References

1. Angeris, G., Kao, H.T., Chiang, R., Noyes, C., Chitra, T.: An analysis of uniswap markets. arXiv preprint arXiv:1911.03380 (2019)
2. Auer, R., Haslhofer, B., Kitzler, S., Saggese, P., Victor, F.: The technology of decentralized finance (DeFi). Digit. Finance **6**(1), 55–95 (2024)
3. Bisq DEX: Bisq-DEX (2025). https://bisq.wiki/Bisq_1. Accessed 06 Mar 2025
4. Bisq2 DEX: Bisq2-DEX (2025). https://bisq.wiki/Bisq_2. Accessed 06 Mar 2025
5. Brechlin, A., Schäfer, J., Armknecht, F.: Buy crypto, sell privacy: investigating the cryptocurrency exchange evonax. In: 2024 IEEE International Conference on Blockchain and Cryptocurrency (ICBC), pp. 1–7. IEEE (2024)
6. Brechlin, A., Schäfer, J., Armknecht, F.: Buy crypto, sell privacy: an extended investigation of the cryptocurrency exchange evonax. Int. J. Network Manage **35**(1), e2325 (2025)
7. Decred Atomic Swaps: Atomic swaps decred style (2018). https://github.com/decred/atomicswap. Accessed 18 Feb 2025
8. European Union: Regulation (EU) 2023/1114 of the European parliament and of the council of 31 may 2023 on markets in crypto-assets, and amending regulations (EU) no 1093/2010 and (EU) no 1095/2010 and directives 2013/36/EU and (EU) 2019/1937 (2023). https://eur-lex.europa.eu/eli/reg/2023/1114/oj
9. Financial Action Task Force: Updated guidance for a risk-based approach to virtual assets and virtual asset service providers (2021). https://www.fatf-gafi.org/content/dam/fatf-gafi/guidance/Updated-Guidance-VA-VASP.pdf
10. Goodell, B.: History and state of Monero security analysis (2024). https://github.com/cypherstack/pup-monero-analysis/releases/download/final/final.pdf

11. Gugger, J.: Bitcoin-Monero cross-chain atomic swap. Cryptology ePrint Archive, Paper 2020/1126 (2020). https://eprint.iacr.org/2020/1126
12. Hammad, N., Victor, F.: Monero traceability heuristics: wallet application bugs and the Mordinal-P2Pool perspective. In: 2024 IEEE International Conference on Blockchain and Cryptocurrency (ICBC), pp. 540–548. IEEE (2024)
13. Haveno DEX: Haveno-DEX (2025). https://github.com/haveno-dex. Accessed 18 Feb 2025
14. Hickey, L., Harrigan, M.: The bisq DAO: on the privacy cost of participation. In: 2020 IEEE Symposium on Computers and Communications (ISCC), pp. 1–6. IEEE (2020)
15. Hickey, L., Harrigan, M.: The Bisq decentralised exchange: on the privacy cost of participation. Blockchain Res. Appl. **3**(1), 100029 (2022)
16. Hinteregger, A., Haslhofer, B.: Short paper: an empirical analysis of Monero cross-chain traceability. In: Goldberg, I., Moore, T. (eds.) FC 2019. LNCS, vol. 11598, pp. 150–157. Springer, Cham (2019). https://doi.org/10.1007/978-3-030-32101-7_10
17. Hoenisch, P., Mazumdar, S., Moreno-Sanchez, P., Ruj, S.: LightSwap: an atomic swap does not require timeouts at both blockchains. In: International Workshop on Data Privacy Management, pp. 219–235. Springer (2022)
18. Hoenisch, P., del Pino, L.S.: Atomic swaps between bitcoin and Monero. arXiv preprint arXiv:2101.12332 (2021)
19. libp2p: libp2p-protocol (2025). https://docs.libp2p.io/concepts/discovery-routing/rendezvous/. Accessed 06 Mar 2025
20. Möser, M., et al.: An empirical analysis of traceability in the Monero blockchain. In: Proceedings on Privacy Enhancing Technologies (2018)
21. Particl Academy: BSX-DEX (2024). https://academy.particl.io/en/latest/index.html. Accessed 06 Mar 2025
22. RetoSwap: RetoSwap (2024). https://github.com/retoaccess1/haveno-reto. Accessed 18 Feb 2025
23. Thyagarajan, S.A., Malavolta, G., Moreno-Sanchez, P.: Universal atomic swaps: secure exchange of coins across all blockchains. In: 2022 IEEE Symposium on Security and Privacy (SP), pp. 1299–1316. IEEE (2022)
24. UnstoppableSwap: unstoppableswap-dex (2025). https://github.com/UnstoppableSwap/core. Accessed 18 Feb 2025
25. Warren, J.: Bitmessage: a peer-to-peer message authentication and delivery system. White paper (2012). https://bitmessage.org/bitmessage.pdf
26. Xu, J., Paruch, K., Cousaert, S., Feng, Y.: SoK: decentralized exchanges (DEX) with automated market maker (AMM) protocols. ACM Comput. Surv. **55**(11), 1–50 (2023). https://doi.org/10.1145/3570639. http://dx.doi.org/10.1145/3570639
27. Yousaf, H., Kappos, G., Meiklejohn, S.: Tracing transactions across cryptocurrency ledgers. In: 28th USENIX Security Symposium (USENIX Security 2019), pp. 837–850 (2019)

Toward a Secure Tokenized Green Credit Management System: Case Study of WREGIS

Mahmudun Nabi[✉] and Reihaneh Safavi-Naini

University of Calgary, Alberta, Canada
{mahmudun.nabi1,rei}@ucalgary.ca

Abstract. Renewable energy (RE) registries are centralized systems that track and manage Renewable Energy Certificates (RECs) that provide a proof that the claimed RE activity has occurred. In this work, we study the Western Renewable Energy Generation Information System (WREGIS), a widely used web-based tracking system in the western United States and Canada, and motivate the need for decentralization. We then propose a blockchain-based system for green credit management for WREGIS that uses a combination of private and public blockchains to remove the intermediaries, to allow small producers to directly receive green credit tokens for their energy production and be able to participate in the renewable energy market. The system allows verification of users' claims and issuance of tokens using smart contracts on a private and public blockchains, respectively. We show the correctness and security of the token generation process, and that the system provides a high level of privacy for energy producers. We give descriptions of smart contracts in the two chains and details of our proof-of-concept implementation of the system, and evaluate transaction costs and efficiency of the system. Our work serves as an approach to the tokenization of other green credit systems.

Keywords: Blockchain and Smart Contract · Renewable Energy · Green Credit Tokenization

1 Introduction

The renewable energy (RE) market encompasses the production, distribution, and trade of energy generated from sustainable sources such as solar, wind, hydro, geothermal, and biomass. This market has experienced rapid growth in recent years due to increasing concerns about climate change, energy security, and the declining costs of renewable technologies. According to the International Energy Agency (IEA), renewables accounted for nearly 30% of global electricity generation in 2022, with solar and wind energy leading the expansion [18]. Governments worldwide have implemented policies, subsidies, and incentives to accelerate the adoption of clean energy, while corporations and investors are increasingly committing to net-zero goals. Technological advancements, improved energy storage solutions, and growing consumer awareness have further fueled the market's expansion, making renewables a dominant force in the global energy transition [33].

A credit system that rewards renewable energy production provides incentives for individuals and businesses to generate clean energy by issuing renewable energy certificates (RECs) or carbon credits. These credits represent proof that a certain amount of electricity was generated from renewable sources and can be traded or sold in environmental markets. For example, in the REC system used in the U.S., solar or wind energy producers receive RECs for each megawatt-hour (MWh) of electricity they generate. These RECs can then be sold to companies seeking to offset their carbon footprint, creating a financial incentive for renewable energy production.

In line with *Web3* applications, which emphasize decentralization, transparency, and user participation, small renewable energy producers must be empowered to actively participate in the energy market. By leveraging peer-to-peer (P2P) energy trading, blockchain-based smart contracts, and decentralized energy exchanges, small producers can have greater market access, receive fair compensation, and contribute to energy democratization. This will not only enhance grid resilience, reduce reliance on large utilities, and promote sustainability by incentivizing local clean energy generation. It will incentivize new economic activities through the sharing of resources and exchanges between neighborhoods.

The growing call for sustainable development and RE has attracted an increasing number of households to participate in renewable energy generation using micro-generation technologies [34,38]. RECs, however, do not provide support for small providers to enter the energy market, nor fairly reward them for their contribution to sustainability and the green economy. In a basic *green credit system*, RE producers report their energy generation data to a *credit-issuing authority*, which verifies their claims and issues credits. Since many credit-issuing agencies impose a minimum threshold on energy generation, small-scale producers rely on *aggregator service* to combine and verify claims and submits them in a batch, reaching the required minimum. Aggregators, often local electricity retailers or intermediaries (with infrastructure to verify a RE generation claim), receive RECs from the credit-issuing authority, which may not be passed to the producers. In many cases, including the case of Alberta's[1] micro-generation system [3] that is implemented following WREGIS (Western Renewable Energy Generation Information System) and is the case study considered in this paper, aggregators do not distribute the received RECs to individual producers. Thus while the producers will have lower energy bills (based on a fixed rate), it is the aggregators that collect green credit rewards from the grid owner (e.g., the local government) and are able to trade the RECs in energy markets. This effectively excludes small producers from today's vibrant energy market. Credit issuing process may involve other intermediaries. In WREGIS [39], RE data must be submitted through verified entities such as Qualified Reporting Entities (QREs), which, like aggregators, are registered with the credit-issuing authority.

Introducing multiple levels of intermediaries, while important to provide verifiability for generation claims, creates complexity in the system as well as opportunities for misuse of the system. Intermediaries may find incentives to collude

---

[1] A province of Canada.

with energy producers in incorrect reporting of RE generation data and ultimately generation of RECs for invalid claims. In other words, the existing architecture is a distributed system that, for correct functioning, requires many points of the system to be trusted, while there are incentives for the participants to deviate from their assigned roles.

Blockchain-Based Credit Management. One of the main applications of blockchain in today's information management systems is to remove intermediaries, empowering individual nodes to participate in wide exchanges with other nodes. Blockchain-based solutions for energy credit management, including Toucan [37] and Moss [25], aim to decentralize carbon credit management by leveraging Web3 technology to tokenize carbon credits and enable automated peer-to-peer (P2P) trading through smart contracts. However, these systems primarily focus on tokenization and credit trading after the producers' claims have been verified by a traditional trusted human-centered verification system. Similarly, systems such as Brooklyn Microgrid [13], that enables peer-to-peer trading of solar energy, and UrbanChain [21], which facilitates peer-to-peer energy exchange, focus mainly on energy trading rather than the full automation of REC generation, trading and management (see Appendix A for more details on these schemes).

Our Work. Our goal is to explore and identify the challenges of *tokenizing* green credit systems through a concrete case study. We consider a web-based renewable energy tracking system that is currently deployed in Canada[2] and uses the WREGIS, a leading independent renewable energy tracking system that is designed to support the creation, verification, and trading of RECs across the Western Electricity Coordinating Council (WECC) region, with the goal of ensuring transparency and accountability in renewable energy markets.

(i) Architecture. In Sect. 3.1, we review the WREGIS workflow and propose a *hybrid blockchain architecture* (in Sect. 3.2) that combines a public and a private blockchains. This hybrid architecture achieves the same goal as WREGIS and ensures: (i) the correct issuance of credits and (ii) user privacy in the blockchain-based green credit management system. The private blockchain and its associated smart contracts and oracles are used to verify users' energy generation claims. Once verified, these claims are presented to the public blockchain, in a verifiable form, where *Green Tokens (GTs)* are issued to the users using a `GToken` smart contract on the public chain. The system effectively reduces reliance on intermediaries by leveraging Oracle smart contracts, which validate users' claims by querying local electricity providers that directly interact with energy producers. By utilizing smart contracts within the private blockchain, the entire verification process for REC generation is automated, enhancing both transparency and efficiency.

(ii) User privacy. Ensuring that users' energy generation history remains private introduces efficiency challenges that ultimately have led us to use a hybrid architecture. In particular, using cryptography can ensure user privacy using a single (public) chain but at the high computational cost of zero-knowledge

---

[2] Province of Alberta.

proofs for verifiability. Additionally, using a public chain only will increase the delay because of transaction confirmation time. Using hybrid architecture allows us to use more efficient cryptographic primitives to provide user privacy while providing the ability to "open" the required information to the public blockchain in a verifiable way, as required by the token generation process. It also substantially reduces transaction delays. We use BBS+ Signature scheme, [35], a cryptographic scheme that enables efficient and privacy-preserving signing of a set messages. BBS+ allows a signing authority to sign a set of messages, from which the recipient can selectively disclose and prove the correctness of subsets of the messages without revealing the entire set. BBS+ has been used for privacy-enhancing applications such as anonymous credentials and verifiable credentials in decentralized identity systems. We use BBS+ for *selective disclosure* of subsets of verified attributes of energy producers' claims (e.g., the amount of generation without disclosing the producer's identity). Our system design is detailed in Sect. 4.

(iii) Analysis. In Sect. 4.4, we provide a systematic security and privacy analysis of our proposed design. We consider the system entities and their incentives to misuse the system individually or in collusion with others, and show that using smart contracts effectively removes the ability of bad actors to result in an incorrect issuance of tokens. We use *unlinkability of a user's transactions* as the main notion of privacy and define *single-chain unlinkability*, which captures the unlinkability of a user's transaction against a node of a chain, and *cross-chain unlinkability* against an adversary that has nodes in both chains. We argue that our proposed construction satisfies single-chain unlinkability for individual chains, as well as cross-chain unlinkability.

We also provide a proof-of-concept implementation of our system to show the applicability of the design in practice. We design and implement (in Solidity) a set of two smart contracts for data verification on the private chain and one smart contract (`GToken`) for token generation on the public blockchain. To estimate the overhead of the cryptographic components of the system in practice, we use a web-based tool [27] to generate BBS+ signature and proof of ownership of the signature. The signature is used in a verifiable credential that we implemented in the W3C standard [23]. This allows us to evaluate the computation and storage cost of the public blockchain for issuing tokens. Our results are presented in Tables 1 and 2 of Sect. 5.

Organization. Section 2 is preliminaries. Section 3.1 and 3.2 provide WREGIS outline and our blockchain-based design. Section 4 outlines our green token generation scheme, including its security and privacy analysis. Section 5 presents implementation and evaluation results, and Sect. 6 concludes the paper.

2 Preliminaries

Blockchain and Smart Contracts. Blockchain is a decentralized, distributed ledger system that securely records transactions across multiple nodes in a network. It ensures data transparency and that the data cannot be altered by any participant without the consensus of the network participants. This work uses two types of blockchains- *public* and *private*. Public blockchains are fully decentralized networks where participants can join and validate transactions, such as Bitcoin [26] and Ethereum [9]. In contrast, private blockchains such as R3 Corda [7], Hyperledger [10] operate within a more controlled environment, with access restricted to specific participants, offering greater control, efficiency, and privacy. Blockchains such as Ethereum also support smart contracts, which are self-executing programs that automate transactions based on predefined rules and allow the development of blockchain-based decentralized applications (dApps). One key blockchain application is tokenization, where assets are represented as digital tokens. The ERC-20 standard, widely used in Ethereum-based tokenization, defines a common set of functions (*totalSupply, balanceOf, transfer, approve,* and *transferFrom*) for new token generation.

BBS+ Signature Scheme. The BBS+ signature is a multi-message digital signature protocol that enables signing multiple messages with a single signature while supporting selective disclosure [11,35]. It operates on a pairing-friendly bilinear group where a signer generates a secret-public key pair and signs messages using random generators and cryptographic pairing operations. Verification ensures the signature's validity via bilinear equality checks. Additionally, BBS+ proofs allow proving possession of a valid signature while revealing only a subset of signed messages, maintaining unlinkability and proof of possession. Appendix B provides further details on its main functions with an example.

Verifiable Credential (VC). A *credential* is a digital representation of *claims* (e.g., specific attributes or facts) about a *subject* (e.g., a person or organization), similar to a driver's license or passport. A **verifiable credential** (VC), following World Wide Web Consortium (W3C) standards [23], uses cryptographic proofs (e.g., digital signatures) to confirm the issuer and ensure data integrity. The W3C VC ecosystem [23] has three parties: (i) *issuer*, who creates and issues the VC; (ii) *holder*, who requests, stores, and shares the VC; and (iii) *verifier*, who authenticates the VC by verifying its digital signature. The holder can create a verifiable presentation (VP) to share full or partial VC data securely. Figures 4a and 4b in Appendix C show the VC issuance and presentation process and its core components: *metadata* (credential details), *attributes* (subject claims), and *proof* (issuer's digital signature on metadata and claims), respectively. A VC is encoded in JSON [5] or JSON-LD [24] formats.

3 A Blockchain-Based Approach to WREGIS

We first introduce WREGIS, and then design a hybrid blockchain-based system that achieves the same functionality.

3.1 WREGIS

WREGIS [39] is an independent, web-based tracking system designed to issue RECs. A REC serves as proof that 1 megawatt-hour (MWh) of electricity was

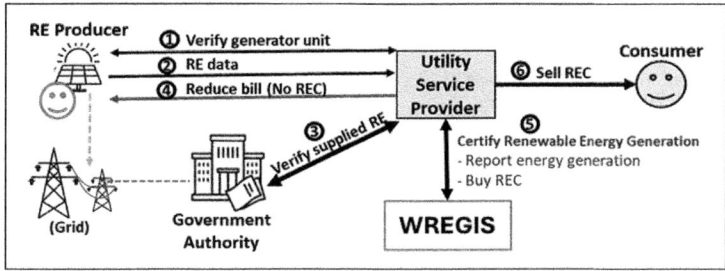

Fig. 1. Workflow of a micro-generation credit system [3].

generated from an eligible renewable energy source. Each REC includes information such as the type of renewable fuel used (e.g., solar, wind, water), the month and year the MWh was generated, the facility location, the customer to whom the REC is issued, and the issuer's signature.

WREGIS consists of the following entities: (1) *Users*, which include individual customers (small-scale unit owners), aggregators (managing multiple small units), and organizations (operating large-scale facilities); (2) *Qualified Reporting Entities (QREs)*, third parties tasked with verifying and submitting generation data to WREGIS for certificate creation; (3) *WREGIS Administrator (WA)*, responsible for overseeing system operations, ensuring compliance, and managing user registration; and (4) *Program Administrators (PAs)*, who manage renewable energy programs, certify generating units and meters, and resolve disputes. At a high level, WREGIS operates as follows (see Fig. 5 in Appendix D): A user registers with WREGIS and authorizes a Qualified Reporting Entity (QRE) to report generation data. The WREGIS administrator verifies the data's validity and issues REC to the user's account if valid. If the data is invalid, the user needs to submit correct data verified by the program administrator, with non-compliance leading to the removal of the generating unit from the system. Figure 1 shows the operation of a traditional *micro-generation credit system*, such as the one in Alberta, Canada [3], utilizing WREGIS where the utility service providers offer the aggregator service to micro RE producers (details in Appendix D).

We identify the following key issues: **(i)** *Micro RE generators cannot report data directly to WREGIS and depend on intermediaries like aggregators or QREs*; **(ii)** *The traditional credit system is centralized and not user-centric, limiting fair compensation for small-scale RE generators supplying surplus energy to the grid*; and **(iii)** *Small RE producers cannot directly participate in energy markets for credit exchange as WREGIS is not connected with other credit systems, does not support credit transfers outside its framework, and typically issues credits to aggregators instead of individual generators.* These issues are discussed further in Appendix D with the assumption on WREGIS entities.

3.2 Designing a Blockchain-Based System for WREGIS

To modernize the WREGIS system by automating renewable energy data verification and certificate generation, we propose a hybrid blockchain-based architecture that combines private and public blockchains for secure green credit management. The *private blockchain* securely stores and verifies RE generation data, ensuring data integrity and confidentiality, while the *public blockchain* executes the application smart contract for '**green token**' (GT) generation. The system consists of the following main entities:

1. **Users.** The (micro) renewable energy producers who own small renewable energy generating units (such as rooftop solar panels) and want to receive credit for surplus RE generation.
2. **Registry administrator (RA).** Manages user identities and registration on the registry platform, verifies RE data via smart contracts and deploys an application smart contract for tokenizing RECs.
3. **Governance authority (GA).** Oversees RE regulations, certifies meters, compensates service providers for crediting RE producers, and resolves disputes with on-chain smart contract coordination.
4. **Blockchain.** We use a hybrid model with both private and public blockchains. Users, RA, and GA are nodes on both chains (via client applications).
    a) *Private chain.* A group of stakeholders (e.g., government agencies, utility companies, registries, etc.) can jointly run the private chain by their authorized representatives (e.g., RAs). It includes:
        (i) **Validator nodes** (RAs). Manage node admission (e.g., user and Oracle nodes) and validate transactions.
        (ii) **Edge nodes** (Users). Interact with Validator nodes and authorized smart contracts (Fig. 2).
        (iii) **Oracle nodes** (part of the Oracle service). Facilitate communication between the private blockchain and external systems.
    b) *Public chain.* Receives verified RE data and uses application smart contracts (e.g., GToken) for token issuance based on the verified information.
5. **Smart contracts.**
    a) *System contracts.* (Details in Sect. 4.2.)
        (i) MetReg (Meter Registry). Deployed by the GA in the private chain to store meter certificates.
        (ii) DataVer (Data Verification). Deployed by the RA on the private chain to store hashed generation data, verifiable credentials (VCs), and Oracle verification results to validate the authenticity of issued VCs.
    b) *Application contract.*
        (i) GToken (Green Token). Deployed by the RA on the public chain to verify and issue tokens for valid requests.
6. **Oracle service.** Used by the RA to verify the user's RE generation claims. It includes an on-chain Oracle contract and off-chain Relay entities (registered as Oracle nodes) that fetch data from trusted external sources (e.g., service providers). Town Crier [40], Muscle [20], Chainlink's Oracle network [6], etc., are some examples of existing Oracle services that employ authenticated data feed protocols to ensure secure and reliable data verification.

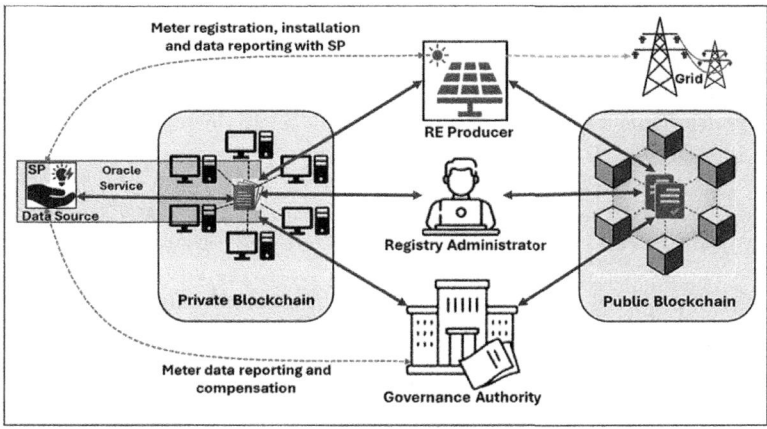

Fig. 2. Overview of Blockchain-based green token system.

4 A Green Token Generation Protocol for WREGIS

Trust Assumptions. We make the following trust assumptions:

1. The end users on the private blockchain (e.g., RE producers) are **untrusted**.
2. The registry administrators (RAs) on the private blockchain are **honest-but-rational** and generally follow the protocol as prescribed. However, external incentives, such as financial gain from collusion with a dishonest user, may tempt an RA to deviate from honest protocol participation and issue a verifiable credential (VC) to the user with incorrect RE data.
3. The governance authority (GA) is **trusted** to certify a RE producer's meter (e.g., verify the meter's capacity and link the meter to the owner), enforce policies, and audit other entities in the system.
4. The Oracle system output in private blockchain is **trusted**. Note that in this work, we do not provide a description of any specific Oracle mechanism, as it is outside the scope of this paper. Any existing Oracle system, such as [6,20,40], which guarantees the authenticity of external data, can be adopted.
5. The user's identity and meter information are verified through a trusted authentication process prior to their registration in the private blockchain.
6. Public blockchain observers who do not have access to the private blockchain (i.e., external observers) are **untrusted**.
7. Cryptographic operations such as *BBS+ signature* scheme, verifiable credential (VC), and smart contracts are correctly implemented by the respective entities, and results from smart contract executions are always correct.

Communication Model. We consider the following setup.

1. Communication between the user (RE producer) and the RA happens through a secure channel (e.g., using TLS).

2. Communication between smart contracts (on both public and private chains) and the RA or user takes place over public channels. Furthermore, we assume that a user interacting with smart contracts on the public blockchain can employ multiple pseudonyms derived from a single public key (e.g., to hide their identity).

Threat Model

1. **Adversaries and Capabilities.** We divide adversaries into the following two categories with their capabilities:
   a) *Private chain adversaries.* The **registered users** in the private blockchain are considered as the potential adversaries in the private network. They have the following capabilities:
      (i) Dishonest users can submit incorrect RE generation data or send the same data multiple times (e.g., send the same RE quantity with a different timestamp) to RA for verification.
      (ii) A dishonest user can forge a verifiable credential by combining arbitrary RE data with a signature from an old VC and request a token to the public blockchain based on this forged VC.
      (iii) A dishonest user can collude with a registry administrator (RA) to get a VC on incorrect data.
      (iv) Private chain users can observe verification transactions data (submitted to the Oracle contract) on the private chain and token requests (submitted to the GToken contract) on the public chain and can attempt to correlate them to compromise RE producers' privacy.
   b) *Public chain adversaries.* External observers of the public blockchain who do not have access to the private chain and can see only the data submitted in a token request.

2. **Adversarial Goals**
   a) *Incorrect data submission, double counting* and *VC forgery* attacks by *dishonest private chain user.* Smart energy meters equipped with Advanced Metering Infrastructure (AMI) technology are typically installed by service providers (SPs) at renewable energy facilities to enable secure, two-way remote communication between SPs and individual meters [16]. As a result, when reporting generation data to the registry administrator (RA), users need to manually read the data from the meter and submit it to the RA, creating opportunities for dishonest RE producers to submit incorrect generation data for verification.

   A malicious user may also attempt a *double-counting attack* by reusing the same generation data multiple times to claim excess credits. This can occur in two ways:
      (i) **Off-chain double-counting.** A dishonest user submits the same RE data to the RA multiple times to claim credits repeatedly.
      (ii) **On-chain double-counting.** A malicious user, after obtaining a valid verifiable credential (VC) from the RA, can attempt to submit multiple token requests using the same underlying signature but generating distinct *BBS+ proofs* by blinding each proof with different randomness, making the proofs unlinkable.

Additionally, a malicious user can *create a forged verifiable credential* by pairing arbitrary RE generation data with a RA's signature extracted from an old VC and make a token request to fraudulently obtain green tokens.

b) *Collusion fraud by the registry administrator.* The RA may collude with a dishonest RE producer if it leads to increased earnings. A colluding RA can attempt to issue a verifiable credential to the dishonest user with incorrect data in different ways. For example, *incorrect data submission to Oracle SC*, submitting multiple verification requests for the same RE data to the Oracle system (i.e., *double-counting attack*), *fraudulent certificate issuance* without performing proper verification, etc., are some of the ways RA can deviate from the original protocol.

c) *Linkability.* In our hybrid architecture, linkability can occur in two forms:
  (i) **Single-chain linkability.** In a blockchain, an adversary may attempt to link multiple transactions belonging to the same user. In the private blockchain, this attack is mitigated through security measures such as encryption and hashing, making transaction linkage infeasible. However, on the public blockchain, adversarial nodes can observe disclosed RE data associated with a token request, potentially linking transactions.
  (ii) **Cross-chain linkability.** An adversary operating nodes on both the private and public blockchains (i.e., a private blockchain adversary) may attempt to correlate private chain data with publicly submitted token request data from the same user, thereby compromising user privacy.

4.1 Security and Privacy Goals

Security Goals

1. Ensure that a green token (GT) is issued only if the RE generation data originates from a certified meter and is reported by its rightful owner.
2. Prevent multiple GT issuances for the same RE data.

Thus, a green token will only be issued to a requester (e.g., a renewable energy producer) if the generation data is authentic, unaltered by adversaries, and accurately reported to the GToken smart contract for token generation, a concept known as *Veracity* of data [4]. This protects against adversarial threats, including *incorrect data submission*, *double counting*, *credential forgery*, and *collusion fraud*. The following conditions must be met to achieve our security goals:

(i) *Meter verification.* Ensuring that the meter used for data reporting is authentic (i.e., certified by a trusted certificate authority) and owned by the RE producer reporting the data.
(ii) *Data reading verification.* Validating whether the reported generation data (by both RA and RE producers) accurately reflects the original data.

(iii) *Verifiable data portability across blockchain networks.* Ensuring that verified data can be securely and verifiably transferred from the private blockchain to the public blockchain for token generation.

Privacy Goals. We consider the following privacy requirements:

1. (*Cross-chain unlinkability*) Private chain adversaries should not be able to link an RE producer's token request on the public blockchain to a corresponding data verification request on the private blockchain.
2. A public blockchain adversary must not be able to infer an RE producer's *meterID*, facility location (e.g., *siteID*), or any other identifiable attribute by observing a token request.
3. (*Single-chain unlinkability*) Both private and public blockchain adversaries should not be able to correlate whether multiple token requests originate from the same RE producer by observing and analyzing the disclosed data.

For privacy analysis, we consider two scenarios for the adversary's access to data.
(i) *Private chain interactions.* A registered RE producer submits RE generation data to the RA, which verifies it via `MetReg` and an Oracle service. Upon validation, the RA issues a verification certificate to the user, which is then used to request token issuance on the public chain.
(ii) *Public chain interactions.* A token requester (e.g., RE producer) submits token issuance requests to the `GToken` contract on the public chain and receives green tokens in return.

4.2 Smart Contracts (SCs) for Token Generation

The details of the contracts are given below (see Appendix E for the abstract of the contracts).

1. **Meter registry (`MetReg`).** Deployed and maintained by the governance authority (GA) in the private blockchain. It stores a meter's digital certificate (signed by the GA) and its status (active/inactive), enabling the registry administrator (RA) to verify meter information upon receiving RE data from a producer. This contract has the following main functions:
   a) *registerMeter():* is called by the GA to register a new meter by providing the digital meter *certificate* and sets the initial status of the meter, such as *active* or *inactive*.
   b) *verifyMeter():* is called by RA to initiate meter verification. If the meter has an active status, then the contract verifies the meter's certificate using GA's public key. If successful, it returns *true*; otherwise, *false*.
   c) *updateMeterStatus():* allows GA to update the status of a meter.
   d) *verifyGASignature():* a private helper function to verify GA's signature.
2. **Data verification (`DataVer`).** Deployed by the RA on the private blockchain, it serves as a directory to store the verification requests. The main functions of this SC are:

a) *submitRECommitment()*: is called by a user to submit a hashed commitment of generation data for verification.
b) *submitOracleVerification()*: is called by the Oracle SC to submit verification output after external verification.
c) *storeVCCommitment()*: is called by RA to store the hashed verifiable credential (VC) after successful verification.
d) *matchVerificationRequest()*: is called internally by the `storeVCCommitment()` function to verify if the user's commitment matches the Oracle's output for which the VC was issued. If the match is valid, it returns *true*; otherwise, it returns *false*. If *false* is returned (e.g., the user's commitment is not found or the Oracle's output is invalid), the VC is discarded as incorrect, and the Government Authority (GA) is notified (by emitting a dispute message) to resolve the dispute.

3. **Green token generation (GToken).** Deployed by RA in the public blockchain and responsible for verifying token requests and, if valid, issuing ERC-20 compliant green token(s) to the requester. The key functions are:
   a) *requestGToken()*: It allows a user to submit a valid BBS+ proof to request green tokens (GTs). It verifies the proof, and if valid, it calls the `issueToken()` function internally for token issuance. It calls the `verifyRequestCommitment()` function internally to check for double reporting of the same data.
   b) *verifyBBSProof()*: It verifies the BBS+ proof to ensure that the token requester has valid data (e.g., valid signature from RA on verified RE data). It returns *true* if the proof is valid, *false* otherwise.
   c) *issueToken()*: After successful proof verification, this function is called inside `requestToken()` to issue new green tokens to the requester's address. It uses the relevant ERC-20 function(s) for this token issuance.

4.3 User Interactions in Green Token Generation

There are three stages in our token generation scheme:

1. **Registration.**
   a) *User registration*: RA verifies each user's identity through a trusted identity verification process (e.g., verifying a government-issued ID) and issues a login credential to interact with the private blockchain.
   b) *Meter registration*: The GA verifies and certifies electric meters through in-person inspections and creates a certificate $Cert^{GA}_{meterID}$ containing hashed meter, owner, and site IDs, meter attributes, a timestamp, and GA's signature ($Cert^{GA}_{meterID} = \{H(meterID), H(ownerID), H(siteID), meterAttributes, verificationDate, \sigma_{GA}\}$). GA registers the meter as "*active*" by calling the *registerMeter()* function in the MetReg SC.

2. **Data reporting and verification in private blockchain.**
   a) *Data reporting to RA*: Registered users (RE producers) send ($generationData, \sigma_{User}$) to RA for verification through secure off-chain channel and publish $H(generationData)$ on the private chain via the `DataVer` SC as a commitment. Here, $generationData = \{ownerID, meterID, siteID,$ timestamp (start date, end date), REType, REQuantity$\}$ and $\sigma_{User} = Sign_{User_{SK}}(generationData)$.
   b) *Data verification using Oracle*:
      (i) RA verifies the meter's validity using the *verifyMeter()* function in the `MetReg` contract. If valid, RA encrypts $generationData$ with the service provider's (i.e., external data source) public key PK_{SP}, gets $c_{\mathcal{GD}} = \mathsf{Enc}(PK_{SP}, generationData)$ and sends $c_{\mathcal{GD}}$ to Oracle SC for external verification. The Oracle SC first checks if $c_{\mathcal{GD}}$ already exists in its storage. If it does, reject the verification request identifying it as a "*Duplicate Request*". Otherwise, forwards $c_{\mathcal{GD}}$ to SP.
      (ii) The SP decrypts $c_{\mathcal{GD}}$, validates $generationData$ and returns ($True$, $H(generationData)$, σ_{SP}) to `DataVer` SC via the Oracle contract, where σ_{SP} is the digital signature of SP on the hashed $generationData$. Otherwise, SP returns $False$.
      (iii) If valid, RA issues $VC_{ownerID} = \{metadata, generationData, \sigma_{RA}\}$ to the user, where $metadata$ includes VC details like type, issue date, and expiration date, while σ_{RA} is RA's BBS+ signature on $metadata$ and $generationData$.
      (iv) RA then publishes $(H(VC_{ownerID}), H(generationData))$ to `DataVer` SC for each VC issued against a verified $generationData$.

3. **Token request on public blockchain by user (VC holder).**
   a) User first verifies RA's signature σ_{RA} on VC and sends a *token_request* (=$\{proof, M_{Disclosed}, public\ parameters\}$) to `GToken` SC, where *proof* is BBS+ proof on $VC_{ownerID}$ contents, $M_{Disclosed}$ is the revealed data subset and *public parameters* are for σ_{RA} and *proof* verifications.
   b) The `GToken` SC: (i) Computes $H(M_{Disclosed})$ and verifies whether this hash already exists in its storage. If not, it stores the hash as a commitment to the token request; otherwise, it rejects *token_request*. (ii) Checks the signature and the *BBS+ proof*. If valid, it issues green token(s) to the user. Otherwise, it rejects the *token_request*.

Figure 7 in Appendix F shows the flowchart of the above interactions.

4.4 Security and Privacy Analysis

Security Analysis. The following statement holds for our green token generation protocol:

Statement: *The green token generation protocol ensures secure token issuance by guaranteeing that only authentic, verifiable, and tamper-proof renewable energy data is used, effectively preventing incorrect data submission, VC forgery, collusion fraud, and double counting.*

Required security conditions (mentioned in Sect. 4.1) are satisfied as below:

1. **Verified meter.** Meter verification occurs on the private chain via the `MetReg` SC. A meter is valid if (a) it is certified by the GA and (b) it is operated by its rightful owner. The RA verifies the GA's signature (σ_{GA}) using the GA's public key, ensuring data originates from a certified meter and its owner.
2. **Verified data reading.** RE generation data accuracy is ensured through (i) meter verification (condition (1)) and (ii) Oracle-based cross-verification against trusted external sources. This prevents:
   a) *Incorrect data submission by a dishonest user or colluding RA.* Oracle verification fails for any incorrect data submission
   b) *Off-chain double counting by a dishonest user.* The `DataVer` SC's *submitRECommitment()* function ensures unique commitments, rejecting duplicates.
   c) *Double counting by a colluding RA.* The Oracle SC rejects any duplicate encrypted data.
   d) *Fraudulent certificate issuance by a colluding RA.* The `DataVer` SC's *matchVerificationRequest()* function ensures VCs are only issued for verified data.
3. **Secure data transfer across chains.** The RA signs validated generation data using the BBS+ signature scheme, included in a verifiable credential (VC). Users generate a BBS+ proof from the VC and submit it to the `GToken` SC with a *token_request* containing disclosed RE data ($M_{Disclosed}$) and public parameters. This prevents:
   a) *Credential forgery and arbitrary data submission during token request.* BBS+ signature scheme ensures that adversaries cannot forge VCs or link arbitrary data to RA signatures (e.g., by linking arbitrary RE generation data with a previously extracted RA signature from an old VC), causing proof verification to fail and token requests to be rejected.
   b) *On-chain double counting by malicious RE producer.* The `GToken` SC's *verifyRequestCommitment()* function checks for duplicate $M_{Disclosed}$ hashes and rejects an on-chain *token_request* if a match is found.

Privacy Analysis. For privacy analysis of the proposed green token generation process, we examine the views of users and other entities in the system to determine what information can be inferred. Tables 3 and 4 in Appendix G detail the visible information during private and public blockchain interactions (as defined in Sect. 4.1). Our protocol ensures privacy by combining verifiable credentials (VCs), BBS+ signatures for selective disclosure, and a hybrid blockchain model, fulfilling the privacy requirements outlined in Sect. 4.1.

(i) **Privacy goal (1)** is ensured because:
   a) *For meter verification*, the RA checks the meter's certification details and validates GA's signature (σ_{GA}) by querying the `MetReg` smart contract using the hashed *meterID*, hiding the *meterID* from other users.

b) *During data verification*, RA submits encrypted RE data $c_{\mathcal{GD}}$ to the Oracle system, which is decrypted off-chain by the trusted external data source, and only a binary verification result (valid/invalid) is posted on-chain. The RA then sent a BBS+ signed VC to the producer off-chain.

Thus, RE producer identity and *generationData* remain hidden during both verifications, and observers cannot link private chain requests to public chain token requests, ensuring *cross-chain unlinkability*

(ii) **Privacy goal (2)** is guaranteed because the *token_request* includes a *BBS+ proof* derived from a BBS+ signed VC and a subset of *generationData*. The GToken SC verifies the proof, confirming that the user possesses a valid BBS+ signature from the RA and the disclosed subset of RE data is signed as part of that signature. The *selective disclosure* property of BBS+ allows hiding sensitive data (e.g., *meterID*, *siteID*, *ownerID*) while revealing only necessary details (e.g., *timestamp*, *REType*, *REQuantity*), preventing public chain observers from linking the token request to a specific meter, location, or producer.

(iii) **Privacy goal (3)** is satisfied by the use of BBS+ signature scheme. Each BBS+ proof in a *token_request* is unique due to varying *generationData* (e.g., different *REQuantity* values at different *timestamp*). Additionally, public chain users can use multiple pseudonyms from a single public key, preventing public chain observers from linking multiple requests to the same RE producer, ensuring *single-chain unlinkability*.

5 Implementation

We provide a proof-of-concept implementation to estimate costs and evaluate the practicality of the proposed token generation process by measuring the *computational time and storage overhead of cryptographic operations* and *gas costs* for executing smart contract functions on the public blockchain. The smart contracts are developed in Solidity using the Remix IDE [17], with Ganache [14] employed for local Ethereum blockchain simulation. A web-based tool [27] is used to generate BBS+ signatures and proofs. Verifiable credentials (VCs) are implemented in Python, following the W3C data model [23] that takes renewable energy attributes and a BBS+ signature as input and outputs a VC in JSON format. Performance evaluation is conducted on a Windows 11 machine with an Intel(R) Core(TM) i7 CPU @ 3.60 GHz and 8 GB RAM.

GToken Contract Implementation Challenge and Our Choice of Solution. The GToken contract integrates BBS+ proof verification and ERC-20 token generation. Since Solidity lacks native support for pairing-friendly elliptic curves like BN254 or BLS12-381, implementing an exact BBS+ proof verifier on-chain is challenging. To address this, we use OpenZeppelin's bn256Pairing library for ZKP verification in Solidity, enabling gas cost estimation for proof verification on the public blockchain. See Appendix H for system setup details and VC generation pseudocode.

Table 1. Cost of cryptographic operations.

Component	Computing Entity	Size (bytes)	Time (ms)
BBS+ Signature	RA	160	NA
Verifiable Credential	RA	1260	0.25
BBS+ Proof *	RE Producer	384	NA

Table 2. Token request verification and token issuance cost (in gas) in the public chain.

Operation	Gas Cost
ZKP Verification	160,060 gas
Minting GT	67,200 gas
Total cost (estimated)	227,260 gas

Evaluation and Performance Analysis. We implemented a sample renewable energy generation scenario in which a RE producer has a dataset $M = \{$"$did : example : owner789$", "$meter - 56789$", "$site - 34567$", "$Solar$", "$100kWh$", "$2025 - 02 - 15T12 : 00 : 00Z$"$\}$. We measured the computational cost (execution time in milliseconds) and storage overhead (data size in bytes) for cryptographic mechanisms like verifiable credentials (VCs), BBS+ signatures, and zero-knowledge proofs (BBS+ proofs). The results are summarized in Table 1, where- (i) BBS+ signature computational time is excluded (denoted as *NA*) as it uses a web-based implementation [27], (ii) the (*) symbol next to BBS+ proof indicates that the proof size varies based on the number of undisclosed (hidden) messages, and (iii) Oracle service costs are excluded since it is not implemented, but services such as [6,20,40] can be integrated, with costs varying based on the Oracle service provider.

After data verification, the producer receives a VC from the RA. When submitting a token request to the GToken contract, the producer discloses $M_{Disclosed} = \{$"$Solar$", "$100kWh$", "$2025 - 02 - 15T12 : 00 : 00Z$"$\}$ while keeping the remaining attributes $M_{Hidden} = \{$"$did : example : owner789$", "$meter - 56789$", "$site - 34567$"$\}$ private. We measured the gas cost of ZKP verification and token issuance (using OpenZeppelin's ERC-20 library) on the Ethereum test network. Table 2 shows the gas costs for these operations, totaling approximately 0.63% of Ethereum's block capacity[3].

The results in Tables 1 and 2 show that our token generation approach achieves a balance between security and efficiency, with reasonable computational overhead for RE data verification, and the gas cost for on-chain token request verification and issuance is not high. These results validate the practicality of our model, making it adaptable to various EVM-based blockchain ecosystems.

6 Concluding Remarks

Green credit is an important mechanism to incentivize users towards renewable energy generation and, ultimately, a more sustainable environment. We motivated the need for decentralization of REC issuance using blockchains with the

---

[3] Based on block gas limit from etherscan.io/chart/gaslimit on March 01, 2025.

aim of including small producers in the energy credit systems and the opportunity for trading and engagement in the financial market that is built around that.

Our proposed blockchain-based design of WREGIS is a step towards stronger incentivization of small producers and democratization of the energy market. Our design uses a hybrid architecture consisting of a private and a public blockchain. The private blockchain can be run by a combination of authorities that can include local and provincial government authorities, regulatory bodies, or other trusted stakeholders that participate in the system.

Interesting open questions are formal security and privacy analysis of our protocols, and the design and analysis of secure exchange systems for different types of green credit.

A   Related Work

Several greenhouse gas emission tracking and credit systems exist to support sustainability, both blockchain-based and non-blockchain-based. Non-blockchain systems, such as web-based platforms for carbon offset credits [1,12,19,32] and renewable energy tracking [2,22,29], rely on trusted intermediaries (e.g., aggregators) or centralized entities (e.g., local energy providers) for data reporting and verification. This limits small-scale RE producers' ability to participate directly in energy trading.

Blockchain technology and smart contracts have gained significant attention in recent years for their inherent characteristics, such as transparency, decentralization, and immutability in various domains, including renewable energy and sustainability. Several blockchain-based systems are being implemented for managing renewable energy certificates (RECs), and enabling peer-to-peer (P2P) energy trading such as [8,13,21,30,31]. [30,31] facilitates P2P energy trading and REC management using blockchain tokens, allowing consumers and producers to trade energy directly. [8] is another blockchain-based platform that allows renewable energy producers to tokenize their energy production and sell it directly to consumers. Brooklyn Microgrid [13], a project of LO3 Energy, is another example system that enables residents to trade solar energy within their community using blockchain technology. UrbanChain [21] is another peer-to-peer energy exchange services in the United Kingdom (UK) that enables consumers and producers to trade renewable energy directly. While innovative, these platforms- do not fully address the challenges of automated, tamper-proof REC verification and issuance, primarily focus on energy trading rather than REC management, or often rely on intermediaries or centralized components.

Blockchain has also been applied to sustainability and carbon credit[4] management [25,37]. These systems aim to develop a decentralized solution and address the issues in traditional tracking systems such as double-counting and incorrect data submission. These systems use Web3 technology to tokenize carbon

---

[4] Carbon credits are tradable certificates representing a reduction, removal or avoidance of one metric ton of greenhouse gas emissions from the atmosphere [15].

credits and enable automated P2P trading[5] through smart contracts. However, despite being a leading blockchain-based solution for carbon credit tokenization, Toucan [37] remains centralized and human-dependent [36], where each carbon credit brought on-chain as a TCO2 token (an ERC-20 standard token) undergoes a verification process carried out by a Toucan verifier, who must be a trusted member of the Toucan community.

B The BBS+ Signature Scheme

It is a multi-message digital signature protocol that allows a signer to sign multiple messages while producing a single digital signature [11,35]. The main functions of this scheme (as defined in [35]) are explained below following the notation of [11]:

1. **Key generation:** Let $(\mathbb{G}_1, \mathbb{G}_2)$ be a bilinear group pair of some prime order p, and g_1, g_2 are two base points on $\mathbb{G}_1$ and $\mathbb{G}_2$, respectively (generated using a *setup* algorithm). The key generation function randomly generates $x \leftarrow \mathbb{Z}_p$ as the *secret key* and computes $w \leftarrow g_2^x$ as the corresponding *public key*.
2. **Signature generation:** The *Sign* function takes the secret key x, public key w and the set of messages $M = \{m_1, m_2, m_3, \ldots, m_L\}$ as input and generates a signature σ. The signature generation process involves the following steps: (i) generate a random generator for each message $\{h_1, h_2, \ldots, h_L\} \leftarrow \mathbb{G}_1$, (ii) generate a random number $\epsilon \leftarrow \mathbb{Z}_p$, (iii) compute $A = (g_1 \prod_{i=1}^{L} h_i^{m_i})^{\frac{1}{\epsilon + x}}$ and (iv) output the signature $\sigma = (A, \epsilon)$.
3. **Signature verification:** The *Verify* function checks the validity of the signature against a public key. Given the public parameters $(g_1, g_2, h_1, \ldots, h_L, w)$, messages $\{m_1, m_2, m_3, \ldots, m_L\}$ and signature $\sigma = (A, \epsilon)$, the signature verification is done by checking the equality $e(A, wg_2^\epsilon) = e(g_1 \prod_{i=1}^{L} h_i^{m_i}, g_2)$. Here, e is a bilinear map that satisfies the following properties [11]: bilinearity (e.g., $e(g_1^x, g_2^x) = e(g_1, g_2)^{xy}$), non-degeneracy (i.e., $e(g_1, g_2) \neq 1$) and efficiency.
4. **Proof generation:** The *ProofGen* operation generates a *BBS+ proof*, which is a zero-knowledge proof-of-knowledge of a BBS+ signature with a disclosed subset of the signed messages. It blinds the signature and undisclosed messages with random scalars, with a strict requirement of maintaining the (signed) message order and the indexes of disclosed messages.
5. **Proof verification:** The *ProofVerify* function validates a *BBS+ proof* (the blinded values), given the Signer's public key, and the disclosed messages and their generators. This verification ensures- (i) the prover has possession of a valid signature and (ii) the disclosed messages are signed as part of the original signature.

The BBS+ signature scheme [35] has three key properties:

---

[5] Peer-to-peer (P2P) trading involves the direct exchange of surplus electricity between two parties on a connected grid.

(i) *Selective disclosure*: Allows a prover who has the messages, the signature, and group generators used for signing the messages to create a proof by choosing a subset of messages to disclose, while keeping the remaining messages and the signature hidden.

(ii) *Unlinkable proofs*: Proof created by the prover are zero-knowledge proofs of knowledge of the signature. It ensures that multiple proofs derived from the same signature cannot be linked.

(iii) *Proof of possession*: Verifies that the prover holds a valid signature and its signed messages, without revealing the signature itself (Fig. 3).

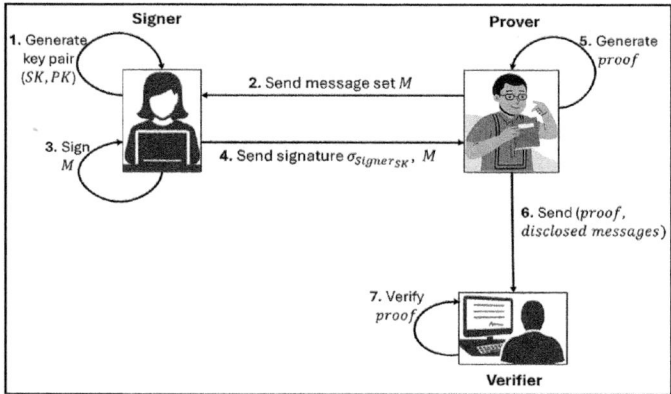

Fig. 3. BBS+ signature scheme [35], where SK and PK are Signer's secret key and public key, respectively, M denotes the message set and $proof$ is a BBS+ proof created using the proof generation function (ProofGen) in [35].

An Example of BBS+ Signature Scheme. Consider a scenario where a user (Prover) has three messages, $M = \{m_1, m_2, m_3\}$, which were sent to a Signer. The Signer generates a BBS+ signature, σ, on the message set M and returns it to the user along with the messages. If the user wants to reveal m_2 to a Verifier while keeping m_1 and m_3 private, the BBS+ signature scheme [11,35] enables the user to selectively disclose specific signed messages. Using this scheme, the user can create a zero-knowledge proof that shows possession of a valid signature σ, while revealing only m_2 and keeping the remaining messages (m_1, m_3) and the signature σ hidden from the Verifier. The steps are given below:

(*Signature Generation by Signer and Verification by Prover*)

1. *Key generation*: Signer generates *secret key* x and *public key* $w = g_2^x$.
2. Prover sends messages $M = \{m_1, m_2, m_3\}$ to Signer.
3. Signer:
   (a) generates message generators $\{h_1, h_2, h_3\}$
   (b) picks random numbers ϵ

(c) computes $A = (g_1 h_1^{m_1} h_2^{m_2} h_3^{m_3})^{\frac{1}{\epsilon+x}} = B^{\frac{1}{\epsilon+x}}$, where $B = (g_1 h_1^{m_1} h_2^{m_2} h_3^{m_3})$
(d) outputs signature, $\sigma = (A, \epsilon)$
4. Signer sends $(\sigma, M, \{h_1, h_2, h_3\})$ to Prover

(**Proof generation by Prover and Proof Verification by Verifier**)
(Proof generation) Suppose the Prover discloses the message $\{m_2\}$ and keeps $\{m_1, m_3\}$ hidden to a Verifier. Then the Prover creates a signature proof of knowledge (SPK) where certain messages are disclosed and others remain hidden as follows:

1. generate random numbers r_1, r_2
2. compute $B = (g_1 h_1^{m_1} h_2^{m_2} h_3^{m_3})$
3. (to blind A) compute $\acute{A} = A^{r_1 r_2}$ [**eq (i)**]
4. (to blind B) compute $D = B^{r_2}$ [**eq (ii)**]
5. compute $\acute{B} = D^{r_1} \acute{A}^{-\epsilon}$ $(= \pi_1)$ [**eq (iii)**]
6. compute $g_1 h_2^{m_2} = D^{r_2^{-1}} h_1^{-m_1} h_3^{-m_3}$ $(= \pi_2)$ [**eq (iv)**]
7. compute $\pi = SPK\{(\epsilon, r_1, r_2^{-1}, m_1, m_3) : \pi_1 \wedge \pi_2\}$. π denotes a proof of knowledge of integers $(\epsilon, r_1, r_2^{-1}, m_1, m_3)$ such that π_1 and π_2 holds.

So, the **proof** is: $(\acute{A}, \acute{B}, D, \pi)$ that the Prover sends to the Verifier along with the disclosed message $\{m_2\}$.
[At this point: private values are: $(x, \epsilon, r_1, r_2^{-1}, \{m_1, m_3\}, A, B$, and the public values are: $(g_1, g_2, h_1, h_2, h_3, w), (\acute{A}, \acute{B}, D, \pi), m_2]$

1. (Proof verification) Upon receiving the proof the Verifier checks the following (using the public parameters):
   (a) **Verify the signature** σ is valid by checking $e(\acute{A}, w) = e(\acute{B}, g_2)$
   (b) **Verify that the disclosed message $\{m_2\}$ is signed as part of the signature** σ. (i.e., Validate π by checking whether equations (iii) and (iv) holds or not)

C W3C Verifiable Credential

The basic components of a verifiable credential (VC) data model and its lifecycle (as defined by W3C in [23]) are shown in Fig. 4a. In Fig. 4b, the *metadata* provides information about the credential, *attributes* represent claims about the subject, and *proof* is the cryptographic evidence, ensuring integrity through the issuer's digital signature on both metadata and attributes.

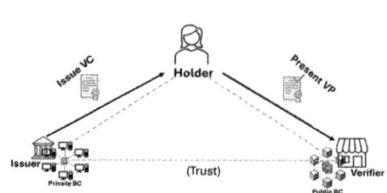
(a) VC issuance and presentation.

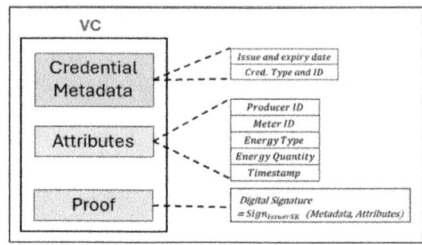
(b) Basic VC components with sample values.

Fig. 4. W3C Verifiable Credential (VC) [23].

D Issues in WREGIS

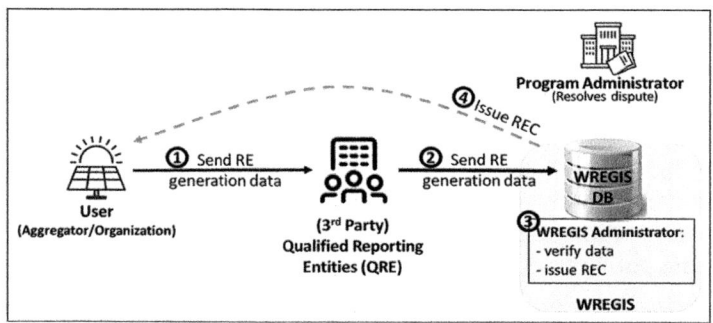

Fig. 5. WREGIS data reporting and REC issuance process.

Figure 5 shows how WREGIS works and Fig. 1 in Sect. 3.1 illustrates an example scenario of how a traditional micro-generation credit system works utilizing the tracking system, showing the flow of interactions among different participants - the producer (micro-generator owner), consumer, local service provider (e.g., Enmax), and the tracking system (e.g., WREGIS). The RE producer (e.g., rooftop solar panel owner) registers with a local utility service provider (SP), supplies excess energy to the grid, and reports the RE quantity to SP. The SP verifies the data from the government authority and issues compensation credit at a preset fixed rate to the RE producer for the supplied electricity. The SP then reports the generation data to a tracking system (e.g., WREGIS) and receives RECs in return (as shown in Fig. 5). Finally, the SP sells renewable energy to consumers at its own rate and retires one REC for every 1000 kWh of renewable energy sold.

Issues in Traditional Micro-generation Credit System: Based on WREGIS assumption on its entities (Fig. 6), WREGIS operation, the workflow of the

Entities	Trust Assumption
Individual Customer	Untrusted
Aggregator	Untrusted
Organization	Untrusted
Qualified Reporting Entity (QRE)	Untrusted
WREGIS Administrator	Trusted
Program Administrator	Trusted

Fig. 6. WREGIS entities and trust assumptions.

traditional micro-generation credit system and the interactions between the involved entities, we have identified the following issues:

1. **Need for a trusted intermediary**: Every WREGIS customer requires a trusted third party, such as a Qualified Reporting Entity (QRE), to report their renewable energy generation data. However, there is a risk that the QRE could collude with an untrustworthy customer to manipulate the reported data. While still meeting WREGIS's minimum standards, they could falsely report a higher generation amount than what was actually produced. As a result, the WREGIS administrator might issue a REC on incorrect data.
2. **Centralized and less user-focused credit system**: Individual or small-scale renewable energy producers must register with a local energy service provider, which acts as an aggregator. The aggregator registers with WREGIS as a customer and reports the combined energy generation data through the QRE. As a result, the REC is issued to the aggregator rather than the original producer. The aggregator then sells the REC at their own price, while the original producer receives credit from the aggregator at a pre-set price.
3. **Lack of exchange facility**: RECs can only be transferred between WREGIS-registered customer accounts. RECs issued to one account for a specific fuel type (e.g., solar) *cannot be exchanged* with RECs generated to another account from a different fuel type (e.g., water). This is important because the ability to exchange RECs from one fuel type for another allows energy producers to optimize their production costs for a specific type of fuel and enables consumers to meet their energy demands based on the available supply from different sources. For example, a solar energy producer might want to exchange the solar tokens for water tokens during periods of low solar generation, such as during winter or cloudy days, to ensure a continuous supply of energy. Conversely, a water energy producer might want to exchange water tokens for solar tokens during dry seasons when water flow is reduced to meet the energy needs. Additionally, this exchange allows both parties to balance their energy production cost and consumption effectively.
4. **Double counting issue**: As per the agreement, a micro-generator must report 100% of its renewable electricity generation to the tracking system

it is registered with and claim the RECs associated with it. However, the same micro-generator unit might register with a different tracking system and claim RECs for the same renewable electricity output. Therefore, the same generator can claim RECs from different registries for the same generated green power.

5. **Incorrect data issue**: If the characteristics of a green energy generating unit significantly change and these changes are not reported to WREGIS in an update, or if inaccurate data is submitted, it may result in faulty creation of certificates for that generating unit.

E Smart Contracts (SCs) in Our System

We have two system smart contracts `MetReg` and `DataVer` for the private chain and an application smart contract `GToken` for token generation on the public chain. The abstract of these contracts are given below (cf. Algorithms 1 to 3).

Algorithm 1 Abstract `MetReg` smart contract.

---

contract MetReg {
    modifier (onlyGA, onlyRA);
    function registerMeter (bytes32 $meterIDHash$, bytes[] $certificate$, bool $isActive$) external onlyGA
    function verifyMeter(bytes32 $meterIDHash$) external view onlyRA returns (bool)
    function updateMeterStatus(bytes32 $meterIDHash$, bool $isActive$) external onlyGA
    function verifyGASignature(bytes32 $certificate$, bytes32 $GAsignature$) internal view returns (bool) }

Algorithm 2 Abstract `DataVer` smart contract.

---

contract DataVer {
    modifier (onlyRA, onlyOracle);
    function submitRECommitment (bytes32 $RECommitment$) external
    function submitOracleVerification(bool $isValid$, bytes32 $generationDataHash$, bytes $SPSignature$) external onlyOracle
    function storeVCCommitment(bytes32 $vcHash$, bytes32 $generationDataHash$) external onlyRA
    function matchVerificationRequest(bytes32 $userDataCommitment$, bytes32 $oracleResult$) internal view returns (bool) }

F Interactions in Green Token Generation

Figure 7 shows the user interaction flowchart in the green token generation process.

Algorithm 3 Abstract GToken smart contract.

contract GToken {
    constructor (address $Contract\_Owner$);
    modifier (onlyRA);
    (ERC-20 Token standard functions:) totalSupply, balanceOf, transfer, allowance, approve, transferFrom;
    function requestGToken (bytes $proof$, bytes[] $disclosedData$, bytes[] $publicParams$) external;
    function verifyBBSProof (bytes $proof$, bytes[] $disclosedData$, bytes[] $publicParams$) internal pure returns (bool);
    function verifyRequestCommitment(bytes32 $disclosedDataHash$) internal pure returns (bool);
    function issueToken(address $ownerID$, uint256 $amount$, bytes32 $AuxiliaryTokenData$) internal }

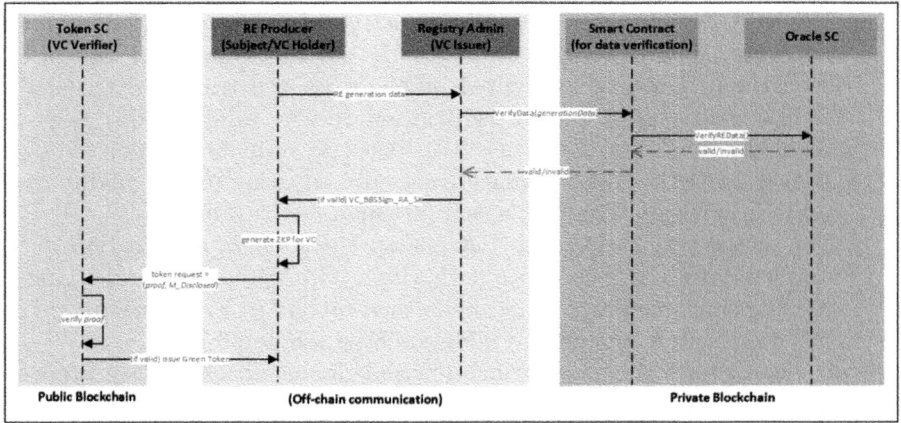

Fig. 7. Green token generation flowchart.

Table 3. View of entities during user interaction in private blockchain.

Entity	Accessible (Visible) Data
RE producer	$generationData_{REProducer}$, $VC_{BBSSign_{RA}}$ and public parameters to verify BBS+ signature, Meter certificate(s)
Registry administrator (RA)	$generationData_{REProducer}$, $VC_{BBSSign_{RA}}$ and public parameters to verify BBS+ signature, Meter certificate(s)
Governance authority (GA)	$Enc(generationData_{REProducer})$, Meter certificate(s)
Other Registered users	$Enc(generationData_{REProducer})$
Oracle system	$Enc(generationData_{REProducer})$

G Entity Views and Privacy in Token Generation Protocol

The views of different entities in the token generation process during private and public blockchain interactions are given in Tables 3 and 4, respectively.

Privacy Analysis Detailed Discussion. The privacy analysis of the proposed green token generation system is based on capturing the views of users and other entities in the system and inferring what can be inferred from these views.

View of Interaction During Token Generation Protocol: The information visible to each entity during the two interaction scenarios, private and public blockchain interactions (as mentioned in Sect. 4.1)—are presented in Tables 3 and 4, respectively. Based on these views, we provide our argument regarding the privacy requirements outlined in Sect. 4.1.

Our token generation protocol ensures that the privacy requirements are fulfilled through a combination of verifiable credentials (VCs), BBS+ signatures for selective disclosure, and a hybrid blockchain model.

1. **Privacy goal (1)** is guaranteed because of the followings:
    a) For the data verification, the registry administrator (RA) submits encrypted RE *generationData* to the Oracle system on the private blockchain, which is decrypted off-chain by the trusted external data source, and only a binary verification result (valid/invalid) is posted on-chain. Once verified, the RA issues a verifiable credential (VC), signed using the BBS+ signature scheme, attesting to the validity of the *generationData*. This VC is sent off-chain to the producer.
    b) For meter verification, the RA checks the meter's certification details and validates the governance authority's (GA) signature by querying the MetReg smart contract using the hashed *meterID*. Since the *meterID* is not disclosed, it remains invisible to other registered users.

   Thus, during both the data verification and the meter verification processes, the identity of the RE producer and its *generationData* remain hidden from the private chain adversaries (as defined in the threat model in Sect. 4). Registered users and Oracle system entities can only see the encrypted RE data. As a result, when the producer submits a *token_request* on the public blockchain revealing only a subset of *generationData*, observers (who are also registered users of the private chain) cannot link private chain verification requests to public chain token requests, satisfying the *cross-chain unlinkability* property.

2. **Privacy goal (2)** is guaranteed because the *token_request* includes a *BBS+ proof* derived from a BBS+ signed Verifiable Credential (VC) along with a subset of data from *generationData*. The Verifier (i.e., the GToken smart contract) checks the validity of the BBS+ proof, proving the user's possession of a valid BBS+ signature from RA (the Issuer of VC) and the disclosed subset of RE data is signed as part of that signature. Validating the proof guarantees the authenticity and integrity of the disclosed and hidden data and the knowledge of the BBS+ signature. Note that, the disclosed data must be supplied to the Verifier in the same order as they were as part of the *generationData* given to the RA for verification. Otherwise, the proof verification will fail. The *selective disclosure* property of the BBS+ signature scheme [11,35] enables the requester to hide sensitive RE data such as *meterID*, *siteID*, or *ownerID*, and reveal only the necessary subset of data (e.g., *timestamp, REType, REQuantity*) on the public blockchain for token generation, ensuring that no observer can link the token request to a specific meter/facility location/RE producer.

3. The use of BBS+ signature scheme ensures **privacy goal (3)** is satisfied. Each BBS+ proof (e.g., a zero-knowledge proof of knowledge of the signature) submitted by a user to the Verifier with a *token_request* is unique. This uniqueness arises from the varying attribute values in *generationData* (e.g., different *REQuantity* values at different *timestamp*). Additionally, a public blockchain user can employ multiple pseudonyms derived from a single public key to hide their identity. As a result, even if multiple requests come from the same RE producer, public chain observers cannot correlate them, guaranteeing *single-chain unlinkability*.

Table 4. View of entities during a token request in the public blockchain.

Entity	Accessible (Visible) Data
Token requester (VC holder)	$generationData_{REProducer}$ (= {Disclosed data + Hidden data}), *BBS+ Proof* Public parameters for signature and proof verification, *Green Token, Requester pseudonym*
Registry administrator (RA)	*token_request* = (*BBS+ Proof*, Disclosed data, Public parameters for signature and proof verification), *Green Token, Requester pseudonym*
Governance authority (GA)	*token_request* = (*BBS+ Proof*, Disclosed data, Public parameters for signature and proof verification), *Green Token, Requester pseudonym*
Public blockchain observers	*token_request* = (*BBS+ Proof*, Disclosed data, Public parameters for signature and proof verification), *Green Token, Requester pseudonym*

H   Implementation Details

System Setup. The setup phase involves initializing the necessary components and deploying the necessary smart contracts for the token generation process.

(i) *Blockchain networks*: Our implementation is designed to be general and applicable to any EVM-based private-public blockchain setting. For testing, we used *Ganache* [14], a widely used framework to simulate the EVM and Ethereum blockchain on a local computer.

(ii) *Verifiable credential (VC)*: We implemented verifiable credentials (VC) following the W3C data model [23] in Python (`VC.py`, pseudocode is given in Algorithm 4). The VC includes *credential metadata, attributes of renewable energy* (i.e., claims), and *a digital signature* on the metadata and attributes (as proof), encoded in JSON format. For signature (i.e., proof) generation, we utilized a browser-based BBS+ signature demo [27], which implements core functions such as key generation, signature generation and verification, and BBS+ proof generation and verification in JavaScript. This web-based tool was used to create BBS+ signatures on manually provided metadata and RE attribute values. The resulting BBS+ signature value, along with the credential metadata and RE data, is fed into the `VC.py` program, which outputs a digital credential in JSON format.

(iii) *Smart contracts and deployment*: We implemented the `MetReg`, `DataVer` and `GToken` smart contracts in *Solidity* language using the Remix IDE [17].

(iv) The `GToken` contract, upon receiving necessary RE verification data such as *BBS+ proof, disclosed data,* and *public parameters* - (1) validates the zero-knowledge proof (ZKP) generated from the BBS+ signature in VC and (2) mints green tokens upon successful verification. The contract follows the ERC-20 token standard by importing key ERC-20 functions from the OpenZeppelin library [28].

(v) The `MetReg` contract stores meter certification data from the governance authority (GA) and allows the registry administrator (RA) to retrieve data from it for meter verification.

(vi) *Device specification*: We evaluated the performance of our system on a machine running Windows 11 with Intel(R) Core(TM) i7 CPU @ 3.60 GHz and 8 GB RAM.

GToken Contract Implementation Challenge and Our Choice of Solution. The GToken contract integrates both a BBS+ proof verifier function and an ERC20 token generation functions. The BBS+ proof is a non-interactive zero-knowledge proof (NIZK) and relies on pairing-friendly elliptic curves like BN254 or BLS12-381, which Solidity does not natively support. Additionally, for the proof-of-concept, we use a web-based tool [27] for BBS+ signature and proof generation,

---

Algorithm 4 W3C Verifiable Credential (VC) Construction (`VC.py`)

Input: Credential metadata, RE attributes, and BBS+ signature
Output VC in JSON format with computation time measured
1: $issuerName, issuerID, VCID \leftarrow$ User input
2: $ownerID, meterID, siteID, REType, REQuantity, timestamp \leftarrow$ User input
3: $BBSplusSignature, publicKey \leftarrow$ User input
4: **Start Timer** T_{start}
5: **Construct VC:**
6:     Initialize VC as an empty dictionary
7:     $VC[\text{``@context''}] \leftarrow$ "https://www.w3.org/2018/credentials/v1"
8:     $VC[\text{``id''}] \leftarrow VCID$
9:     $VC[\text{``type''}] \leftarrow [\text{``VerifiableCredential''}, \text{``RenewableEnergyVC''}]$
10:    $VC[\text{``issuer''}] \leftarrow \{\text{``name''} : issuerName, \text{``id''} : issuerID\}$
11:    $VC[\text{``issuanceDate''}] \leftarrow$ current timestamp
12:    $VC[\text{``credentialSubject''}] \leftarrow \{\text{``ownerID''} : ownerID, \text{``meterID''} : meterID,$ $\text{``siteID''} : siteID, \text{``REType''} : REType, \text{``REQuantity''} : REQuantity,$ $\text{``timestamp''} : timestamp\}$
13:    $VC[\text{``proof''}] \leftarrow \{\text{``type''} : \text{``BBS + Signature''}, \text{``signatureValue''} :$ $BBSplusSignature,$ $\text{``publicKey''} : publicKey\}$
14: **End Timer** T_{end}
15: Compute Execution Time: $T_{exec} \leftarrow T_{end} - T_{start}$
16: **Store VC in File:**
17: Open file "VC_record.txt" in append mode
18: Write VC as JSON format to file
19: Close file
20: Display VC and Execution Time T_{exec}

which makes it challenging to match and implement the exact proof verification logic within a Solidity smart contract. Instead of implementing the exact BBS+ proof verifier on-chain, we implement a ZKP verification in Solidity using OpenZeppelin's precompiled bn256Pairing library for elliptic curve operations to provide a gas cost estimation for ZKP verification in the public chain.

References

1. Puro earth. https://puro.earth/. Accessed 14 June 2024
2. SU.S. Environmental Protection Agency: Renewable energy tracking systems. https://www.epa.gov/green-power-markets/renewable-energy-tracking-systems. Accessed 14 June 2024
3. Government of Alberta, Canada: Micro-generation. https://www.alberta.ca/micro-generation. Accessed Feb 2025
4. Berti-Equille, L., Borge-Holthoefer, J.: Veracity of Data. Springer, Cham (2022). https://doi.org/10.1007/978-3-031-01855-8
5. Bray, T.: The JavaScript Object Notation (JSON) Data Interchange Format. RFC 8259 (2017). https://doi.org/10.17487/RFC8259. https://www.rfc-editor.org/info/rfc8259
6. Breidenbach, L., et al.: ChainLink 2.0: next steps in the evolution of decentralized oracle networks. Chainlink Labs 1, 1–136 (2021)
7. Brown, R.G., Carlyle, J., Grigg, I., Hearn, M.: Corda: an introduction. R3 CEV 1(15), 14 (2016)
8. Bureau, C.: Wepower. https://coinbureau.com/review/wepower-wpr/. Accessed Feb 2025
9. Buterin, V., et al.: A next-generation smart contract and decentralized application platform. White paper (2014)
10. Cachin, C., et al.: Architecture of the hyperledger blockchain fabric. In: Workshop on Distributed Cryptocurrencies and Consensus Ledgers, Chicago, IL, vol. 310, pp. 1–4 (2016)
11. Camenisch, J., Drijvers, M., Lehmann, A.: Anonymous attestation using the strong Diffie Hellman assumption revisited. In: Franz, M., Papadimitratos, P. (eds.) Trust 2016. LNCS, vol. 9824, pp. 1–20. Springer, Cham (2016). https://doi.org/10.1007/978-3-319-45572-3_1
12. Government of Canada: Canada's greenhouse gas offset credit system. https://www.canada.ca/en/environment-climate-change/services/climate-change/pricing-pollution-how-it-will-work/output-based-pricing-system/federal-greenhouse-gas-offset-system.html. Accessed 14 June 2024
13. Brooklyn Energy: Brooklyn microgrid. https://www.brooklyn.energy/. Accessed Feb 2025
14. Ganache (2019). https://www.trufflesuite.com/ganache
15. Internation Emissions Trading Association (IATA): Carbon credit 101. https://ieta.b-cdn.net/wp-content/uploads/2023/09/IETA_101_CarbonCredits_Sept2023.pdf. Accessed 16 June 2024
16. IBM: What is advanced metering infrastructure (AMI). https://www.ibm.com/think/topics/advanced-metering-infrastructure. Accessed Feb 2025
17. Remix-solidity IDE (2019). https://remix.ethereum.org
18. International Energy Agency (IEA): Renewables 2023: Analysis and forecasts to 2028 (2024). https://www.iea.org/reports/renewables-2023

19. Winrock International: American carbon registry. https://acrcarbon.org/acr-registry/. Accessed 14 June 2024
20. van der Laan, B., Ersoy, O., Erkin, Z.: Muscle: authenticated external data retrieval from multiple sources for smart contracts. In: Proceedings of the 34th ACM/SIGAPP Symposium on Applied Computing, pp. 382–391 (2019)
21. UrbanChain Ltd: Urbanchain. https://www.urbanchain.co.uk/. Accessed Feb 2025
22. M-RETS: M-ret. https://www.mrets.org/about/mission-vision-values/. Accessed 14 June 2024
23. Manu Sporny, D.L., Chadwick, D.: Verifiable credentials data model v1.1 (2022). https://identity.foundation/bbs-signature/draft-irtf-cfrg-bbs-signatures.html#name-generators
24. Sporny, M., Longley, D., Kellog, G., Lanthaler, M., Champin, P.-A., Lindstrám, N.: JSON-LD 1.1 (2020). https://www.w3.org/TR/json-ld11/
25. MOSS: Moss whitepaper. https://v.fastcdn.co/u/f3b4407f/54475626-0-Moss-white-paper-eng.pdf. Accessed 14 June 2024
26. Nakamoto, S.: Bitcoin: a peer-to-peer electronic cash system (2008)
27. Networking, G.: BBS signature demo. https://www.grotto-networking.com/BBSDemo/
28. OpenZeppelin: ERC-20. https://github.com/OpenZeppelin/openzeppelin-contracts/tree/master/contracts/token/ERC20
29. Patel, S.: A guide to renewable energy credits (RECs). https://esg.conserve.com/guide-to-renewable-energy-credits/. Accessed 14 June 2024
30. PONTON: Enerchain. https://www.ponton.de/enerchain. Accessed Feb 2025
31. Powerledger: Powerledger. https://powerledger.io/. Accessed Feb 2025
32. Registry, V.: Verra. https://registry.verra.org/?_gl=1*1e9wpvm*_ga*MTg0MDg5MzE1Ni4xNzEzMjk2NDI1*_ga_2VGK901B6P*MTcxMzI5NjQyNS4xLjEuMTcxMzI5NjU5NS4wLjAuMA. Accessed 14 June 2024
33. REN21: Renewables 2023 global status report (2023). https://www.ren21.net/gsr-2023/
34. Scarpa, R., Willis, K.: Willingness-to-pay for renewable energy: primary and discretionary choice of British households' for micro-generation technologies. Energy Econ. **32**(1), 129–136 (2010)
35. Looker, T., Kalos, V., Whitehead, A., Lodder, M.: The BBS signature scheme (2024). https://identity.foundation/bbs-signature/draft-irtf-cfrg-bbs-signatures.html#name-generators
36. Toucan: Carbon-credit bridging approval process in toucan. https://docs.toucan.earth/toucan/carbon-bridge/puro-carbon-bridge/await-approval. Accessed 14 June 2024
37. Toucan: Toucan. https://docs.toucan.earth/. Accessed 14 June 2024
38. Willis, K., Scarpa, R., Gilroy, R., Hamza, N.: Renewable energy adoption in an ageing population: heterogeneity in preferences for micro-generation technology adoption. Energy Policy **39**(10), 6021–6029 (2011)
39. WREGIS: Western renewable energy generation information system (WREGIS) - operating rules. https://www.wecc.org/Administrative/WREGIS%20Operating%20Rules%20October%202022%20Final.pdf. Accessed 14 June 2024
40. Zhang, F., Cecchetti, E., Croman, K., Juels, A., Shi, E.: Town crier: an authenticated data feed for smart contracts. In: Proceedings of the 2016 ACM SIGSAC Conference on Computer and Communications Security, pp. 270–282 (2016)

Parallel Execution Fee Mechanisms

Abdoulaye Ndiaye[✉][iD]

New York University, New York, NY 10012, USA
andiaye@stern.nyu.edu
https://www.abdoulayendiaye.com/

Abstract. This paper investigates how pricing schemes can achieve efficient allocations in blockchain systems featuring multiple transaction queues under a global capacity constraint. We model a capacity-constrained blockchain where users submit transactions to different queues—each representing a submarket with unique demand characteristics—and decide to participate based on posted prices and expected delays. We find that revenue maximization tends to allocate capacity to the highest-paying queue, whereas welfare maximization generally serves all queues. Optimal relative pricing of different queues depends on factors such as market size, demand elasticity, and the balance between local and global congestion. My results have implications for the implementation of local congestion pricing for evolving blockchain architectures, including parallel transaction execution, directed acyclic graph (DAG)-based systems, and multiple concurrent proposers.

Keywords: Blockchain · Fintech · Transactions · Parallel Execution · Fee Markets · Consensus

1 Introduction

Blockchain technology is rapidly reshaping the global financial landscape. In the United States, a notable milestone occurred in January 2024 when the Securities and Exchange Commission approved the trading of Bitcoin ETFs on public exchanges [17]. Cryptocurrencies such as Bitcoin and Ethereum have gained widespread adoption, enabling peer-to-peer transactions without the need for traditional intermediaries like banks. On platforms like Ethereum, smart contracts—self-executing agreements with conditions encoded in software—facilitate various financial services, from loans and insurance to decentralized exchanges.

Blockchain technology operates by executing transactions in a decentralized manner, ensuring that transactions are ultimately *executed* (liveness) and that a decentralized network of computers—referred to as miners in proof-of-work systems or validators in proof-of-stake systems—can agree on the state of the blockchain after execution (safety). Despite the growing importance of blockchain technology, there are still significant limitations in their scalability, particularly in the efficient execution of transactions in the presence of congestion. As blockchain applications expand beyond cryptocurrencies into decentralized finance (DeFi), supply chain management, and digital identity, the efficient allocation of blockchain resources has become increasingly critical.

Traditional blockchain protocols often rely on simple fee-based models where users attach fees to their transactions, and miners or validators prioritize transactions based on these fees. While straightforward, such Transaction Fee Mechanisms (TFMs) can lead to inefficiencies, including congestion of parts of the blockchain state, high transaction fees during peak demand, and suboptimal resource allocation.[1] Moreover, as blockchains evolve to allow for parallel transaction settlement and support complex decentralized applications, the need for more sophisticated mechanisms that can handle heterogeneous transaction types becomes apparent.

While TFMs that guarantee the inclusion of a transaction in the next block are well-studied [5,9,13–15,18], little is known about the design of Execution Fee Mechanisms (EFMs). EFMs refer to the protocols and systems that determine the order and manner in which transactions are processed and finalized on a blockchain network. In any decentralized system like blockchain, transactions are submitted by multiple users, often simultaneously. The mechanism by which these transactions are sequenced and confirmed is crucial for maintaining the network's integrity, security, and performance.

Parallel EFMs are at the heart of several emerging blockchain systems, including parallel execution blockchains, Directed Acyclic Graph (DAG)–based blockchains, and blockchains with multiple concurrent proposers.

For instance, parallel execution blockchains[2] divide the state represented by the blockchain into multiple, non-overlapping partitions or *local fee markets*, each of which can handle transactions independently.[3] Optimal pricing of these local markets can allow for a EFM where fees are determined by the demand within each partition rather than the entire network. In DAG-based blockchains[4], transactions are included in a graph of blocks without requiring them to be ordered in a single chain. However, their EFM is crucial for organizing the unordered transactions into a logical sequence for execution and achieving consensus on the final state across the entire network.[5] Lastly, in blockchains with multiple

---

[1] For three hours on April 30, 2022, it cost at least $6500 to send any transaction on the Ethereum blockchain because of a single anticipated NFT collection release; see https://www.coindesk.com/business/2022/05/01/bayc-team-raises-285m-with-otherside-nfts-clogs-ethereum/.

[2] Such as Solana, Avalanche, or the planned upgrade to the Ethereum blockchain.

[3] Note that one may argue that parallel execution is already the case in Ethereum, given the proliferation of Ethereum Layer 2s, or the co-existence of regular transactions and blobs.

[4] Such as Aptos, Sui, and IOTA.

[5] See [8] for this process of "flattening the DAG" needed for global consensus on transactions.

concurrent proposers[6] a key challenge is to ensure that concurrent proposals do not lead to conflicts or forks that compromise the network's safety. A EFM is, therefore, needed to aggregate proposals from multiple validators or proposers.

In this paper, we embed a general queuing model into the standard price theory framework and study optimal posted-price EFMs for blockchains that can execute independent transactions in parallel. We model a capacity-constrained blockchain execution system as an N-queue system that serves delay-sensitive customers. Each queue represents a submarket or a specific resource requested by transactions.[7] Users submit transactions to these queues and decide upon arrival whether to proceed based on the posted price and expected delays that decrease their utility. A global capacity constraint arises from the need for consensus mechanisms to consider all transactions across queues. A larger volume of transactions leads to propagation delay on consensus security; [3].

In the context of this model, we ask the following research questions: how does revenue maximization affect the allocation of capacity across queues, and under what conditions does it lead to the exclusion of lower-paying queues? What are the welfare implications of different pricing strategies, and how can we design prices that maximize social welfare while accounting for the global capacity constraint? How do market characteristics such as demand elasticity and market size affect the optimal relative pricing across queues?

To address these questions, we first examine the case where the protocol or miners/validators aim to maximize revenue. Formally, such a protocol maximizes the sum of fees collected from all served queues, subject to the local equilibrium conditions in each queue and the global capacity constraint. The local equilibrium condition ensures that, in each queue, the marginal user's expected utility is her outside option—users join a queue if their valuation exceeds the price plus expected delay costs. We find that there exists a threshold capacity level below which allocating all capacity to the highest-paying queue maximizes revenue. This result highlights a potential inefficiency in revenue maximization: the system may exclude transactions from other queues that could contribute positively to social welfare.

Next, we consider the objective of maximizing social welfare. The analysis shows that, in contrast to revenue maximization, the welfare-maximizing allocation generally involves serving all queues. By distributing capacity across all queues, the system ensures that users in different submarkets can access the resources they require. Then we derive the socially optimal relative prices for each queue that implement the welfare-maximizing allocation. These prices are designed as Pigouvian taxes that internalize both the local and global congestion externalities imposed by each executed transaction.

To provide further insights, we specialize the model to a setting where the time between arrivals is exponentially distributed, and execution times are also

---

[6] Such as in current proposals for the Ethereum blockchain, see https://ethresear.ch/t/concurrent-block-proposers-in-ethereum/18777.

[7] Such as a smart contract, a high-level resource that transactions try to access, or a shared object in object-centric blockchains.

exponentially distributed. Each market has an isoelastic demand function characterized by a specific elasticity parameter. We derive explicit formulas for the socially optimal prices as a function of market characteristics such as demand elasticity, market size, and congestion levels.

When the degree of parallelization is high (i.e., the system can process many transactions concurrently), and local congestion dominates global congestion, the ratio of socially optimal prices between any two queues approximates the ratio of their demand intensities normalized by market sizes. In particular, when demand is highly elastic and local congestion effects are strong, the optimal relative price in a queue is approximately proportional to the ratio of demand relative to market size. This implies that setting prices based on the relative demand intensity in each queue approximates the welfare-maximizing solution.

These findings have important implications for the design of Parallel Execution Fee Mechanisms in evolving blockchain architectures. On the one hand, a revenue-maximizing validator favors uniform pricing and serving only the highest-paying user category. On the other hand, by implementing local fee markets—where transactions are assigned to queues with different relative prices based on the resources they access— protocol designers can steer the blockchain closer to efficiency and scalability in transaction execution. In practice, this means that blockchains can define local prices for each state, contract, or program object and employ adaptive base fee mechanisms that adjust prices based on local demand conditions.[8] By doing so, the blockchain can prevent high-demand areas from congesting the entire network and ensure that capacity is allocated efficiently across all resources.

1.1 Related Work

This paper contributes to the broader economics literature on the market design of blockchain technology [4,7,10]. [5], and [13,14] study the question of pricing blockspace—that is, determining optimal fee mechanisms for including transactions in blockchain blocks under capacity constraints. [6,15,16,18], and [2] provide foundational analysis of transaction fee mechanisms, focusing on blockchains with linear transaction ordering. This work opens the analysis of transaction execution by modeling complexities introduced by parallel execution in multi-queue blockchain systems. In doing so, we build on the literature on the pricing of queues [1,11,12] and emphasize the balance between global and local congestion. Beyond the theoretical contributions, our results have practical implications for blockchain system design and can help improve the efficiency and scalability of both new and existing blockchain technologies. My framework is applicable to other settings where multi-queue systems are present, and there is potential for congestion, such as supply chain management, cloud computing, and online service platforms.

The remainder of the paper is organized as follows. Section 2 highlights the limits of traditional blockchain fee models with a two-queue example. Section 3

---

[8] Such as Ethereum's EIP-1559 fee mechanism studied in [16] and [13].

presents the model setup, including users, local equilibrium conditions, and global inclusion constraints. In Sect. 4.1, we analyze the revenue maximization problem and derive the conditions under which capacity allocation favors the highest-paying queue. Sections 4.2 and 4.3 focus on welfare maximization, characterizing the socially optimal pricing strategies and their implications. Finally, Sect. 5 concludes the paper and suggests avenues for future research.

2 The Problem of Execution in Standard TFMs: An Example

In this section, we illustrate the challenges associated with executing transactions in standard Transaction Fee Mechanisms (TFMs) through a simple example. Consider a blockchain system with two separate queues, Queue A and Queue B, each holding three transactions awaiting inclusion and execution in the blockchain. The expected values of the transactions in Queues A and B are $\mathbb{E}[v_a] = 10$ and $\mathbb{E}[v_b] = 6$, respectively.

Figure 1 depicts the state of the two queues. In each period, two new transactions arrive in each queue. However, due to the necessity for global consensus, the blockchain can collect and process up to *five* transactions at a time.

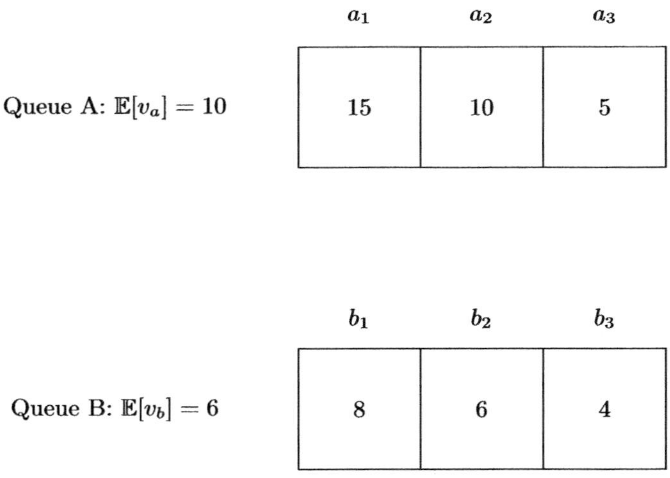

	a_1	a_2	a_3
Queue A: $\mathbb{E}[v_a] = 10$	15	10	5

	b_1	b_2	b_3
Queue B: $\mathbb{E}[v_b] = 6$	8	6	4

Fig. 1. Example Transaction Queues

In Queue A, there are three transactions denoted as a_1, a_2, and a_3, with individual values of 15, 10, and 5, respectively. Similarly, Queue B contains transactions b_1, b_2, and b_3, with values of 8, 6, and 4. The higher expected value in Queue A indicates that, on average, transactions in this queue are more valuable to the network or its users compared to those in Queue B.

2.1 The Problem with Global Ordering and a Uniform Price

Under a standard TFM, the selection of transactions for inclusion is typically based on the fees attached to them. With a uniform price for inclusion and a global ordering for all transactions, the global capacity constraint can lead to an imbalance in how transactions from different queues are executed. Specifically, more transactions from Queue A are processed than those from Queue B, even though transactions from both queues could be executed in parallel without interference. This results in Queue B becoming underserved, causing its backlog to grow over time. Figure 2 illustrates this scenario.

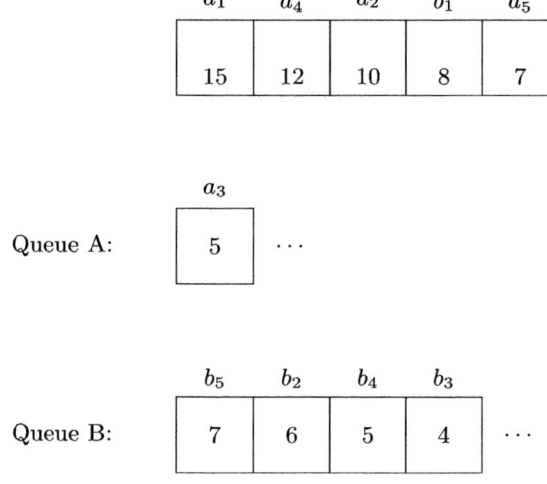

Fig. 2. Global Ordering under Uniform Price. Newly arrived and executed transactions are highlighted in red and starred. (Color figure online)

The top portion of the figure represents the global execution order, where transactions from both Queue A and Queue B are interleaved based on their arrival times and values. Transactions a_1, a_2, and b_1 are included in the execution queue. Additionally, new higher-value transactions a_4^* and a_5^* (highlighted in red and starred) arrive in Queue A with values of 12 and 7, respectively. Due to their higher values, these transactions are immediately prioritized in the global ordering.

The middle section shows Queue A's state. Transaction a_3 remains in the queue with a value of 5. While some transactions from Queue A are being executed, new higher-value transactions continue to arrive, maintaining its dominance in the execution queue.

The bottom section illustrates Queue B's state. Transactions b_2 to b_5 accumulate in the queue with values ranging from 4 to 7. Despite the continuous arrival of transactions, Queue B's transactions are not prioritized in the global execution order due to their lower values compared to those in Queue A.

Because of the global capacity constraint—only five transactions can be executed at a time—the mechanism tends to favor transactions with higher values to maximize immediate throughput or revenue. Transactions from Queue B could be processed in parallel with those from Queue A without any conflicts or interference. However, the global ordering does not account for this possibility, resulting in suboptimal use of the system's parallel processing capabilities.

2.2 A Potential Solution: Market Value-Weighted Ordering

To address the issues above, we study a potential solution we will call *Market Value-Weighted Ordering*. Suppose that the expected values of transactions in Queues A and B, denoted by $\mathbb{E}[v_a]$ and $\mathbb{E}[v_b]$ respectively, are known or can be reliably estimated. This information could be derived from historical data, statistical analysis, or real-time monitoring of transaction patterns.

The key idea is to adjust or normalize the bids of transactions in each queue according to the expected value of that queue. Specifically, we treat each transaction as if its bid is scaled by the inverse of the expected value of its queue. For transactions in Queue A and Queue B, we adjust their bids as follows:

$$a'_i = \frac{a_i}{\mathbb{E}[v_a]}, \quad b'_i = \frac{b_i}{\mathbb{E}[v_b]}.$$

By scaling the bids in this manner, we standardize the bids across queues, allowing for a comparison of transactions based on their relative value within their respective queues. Figure 3 illustrates these adjusted bids.

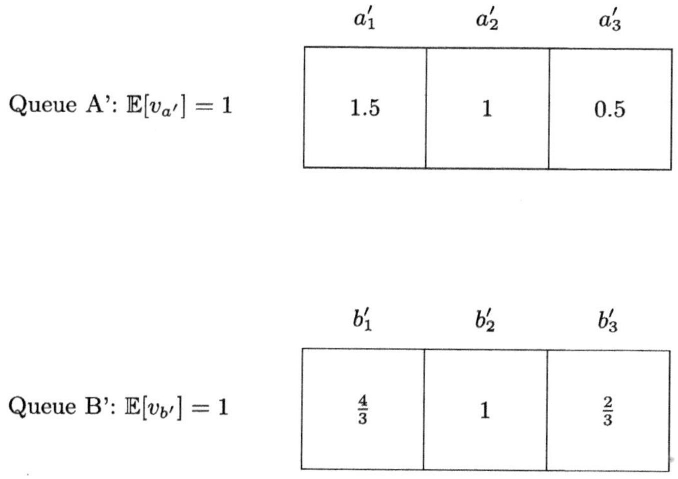

	a'_1	a'_2	a'_3
Queue A': $\mathbb{E}[v_{a'}] = 1$	1.5	1	0.5

	b'_1	b'_2	b'_3
Queue B': $\mathbb{E}[v_{b'}] = 1$	$\frac{4}{3}$	1	$\frac{2}{3}$

Fig. 3. Market Value-Weighted Ordering. Each transaction is treated *as if* its bid is $a_i/\mathbb{E}[v_a]$ or $b_i/\mathbb{E}[v_b]$

Under this Market Value-Weighted Ordering, the system evaluates transactions based on their adjusted bids, resulting in a more balanced execution of transactions from both queues. Figure 4 illustrates how transactions are selected for execution under this mechanism.

Transactions a'_1, b'^*_1, a'_4, b'^*_5, and a'_2 are selected for execution. Transactions from Queue B' that are executed are highlighted in blue. The lower-value transactions remain in their respective queues, awaiting future execution based on their adjusted bids and arrival times.

This example demonstrates the potential social value of relative pricing and suggests that value-weighted relative pricing of different queues can be approximately welfare-maximizing. In the remainder of this article, we will generalize this idea in a model of a blockchain with parallel execution and a global capacity constraint due to consensus.

3 Model

In this section, we present a formal model of a capacity-constrained blockchain execution system. The system is modeled as an N-queue system that serves delay-sensitive customers. These queues can be associated with each smart contract, each high-level resource that transactions try to access, or each shared object in the case of object-centric blockchains.

Setup. We assume that execution times are independently and identically distributed (i.i.d.) with unit mean.[9] Each user submits a transaction that arrives in one of the queues $i \in \{1, \ldots, N\}$, following an exogenous Poisson process with rate (or market size) Λ_i. Since the consensus mechanism takes into account transactions in all queues, there is a global capacity constraint for inclusion, meaning that the total number of transactions that can be included across all queues is limited. For simplicity, we consider mechanisms with posted prices p_i for each submarket or queue i. Upon arrival and observing the posted prices, users decide whether or not to submit their transaction at the posted price p_i, taking into account potential delays and their own valuations.

User Valuations. Users are considered to be atomistic relative to the market size, meaning that each individual user's actions have a negligible impact on the overall system. They differ in their valuations v, representing their willingness to pay for immediate execution without delay. For each submarket i, valuations are independently and identically distributed (i.i.d.) draws from a continuous distribution Φ_i (independent of arrival and execution times) with probability density function ϕ_i. We assume that ϕ_i is strictly positive and continuous on the positive interval $[\underline{v}, \bar{v}]$. Let $\bar{\Phi}_i(v) = 1 - \Phi_i(v)$ denote the complementary cumulative distribution function, representing the probability that a user's valuation exceeds v. If all transactions with values greater than v join queue i, the arrival (or demand) rate in market i will be $\lambda_i = \Lambda_i \bar{\Phi}_i(v)$. Conversely, when the arrival

---

[9] For transactions with different execution times, we can interpret the derived prices below as gross prices rather than per-unit prices. This simplification allows us to focus on the core dynamics without loss of generality.

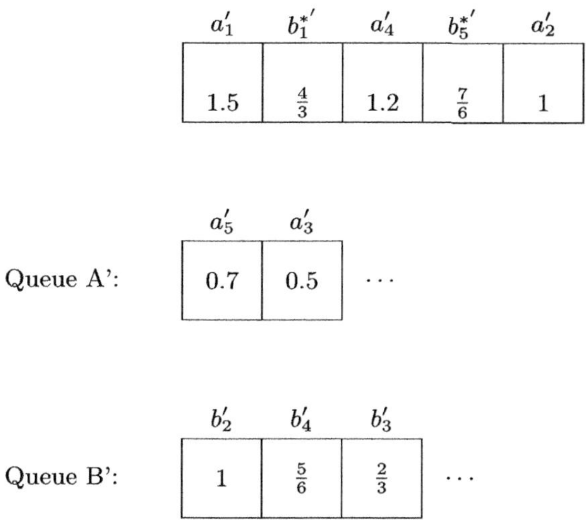

a'_1	$b^{*'}_1$	a'_4	$b^{*'}_5$	a'_2
1.5	$\frac{4}{3}$	1.2	$\frac{7}{6}$	1

Queue A':

a'_5	a'_3	
0.7	0.5	...

Queue B':

b'_2	b'_4	b'_3	
1	$\frac{5}{6}$	$\frac{2}{3}$	...

Fig. 4. Execution under Market Value-Weighted Ordering. Executed transactions from queue B' are highlighted in blue and starred.

rate is λ_i, the marginal value v is equal to $\bar{\Phi}_i^{-1}(\lambda_i/\Lambda_i)$, where $\bar{\Phi}_i^{-1}$ is the inverse of $\bar{\Phi}_i$.

Following [1], let $V_i(\lambda_i)$ denote the expected aggregate (gross) value in submarket i per unit of time without delay. Then, the downward-sloping marginal value (or inverse gross demand) function $V'_i(\lambda_i) \equiv \bar{\Phi}_i^{-1}(\lambda_i/\Lambda_i)$ defines a one-to-one mapping between the demand rate λ_i and the marginal value $V'_i(\lambda_i)$. Each V_i is increasing and is assumed to be strictly concave, $V'_i(\lambda_i) > 0, V''_i(\lambda_i) < 0$ for $\lambda_i < \Lambda_i$.

Delay Costs. Users are sensitive to delays in transaction execution. We consider the following utility function for a user with valuation v who pays a price p and experiences a delay of t units of time:

$$u(v, t, p, i) = v \cdot D_i(t) - C_i(t) - p \qquad (1)$$

In this expression, p is the price paid by the user to submit the transaction. The term $D_i(t)$ is a multiplicative delay discount function for queue i, capturing how the user's valuation decreases with delay. For example, $D_i(t)$ could be a discount factor like $e^{-d_i t}$, where d_i is the discount rate. The term $C_i(t)$ is an additive delay cost function for queue i, representing additional costs incurred due to delay, such as opportunity costs or penalties. These costs capture a variety of losses that can occur due to the deterioration of execution performance with delay.[10]

---

[10] Typical costs due to slow execution can be the failure to purchase a good, loss of an arbitrage opportunity, sandwich-attacked transactions, and other MEV attacks.

Let $\boldsymbol{\lambda} \equiv (\lambda_1, \ldots, \lambda_N)$ denote a vector of demand rates in each submarket. Each user in queue i maximizes her own expected utility, which she forecasts using the distribution of the steady-state delay $\tilde{W}(\lambda_i)$. The delay depends on the set of paying users only through the resulting demand rate λ_i and is not affected by the actions of an individual atomistic user. In addition, we allowed the individual delay costs $D_i(t)$ and $C_i(t)$ to depend directly on i, which can reflect the selection of different types of users in queues. Let $\overline{D}_i(\lambda_i) \equiv \mathbb{E}[D_i(\tilde{W}(\lambda_i))]$ and $\overline{C}_i(\lambda_i) \equiv \mathbb{E}[C_i(\tilde{W}(\lambda_i))]$ be the expected delay discount and delay cost functions, respectively. Given λ_i, a user with value v_i for submarket i who pays p_i has expected utility

$$u(v_i|p_i, \lambda_i) \equiv v_i \cdot \overline{D}_i(\lambda_i) - \overline{C}_i(\lambda_i) - p_i. \tag{2}$$

Local Equilibrium Demand. We now consider the equilibrium behavior of users in each queue. Let $i \in \{1, \ldots, N\}$ and p_i the price in submarket i. Suppose V_i is continuously differentiable in $\mathbb{R}^+$ and that the net value to the highest value user of being served immediately in each queue is positive, that is $V_i^{'}(0)\overline{D}_i(0) - \overline{C}_i(0) > 0$. This condition ensures that there is a positive net benefit to participating in the market for at least some users. Without loss of generality, we index the queues in decreasing order (without ties) of their net value of being served immediately: $V_1^{'}(0)\overline{D}_1(0) - \overline{C}_1(0) > V_2^{'}(0)\overline{D}_2(0) - \overline{C}_2(0) > \cdots > V_N^{'}(0)\overline{D}_N(0) - \overline{C}_N(0)$. Given a price p_i, queue i is active (i.e., has positive demand) if the highest-value user obtains positive expected utility when served immediately: $V_i^{'}(0) \cdot \overline{D}_i(0) - \overline{C}_i(0) > p_i$. The marginal user has valuation $V_i^{'}(\lambda_i(p_i))$ and zero expected utility in equilibrium. That is, in any Nash equilibrium, users join if, and only if demand in market i, $\lambda_i(p_i)$, satisfies

$$u(V_i^{'}(\lambda_i(p_i))|p_i, \lambda_i) = V_i^{'}(\lambda_i(p_i)) \cdot \overline{D}_i(\lambda_i) - \overline{C}_i(\lambda_i) - p_i = 0 \tag{3}$$

This equilibrium condition can be interpreted in at least two ways. If users can choose which queue to join, entry and exit occur *across* queues in equilibrium until the expected utility from joining any queue equals their outside option (which is normalized to zero).[11] Second, if the protocol dictates which queue transactions are assigned to (e.g., based on transaction type or resource accessed), entry and exit occur *within* each queue, and the expected utility for the marginal user in each queue equals zero. Users decide whether to participate based on the conditions in their assigned queue. Thus, the equilibrium condition maps the demand rate λ_i to the price in queue i and vice-versa for queues that are active. Henceforth, we will write such expression as $p_i(\lambda_i)$.

Global Inclusion Constraint. Because the consensus process must weigh every transaction, an excessive volume introduces network latency, creating an effective global cap on how many can be admitted. Let κ denote the global capacity of

---

[11] This would be, for instance, the case of multi-proposer consensus, or DAG-based blockchains where users choose to which part of the graph they send their transactions.

transactions that can be served per unit of time. The capacity constraint is then

$$\sum_{i=1}^{N} \lambda_i \leq \kappa : \qquad (4)$$

This constraint implies that the sum of the demand rates across all queues cannot exceed the global capacity κ. It reflects limitations such as block size, network bandwidth, and the need for synchronization across the network.

In this analysis, we focus on instances where the global capacity constraint is *binding*, meaning that the total demand equals the capacity. This situation is common in blockchain systems during periods of high demand. The problem of variable global capacity would deliver similar results.

4 Results

In this section, we analyze the implications of the model for revenue maximization and welfare maximization.

4.1 Revenue Maximization

We begin by examining how a protocol or miners/validators aiming to maximize revenue would set prices and allocate capacity across the different queues.

Revenue. Let $\mathcal{S}$ denote the set of *served queues*, i.e., the queues that are active and receive a positive capacity allocation. The protocol's revenue is the total fees collected from all served queues, which can be expressed as $\sum_{i \in \mathcal{S}} \lambda_i p_i(\lambda_i)$, where λ_i is the demand rate in queue i, and $p_i(\lambda_i)$ is the price charged in queue i as a function of the demand rate. Using the equilibrium condition from Eq. (3), the revenue maximization problem can be expressed in terms of demand rates. For simplicity of notation, we assume here that all queues are served.[12]

$$\Pi = \max_{(p_1,\ldots,p_N)} \sum_{i=1}^{N} \lambda_i V_i^{'}(\lambda_i) \cdot \overline{D}_i(\lambda_i) - \lambda_i \cdot \overline{C}_i(\lambda_i) \qquad (6)$$

Our objective is to find the set of prices $(p_1, p_2, \ldots, p_N)$ and served queues $\mathcal{S}$ that maximize revenue Π, subject to the local equilibrium condition (3) for all served queues and the global capacity constraint (4). We consider uniform pricing where $p_1 = \cdots = p_N = p \in \mathbb{R}_+$ and optimal relative prices $(p_1, \ldots, p_N) \in \mathbb{R}_+^N$. The following proposition characterizes the revenue-maximizing allocation under both pricing strategies.

---

[12] The general expression is

$$\Pi = \max_{\mathcal{S},(p_i; i \in \mathcal{S})} \sum_{i \in \mathcal{S}} \lambda_i V_i^{'}(\lambda_i) \cdot \overline{D}_i(\lambda_i) - \lambda_i \cdot \overline{C}_i(\lambda_i). \qquad (5)$$

Proposition 1. *There exists a threshold capacity $\underline{\kappa} \in (0, +\infty)$ such that for all total capacities $\kappa \leq \underline{\kappa}$, the revenue-maximizing uniform price and the revenue-maximizing relative prices allocate all capacity to the highest price queue, i.e., $S = \{1\}$.*

Proof. The idea of the proof is to construct a small capacity (or equivalently, a large enough level of congestion and price for queue 1) so that no customers will be willing to join queues $2, \ldots, N$ and net revenue from queue one is increasing in its allocated capacity. In these conditions, allocating all capacity to queue one is revenue maximizing. Since $V_1'(0)\overline{D}_1(0) - \overline{C}_1(0) > V_2'(0)\overline{D}_2(0) - \overline{C}_2(0) > \cdots > V_N'(0)\overline{D}_N(0) - \overline{C}_N(0)$ without loss of generality, and $V_i'(\lambda)\overline{D}_i(\lambda) - \overline{C}_i(\lambda)$ is continuously decreasing in λ for all i, there exists $\kappa_1 \in (0, +\infty)$ such that $V_1'(\kappa_1)\overline{D}_1(\kappa_1) - \overline{C}_1(\kappa_1) > V_2'(0)\overline{D}_2(0) - \overline{C}_2(0) > \cdots > V_N'(0)\overline{D}_N(0) - \overline{C}_N(0)$. Denote gross revenue from queue 1 absent any delays as $R_1(\lambda_1) = \lambda_1 V_1'(\lambda_1)$, the marginal net revenue from this queue is $R_1'(\lambda_1)\overline{D}_1(\lambda_1) - \overline{C}_1(\lambda_1) + \lambda_1 V_1'(\lambda_1)\overline{D}_1'(\lambda_1) - \lambda_1 \overline{C}_1'(\lambda_1)$. Evaluated at $\lambda_1 = 0$ yields $R_1'(0)\overline{D}_1(0) - \overline{C}_1(0) = V_1'(0)\overline{D}_1(0) - \overline{C}_1(0) > 0$, therefore, by continuity, the marginal net revenue from queue 1 is increasing in a neighborhood of 0. That is, $\exists\, 0 < \underline{\kappa} \leq \kappa_1$ such that $V_1'(\underline{\kappa})\overline{D}_1(\underline{\kappa}) - \overline{C}_1(\underline{\kappa}) > V_2'(0)\overline{D}_2(0) - \overline{C}_2(0) > \cdots > V_N'(0)\overline{D}_N(0) - \overline{C}_N(0)$ and the net revenue function $\kappa \mapsto \kappa[V_1'(\kappa)\overline{D}_1(\kappa) - \overline{C}_1(\kappa)]$ is increasing in $[0, \underline{\kappa}]$. In both the relative price and uniform price case, for capacity below $\underline{\kappa}$ it is revenue maximizing to allocate all capacity to queue 1, since at those capacities and prices, no customers will be willing to join queues $2, \ldots, N$ and the total capacity is used since net revenue from queue one is increasing in this segment.

This proposition highlights a potential inefficiency in revenue maximization: when capacity is limited, the system tends to favor the queue with the highest-paying users, potentially excluding transactions from other queues that could contribute positively to social welfare.

4.2 Welfare Maximization

Next, we consider the objective of maximizing social welfare, which takes into account the total net benefit to all users across all queues rather than focusing solely on revenue. The protocol's social welfare over all queues[13]

$$SW = \max_{\lambda_i \in [0, \Lambda_i)^N} \sum_{i=1}^{N} V_i(\lambda_i) \cdot \overline{D}_i(\lambda_i) - \lambda_i \cdot \overline{C}_i(\lambda_i) \tag{8}$$

---

[13] The general problem is

$$SW = \max_{S, \lambda_i \in [0, \Lambda_i)^N, i \in S} \sum_{i \in S} V_i(\lambda_i) \cdot \overline{D}_i(\lambda_i) - \lambda_i \cdot \overline{C}_i(\lambda_i). \tag{7}$$

Subject to the local equilibrium condition (3) and the global inclusion constraint (4). The protocol's social welfare is defined as the sum of the expected net values to all users across all queues, accounting for delay costs. Under welfare maximization, setting optimal relative prices $(p_1, \ldots, p_N) \in \mathbb{R}_+^N$ is equivalent to a planner choosing the demand rates $\lambda_i \in [0, \Lambda_i)^N, i \in \mathcal{S}$ directly subject to local equilibrium conditions (3) in all served queues and the global capacity constraint (4). The following proposition shows that the relative price social optimum generically serves all queues.

Proposition 2. *Suppose that the discount rate and linear delay cost functions are so that the net utility function from queue i, that is $W_i \equiv \lambda_i \mapsto V_i(\lambda_i) \cdot \overline{D}_i(\lambda_i) - \lambda_i \cdot \overline{C}_i(\lambda_i)$ is strictly concave, and $\exists \nu > 0$ such that $W_i'(0) > \nu$ for all i, and $\sum_{i=1}^{N}(W_i')^{-1}(\nu) = \kappa$ then in the relative price social optimum, capacity is allocated in all queues, $\mathcal{S} = \{1, \ldots, N\}$.*

Proof. Since each W_i is strictly concave, their sum is strictly concave. Let λ^* be an optimal solution to the problem. By the KarushKuhnTucker conditions, $\exists \mu \geq 0$ such that $W_i'(\lambda_i^*) = \mu$ if $\lambda_i^* > 0$ and $W_i'(\lambda_i^*) \leq \mu$ if $\lambda_i^* = 0$ Suppose, for contradiction, that $\exists j$ such that $\lambda_j^* = 0$. Then, $W_j'(0) \leq \mu$. But we know that $W_j'(0) > \nu$, therefore, $\mu > \nu$. There exists at least one index i so that $\lambda_i^* > 0$, otherwise total capacity would be zero. For all i where $\lambda_i^* > 0$, we have $W_i'(\lambda_i^*) = \mu > \nu$. Since W_i is strictly concave, W_i' is strictly decreasing. Therefore, $\lambda_i^* < (W_i')^{-1}(\nu)$ for all i where $\lambda_i^* > 0$. This implies that $\sum_{i=1}^{N} \lambda_i^* < \sum_{i=1}^{N}(W_i')^{-1}(\nu) = \kappa$. But this contradicts the optimality of λ^* because we can increase the objective function by increasing λ_j^* slightly while still satisfying the constraint. Therefore, our assumption of the existence of j is a contradiction, and we conclude that $\lambda_i^* > 0$ for all i. That is, all queues are allocated non-zero capacity.

This proposition indicates that, under welfare maximization, it is optimal to serve all queues, distributing capacity across them in a way that balances the marginal social welfare contributions. This contrasts with the revenue-maximizing allocation, which may exclude some queues to maximize revenue.

4.3 Welfare Maximizing Relative Pricing

Having established that welfare maximization leads to capacity allocation across all queues, we now derive the welfare-maximizing relative prices that support this allocation under the conditions of Proposition 2. Let μ denote the Lagrange multiplier associated with the global capacity constraint (4). Economically, μ represents the shadow price of including an additional transaction in the system; it reflects the marginal social cost of capacity constraints. The following propositions link the socially optimal prices in each queue to this shadow price and demand characteristics.

Proposition 3. *The socially optimal relative prices are given by*

$$p_i = -V_i(\lambda_i)\overline{D}_i^{'}(\lambda_i) + \lambda_i \overline{C}_i^{'}(\lambda_i) + \mu \qquad (9)$$

This proposition emerges from the first order condition for λ_i and replacing p_i from (3). This expression shows that the socially optimal price in queue i includes three components. First, the local delay externality $-V_i(\lambda_i) \cdot \overline{D}'_i(\lambda_i)$ captures the negative impact of increased demand on the expected delay discount. As λ_i increases, the expected delay increases (since the system becomes more congested), reducing the net value for all users in queue i. Second, the local additive delay cost $\lambda_i \cdot \overline{C}'_i(\lambda_i)$ represents the additional additive delay costs incurred due to increased demand. Third, the global capacity externality μ reflects the marginal cost of consuming limited capacity that could have been used by other queues.

At the socially optimal prices, the marginal user's expected net value is equal to the total externality they impose on the system. This ensures that users internalize the full social cost of their participation, leading to an efficient allocation of resources.

To gain further insights, we specialize the model to a setting where the time between arrivals is exponentially distributed, and the execution times for each user also follow an exponential distribution. Each market has size Λ_i each with a different isoelastic marginal value function $V'_i(\lambda_i) = (\lambda_i/\Lambda_i)^{-1/\varepsilon_i}$ where $\varepsilon_i > 1$ represents demand elasticity for queue/resource i. In this setting, $V_i(\lambda_i) = \frac{(\lambda_i/\Lambda_i)^{1-1/\varepsilon_i}}{1-1/\varepsilon_i}$.

Assuming that the delay discount function is exponential, $D(t) = e^{-dt}$ and the additive delay cost is linear $C(t) = c \times t$ where $c, d > 0$, we have (see Appendix A for detailed derivations)

$$\overline{C}_i(\lambda_i) = \frac{c}{1-\lambda_i}$$

$$\overline{D}_i(\lambda_i) = \frac{1-\lambda_i}{1+d-\lambda_i} \qquad (10)$$

Approximation Under High Parallelization. Suppose that the demand rates λ_i and λ_j are small relative to 1 and the discount rate d, reflecting a high degree of parallelization (i.e., the system can process many transactions concurrently). Under this assumption, we can approximate the socially optimal relative prices.

Corollary 1. *Under the above assumptions, the ratio of the socially optimal prices in queues i and j is approximately*

$$\frac{p_i}{p_j} \approx \frac{\frac{(\lambda_i/\Lambda_i)^{1-1/\varepsilon_i}}{1-1/\varepsilon_i} \cdot \frac{d}{(1+d)^2} + c\lambda_i + \mu}{\frac{(\lambda_j/\Lambda_j)^{1-1/\varepsilon_j}}{1-1/\varepsilon_j} \cdot \frac{d}{(1+d)^2} + c\lambda_j + \mu} \qquad (11)$$

Proof. First, we compute the derivatives: $V'_i(\lambda_i) = \Lambda_i \lambda_i^{-1/\varepsilon_i}, \overline{D}'(\lambda_i) = -\frac{d}{(1+d-\lambda_i)^2}, \overline{C}'(\lambda_i) = \frac{c}{(1-\lambda_i)^2}$. Substitute into the equation for p_i, $p_i = \frac{(\lambda_i/\Lambda_i)^{1-1/\varepsilon_i}}{1-1/\varepsilon_i} \cdot \left(\frac{d}{(1+d-\lambda_i)^2}\right) + \lambda_i \cdot \frac{c}{(1-\lambda_i)^2} + \mu$. Consider the ratio p_i/p_j. Assuming λ_i and λ_j are small compared to 1 and d we have $(1+d-\lambda_i)^2 \approx$

$(1+d)^2, (1-\lambda_i)^2 \approx 1$, replacing in the expression for relative prices yields
$$\frac{p_i}{p_j} \approx \frac{\frac{(\lambda_i/\Lambda_i)^{1-1/\varepsilon_i}}{1-1/\varepsilon_i} \cdot \frac{d}{(1+d)^2} + c\lambda_i + \mu}{\frac{(\lambda_j/\Lambda_j)^{1-1/\varepsilon_j}}{1-1/\varepsilon_j} \cdot \frac{d}{(1+d)^2} + c\lambda_j + \mu}.$$

The approximate price ratio reveals how the optimal prices depend on queue-specific characteristics such as market size Λ_i, demand elasticity ε_i, and demand rates λ_i. When μ is small relative to the other terms (i.e., when local congestion effects dominate global capacity constraints), the price ratio is primarily determined by these queue-specific factors. As μ increases (i.e., when global congestion becomes more significant), its effect is to push the price ratio closer to 1, reducing price differentiation across queues.

Corollary 2. *Suppose, in addition to the assumptions of Corollary 1, that local congestion dominates global congestion (μ is negligible compared to p_i and p_j), and demand is perfectly elastic ($\varepsilon_i, \varepsilon_j \to \infty$). Then, the price ratio is simplified to*

$$\frac{p_i}{p_j} \approx \frac{\lambda_i}{\lambda_j} \cdot \frac{\Lambda_j}{\Lambda_i} \tag{12}$$

This limit expression offers several insights. First, in the case of perfectly elastic demand, the optimal prices are proportional to the ratio of demand rates normalized by market sizes (λ_i/Λ_i). This suggests that setting prices based on the relative demand intensity in each queue approximates the welfare-maximizing solution. Second, as the market size Λ_i for a congested queue decreases, the optimal price for that queue diverges from a uniform price, reflecting the higher marginal value of capacity in smaller markets.

5 Conclusion

In this paper, we investigated posted-price Parallel Execution Fee Mechanisms within a capacity-constrained blockchain system characterized by multiple queues or local fee markets. My model captures the essential features of parallel execution in blockchain networks, where transactions may access different resources or contracts and can be processed concurrently. A key aspect of our analysis was the global inclusion constraint imposed by the consensus mechanism. This constraint necessitates that all transactions, regardless of their queue, must be considered collectively for inclusion.

The analysis reveals several key insights. When the objective is to maximize revenue, especially under limited capacity, the system tends to allocate all capacity to the queue with users willing to pay the highest fees. In contrast, when the objective is to maximize social welfare, the optimal allocation generally involves serving all queues. We found that the optimal relative pricing across different queues depends on several factors, including market size, demand elasticity, and the balance between local and global congestion. In settings where demand elasticity is high, and local congestion effects dominate, pricing individual queues proportional to demand relative to market size is approximately welfare-maximizing.

The findings suggest that implementing local fee markets within such blockchains can improve overall system efficiency. By defining local values for each state, contract, or object and employing an adaptive base fee mechanism for inclusion, transactions can be assigned to queues with different relative prices. As blockchain technologies evolve towards more complex architectures, such as parallel execution, Directed Acyclic Graph (DAG)-based systems, and multiple concurrent proposers, this paper provides valuable insights for protocol designers.

While this study provides a foundational model for efficient parallel execution fee mechanisms, we have abstracted from several aspects of transaction execution on blockchains.

One important extension is the study of optimal local priority auctions. In such a setting, customers could participate in a two-stage bidding process for entering queues in a system with multiple service points. Initially, users might bid for priority in a global queue, reflecting the capacity constraints of the consensus mechanism. Subsequently, they could bid for specific services in parallel queues, corresponding to different resources or contracts. Studying how to design such auctions to optimize for social welfare or revenue maximization would be a promising area for further research.

Another area for future research is the development of dynamic pricing mechanisms that adapt to changing network conditions, user behaviors, and congestion levels in real time. While a comprehensive examination of these complex issues lies beyond the scope of this paper, they offer promising opportunities for future research and further refinement of our analysis.

A Appendix

A.1 Expression of Delay Costs

Proof. We begin by considering the definitions of $\overline{C}_i(\lambda_i)$ and $\overline{D}_i(\lambda_i)$:

$$\overline{C}_i(\lambda_i) = \mathbb{E}[C(T_i)] = \int_0^\infty C(t) f_{T_i}(t) dt \tag{13}$$

$$\overline{D}_i(\lambda_i) = \mathbb{E}[D(T_i)] = \int_0^\infty D(t) f_{T_i}(t) dt \tag{14}$$

where $f_{T_i}(t)$ is the probability density function of the exponential distribution with rate parameter λ_i:

$$f_{T_i}(t) = \lambda_i e^{-\lambda_i t} \tag{15}$$

For $\overline{C}_i(\lambda_i)$, we substitute $C(t) = ct$ and solve:

$$\overline{C}_i(\lambda_i) = \int_0^\infty ct\lambda_i e^{-\lambda_i t} dt \tag{16}$$

$$= c\lambda_i \int_0^\infty t e^{-\lambda_i t} dt \tag{17}$$

$$= c\lambda_i \left[-\frac{t}{\lambda_i} e^{-\lambda_i t} \Big|_0^\infty - \int_0^\infty -\frac{1}{\lambda_i} e^{-\lambda_i t} dt \right] \tag{18}$$

$$= c\lambda_i \left[0 + \frac{1}{\lambda_i^2} \right] \tag{19}$$

$$= \frac{c}{\lambda_i} = \frac{c}{1 - \lambda_i} \tag{20}$$

For $\overline{D}_i(\lambda_i)$, we substitute $D(t) = e^{-dt}$ and solve:

$$\overline{D}_i(\lambda_i) = \int_0^\infty e^{-dt} \lambda_i e^{-\lambda_i t} dt \tag{21}$$

$$= \lambda_i \int_0^\infty e^{-(d+\lambda_i)t} dt \tag{22}$$

$$= \lambda_i \left[-\frac{1}{d+\lambda_i} e^{-(d+\lambda_i)t} \Big|_0^\infty \right] \tag{23}$$

$$= \lambda_i \left[0 + \frac{1}{d+\lambda_i} \right] \tag{24}$$

$$= \frac{\lambda_i}{d+\lambda_i} = \frac{1-\lambda_i}{1+d-\lambda_i} \tag{25}$$

Thus, when the delay discount function is exponential $D(t) = e^{-dt}$ and the additive delay cost is linear $C(t) = c \times t$ where $c, d > 0$, the following equations hold:

$$\begin{aligned} \overline{C}_i(\lambda_i) &= \frac{c}{1-\lambda_i} \\ \overline{D}_i(\lambda_i) &= \frac{1-\lambda_i}{1+d-\lambda_i} \end{aligned} \tag{26}$$

References

1. Afeche, P., Mendelson, H.: Pricing and priority auctions in queueing systems with a generalized delay cost structure. Manage. Sci. **50**(7), 869–882 (2004)
2. Bahrani, M., Garimidi, P., Roughgarden, T.: Transaction fee mechanism design in a post-MEV world. In: Böhme, R., Kiffer, L. (eds.) 6th Conference on Advances in Financial Technologies (AFT 2024). Leibniz International Proceedings in Informatics (LIPIcs), vol. 316, pp. 29:1–29:24. Schloss Dagstuhl – Leibniz-Zentrum für Informatik, Dagstuhl (2024). https://doi.org/10.4230/LIPIcs.AFT.2024.29. https://drops.dagstuhl.de/entities/document/10.4230/LIPIcs.AFT.2024.29

3. Bonneau, J., Felten, E., Miller, A., Goldfeder, S.: Bitcoin and cryptocurrency technologies Arvind Narayanan. Netw. Secur. **2016**(8), 4 (2016)
4. Budish, E.: Trust at scale: the economic limits of cryptocurrencies and blockchains*†. Q. J. Econ., qjae033 (2024). https://doi.org/10.1093/qje/qjae033
5. Buterin, V.: Blockchain resource pricing (2018). https://ethresear.ch/uploads/default/original X **2**
6. Chung, H., Shi, E.: Foundations of transaction fee mechanism design. In: Proceedings of the 2023 Annual ACM-SIAM Symposium on Discrete Algorithms (SODA), pp. 3856–3899. SIAM (2023)
7. Halaburda, H., Haeringer, G., Gans, J., Gandal, N.: The microeconomics of cryptocurrencies. J. Econ. Lit. **60**(3), 971–1013 (2022). https://doi.org/10.1257/jel.20201593. https://www.aeaweb.org/articles?id=10.1257/jel.20201593
8. Keidar, I., Kokoris-Kogias, E., Naor, O., Spiegelman, A.: All you need is DAG. In: Proceedings of the 2021 ACM Symposium on Principles of Distributed Computing, pp. 165–175 (2021)
9. Kiayias, A., Koutsoupias, E., Lazos, P., Panagiotakos, G.: Tiered mechanisms for blockchain transaction fees (2023). https://arxiv.org/abs/2304.06014
10. Leshno, J.D., Strack, P.: Bitcoin: an axiomatic approach and an impossibility theorem. Am. Econ. Rev. Insights **2**(3), 269–86 (2020). https://doi.org/10.1257/aeri.20190494. https://www.aeaweb.org/articles?id=10.1257/aeri.20190494
11. Mendelson, H.: Pricing computer services: queueing effects. Commun. ACM **28**(3), 312–321 (1985). https://doi.org/10.1145/3166.3171. https://dl.acm.org/doi/10.1145/3166.3171
12. Naor, P.: The regulation of queue size by levying tolls. Econometrica J. Econ. Soc., 15–24 (1969)
13. Ndiaye, A.: Why bitcoin and ethereum differ in transaction fees: a theory of blockchain fee policies. CEPR Discussion Paper No. 18890 (2024). https://cepr.org/publications/dp18890
14. Ndiaye, A.: Blockchain price vs. quantity controls. Working Paper (2023)
15. Roughgarden, T.: Transaction fee mechanism design for the ethereum blockchain: an economic analysis of EIP-1559. arXiv preprint arXiv:2012.00854 (2020)
16. Roughgarden, T.: Transaction fee mechanism design. ACM SIGecom Exchanges **19**(1), 52–55 (2021)
17. SEC: Statement on the approval of spot bitcoin exchange-traded products (2024). https://www.sec.gov/newsroom/speeches-statements/gensler-statement-spot-bitcoin-011023. Accessed 22 Oct 2024
18. Shi, E., Chung, H., Wu, K.: What can cryptography do for decentralized mechanism design? In: Tauman Kalai, Y. (ed.) 14th Innovations in Theoretical Computer Science Conference (ITCS 2023). Leibniz International Proceedings in Informatics (LIPIcs), vol. 251, pp. 97:1–97:22. Schloss Dagstuhl – Leibniz-Zentrum für Informatik, Dagstuhl, Germany (2023). https://doi.org/10.4230/LIPIcs.ITCS.2023.97. https://drops.dagstuhl.de/entities/document/10.4230/LIPIcs.ITCS.2023.97

SoK: Modelling Data Storage and Availability

Carlo Brunetta[1]( ) and Massimiliano Sala[2]

[1] Independent Researcher, Bagnolet, France
brunocarletta@gmail.com
[2] Department of Mathematics, University of Trento, Trento, Italy
massimiliano.sala@unitn.it

Abstract. Our digital society's ever-increasing demand for data storage has driven up costs and security concerns, particularly with the shift towards outsourced third-party storage providers. This transition raises critical issues regarding privacy, trust, and data availability, i.e. the assurance that stored data remains accessible and retrievable.

This paper introduces a novel model that abstracts data-storage mechanisms by identifying distinct entities, each with a specific role in managing the data flow. Our model is designed to describe storage mechanisms, ranging from centralized to fully-decentralized systems, together with some data availability guarantees.

We highlight the underlying trust assumptions, providing a guideline for understanding application requirements and systematizing knowledge on data storage and availability. To illustrate our model usefulness, we examine several real-world data-storage-and-availability solutions, classifying them within our model as well as showcasing advantages and disadvantages. We conclude by comparing these solutions, which lets us propose open questions and future research directions for data-storage-and-availability methodologies.

Keywords: Data Storage · Data Availability · Decentralization · Blockchain

1 Introduction

Our society has become deeply integrated with digital services designed to understand our needs, anticipate them and better align with our individual requirements. This level of customization is the new expected norm, shaping our interactions with technology and influencing our daily lives. The vast amount of data we generate and own is the driving force behind this digital experience. This data describes everything about our online activities and can come from any device connected to the web. This sheer volume of information highlights a significant engineering challenge: how to handle this ever-growing data flow.

Data management is not merely about quantity, since data might be highly confidential, thus requiring robust privacy guarantees and clear access controls, to ensure that only authorized entities can obtain or modify such confidential data. Moreover, despite its digital representation, data must be physically stored somewhere. This fundamental requirement is sometimes neglected, but it is crucial for ensuring the availability, reliability, and integrity of data. These aspects are mere examples of the multifaceted nature of data management.

Our Contribution. This paper aims to introduce a novel abstract model for both the data-storing process and the availability-verification process. Our model identifies several roles and procedures involved in data storage, providing a clear framework for comparing storage strategies. By design, our model categorizes storage-and-availability processes, ranging from local and centralized solutions to fully-decentralized protocols, together with different levels of trust, from high-trust to trust-less domains.

Our model provides a taxonomy of the solutions' landscape, enabling a better understanding of each approach. To illustrate this, we provide examples of real-world storage-and-availability solutions and classify them into the model, so that we can discuss the pros and cons of alternative methodologies. Our ultimate goal is to provide a guideline to empower developers and engineers to make informed choices on the most appropriate data storage solution required by their applications.

Related Work. Our paper joins a collection of recent systematization-of-knowledge works in the area of data storage and availability. Unsurprisingly given the strong link between blockchain technology and cryptography [10,24], they mainly focus on blockchain-based approaches. Raikwar *et al.* [22] analyse the cryptographic primitives/protocols used in the blockchain domain, where some are related to the confidential storage and availability of stored data, e.g. they explain proof of retrievability (PoR), how this primitive is used to verify the retrievability of stored data, and they describe a specific instantiation for Bitcoin called **Retricoin** [25]. Zahed Benisi *et al.* [32] provide a comprehensive overview on the distributed and decentralized storage solutions with a major focus on the possible applications, e.g. rollups, outsourcing data storage while maintaining verifiable traceability, as well as some open challenges. Ernstberger *et al.* [11] provide a thorough analysis on data sovereignty, i.e. the ability to have control on the data, and how this is achieved or guaranteed in decentralized solutions. Li *et al.* [16] collect known decentralized storage solutions and provide a comparison of the technical cryptographic primitives/protocols they use.

We complete these works with our abstract model which provides a more precise characterization of each solution and which can categorize any solution, even centralized ones, thus creating a guideline for evaluating data-storage systems. All of these applications are extensively described in further works such as Gudgeon *et al.* [12] and their taxonomy of layer-2 solutions, where decentralized storage with rigorous availability verification is paramount.

Paper Organization. Section 2 describes our data storage model and classifying properties, of which we provide an explanation. It also includes some assumptions, conjectures and (possibly mandatory) cryptographic primitives. Section 3 lists real examples, how they are designed and how they fit into the data storage model. We place a strong emphasis on decentralized solutions and their design choices. Section 4 summarizes our findings by providing a comparison of the previous examples, along with some open questions and future research directions.

2 Abstract Data Storage Model

This section introduces our data storage model, the entities composing it and the essential properties used to classify applications. Regarding the essential properties, we focus on *data availability* being the main requirement for any realistic application, i.e. if data is not available, no other property makes sense.

As depicted in Fig. 1, our model identifies conceptually different entities representing separated data-handling phases:

▷ *Owner* $\mathcal{O}$: this entity owns the data and is the one requesting the data to be stored. The owner is responsible for preparing the data to store and for finding a contractual agreement with other entities. This agreement outlines how the handling will be conducted and the guarantees that must be provided, e.g. encryption requirements, distribution process to multiple storing nodes, availability guarantees, etc.
▷ *Handler* $\mathcal{H}$: the handler plays the role of a *file-system*, i.e. it coordinates the owner's storage requests, finds the appropriate storage nodes, keeps track of the location of stored data, probes the storage for availability, etcetera.
▷ *Storage Node (storer)* $\mathcal{S}$: this entity is responsible for physically storing the data and for retrieving it whenever requested by the handler.
▷ *Retriever* $\mathcal{R}$: the retriever is the designated entity that receives the owner's data from the handler. The retriever is allowed to request the designated data from the handler.

All these entities and their differentiated roles must coordinate to allow the correct, safe and trustworthy data storage. This coordination can be classified by specific *flavoured* properties, later discussed in detail:

○ *Access Control*: describing who has the right to access the data and if this data must preserve confidentiality during the storage, either from potential leaks or from a malicious handler/storer. All these are effectively metadata policies that the owner requests as part of the storage agreement. The access control allows a clear distinction of the scenarios where the receiver and the owner are the same entity or not.
○ *Data Handling Technique*: the Handler has the task of mapping the data's retrieval request to a concrete storage location, thus creating a mapping between requests and where data is stored, basically a *file-system* instantiation. This process can be made via as a centralized, distributed or full decentralized protocol.
○ *Data Storage Technique*: once the data arrives at the Storage Node, this must effectively be stored on a physical medium. Similarly to data handling, this phase can be made via either centralized, distributed or decentralized solutions. Furthermore, each storage node might use different storing methodology to provide a higher level of resilience against faulty storage media.
○ *Proving Data Availability*: whenever the data is stored, the owner (or receiver) might request a proof that the data is available for retrieval. This proof can

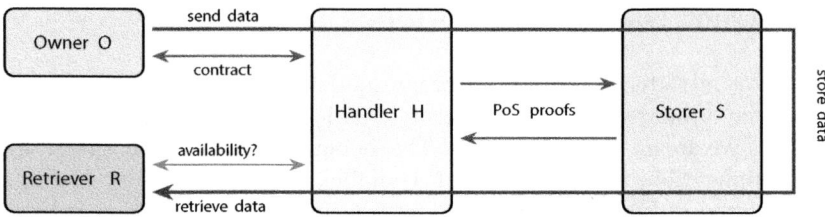

Fig. 1. Our abstract storage model with the fundamental actions between the entities as arrow. A major (blue) highlight of the data-flow is given. (Color figure online)

be used to coordinate a recovery procedure, to halt rewarding to the storage node, to alert the receiver for the lost of stored data or for other application-oriented responses.

2.1 Centralized, Distributed and Decentralized

Except for the owner which we assume to always be solo, all the other entities can be composed of *single or multiple* parties, hence introducing a trade-off between trust and resilience. Having single or multiple parties suggests concepts such as *centralized, distributed* and *decentralized* and, despite being often used interchangeably, we make a clear distinction between the terminologies:

▷ a *centralized* entity is defined by a single party representing the whole;
▷ a *distributed* entity is a *selected group* of parties where new members might join only according to strict rules (to build up a trust baseline);
▷ a *decentralized* entity is composed by an *open group* of parties which have limited trust between each other since everyone is (mostly) free to join.

In other words, a centralized entity is composed by a single party, while both a distributed and decentralized entity are composed by several parties interacting with each other to accomplish their goals. The difference between distributed and decentralized is found in the *underlying trust* between the parties and in the related enrolement's procedure. We define an entity to be decentralized if *anyone* can join the entity without specific prerequisites or trust requirements, similarly to how anyone can join a decentralized blockchain network by merely running a specific protocol's code. While, if the enrolement's procedure comprehends only *selected* individuals, we define such an entity to be distributed because the member selection process might not follow fair or transparent principles.

2.2 Data Availability

A fundamental requirement for any application is *data availability* (DA) which can be described as the concept that *"data must be proved available"* meaning that it should be possible to prove that any data stored is indeed available and can be retrieved by the designated receiver. Differently from other works, we use interchangeably the concept of *availability* and *retrievability* since, in our model, if data is retrievable by the correct receiver, then data must be available. For completeness, *data immutability* is an orthogonal fundamental property which we assume to hold at all time since *"data should not be (maliciously) modifiable"* guaranteeing the retrieval of the original data.

Before moving to known mechanism used to guarantee data availability, let us collect precise goals or properties for the proving mechanism:

DA.1 *formal verification* denotes that the proving mechanism provides a computationally verifiable proof of data availability, e.g. by using well-established cryptographic primitives such as Merkle trees;

DA.2 *timed proving* indicating that the verification procedure should formally prove the data availability at the exact time of proving and not before, i.e. the proof request acts as an unpredictable challenge forcing the proving mechanism to maintain the data available;

DA.3 *selective verification* indicating the possibility to prove the availability of a selected portion of the data. This can be useful when multiple files are stored and only a subset of them must be checked or if the data is too heavy, e.g. the availability proof might be reduced to uniform randomly selected pieces, thus providing a measurable probability of the whole data being available;

DA.4 *distributed storage* meaning that storage should be distributed between different nodes that interact to improve efficiency, rather than merely replicating the storage. Adding a network of storing nodes introduces security and protocol's complexity with the advantage of (hopefully) achieving more advanced features, e.g. threshold procedures or costs offloading;

DA.5 *proving resilience* denoting that if multiple storage nodes actively cooperate to store data, they are able to prove the data's availability even if some of the nodes are unavailable;

Important aspects when considering data availability are the data *confidentiality* (depending on the trust model required), the *time-frame* considered or the *storage duration* for which the data is requested to be available (outside this window, there might not be any guarantees).

Any DA solution is defined by some general procedures, designed to commit some sort of verification material connected to the data stored, which create a random computational challenge for the storer that can be answered only if they have the stored data available.

In the literature, there are many examples of protocols providing DA guarantees, each with a specific twist required by their application [7,20,21,26], e.g. provable-data-possession [2], proof-of-storage [4,31], proof-of-retrievability [25], proof-of-ownership [13], proof-of-space-time [3,19,33], or similar [8]. While each solution has its own techniques, we identify some common ones:

o *erasure codes* [6] are often used to extend data into a longer version, from which some shards are generated and distributed to some storage nodes. The main reason is that by correctly tweaking the code's parameters, the data might be retrievable even with a smaller amount of shards, hence providing resilience against many attacks on/from the storage nodes.

- *Merkle trees* (or similar hash-based data structure) are used to compress DA proofs based on hash-evaluation into a more compact format while providing paramount immutability guarantees. These solutions offer high throughput at the cost of limited feature-extensions capability, e.g. many solutions have private verifiability (only the receiver can verify the DA).
- *Zero-Knowledge* (ZK), as in succinct non-interactive/transparent argument of knowledge (SNARK/STARK) [17], provide a more computationally-expensive proving protocol at the benefit of allowing higher degree of expressibility. For example, differently from the hash-based solutions, many ZK solutions are designed to permit public DA verifiability.
- *Commit-and-open* solutions, especially via Kate et al. [15] polynomial commitment scheme, where the idea is to encode data into a secret polynomial, which is publicly committed and provided to the storage node. To generate a DA proof, the receiver requests the evaluation of the polynomial on some challenge points, which allows the verification of the polynomial's knowledge (this knowledge implies the availability of stored data).

Typically, these solutions are considered in a DA *layer* which is the network of interacting entities that creates, handles and verifies the DA proof requests. In the vast majority of known approaches, this network is based on a (public) ledger to allow for a sequential and traceable transcript of the stored data's history. This ledger also provides an easier computational control of the verification process by means of smart contracts (or similar programs) that automatically verify DA cryptographic proofs.

2.3 Rewarding Mechanism

Both storing and proving data availability have a non-negligible computational cost, which must be considered in applications, thus requiring the introduction of a *rewarding mechanism*, i.e. how the effort by any entity should be rewarded (and by whom).

Intuitively, the owner $\mathcal{O}$ and retriever $\mathcal{R}$ should pay for the storage and availability service, but they should be compensated by the handler if their data is lost (or turns out to be not available in the agreed availability-window). This suggests $\mathcal{O}$ and $\mathcal{R}$ pay the handler $\mathcal{H}$, the storer $\mathcal{S}$, or both, depending on the entities' independence and the (agreed) work compensations. The total compensations should consider: the effective costs for the data storage, all the DA proofs computed by the storage nodes, the handler's proof verification and also some management overhead.

As later showcased by the examples in Sect. 3, the burden of these costs can be effectively addressed in centralized or distributed scenario, where payments can be done at the final verification of the correct execution of the service and, if something goes wrong, the entities are supposed to follow the agreed contract (which is often legally binding). For example, if $\mathcal{S}$ loses the data, $\mathcal{R}$ and $\mathcal{O}$ will request a refund from $\mathcal{H}$ which must compensate them with an amount demanded to $\mathcal{S}$ for breaching the agreement between $\mathcal{S}$ and $\mathcal{H}$.

The decentralized scenario follows the same payments and claims requirements but, depending on the technology used to obtain the decentralization, the costs might be required to be provided upfront by $\mathcal{O}$. This problem demands a stricter automatic mechanism to ensure the correct protocol's execution. The same might apply to $\mathcal{H}$ or $\mathcal{S}$ whenever involved in the DA verification process, e.g. these entities might lock a deposit that will be returned if the verification is done correctly (together with the appropriate compensation for the work). Otherwise, the deposit is used as collateral, i.e. to refund $\mathcal{O}$ for the data loss.

The rewarding mechanism must therefore provide a cleverly designed incentive that avoids favouring malicious behaviour, otherwise malicious entities would never be punished. Furthermore, it is convenient to publicly maintain an immutable trace of the rewards, at the advantage of a traceable reputation mechanism, and to favour algorithmically-defined procedures that automatically partitions the rewards, e.g. via smart contracts.

3 Classifying Known Solutions

In this section we classify several known solutions in our model. We also provide explanations on the used methodologies/technologies, together with: some considerations on costs, the control over data and the required trust level. The examples are sorted according to the degree of decentralization.

3.1 Autonomous Storage

The simplest solution is to have a unique party acting in all the entities roles, i.e. the party self-hosts and manages its own data storage and availability.

Such a solution is clearly fully centralized, while confidentiality and resilience highly depend on the choices made. For example, the storage can be setup as a RAID system to increase redundancy and resilience against failing hard-drives. Availability verification does not require any specific procedure, since the owner has direct (or close enough) access to the storage system. All the costs, both hardware and management, are on the owner. There is no effective trust required, except possibly for the hardware itself, which might contain a backdoor.

3.2 Self-handled Storage

The second-simplest solution considers an owner that outsources its storage to either a single or multiple storage nodes, in some sort of *storage renting* where the owner takes the additional role of the data handler.

We classify self-handled storage to be a centralized handler with distributed storage. DA mechanisms can be implemented since they are specific protocols. In this scenario, the data owner *autonomously* decides to reward verified DA proofs and all the rewarding rights/guarantees are executed as per contract. To have a more algorithmic rewarding mechanism, the DA verification might be executed over any public ledger and with a smart contract. On the other hand, this latter idea would defy the purpose of *keeping-it-simple*, since it would turn the whole system into a sort of decentralized storage solution, discussed later.

3.3 Cloud Storage

Whenever the data owner outsources the data handling to an either centralized or distributed entity, the scenario depicts the typical cloud storage service where users pay a cloud for storage space without any responsibility on how to prepare data for storage. Usually in such solutions, the storage nodes are under the full control of the handler, which is a unique bigger entity that coordinates the storage as it better fits its infrastructure. This leads to more efficiency, as for example a storage contract with fewer retrievability guarantees creates an opportunity for the cloud server to save in storage-hardware costs, with the saving going for investment in some other parts of its system (e.g., cyber security).

Data availability proofs are usually not provided for cloud storage service, since any data loss is often handled according to some contractual agreements (e.g., monetary compensation via an insurance). Yet, this cost-efficient strategy relies on completely trusting the cloud's promise to keep the data available.

Similarly to self-handled storage, we classify any common cloud storage to be a centralized handler with distributed storage or distributed handler and storage. DA guarantees are (usually) not provided because a legally binding contract is often used to handle the scenario of a data loss. Internally, most probably the cloud storage services have mechanisms to distribute the stored data to minimize space costs and to create redundancy to verify that all the data is available (DA.4, DA.5). Unfortunately, this information is not provided to the data owner.

3.4 Decentralized Storage

The final class considered are decentralized storage solutions, commonly referred as *data availability layers*. The conceptual difference from the other examples is that anyone can join the decentralized network by providing computational power for data handling or storage space. However, data availability verification is paramount, since there is no underlying trust among potentially anonymous parties. These observations lead to consider a public ledger that algorithmically coordinates at least the reward protocol (if not the entire system), which must compute and distribute the economic incentives to honest-behaving entities.

The management costs are obviously higher than those of other solutions, since the coordinating protocols must build trust from scratch, which is known to be a very expensive process. Fortunately, the security guarantees are stronger, formally proven and verifiable (at least in principle). Additionally, the rewards themselves, typically awarded via cryptocurrencies or specific crypto-tokens, can increase their intrinsic value with the increase of demand for the decentralized storage service. The value growth pushes more participation in the storage service, providing higher stability and resilience for the underlying decentralized network.

Differently from other solutions, a decentralized storage based on a public ledger can more easily be used for *roll-ups scaling* mechanism. With a roll-up we mean a protocol aiming for a higher transaction throughput by performing an aggregation of several transactions into a single transaction. We consider only roll-ups that also provide an aggregation proof that is effectively reported and verified (possibly on the main ledger). Any such (aggregated) transaction plus its proof needs significantly less space than all initial transactions combined. This space saving opens the door to the scaling down of transaction throughput on the main blockchain. Without entering into the discussion of computational costs for such scaling solutions, which is abundantly discussed in the research community (see e.g., [12,14,23]), in any case the initial transactions must be stored somewhere (i.e., in a DA) and must remain available for verifiers, who can determine later the correctness of the aggregated transaction and its proof.

From the extensive solution space of DA layers [1,7,16,26,32], for our analysis we select Storj [29], FileCoin [21], Avail [5], Sia [28], Arweave [30] and Celestia [9], checking their techniques to achieve DA guarantees.

Storj. Storj is a cloud-storage service that allows users to store their data in a distributed cloud system. Storing devices are awarded for the space (and time) provided and used. Storj's network is composed by three types of nodes: clients of the service, Storj's nodes, which in practice compose the DA layer, and some special network's coordinators, which keep note on both the storage network's distribution and the rewards accrued by the network's nodes.

From a technical point of view [29], the owner $\mathcal{O}$ encrypts via a symmetric encryption scheme, e.g. AES256 − CTR, their data m and obtains an encrypted ciphertext c which is split into specific-size shards $\{c_i\}_{i \in I}$. For each shard, the storage node $\mathcal{S}$ provides a root node and a specific tree level, so that the owner instantiates a proof-of-retrievability (PoR) by computing, intuitively, a salted Merkle tree with all shards of $\mathcal{O}$'s interest. To allow resilience against failing storage nodes, Storj suggests the shard to either be replicated to multiple nodes or to use erasure-encoding schemes. To select $\mathcal{S}$, Storj is based on a distributed hash table called Kademlia [18], which creates and maintains a distributed message routing among nodes, together with some security guarantees. This primitive allows the association of a unique shard's identifier, e.g. a digest of the shard, with a unique node $\mathcal{S}$ that is responsible for the storage, up to coordinated modifications to the distributed hash table's key-value entries.

The DA verification is done via a challenge-response protocol, where $\mathcal{O}$ provides to $\mathcal{S}$ a random salt used during the PoR's initialization. If the file is available, $\mathcal{S}$ can provide a Merkle proof thus guaranteeing the retrievability of its shard. The verification process is not automatic and it is intrinsically limited by the number of salt values chosen during initialization.

Regarding the handler's role, Storj considers a software solution that should facilitate networks communications together with the contractual agreements with the storer for their service (which are coordinated on a public ledger). Their idea is to detach such responsibilities to a software, which can either be hosted locally or outsourced to a trusted party.

We classify Storj as a centralized handler with decentralized storage able to provide non-timed formal DA proofs of the whole encrypted data (DA.1). The storage is distributed between the nodes and can be made more resilient (DA.4, DA.5). Access control is completely left to the owner's control and, without major modification to the protocol, it is not trivial to integrate a protocol that allows new access permissions after-storing, e.g. via proxy re-encryption.

Arweave. Arweave [30] is a decentralized data storing protocol that aims to provide the infrastructure for the *permaweb*, i.e. a decentralized version of the web where content cannot be easily removed, censored or modified (because distributed over multiple supposedly-independent nodes). The protocol defines an independent blockchain based over a custom proof-of-work mechanism. Any transaction contained in the block defines either some exchange of cryptocurrency between wallets (e.g. payments) or a *data transaction*, i.e. a transaction indicating that some data is requested to be stored by the network (once the transaction is validated, the network distributes the storing of its data).

Arweave opts for an ad-hoc protocol to seek maximal usage efficiency while maintaining storage and computational costs relatively low, at the cost of a more complex tokenomics design (which is well motivated in their documentation [30]). The core DA verification is executed periodically (approximatively every two minutes) via a Succinct Proof of Access (SPoA) that acts similarly to Merkle-tree/hash-based PoS primitive by providing the proof for the whole Merkle-path for some challenged leaf. Differently from other solutions, SPoA is mainly designed to be used in more complex protocols able to prove the availability of replicated data on random offsets and time, by means of a verifiable delay function (VDF). We classify Arweave as a decentralized handler and storage system, designed over an ad-hoc blockchain, which provides timed DA proofs verified by the network and used to mine the next block (DA.1, DA.2, DA.3). Each node decides what data to replicate based on its country's legislation and some tokenomics incentives, needed for the replication of less distributed data (DA.4, DA.5).

Filecoin. FileCoin [21] is a decentralized storage framework that introduces an economically incentivized mechanism on top of the InterPlanetary File System (IPFS) [27], i.e. a decentralized peer-to-peer storage and retrieval network mostly used for decentralized web services. Differently from Storj, FileCoin provides the rewarding infrastructure on top of the already existing IPFS storage layer.

Technically, such an infrastructure is based on a public ledger that stores the agreements between owners and storage nodes. These agreements are created via a *bidding* procedure. More specifically, the owner creates an order specifying the storage and availability requirements, while the storing nodes bid to win the deal which is agreed between the parties via its mutual signature. All the storage costs are therefore independently agreed upon between owner and storage nodes. The protocol enables the handlers to be rewarded for both maintaining the different data-structure required and providing security and fairness guarantees in case of disputation, e.g. if after some time, the stored data is not available or cannot be retrieved.

The IPFS provides *addressable storage-location*, that is, any file in the peer-to-peer system can be uniquely identified by the entire network. Such an identification is specified in the deal, thus clarifying the logical position where the data must be stored. Notably, the file retrieval can be done off-chain by exchanging data chunks for micropayments that can be reported to the ledger for the correct reward (which is managed by the handlers' decentralized network).

Regarding the DA, FileCoin provides a *proof-of-spacetime* primitive that creates PoS proofs for a chosen period, i.e. a proof that the data is retrievable for a specifically chosen window of time. The main idea is to exploit more computational time for the proof generation the proof, while reducing the communication costs (this cost reduction is especially notable when compared with the periodical execution of an entire PoS verification round). Intuitively, the primitive sequentially generates challenges from three inputs: an initial challenge, a counter and the current interaction proof. The computed challenge is used to compute the PoS Merkle proof, in the same spirit as Storj's one, which is the input for a zero-knowledge SNARK that compacts the proof. Providing *"time guarantees"* is obtained by requiring the proving interaction to be executed t times which would require noticeable computational cost (which translates to wall-clock time).

We classify FileCoin as a decentralized handler with decentralized external storage (IPFS) that can provide timed DA proofs verified by the network (via smart-contracts) of the whole or partial data according to IPFS's file management (DA.1, DA.2, DA.3). Even if the storage is distributed over the IPFS's network, there are no (concrete) threshold storing mechanism, rather, the resilience is obtained by having a large replicating network. As per FileCoin, access control is completely left to the owner's control.

Sia. Sia [28] is a framework based on a dedicated blockchain where storage contracts are agreed upon of which design reassembles the Bitcoin blockchain with major differences on the transaction format and goals. In particular, Sia's transaction does not consider a scripting language and mainly focuses on providing the use of a multi-signature scheme where contracts, DA proof and contract updates are the only possible encoded messages. The DA verification are defined using a hash-based PoS and the framework allows for periodic release of rewards without interaction from the data owner, i.e. the contract defines the signing rules for the automatic rewarding of the storage node.

We classify Sia solution as a decentralized handler with a decentralized peer-to-peer storage that provides DA's guarantees on the whole or partial data (DA.1, DA.2, DA.3). As per protocol definition, the storage is not natively distributed, i.e. multiple contracts must be created and the data must be appropriately handled to achieve a somewhat threshold reconstruction mechanism.

Avail. Avail [5] introduces a framework for unifying blockchain networks. For our work, we focus on the underlying DA layer proposed with major interest in how data is prepared and their DA verification mechanism. Avail's DA layer is based on a decentralized blockchain where storage nodes and handlers, called *validators*, maintain trace of all the stored data and agreements between owners and storage nodes made via smart contracts, similarly in spirit to FileCoinbut with a different approach because Avail is not based over IPFS.

The major technical difference is that Avail's ledger stores, together with the entities agreements, the effective DA verification protocol's transcription, i.e. the whole proving is publicly executed and verified on the ledger by strictly following the rules provided in a smart contract. The key point is that the owner is not required to be online to provide a challenge for the verification by the cryptographic primitive. Whenever data must be stored, data is first encrypted (as other solutions) and represented as a matrix of which data chunks for each row is considered as a secret polynomial to be used in the Kate *et al.* [15] polynomial commitment scheme, i.e. the polynomial is homomorphically evaluated on a publicly random secret value, with the related result published as the commitment of the secret polynomial. All the commitments from the rows[1] are posted on the Avail's DA ledger and, if verified, are effectively published.

To prove availability, a smart contract managing the agreement's rewards can be programmed to require a proof over a challenge computed by the current (hash of the) status of the ledger which is (perhaps optimistically) assumed to be unpredictable. Each storer computes the DA proof, composed of the secret polynomial's evaluation on the provided challenge, and the KZG's proof, to allow handlers to verify proofs and correctly execute the smart contract's rewarding mechanism. By cleverly shaping the representation matrix, the protocol allows selective proving, e.g. different files are committed into different polynomials because of their placement in the matrix representation, thus permitting the verification of specific data by requiring the (proved) evaluation of selected polynomials. Such a property enables selective verification that reduces the bandwidth demanded to the network and an increased scalability.

Another technical advantage of using a publicly verifiable scheme, such as KZG, is the possibility to create *light clients*, i.e. handlers in our model that preserve a partial status of the underlying ledger. Each light client can store for a limited time a bounded amount of partial DA proofs. All clients are interconnected into a peer-to-peer network that acts as a *local-cache* of the current DA network. Any of their proofs can be publicly verified, which guarantees that the light clients are not maliciously faking the DA proofs.

The light client's network would offload additional workload from the network allowing any party willing to check the availability of some data to query the local-cache instead. Having lower latency allows a quicker access to the availability proofs and allows a (possible) quicker access to the data/proof.

The natural problems arising are all about correctly handling *cache-lifetime*, e.g. the availability proofs provided by the cache might be different from the real availability which might have consequences, especially if the ledger's handlers

---

[1] The white-paper [5] specifies the usage of an erasure code to extend either the matrix columns or the computed commitments. The paper does not provide a precise formulation thus we limit our description.

decide to provide a DAproof that will survive in the peer-to-peer cache while effectively making the data unavailable.

Avail considers tokenomics for their entities, where requesting to storage is paid by the owner and the DA proofs are used to finalize the payments via a smart contract, where forcing the availability proofs to be stored on the ledger provides accountability. At the same time, honest validators (handlers) are rewarded by the ledger's block-generation fees plus additional estimated expenses to run smart contracts. Notable, only the light clients are not paid for their effort to lowers the systems' demands however, such a rewarding mechanism might be hard to provide by the very nature of the peer-to-peer network and an unintuitive challenge to solve: it is unclear how to provably count the access to valid cached proofs.

We classify Avail's DA layer solution as a decentralized handler with decentralized storage that provides timed DA proofs verified by the network (via smart-contracts) of the whole or partial data (DA.1, DA.2, DA.3). The effective storage is distributed and allows concrete threshold reconstruction mechanism using erasure codes (DA.4). The cached-proofs, stored by the light-clients peer-to-peer network, provide redundancy of the main ledger, systematically offloading efforts on it, which can be better spent into the ledger maintenance (DA.5). As in other solutions, the owner fully controls the access on data.

Celestia. Celestia [9] is a development framework for decentralized application of which data storage and availability layer is based on Al-Bassam [7] and Al-Bassam et al. [8] works. Similarly to other solutions, the DA layer is an independent blockchain with a self-sustaining tokenomics that rewards honest behaviour of the network and storage nodes. Even if the DA guarantees are hash-based, the underlying proving methodology considers a two-dimensional matrix where the data is expanded into a Reed-Solomon Encoded Merkle Tree, i.e. the data is first extended via a Reed-Solomon code and later a Merkle-tree root is evaluated for each column and row for later combining all these values into a single root value. The matrix structure, together with the increased number of Merkle-roots considered, enables the verification of only selected columns/rows and, similarly to Avail, lets light clients reduce the distribution's costs of the DA proofs from the main network.

From the white-paper underlying the protocol [7,8], we classify Celestia's DA layer solution as a decentralized handler and storage that guarantees DA verification of the whole or partial data (DA.1, DA.3). The storage is distributed and the protocol is designed to use erasure codes techniques (DA.4). This way, Celestia obtains the decentralization of the DA proving costs among nodes (DA.5).

4 Discussion and Future Directions

All known solutions introduce some tweaks to better fit the application they are designed for. We report in Table 1 the classification of such solutions into our model and the properties highlighted in Sect. 2. Our model does lead to a systematic classification highlighting differences between these solutions, e.g.:

Table 1. Summary for the examples of Sect. 3, according to our model (Sect. 2). The symbol ✓ indicates presence/compliance, ∼ if optionally implementable, ✗ lack of feature, ? if unknown from the literature, and a dash "–" if not relevant. We denote the owner with $\mathcal{O}$, the handler with $\mathcal{H}$, the storer with $\mathcal{S}$ and the retriever with $\mathcal{R}$.

Protocol	Roles	Access	Storage	Handling	Data Availability
	O H S R	Full O Control / Confidentiality / Designated R / Proxy re-encryption	S Centralized / S Distributed / S Decentralized / DA Proving	H Centralized / H Distributed / H Decentralized / Contractual Market / Redundant Network	DA.1 / DA.2 / DA.3 / DA.4 / DA.5 / Automatic DA / Smart Contract DA / Cryptography
Autonomous	$\mathcal{O}\mathcal{O}\mathcal{O}\mathcal{O}$	✓ – – –	✓ – – ✗	✓ – – ✗ ✗	– – – – – – – –
Self-Handled (single storer)	$\mathcal{O}\mathcal{O}\mathcal{S}\mathcal{O}$	✓ – – –	✓ – – ∼	✓ – – ✓ ✗	∼ ∼ ∼ – – – – As $\mathcal{O}$ desire
Self-Handled (multi storer)	$\mathcal{O}\mathcal{O}\mathcal{S}\mathcal{O}$	✓ – – –	– ✓ – ∼	✓ – – ✓ ✗	∼ ∼ ∼ – – – – As $\mathcal{O}$ desire
Cloud Storage (typical)	$\mathcal{O}\mathcal{H}\mathcal{H}\mathcal{R}$	∼ ✗ ✓ ✗	– ✓ – ✗	✓ ✓[a] – ✓ ✓	– – – ✓ ✓ – – –
Storj	$\mathcal{O}\mathcal{H}\mathcal{S}\mathcal{R}$	✓ ✓ ✓ ∼	– – ✓ ✓	✓ ? – ✓ ✓	✗ ✗ ✓ ✓ ∼ ✓ Hash-based PoS
FileCoin	$\mathcal{O}\mathcal{H}\mathcal{S}\mathcal{R}$	✓ ✓ ✓ ∼	– – ✓ ✓	– – ✓ ✓ ✓	✓ ✓ ✓ – – ∼ ∼ PoS and SNARK
Avail	$\mathcal{O}\mathcal{H}\mathcal{S}\mathcal{R}$	✓ ✓ ✓ ∼	– – ✓ ✓	– – ✓ ✓ ✓	✓ ✓ ✓ ✓ ✓ ✓ ✓ KZG
Arweave	$\mathcal{O}\mathcal{H}\mathcal{S}\mathcal{R}$	✓ ✓ ✓ ∼	– – ✓ ✓	– – ✓ ? ✓	✓ ✓ ✓ ✓ ✓ ✓ ? Hash SPoA, VDF
Sia	$\mathcal{O}\mathcal{H}\mathcal{S}\mathcal{R}$	✓ ✓ ✓ ∼	– – ✓ ✓	– – ✓ ✓ ✗	✓ ✓ ✓ ✗ ✗ ✓ ✓ Hash-based PoS
Celestia [7,8]	$\mathcal{O}\mathcal{H}\mathcal{S}\mathcal{R}$	✓ ✓ ✓ ∼	– – ✓ ✓	– – ✓ ? ✓	✓ ✓ ? ✓ ✓ ? ?[b] Merkle Matrix

[a] Cloud storage providers might distribute their workload or provide multiple access point for the storage service. We identify both as possible without separating the table's entry.

[b] From the research articles, it is not specified if the DA verification can be spontaneously requested by the network, if the proofs can effectively be prepared before hand and/or if the layer provides smart contracts to create a contract.

- Differently from other protocols, Storj seems to prefer a (software) centralized solution. One of their future goal is to provide a (software) decentralized solution to align with similar different solutions.
- Differently from Avail and Storj, FileCoin does not develop specific redundancy/threshold mechanism to protect against the loss of data shares (because this should be handled by the underlying IPFS layer).
- FileCoin is designed for direct coordination between $\mathcal{O}$'s storage demand and store nodes, while Storj and Avail focusses more on an offer-framework where the deals are agreed upon a market which is available on the public ledger.
- Avail is the only protocol to define a peer-to-peer network composed of light clients that crate an effective cache of the DA layer. This idea provides clear intra-network optimizations that improve with the increase of the peers network. However, the white-paper [5] does not offer enough details to under-

stand the limitations, how natural cache-memory problems are solved and which security assumptions are proved.[2]

4.1 Further Comments

While investigating the literature, we noted that no PoS/DA solution (with detailed technical white-paper) is designed around the idea of utilizing the periodical DA proofs as a possible mechanism to facilitate a possible data-recovery procedure. For specific scenarios where the data is not too big, imagine the handler verifies and stores t DA proofs on the ledger which are exactly the amount of proof requested by a contractual agreement. The consecutive protocol's execution would suggest that the storage node provides to the retriever the data. However, a malicious retriever might act as the data is corrupted thus forcing a rewarding resolution based on the smart contract's code.

Following our previous discussion, what we suggest is to have a reconstruction algorithm that takes the verified DA proofs and outputs the data. For example, Avail uses KZG polynomial evaluations as proofs which, by algebraic properties, would allow the reconstruction of the whole polynomial if the correct amount of evaluations is known, i.e. one more than the degree of the polynomial. Therefore, a timed mechanism that publicly releases proofs and, after a pre-defined number of periods, automatically permits recovery of committed data.

4.2 Conclusions

The domain of data storage and availability is a rapidly evolving environment where new ideas and techniques often mixes with specialized features oriented to real-world applications. Our model leads to a precise classification of these solutions (and more traditional ones), providing both help for comparing storage systems and a guideline for developers searching the best-fitting framework (that achieves their requirement without introducing additional complexity).

Acknowledgment. The authors would like to thank Ripple's University Blockchain Research Initiative, Amit Chaudhary and the Palliora project (https://www.palliora.org).

---

[2] If both the DA proving periodicity and the cache have a lifetime of Δ, then a handler $\mathcal{H}$ may give partial proofs of some data m to the light client's network *exactly* at the same time as the last DA proof is published. If $\mathcal{H}$ is malicious, it might delete m, sell its space for a timespan $< \Delta$, which would let $\mathcal{H}$ query from the cache-network the partial proofs and reconstruct m thus fraudulently fulfilling its DA obligations. $\mathcal{H}$ would gain almost twice the reward at the cost of the light client's network, which are not rewarded.

References

1. 0G Labs, 0G: Towards Data Availability 2.0 (2024). https://0g.ai
2. Ateniese, G., et al.: Provable data possession at untrusted stores. In: Nissing, P., De Capitani di Vimercati, S., Syverson, P.F. (eds.) ACM CCS 2007, pp. 598–609. ACM Press (2007). https://doi.org/10.1145/1315245.1315318
3. Ateniese, G., Chen, L., Eternad, M., Tang, Q.: Proof of storage/time: efficiently checking continuous data availability. In: NDSS 2022. The Internet Society (2022). https://doi.org/10.14722/ndss.2022.24037
4. Ateniese, G., Kamara, S., Katz, J.: Proofs of storage from homomorphic identification protocols. In: Matsui, M. (ed.) ASIACRYPT 2009. LNCS, vol. 5912, pp. 319–333. Springer, Heidelberg (2009). https://doi.org/10.1007/978-3-642-10366-7_19
5. Avail Team, Avail: A Unifying Blockchain Network, version 2.1 (2024). https://www.availproject.org
6. Balaji, S., Krishnan, M.N., Vajha, M., Ramkumar, V., Sasidharan, B., Kumar, P.V.: Erasure coding for distributed storage: an overview. Sci. China Inf. Sci. **61**, 1–45 (2018)
7. Al-Bassam, M., LazyLedger: A Distributed Data Availability Ledger With Client-Side Smart Contracts (2019). arXiv: 1905.09274 [cs.CR]. https://arxiv.org/abs/1905.09274
8. Al-Bassam, M., Sonnino, A., Buterin, V.: Fraud and Data Availability Proofs: Maximizing Light Client Security and Scaling Blockchains with Dishonest Majorities (2019). arXiv: 1909.09267 [cs.CR]. https://arxiv.org/abs/1909.09267
9. Celestia Labs, Celestia (2025). https://celestia.org
10. Cimatti, A., et al.: J. Math. Cryptol. **19**(1), 20040045 (2025). https://doi.org/10.1515/jmc-2024-0045
11. Ernstberger, J., et al.: SoK: data sovereignty. In: 2023 IEEE European Symposium on Security and Privacy, pp. 122–143. IEEE Computer Society Press (2023). https://doi.org/10.1109/EuroSP57164.2023.00017
12. Gudgeon, L., Moreno-Sanchez, P., Roos, S., McCorry, P., Gervais, A.: SoK: layer-two blockchain protocols. In: Bonneau, J., Heninger, N. (eds.) FC 2020. LNCS, vol. 12059, pp. 201–226. Springer, Cham (2020). https://doi.org/10.1007/978-3-030-51280-4_12
13. Halevi, S., Harnik, D., Pinkas, B., Shulman-Peleg, A.: Proofs of ownership in remote storage systems. In: Chen, Y., Danesiz, O., Simsatkov, V. (eds.) ACM CCS 2017, pp. 491–504. ACM Press (2017). https://doi.org/10.1145/3092701.3092765
14. Huang, C., Song, R., Xiao, J., Guo, J., Nian, B.: Data Availability and decentralization: new techniques for zk-rollups in layer 2 blockchain networks (2024). arXiv: 2403.10828 [cs.CR]. https://arxiv.org/abs/2403.10828
15. Kate, A., Zaverucha, G.M., Goldberg, I.: Constant-size commitments to polynomials and their applications. In: Abe, M. (ed.) ASIACRYPT 2010. LNCS, vol. 6477, pp. 177–194. Springer, Heidelberg (2010). https://doi.org/10.1007/978-3-642-17373-8_11
16. Li, C., Xu, M., Zhang, J., Guo, H., Cheng, X.: SoK: decentralized storage network. High-Confidence Comput. **4**(3), 100239 (2024). https://doi.org/10.1016/j.hcc.2024.100239
17. Liang, J., Hu, D., Yu, W., Yang, P., Shen, Q., Wu, Z.: SoK: understanding zk-SNARKs: the gap between research and practice. Cryptology ePrint Archive, Paper 2025/172 (2025). https://eprint.iacr.org/2025/172

18. Maymounkov, P., Mazières, D.: Kademlia: a peer-to-peer information system based on the XOR metric. In: Druschel, P., Kaashoek, F., Rowstron, A. (eds.) IPTPS 2002. LNCS, vol. 2429, pp. 53–65. Springer, Heidelberg (2002). https://doi.org/10.1007/3-540-45748-8_5
19. Moran, T., Orlov, I.: Proofs of space-time and rational proofs of storage. Cryptology ePrint Archive, Report 2016/035 (2016). https://eprint.iacr.org/2016/035
20. Movement Labs, Movement Network: High-Throughput Fast Finality Move-based Chains Secured by Ethereum, version 0.2.7 (2025). https://www.movementnetwork.xyz/whitepaper/movement-whitepaper_en.pdf
21. Protocol Labs, Filecoin: A Decentralized Storage Network (2017). https://filecoin.io/filecoin.pdf
22. Mamounas, M., Gligoroski, D., Kralevaka, K.: SoK of used cryptography in blockchain. IEEE Access **7**, 148566–148575 (2019). https://doi.org/10.1109/ACCESS.2019.2945653
23. Saif, M.B., Migliorini, S., Spoto, F.: A survey on data availability in layer 2 blockchain rollups: open challenges and future improvements. Future Internet **16**(9) (2024). https://doi.org/10.3390/fi16090315, https://www.mdpi.com/1999-5903/16/9/315
24. Scafuro, A.: Blockchains and cryptography. In: Advanced Cryptographic Protocols, pp. 100–130. De Cifris Press (2024). http://doi.org/10.69091/koine/vol-4-P05
25. Sengupta, H., Bag, S., Ruj, S., Sakurai, K.: Retricoin: bitcoin based on compact proofs of retrievability. In: Proceedings of the 17th International Conference on Distributed Computing and Networking. Association for Computing Machinery, New York, NY, USA (2016). https://doi.org/10.1145/2833312.2833317
26. Skidanov, A., Poloniukhin, I., Wang, H.: Nightshade: Near Protocol Sharding Design 2.0 (2024). https://near.org/papers/nightshade
27. Trautwein, D., et al.: Design and evaluation of IPFS, a storage layer for the decentralized web. In: Proceedings of the ACM SIGCOMM 2022 Conference. Association for Computing Machinery, New York, NY, USA (2022). https://doi.org/10.1145/354216.3544252
28. Vorick, D., Champine, L.: Sia: Simple Decentralized Storage (2014). https://sia.tech/sia.pdf
29. Wilkinson, S., et al.: Storj: A Peer-to-Peer Cloud Storage Network (2016). https://storj.io/storjv2.pdf
30. Williams, S., Kedin, A., Berman, L., Campos-Groth, S.: Arweave: The Permanent Information Storage Protocol (2023). https://arweave.org
31. Xu, J., Yang, A., Zhou, J., Wong, D.S.: Lightweight and Privacy-Preserving Delegatable Proofs of Storage. Cryptology ePrint Archive, Report 2014/395 (2014). https://eprint.iacr.org/2014/395
32. Zahed Benisi, N., Aminian, M., Javadi, B.: Blockchain-based decentralized storage networks: a survey. J. Netw. Comput. Appl. **162**, 102656 (2020). https://doi.org/10.1016/j.jnca.2020.102656
33. Zhang, C., Li, X., Xu, M.H.: ePoS: practical and client-friendly proof of storage-time. IEEE Trans. Inf. Forensics Secur. **18**, 1052–1063 (2023). https://doi.org/10.1109/TIFS.2022.3233780

Open Access This chapter is licensed under the terms of the Creative Commons Attribution 4.0 International License (http://creativecommons.org/licenses/by/4.0/), which permits use, sharing, adaptation, distribution and reproduction in any medium or format, as long as you give appropriate credit to the original author(s) and the source, provide a link to the Creative Commons license and indicate if changes were made.

The images or other third party material in this chapter are included in the chapter's Creative Commons license, unless indicated otherwise in a credit line to the material. If material is not included in the chapter's Creative Commons license and your intended use is not permitted by statutory regulation or exceeds the permitted use, you will need to obtain permission directly from the copyright holder.

Author Index

A
Ababneh, Mohammed II-69
Abdallah, Khalid II-309
Al Sadi, Farhan II-309
Al-Chami, Joseph II-196
Almasri, Abdelwahab II-309
Angel, James II-50
Aranha, Diego F. II-281
Araújo, Roberto II-281

B
Bachu, Brad I-78, I-111
Bar-On, Yogev I-137
Bartoletti, Massimo I-147
Ben Aoun, Hichem I-32
Blom, Michelle II-226, II-241
Broby, Daniel II-212
Brunetta, Carlo I-263
Budurushi, Jurlind II-309

C
Clark, Jeremy II-196
Cominetti, Eduardo L. II-281
Conway, Andrew II-297
Culnane, Chris II-297

D
Derka, Martin I-63
Diaconescu, Denisa II-162
Doan, Thi Van Thao II-306
Droll, Jan I-32

E
Ek, Alexander II-226, II-241

F
Friolo, Daniele II-100

G
Gansäuer, Robin I-32
Giustolisi, Rosario II-266
Gogol, Krzysztof M. I-94

Gogol, Krzysztof I-17
Goodell, Geoffrey II-100
Gorzny, Jan I-63
Grötschla, Florian I-1

H
Hartenstein, Hannes I-32
Heimbach, Lioba I-1
Hioki, Leona II-162
Huang, Maozhou II-1

I
Inés Silva, Maria I-17

K
Kemper, Phillip I-63
Kolachala, Kartick II-69
Kopyciok, Yannik I-200
Kraner, Benjamin II-50
Kuehlkamp, Andrey II-138

L
Larangeira, Mario II-1
Lee, Suhyeon I-164
Lenzini, Gabriele II-266
Liao, Gordon I-78
Liu, Dingyue I-78
Livshits, Benjamin I-17, I-47, I-94, I-127

M
Maduakor, Felix II-306
Matias, Paulo II-281
Matsuo, Shin'ichiro II-50
Messias, Johnnatan I-17, I-47
Mitzlaff, Joerg II-306
Moallemi, Ciamac C. I-111
Moallemi, Ciamac I-78

N
Nabi, Mahmudun I-216
Nabrzyski, Jarek II-138
Nakib, Hazem Danny II-100

Ndiaye, Abdoulaye I-245
Nhlabatsi, Armstrong II-309

P

Paruchuri, Rohil II-50
Pekel, Umut II-29
Priyadarshini, Emily I-147

R

Rakeei, Mohammadamin II-266
Richner, Severin I-1
Rønne, Peter B. II-256
Rybakken, Erik II-162

S

Safavi-Naini, Reihaneh I-216
Sala, Massimiliano I-263
Schmid, Stefan I-200
Schneider, Manvir I-94
Silva, Maria Inês I-47, I-127
Silváši, František II-162
Simplicio, Marcos A. II-281
Spoto, Fausto I-180
Stark, Philip B. II-241
Stuckey, Peter J. II-226, II-241
Su, Xiangyu II-1
Sugino, Takaya II-50
Sutherland, Julian II-162

T

Tanaka, Keisuke II-1
Teague, Vanessa J. II-241
Teague, Vanessa II-226, II-297
Tessone, Claudio J. I-94
Toliver, D. R. II-100

V

Valencia Jr., Eduardo T. II-212
Vaughan, Owen II-84
Victor, Friedhelm I-200
Vishwanathan, Roopa II-69
Vukcevic, Damjan II-226, II-241

W

Wan, Xin I-78, I-111
Wattenhofer, Roger I-1
Wilson-Brown, Ty II-297

X

Xu, Jiayu II-122

Y

Yaksetig, Mario II-122, II-162
Yayla, Oğuz II-29
You, Shengwei II-138

Z

Zarouk, Hosam II-309
Zhu, Brian I-78

GPSR Compliance

The European Union's (EU) General Product Safety Regulation (GPSR) is a set of rules that requires consumer products to be safe and our obligations to ensure this.

If you have any concerns about our products, you can contact us on ProductSafety@springernature.com

In case Publisher is established outside the EU, the EU authorized representative is:

Springer Nature Customer Service Center GmbH
Europaplatz 3
69115 Heidelberg, Germany

Batch number: 09218155

Printed by Printforce, the Netherlands